Beginning Windows Phone 7 Development

Second Edition

**Henry Lee and
Eugene Chuvyrov**

Apress®

Beginning Windows Phone 7 Development, Second Edition

ISBN-13 (pbk): 978-1-4302-3596-5

ISBN-13 (electronic): 978-1-4302-3597-2

President and Publisher: Paul Manning
Lead Editor: Ewan Buckingham
Development Editor: James Markham
Technical Reviewer: Fabio Claudio Ferracchiati
Editorial Board: Steve Anglin, Mark Beckner, Ewan Buckingham, Gary Cornell, Jonathan Gennick, Jonathan Hassell, Michelle Lowman, James Markham, Matthew Moodie, Duncan Parkes, Jeffrey Pepper, Frank Pohlmann, Douglas Pundick, Ben Renow-Clarke, Dominic Shakeshaft, Matt Wade, Tom Welsh
Coordinating Editor: Jennifer L. Blackwell
Copy Editor: Mary Behr
Compositor: Bytheway Publishing Services
Indexer: BIM Indexing & Proofreading Services
Artist: April Milne
Cover Designer: Anna Ishchenko

Distributed to the book trade worldwide by Springer Science+Business Media, LLC., 233 Spring Street, 6th Floor, New York, NY 10013. Phone 1-800-SPRINGER, fax (201) 348-4505, e-mail orders-ny@springer-sbm.com, or visit www.springeronline.com.

For information on translations, please e-mail rights@apress.com, or visit www.apress.com.

Apress and friends of ED books may be purchased in bulk for academic, corporate, or promotional use. eBook versions and licenses are also available for most titles. For more information, reference our Special Bulk Sales–eBook Licensing web page at www.apress.com/bulk-sales.

The source code for this book is available to readers at www.apress.com.

To Erica, my beautiful wife, for her love and support. Thank you for always being there for me.

—Henry Lee

To Marianna—my friend, my wife, my muse—and to my parents for their gift of unconditional love.

—Eugene Chuvyrov

Contents at a Glance

Contents

About the Authors

■ **Henry Lee** is the founder of www.ToeTapz.com and http://NewAgeSolution.net and is passionate about technology. He works with various Fortune 500 companies delivering mobile applications and Rich Internet Applications (RIAs). He is focusing his energy on delivering mobile applications on Windows Phone 7, Android, and iPhone. In his spare time, he helps his communities by delivering sessions at technology events. He enjoys discussing current trends in technology with other technologists and sharing business insights with fellow colleagues. You will often find Henry at a local cigar bar, enjoying a cigar and a drink while trying to come up with the next big mobile application.

■ **Eugene Chuvyrov** is an independent .NET consultant in beautiful Jacksonville, Florida. He was lucky enough to start working with Microsoft technologies when he graduated from college in 1998 and has been consistently delivering a positive return on investment to the clients that engage him. His most recent venture is an online event marketing startup, http://packedhouseevents.com, which extends event creation, marketing, and electronic payments to anybody with Internet access. Eugene also facilitates the meetings of the Jacksonville Software Architecture Group, where he enjoys networking and learning from smart people.

As soon as Eugene heard the news that a new mobile platform (Windows Phone 7) was being released by Microsoft, he was intrigued. It was hard to resist the temptation of wide-open possibilities to create smartphone applications using his favorite IDE and all the latest cloud and functional programming-based technologies. This passion, discussed over a cigar with Henry at a local cigar bar, resulted in the book you now hold in your hands. He sincerely hopes you find it useful!

About the Technical Reviewer

■ Fabio Claudio Ferracchiati is a senior consultant and a senior analyst/developer using Microsoft technologies. He works for Brain Force (www.brainforce.com) in its Italian branch (www.brainforce.it).

He is a Microsoft Certified Solution Developer for .NET, a Microsoft Certified Application Developer for .NET, a Microsoft Certified Professional, and a prolific author and technical reviewer. Over the past ten years, he's written articles for Italian and international magazines and co-authored more than ten books on a variety of computer topics.

Acknowledgments

We would like to express our love and gratitude to our wives for encouraging us to finish this book. We are also grateful to Apress for giving us the opportunity to write second edition about what we love to do so that we could share it with the world. The staff at Apress made this book possible by spending many days and nights reviewing and editing the book to meet the tight deadline. Ewan Buckingham provided us with this unique opportunity to share our knowledge. Thank you, Ewan, for believing in us. Also we would like to show our appreciation to the coordinating editor, Jennifer Blackwell, and staff members James Markham, Fabio Claudio Ferracchiati, and Mary Behr. When the first edition was published, we also realized that there were Apress staff members in the marketing department promoting the book; we would like to thank Lisa Lau and the marketing department and Simon Yu for helping us to get in contact with the user groups for speaking engagements.

We also like to thank those who sent us e-mail with comments and those who blogged about our books on the Web with kind remarks. Many online communities helped us improve upon our first edition by offering valuable feedback and we used that feedback to make the second edition better.

Introduction

This is the second edition of this book. We wanted to improve upon the first edition and become the market leader in providing practical knowledge on the fast-coming, latest-and-greatest technology of Windows Phone.

While this second edition was being written, Microsoft and Nokia formally announced their partnership and signed mutual agreement to seal their commitment. It is expected that this partnership between Microsoft and Nokia will bring Windows Phone 7 into the major player arena. We hope that this book will provide developers with the practical knowledge that we gained by developing real world applications; we also hope it will inspire developers to seek growing markets with Windows Phone.

Who This Book Is For

This book assumes that you have basic C# and .NET knowledge. This book will provide you with basic fundamentals and skills that you need to be successful in developing a Windows Phone applications. You don't need previous experience in developing a mobile application—the only thing you need is a desire to learn new technology.

What You Need to Use This Book

In order to write Windows Phone applications and to test out the examples in this book, you'll need to download the tools listed here. All of these are available at no charge from Microsoft. You'll find additional information on how to install and use these tools in Part 1 of this book.

- **Windows Phone Developer Tools RTW** at http://download.microsoft.com/download/1/7/7/177D6AF8-17FA-40E7-AB53-00B7CED31729/vm_web.exe

- **Zune Software** at www.zune.net/en-us/products/software/download/

- **Windows Phone 7 UI Design and Interface Guide** at http://go.microsoft.com/fwlink/?LinkID=183218

- **Windows Phone 7 Marketplace Certification Requirements** at http://go.microsoft.com/?linkid=9730558

- **Microsoft SQL 2008 R2 Express** at www.microsoft.com/express/Database/

- **Azure Tools for Visual Studio 1.2 June 2010** at http://download.microsoft.com/DOWNLOAD/1/F/9/1F96D60F-EBE9-44CB-BD58-88C2EC14929E/VSCLOUDSERVICE.EXE

- **Azure SDK June 2010** at http://www.microsoft.com/windowsazure/sdk/

- **Windows Azure Platform Training Kit September**—for the latest update, please check at http://www.microsoft.com/downloads/en/details.aspx?familyid=413e88f8-5966-4a83-b309-53b7b77edf78

How This Book Is Organized

The book contains 19 chapters broken into two major parts. In Part 1, we will walk you through the development life cycle of the application. You will go from coding the simplest possible "Hello World"–style Windows Phone 7 application to building a full-blown, modern n-tier application that uses both the Windows Phone development platform and the unique cloud services that support it. The section concludes with step-by-step instructions on how to gain certification from Microsoft and offer an application to the public through the Windows Phone Marketplace.

In Part 2, you will learn how to use specific features of Windows Phone devices in your applications, including the accelerometer, location service, application bar, reactive extensions, application hub integration, application life cycle events, isolated storage, Silverlight, XAML, skinning controls, web browser controls, media elements, photos, push notifications, internalization, and security. While each of its chapters is a tutorial, you can also use Part 2 as a reference. Each chapter focuses on a single phone feature and provides step-by-step instructions on how to incorporate it into your application.

Where to Find Sources for the Examples

The source code of all of the examples is available at www.apress.com/ and wp7apress.codeplex.com.

Send Us Your Comments

We value your input. We'd like to know what you like about the book and what you don't like about it. When providing feedback, please make sure you include the title of the book in your note to us.

We've tried to make this book as error-free as possible. However, mistakes happen. If you find any type of error in this book, whether it is a typo or an erroneous command, please let us know about it. Visit the book's web site at www.apress.com/9781430235965 and click the Errata tab. Your information will be validated and posted on the errata page to be used in subsequent editions of the book.

Contacting the Authors

You can contact us directly at the following e-mail addresses:

Henry Lee: Henry.Lee@NewAgeSolution.net

Eugene Chuvyrov: echuvyrov@msn.com

CHAPTER 1

Introducing Windows Phone 7 and the Windows Phone Platform

This is an exciting time for developers as the smartphone race heats up between major players Microsoft Windows Phone, Apple iPhone, and Google Android. As a developer, you are faced with an amazing opportunity to develop a mobile application that can be sold to millions of consumers worldwide using any of the platforms (Windows Phone, iPhone, and Android). By 2014 Gartner predicts that the smartphone market will boom and there will be billions of dollars at stake. This could well be the next big "dot com boom" that everyone's been waiting for.

Recently, Nokia, one of the largest mobile phone makers in the world, announced that it will replace its Symbian-based operating system (OS) with a Windows Phone 7 OS. The partnership between Microsoft and Nokia will potentially boost Windows 7's global market share to 30 percent, making it even more attractive for Windows Phone 7 developers.

The Marketplace for Windows Phone, where consumers can purchase applications, opened in November, 2010. You might consider downloading Zune software from `www.zune.net/en-US/products/software/download/downloadsoftware.htm` to view the current Marketplace. Once you have downloaded the Zune software and fired it up, click marketplace APPS links, and you will be able to see all the Windows Phone applications currently published, as shown in Figure 1–1. You will learn more about the Marketplace in Chapter 5.

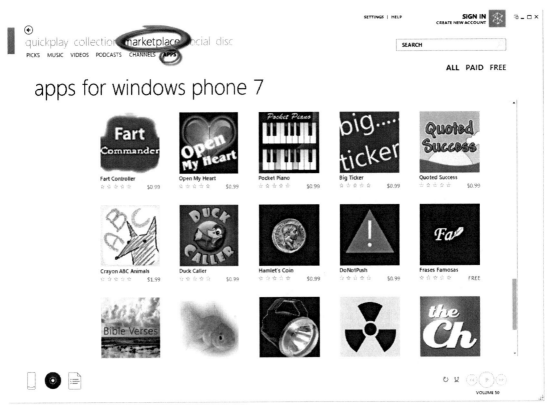

Figure 1–1. Windows Phone Marketplace

There are hundreds of ideas for applications still waiting to be discovered and developed by you. Take a look at QuotedSuccess, DuckCaller, and a MobileBaseball game, shown in Figure 1–2. Which of these will be among the first Windows Phone hits to catch fire with consumers and sell millions of units?

Figure 1–2. Windows Phone applications

What application will you be developing? We've written this book to guide you through the steps it takes to write and launch a successful application to the Marketplace. So what are you waiting for? Let's get started by diving into what Windows Phone has to offer to developers like you.

Windows Phone Overview

Microsoft Windows Phone is a great consumer phone because it has all of the features to which users have become accustomed thanks to the Apple iPhone and Android-powered smartphones like the Motorola Droid and HTC Incredible. These features include multitouch screen, a beautiful user interface (UI) that implements a new modern design named Metro, social networking services like Facebook, and support for popular e-mail accounts such as Yahoo, Hotmail, Google, AOL, and, if you're a corporate user, Microsoft Exchange. Uniquely, the phone ships with a version of Microsoft Office that you can use to read, edit, save, and synch any Word files, Excel spreadsheets, and other Office formats, making it a great phone for those who use Office at home or in the office. Windows Phone can also integrate with Xbox LIVE, making it a great choice for gamers.

Microsoft Windows Phone uses the Zune software to sync installed applications, pictures, music, and back up and flash OS updates. As a developer, you'll also use Zune in conjunction with Visual Studio to debug your applications on a real device; more on that in Chapter 4.

Microsoft also introduces the concept of a *hub* with the Windows Phone: a People hub where users can store all of their contacts and social networking connections; a Music hub where consumers can listen to, download, and purchase music; and an App Hub, also known as the Marketplace, which you will be most interested in since you will be publishing the application you create.

Having a phone that's a hit with consumers is important because the consumer marketplace is where the greatest opportunities lie. One of the great things about Windows Phone is that Microsoft imposes the hardware specifications on the phone manufacturer, making it easy for you to develop an application without worrying about writing special codes for the specific devices. For any future release of the phone, you are guaranteed that the application you write today will work regardless of the brand of the phone.

Naturally, you want to know what language you'll need to master for your work. For Windows Phone, the language of choice today is C# and Visual Basic (VB). As for an application development framework, you have two choices: Silverlight or XNA. Silverlight and XNA both use core .NET Framework. You will learn more about the two frameworks later in this chapter, but first let's take a closer look at the hardware features you can expect on a Windows Phone.

Windows Phone Hardware Specifications

Knowing what's included in the Microsoft Windows Phone hardware specifications will help you prepare for the special needs of the projects you'd like to attempt. Table 1–1 lists the minimum hardware requirements any Windows Phone manufacturer must meet and also includes suggestions as to how they can impact developers like you.

Table 1–1. Windows Phone Minimum Hardware Requirements

Hardware Feature	Description
Must display at WVGA (800 x 480)	Having to worry about only one screen resolution makes it easy to develop an application.
Four-point multi-touch capable	This is unique to the Windows Phone, and you can use this feature to create four-player games. There is definitely room for innovation for using this particular feature.
DirectX 9 hardware acceleration	This means the phone will have a graphical processing unit (GPU), allowing graphically intense tasks to be offloaded to the graphics chips of the phone. This will help you create very smooth and responsive applications and games. This also means 3D games are possible.
GPS	With this, you'll be able to create location-aware applications. See Chapter 14 to learn about location services, how to use Bing Maps, and how to plot GPS data on the map.
Accelerometer	This feature will measure the change of the acceleration in the phone. The accelerometer can be used in games or in creating utility applications, like a level. See Chapter 6 to learn more about this feature.
Compass	With this, you can find north, south, east, and west.
Light	This feature can be used as a flash for the camera.
Digital Camera	This allows you to take pictures and share them on Facebook and other social networking sites. Learn more about this feature in Chapter 16.
Hardware controls: Back, Start, and Search buttons	Every phone will have three buttons on the front of the phone. Keep in mind that you will be required to use Back buttons for going backward in your application, because having separate Back buttons in the application might confuse the user. Learn more about integrating the hardware buttons into the application in Chapter 10.
Support data connections: cellular network and Wi-Fi	This feature allows you to connect to the Internet. You can create web services and consume them from your applications, or you can consume third-party APIs like Twitter or Facebook in your application.
256MB of RAM and 8GM flash storage	Keep in mind that your application can use only 90MB of memory unless the device has more memory than 256MB. If your application does not respect this, it will not pass the Marketplace certification process. See Chapter 5 for more details. Also, the 8GB of flash memory used for storage is shared among other applications, so if you are saving any kind of static data into the Isolated Storage, you must check if the space is available and handle the exception appropriately. See more details on this in Chapter 13.

AT&T had announced it would carry Samsung's Focus, LG's Quantum, and HTC's SurroundTM. And T-Mobile had announced it would carry HTC's HD7. For those who have other cell phone providers, Dell ships its Venue Pro. You can find more information on the release of these phones at www.microsoft.com/windowsphone/en-us/buy/7/phones.aspx.

In the next section, you will learn how the software behind these powerful consumer phones provides a great development platform for developers.

Windows Phone Application Platform

Microsoft did not invent any new languages or frameworks for the Windows Phone application platform. The company simply adapted its existing frameworks. This means that you will be able to program using C# and VB with the .NET Framework). What .NET provides is a common base class library that every Microsoft .NET programmer will be familiar with; it includes support for multithreading, XML, Linq, collections, events, data, exceptions, IO, service model, networking, text, location, reflection, globalization, resources, runtime, security, and diagnostics.

On top of the core .NET Framework, the Windows Phone application platform consists of two major frameworks: Silverlight and XNA. You'll use Silverlight primarily for business applications and simple 2D games. Silverlight uses the Extensible Application Markup Language (XAML), a declarative markup language for creating compelling UI. Designers will have tremendous flexibility in creating UIs for Windows Phone; by using familiar tools like Adobe Illustrator, Photoshop, and Microsoft Expression Design, they can create a vector-based UI that can be easily exported to XAML. XNA is primarily used for creating games; the framework comes with a game engine that allows you to create loop-based games and a 3D engine that allows you to create 3D games.

In the following sections, you will learn more details about the main components of the Windows Phone application platform: Silverlight, XNA, tools, and cloud services.

Silverlight for Windows Phone

The interesting thing about Silverlight is that Silverlight is used in the web technology that is browser plug-in that enables rich Internet application, desktop application quality to be enabled in all major browsers. Silverlight provides you with a sandboxed experience that behaves and abides by the rules of the web browsers; in other words, within a Silverlight application, you can't access the native OS unless you have the necessary APIs. This architecture makes Silverlight very compelling for use in Windows Phone from a security standpoint because Windows Phone provides the same restriction of providing APIs only to developers and limiting access to the native OS.

Another plus is that Silverlight uses XAML, which can be used to declare vector-based graphics and create animations. Any designer familiar with vector-based applications like Adobe Illustrator and Microsoft Expression Design can easily create highly visual elements in vector that can be exported out to XAML. This means the designers have full control over the layout, look and feel, and graphical assets, making Silverlight an extremely powerful choice for creating consumer-oriented applications. Also XAML provides a powerful data binding feature to the controls, making it ideal for creating business oriented applications.

XNA for Windows Phone

Like Silverlight, XNA is not a new technology. XNA is used in creating Xbox games via managed code. It is a natural choice for creating games since Windows Phone has Xbox LIVE integration, allowing XNA-based Xbox games to be easily posted over to Windows Phone. The only thing Xbox game developers have to worry about is screen resolution, which can easily be adjusted and fixed.

XNA provides a rich framework for game developments, including a game loop engine, 2D and 3D engines, and the ability to manage game assets like models, meshes, sprites, textures, effects, terrains, and animations.

Tools

You can download the tools you need for developing Windows Phone applications from http://create.msdn.com/en-us/home/getting_started. The Getting Started page also features rich documentation and tutorials. You should also consider downloading *The UI Design and Interaction Guide* to understand the Metro design guidelines that Microsoft encourages you to follow when developing applications.

Visual Studio

If you don't have a paid version of Visual Studio 2010 on your development machine, then the development tool that you have downloaded from Microsoft will install a free version of Visual Studio 2010 Express for Windows Phone, as show in Figure 1–3. Visual Studio is absolutely necessary because it can be used to design, debug, create projects, package, and automatically generate package manifests. It also includes a phone emulator on which to test the results of your work. In Chapter 5, you will learn to debug and run the emulator from Visual Studio; you will also use Visual Studio to create a package for publication to the App Hub.

Figure 1–3. Microsoft Visual Studio 2010 Express for Windows Phone

Expression Blend

You will need Expression Blend if you want to develop compelling applications using Silverlight for Windows Phone, as shown in Figure 1–4. Typically Expression Blend is used by designers, and many of the Expression Blend functionalities are similar those in Adobe Illustrator, Photoshop, or Expression Design. Note that you can import any Illustrator and Photoshop files into Expression Blend; if you are using Expression Design, you can export Expression Design file directly to an XAML file.

Expression Blend also provides a way to create animation sequences. Although you can create animation in Visual Studio using XAML, it would be very difficult to write complex XAML code to represent complex graphics or animation sequences. It is best to leave complex graphics and animations to Expression Blend.

Figure 1–4. Microsoft Expresion Blend 4 for Windows Phone

Windows Phone Emulator

The Windows Phone emulator, seen in Figure 1–5, is integrated with Visual Studio and simulates a real device. However, there are things you can't do in the emulator. For instance, you can't test any features that require a physical device, such as the accelerometer, GPS, compass, FM radio, SMS, e-mail, phone calling, contact list, and camera.

There is, however, a technique called Reactive Extensions that you can use to simulate the data feed from a real phone. In Chapter 18, you'll learn how to use Reactive Extensions to simulate the accelerometer and GPS readings so that you can work with the emulator without the need of the device.

Figure 1–5. Windows Phone emulator

Documentation and Support

There are many ways to get help if you get stuck on a problem while developing your application. *The Windows Phone 7 Training Kit* at http://create.msdn.com/en-us/home/getting_started contains how-tos on specific technology. You can go to http://forums.silverlight.net/forums/63.aspx to ask Silverlight for Windows Phone–related questions; if you have other Windows Phone-related questions, you can visit http://social.msdn.microsoft.com/Forums/en-US/windowsphone7series. The Windows Phone development team puts out many useful blogs that you can follow at http://windowsteamblog.com/windows_phone/b/wpdev/. Of course, there is Windows Phone documentation at MSDN; go to http://msdn.microsoft.com/en-us/library/ff402535(VS.92).aspx.

Cloud Services

Working with a Windows Phone application that requires saving data to a database is a tricky thing. The first big problem is that you don't know how popular your application will be; if it becomes popular, you might suddenly find millions of users using your application and saving the data to its database at a rate that would require an enterprise-level solution. You also need to find a web service to provide APIs to your application to save to the database, because Windows Phone applications can't directly connect to the database.

This is where the Microsoft Azure cloud comes in. Microsoft Azure provides Windows Azure service for deploying services (WCF, Windows service) and SQL Azure for the database that allows you to scale infinitely as your demand grows larger. You will learn more about the Microsoft Azure cloud in Chapter 3.

There are also Bing Maps services that you can use freely. Bing Maps is free only if you are developing a Windows Phone application. Along with Bing Maps services, Microsoft provides Bing Maps controls in Silverlight that you can use in Windows Phone. You will learn about Bing Maps and location services in Chapter 14.

Push notification services are hosted in the cloud as well; these allow you to push messages to the phone—a very powerful messaging mechanism. You will learn more about this in Chapter 17. Xbox LIVE services also reside in the cloud, which you can take advantage of in your application; however, this topic will not be covered in this book.

You learned a bit about Windows Phone and the Windows Phone platform in the previous sections. In the following sections, you will learn about Windows Phone application development from beginning to end.

Metro Design

Microsoft is targeting Windows Phone 7 toward busy professionals. In order to provide a compelling UI, Microsoft came up with the Metro design. The Metro design derives from the transportation industry typography and visual designs where busy professionals constantly scan and go; because of this, Metro design puts heavy emphasis on simple and clean designs.

Metro design follows five principles. The first principle emphasizes ideas like clean, light, open, and clutter-free and attributes like simple-to-read typography because consumers will be using the phone to read e-mail, SMS, Facebook, and Twitter while on the go. The second principle of Metro design puts the focus on content, where the design premise is geared toward presenting the content. The third principle focuses on seamless integration of hardware and software. The fourth principle puts an emphasis on gestures, where the design enables a world-class multitouch user experience. Lastly, the Metro design concept focuses on an application that is soulful and alive, where information that matters most to the user is presented in a way that is easily accessible by a touch. You can find out more about Metro design by downloading the document provided by Microsoft at
`http://go.microsoft.com/fwlink/?LinkID=183218`.

Application Development Life Cycle

Understanding the application life cycle will help you prepare for it. Much more in-depth discussion, including the certification process, is covered in Chapter 5. Figure 1–6 illustrates a high-level view of the life cycle of an application.

Figure 1–6. Application development life cycle

As a developer, you will start out at the App Hub by registering your Windows Live ID (or you'll create one). Once signed up at the App Hub, you register your physical device so you can debug in the real device. Remember that you can add up to three devices. Using Visual Studio and/or Expression Blend, you will be creating your application and debugging using the emulator or the device you registered. Once the application is created, you need to submit the application to the certification process.

In order to ensure that your application will pass the Marketplace certification process, it's a good idea to read and understand the application certification document found at http://go.microsoft.com/?linkid=9730558. As part of the certification process, your application will go through a series of validations against the application and content policies, packaging, code, phone feature disclosure, language, and images requirements. Your application will also get tested on reliability, performance, resource management, phone functionality uses, and security. The certification process is in place to help promote quality applications to consumers, to protect consumers from malware, and protect Microsoft services.

Once the application passes the certification process, it will be deployed to the Marketplace and then downloaded and used by the consumer. The consumers who use your application will provide ratings and comments; reports can be generated from the App Hub for details on how your application is performing in the Marketplace. Based on the feedback you receive, you can choose to deploy an updated version with bug fixes and new features. Your ultimate goal is to create a compelling application that you know consumers will use and to publish this application to the Marketplace. The Marketplace costs $99 annually; this gives you access to the Windows Phone Marketplace and the Xbox 360 Marketplace. In the Windows Phone Marketplace, you can submit an unlimited number of paid applications and five free applications; additional submissions cost $19.99. In the Xbox 360 Marketplace, you can submit up to ten games.

You will be able to observe any Marketplace activities through the report provided, such as comments, ratings, and number of apps sold, so that you can effectively improve sales and marketing efforts.

When your application is bought by consumers, Microsoft takes 30 percent of the app price; you get to keep 70 percent. You can choose direct deposit so that the money goes directly to your bank account; you will be receiving your payments every first day of the month from Microsoft.

Summary

You have embarked on the journey of developing an application for the Windows Phone Marketplace, which is ready to be explored by developers like yourself. You can be part of a billion-dollar global market; you have a chance to develop an application that can be sold to millions.

This chapter provided a general overview of Windows Phone features, hardware specifications, the development platform, and the Marketplace. In later chapters, you will learn in greater detail about the features and the platform mentioned in this chapter. In Chapter 2, you will build your first Windows Phone application by using tools like Visual Studio, Expression Blend, and the Windows Phone controls.

CHAPTER 2

Building Windows Phone 7 Applications

This chapter will prepare you with everything you will need to get started with Windows Phone 7 development. You will learn about the Windows Phone emulator, Visual Studio 2010, and Microsoft Expression Blend 4. You will use these tools to create your first Windows Phone application.

Before you can write your first application, however, you need to download and install the tools. In the next section, we'll show you how.

Preparing Your Development Machine

At the time of writing this book, Windows Phone 7 developer tool version 1.0 was used. The latest Windows Phone developer tool and patches can be downloaded from http://create.msdn.com/en-us/home/getting_started. The Windows Phone developer tools (vm_web.exe) will install the following:

- *Free version of Visual Studio 2010 Express for Windows Phone*: The programmer's development IDE.

- *Windows Phone emulator*: This is used to run and test the Windows Phone application.

- *Silverlight for Windows Phone*: Silverlight Framework for Windows Phone based on Silverlight 3 technology. See Chapter 1 for the subtle difference between Silverlight 3 and Windows Phone Silverlight framework.

- *Microsoft Expression Blend for Windows Phone*: This can be used to design user interfaces.

- *XNA Game Studio 4*: Tools for developing games.

Once you have installed Windows Phone developer tools, you can start to build your first Windows Phone application.

Building Your First Windows Phone 7 Application

In this section, you'll build a simple "HelloWorld" application using Silverlight framework. Creating the application will provide you with an opportunity to use Visual Studio 2010 Express for Windows Phone, the Windows Phone 7 Emulator, and some Windows Phone Silverlight controls. Later in this chapter, you will use Blend to design Silverlight controls. The final application is displayed in Figure 2–19 at the end of this chapter. A click of its OK button will display the words "Hello World" in a text box. But before you can get started, you must first create a Visual Studio 2010 project.

Creating a Windows Phone Project

To get started, fire up Visual Studio Express 2010 and create a project.

1. To launch Visual Studio 2010 Express, select Windows Start ➤ All Programs ➤ Microsoft Visual Studio 2010 Express ➤ Microsoft Visual Studio 2010 Express for Windows Phone.

2. Create a new project by selecting File ➤ New ➤ Project on the Visual Studio menu, as shown in Figure 2–1.

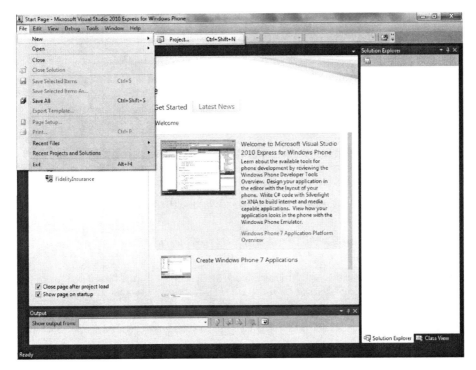

Figure 2–1. Creating a new project

3. From among the three C# templates that Visual Studio displays on its New Project dialog page, select the Windows Phone Application Visual C# template, as shown in Figure 2–2.

■ **Note** There are three different Windows Phone Visual Studio project templates. The Windows Phone Application template is a template for one-page applications. The Windows Phone List Application template uses ListBox control and page navigation framework to create applications with multiple pages. The Windows Phone Class Library template can be used to create a class library that can be referenced by other Windows Phone projects.

4. For the purposes of this exercise, change the name of the new project to HelloWorld by changing the text in the Name box, as shown in Figure 2–2. Also you can change the location where the project will be saved by changing the path in the Location box.

Figure 2–2. Creating a new Silverlight Windows Phone application

5. Finally, select OK on the New Project dialog, and Visual Studio 2010 will build your project, the elements of which are displayed in Figure 2–3.

***Figure 2–3.** HelloWorld Silverlight Windows Phone project*

By default, two TextBlock controls will be placed on the screen; you can see this in the design view on the far left in Figure 2–3.

With a phone project ready to roll, it's time to bring the application to life by adding some functionality and creating a user interface. Let's start with the interface, adding some controls to its blank design surface and some areas where it can display text.

Using Your First Windows Phone Silverlight Controls

The next step is to add Silverlight controls to the HelloWorld Windows Phone application created in the previous steps. You'll be setting the properties of the controls so that the controls can size and position automatically in both Portrait and Landscape mode of Windows Phone.

1. In the Windows Phone Design view window, click MY APPLICATION TextBlock. In the Properties windows at the lower right corner of the Visual Studio IDE, change the Text property from MY APPLICATION to HelloWorld App. Notice that the new text now appears on the Design surface, as shown in Figure 2–4.

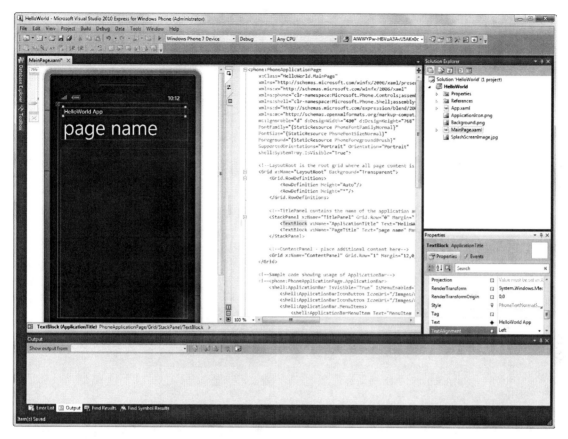

Figure 2–4. Renaming application window title

2. Now open the Visual Studio Toolbox, where you'll find some controls for the HelloWorld user interface. If you can't find the Toolbox, select View Toolbox on the Visual Studio menu. The result of either step, when successful, is to display a list of controls in a vertical panel on the left side of the Visual Studio IDE, as shown in Figure 2–5.

Figure 2–5. *Visual Studio Toolbox containing Windows Phone controls*

The Visual Studio Toolbox contains Windows Phone controls that ship with the Windows Phone developer tools. You'll be using them throughout the book to build increasingly sophisticated user interfaces. You can add any of these to your user interface by dragging it to the Windows Phone Design surface in Visual Studio.

3. To create the interface for the HelloWorld application, let's first add a TextBox to display some text. To do so, drag a TextBox control from the Toolbox to the designer surface directly below the page title TextBlock. When the TextBox control is successfully placed on the phone's designer surface, the TextBox control will be automatically selected. In the Properties window (if you can't find the Properties Window go to View ➤ Properties Window), change the following TextBox properties:

    a. Set Width and Height to Auto.

    b. Set HorizontalAlignment to Stretch.

    c.   Set VerticalAlignment to Top.

    d.   Resize the TextBox width so that there is enough room to its right for an OK button.

    e.   Set Name to txtMessage.

When you properly follow steps a, b, c, and d, you should see the following XAML in the XAML editor area:

```
<TextBox Height="Auto" Margin="0,55,166,0" Name="txtMessage" Text="TextBlock"
VerticalAlignment="Top" HorizontalAlignment="Right" Width="290" />
```

You set Horizontal Alignment to Stretch in step b because you want the TextBox to automatically stretch to fill the extra space created when you rotate the phone emulator to Landscape orientation. Width and Height are set to Auto because you want the TextBox to automatically change its size when Font size increases or decreases. Setting Vertical Alignment to Top will always position the TextBox aligned to the top. You will be able to access the TextBlock control in code by referring to its name, txtMessage.

    4.   Now, let's add the application's OK button to the user interface. To do so, drag and drop a Button control from the Toolbox and drop it to the right of the TextBox. Change the following button properties in Properties Window:

    a.   Set Button Content to OK.

    b.   Set HorizontalAlignment to Right.

    c.   Set VerticalAlignment to Top.

    d.   Set Name to btnOk.

    e.   When steps a, b, and c are properly followed, you should see the following XAML in the XAML editor area. Note that setting the button's horizontal alignment to Right will always align button position to the right side.

```
<Button Content="OK" Height="72" HorizontalAlignment="Right" Margin="308,31,0,0"
Name="btnOk" VerticalAlignment="Top" Width="160" />
```

    5.   Your layout should be done. In XAML view, look for the grid containing the controls you just added. It should look similar to this:

```
<Grid x:Name="ContentGrid" Grid.Row="1">
    <TextBox Height="Auto" Margin="0,55,166,0" Name="txtMessage" Text="TextBlock"
VerticalAlignment="Top" HorizontalAlignment="Right" Width="290" />
    <Button Content="OK" Height="72" HorizontalAlignment="Right" Margin="308,31,0,0"
Name="btnOk" VerticalAlignment="Top" Width="160" />
</Grid>
```

    6.   Figure 2–6 shows the final layout after adding TextBox and Button controls.

Figure 2–6. Final layout of HelloWorld app

Writing Your First Windows Phone Code

In this section, you will be writing C# code that will handle the button click event that will populate the TextBlock named textBlock1 with "Hello World!"

1. To add behavior to the OK button, double-click the OK button on the Design surface of your project. Visual Studio will display MainPage.xaml.cs where you can see that the btnOk_Click method is automatically added (you will add proper code later to handle the button click event).

```
using System.Windows;
using Microsoft.Phone.Controls;

namespace HelloWorld
{
    public partial class MainPage : PhoneApplicationPage
```

```
    {
        public MainPage()
        {
            InitializeComponent();
            // Setting SupportOrientations will control the behavior
            // of the page responding properly to the rotation of the
            // phone. So if you rotate the phone to the landscape
            // your page will change to landscape view.
            SupportedOrientations = SupportedPageOrientation.PortraitOrLandscape
;
        }

        private void btnOk_Click(object sender, RoutedEventArgs e)
        {

        }
    }
}
```

2. In MainPage.xaml, you will notice that the button Click event handler is automatically added to OK button.

```
<Button Content="OK" Height="70"
        HorizontalAlignment="Right" Margin="0,155,-4,0"
        Name="button1" VerticalAlignment="Top" Width="160" Click="button1_Click" />
```

3. In MainPage.xaml.cs replace the button1_click method with the following code:

```
private void button1_Click(object sender, RoutedEventArgs e)
{
    txtMessage.Text = "Hello World!";
}
```

Running Your First Silverlight Windows Phone Application

Your Hello World application is complete. Now it's time to build the application and run it in the Windows Phone 7 emulator.

1. To build the solution, select Build ➤ Build Solution on the Visual Studio menu.

2. To run the application, select Debug ➤ Start Debugging.

3. When the emulator appears, click OK and you will see "Hello World!" as shown in Figure 2–7.

Figure 2–7. Hello World in Windows Phone 7 Emulator

4. Click the rotate control on the Windows Phone 7 emulator, as shown in Figure 2–8.

Figure 2–8. The rotate control

Notice in the Landscape view that the TextBox is automatically resized, stretched out to make full use of the landscape orientation of the device, as shown in Figure 2–9.

Figure 2–9. *Landscape view of Hello World*

5. Stop the application debugging by selecting Debug ➤ Stop Debugging.

■ **Tip**   The Windows Phone 7 emulator can take a long time to start, so you want to avoid closing it down whenever possible. If you need to stop an application in the middle of a debugging run, it's better to use the Visual Studio Debug ➤ Stop Debugging command instead of completely closing down the Windows Phone 7 emulator. Using this technique, the next time the application debugging starts, the project will be loaded into the emulator without first waiting for the emulator to start.

Customizing Your First Windows Phone Application

In the following code walkthrough, you'll learn how to customize the Windows Phone 7 application icon that is displayed to the user and how to change the application's name.

1. In the Solution Explorer, right-click the HelloWorld project and select Add ➤ Existing Item, as shown in Figure 2–10.

Figure 2–10. *Adding a file to the Visual Studio project*

2. Go to where you unzipped the sample codes and choose
\Codes\Ch01\Assets\HelloWorldIcon.png. The Windows Phone 7 application
icon can be any .png file that is 62 x 62. By default, when the Windows Phone
application project is created, the ApplicationIcon.png is used.

3. Right-click the HelloWorld project ➤ Choose Properties.

4. Click the Application tab.

5. In Deployment options ➤ Change the Icon to HelloWorldIcon.png.

6. Change the Title to HelloWorld. Changed properties can be seen in Figure
2–11.

Figure 2–11. Changing the application title and icon

7. Hit F5 to run the application.

8. When the application starts in the Windows Phone 7 emulator, hit the back button on the emulator, as shown in Figure 2–12.

Figure 2–12. Windows Phone 7 back button

9. The list of applications installed on the emulator now includes HelloWorld, as shown in Figure 2–13.

Figure 2–13. Windows Phone 7 application list

Styling Your Application

Either Visual Studio or Microsoft Expression Blend 4 can be used to design XAML-based Silverlight
interfaces. Microsoft Expression Blend 4 provides tools for graphical manipulations and animations,
thus you can create more complex controls than are possible with Visual Studio. Let's look at the basics
of Blend and how Blend makes it easy to style controls.

1. Open Microsoft Expression Blend 4, and select Windows Start ➤ All Programs
   ➤ Microsoft Expression Blend ➤ Microsoft Expression Blend 4 for Windows
   Phone, as shown in Figure 2–14.

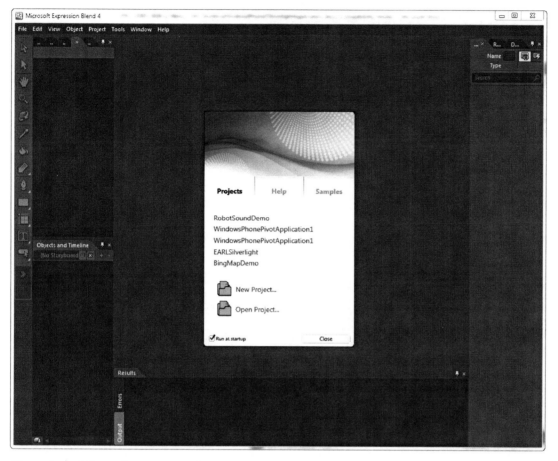

Figure 2–14. Microsoft Expression Blend 4

2. Click Close when you are prompted with the project type selector.

3. In Blend 4, go to File ➤ Open Project/Solution. Browse to the HelloWorld solution you created in the previous steps, as shown in Figure 2–15.

Figure 2–15. Opening an existing project in Blend 4

4.   When the project opens, click the TextBox. In the Properties window, you will see various properties that can be changed, as shown in Figure 2–16. (If you do not see the Properties window, open it by going to Window ➤ Properties.)

Figure 2–16. Properties window in Blend 4 when the control is selected

5. In the Properties window's Brushes category, select Background ➤ choose Gradient brush. Notice that the color editor now has ability to set the gradient color of the TextBox's background color.

6. Choose the first gradient color of blue at 21% and second color of yellow at 64%, as shown in Figure 2–17.

Figure 2–17. *Applying gradient background to TextBox in Blend 4*

7. Go to Project ➤ Run Project.

8. When Change Device Selection window shows, choose Windows Phone 7 Emulator, as shown in Figure 2–18.

Figure 2–18. Change Device Selection window in Blend 4

9. Click OK and the HelloWorld application will start, as shown in Figure 2–19.

Figure 2–19. HelloWorld after being stylized in Blend 4

Summary

In this chapter, you learned how to set up your Windows Phone development environment. You built a simple Windows Phone 7 application using Visual Studio 2010, interacted with the phone emulator, and used Microsoft Expression Blend to style the application.

In the next chapter, you will build an application that can interact with Microsoft SQL Azure in order to store data.

CHAPTER 3

Building Windows Phone 7 Applications Using Cloud Services As Data Stores

There's lots of buzz today about cloud computing technology. The cloud truly empowers you, as the developer, to focus on building an application and off-loading the infrastructure needs to the cloud.

Suppose you have developed an application where businesses can take a picture of invoices and track the money spent, like QuickBooks. In Windows Phone, you can easily use the isolated storage covered in Chapter 13. The problem with isolated storage is that the storage space is tied to the phone; it can differ from manufacturer to manufacturer; and, most importantly, many users will store music, videos, and documents, which can quickly consume the storage space on the phone. A good solution would be to save the invoices information on the database; to do this, you would need a web service that can interact with the database so that the phone can save the invoices, as shown in Figure 3–1.

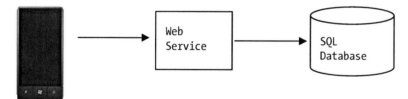

Figure 3–1. Common 3–tier architecture

In order to deploy the solution depicted in Figure 3–1, you need to solve a number of problems. First, you need to consider what type and how many servers to buy to host the web service and database. Once you do, you'll have to purchase and maintain them yourself or pay a hosting service to do the job for you. But this doesn't solve the problem of what you will do to scale up your application if it becomes so popular that millions of consumers want to use it, or if you experience periodic surges in use at, say, the end of each month. Finally, how will you provide for disaster recovery and backup of the database to ensure your service does not go down and disappoint users?

To plan ahead for the huge number of users your application might attract, a more robust architecture must be considered. One example is shown in Figure 3–2, where the load balancer can help accommodate massive concurrent calls to the service; this way, if any of the service goes down, the load balancer will automatically point the request to an available service. On the database side, you have to provide both an active and a passive database in case the main database—the active one—goes down and a switch to the currently passive database becomes necessary. Then you have to worry about disk space, so you will need a storage area network (SAN). Figure 3–2 is your typical Enterprise-grade deployment scenario that provides reliability, scalability, maintenance, and performance but is very expensive and complex.

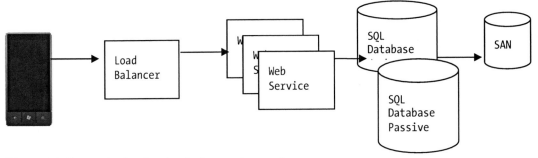

Figure 3–2. *Enterprise-level n-tier deployment scenario*

The architecture in Figure 3-2 might be overkill for the tiny invoice application you're creating, but you don't want to lose the potential that it might be bought by millions of adoring customers. To resolve this dilemma, Microsoft provides Azure service to take care of every single detail of the infrastructure architecture, allowing you to concentrate on developing the best app you can. Microsoft Azure provides peace of mind with a Service Level Agreement of 99.95 uptime, which is equivalent to 4.38 hours downtime per year or 43.2 minutes of downtime per month.

In the remaining sections of this chapter, you will learn to create a simple note-taking application. The application, named Notepad, will implement the n-tier architecture described in Figure 3–2. With the Notepad application, you will be able to create, read, update, and delete notes. The application will consist of three main components: a Windows Phone client (UI), a web service (middle tier) that provides the APIs the UI will use to access a central database, and finally the database itself, which will store the notes the user writes.

Introducing the MVVM Pattern

In developing the Notepad phone application, you will be using the increasingly popular Model-View-ViewModel (MVVM) pattern. MVVM is a design pattern that provides a clear separation between the UI, the application logic, and the data of an application. The models maintain the data, the views display the data or provide the UI for user interaction, and the view-model acts as the controller, or brain, that handles the events that affect either the data or the view. Figure 3–3 illustrates the elements of the MVVM pattern and their relationships.

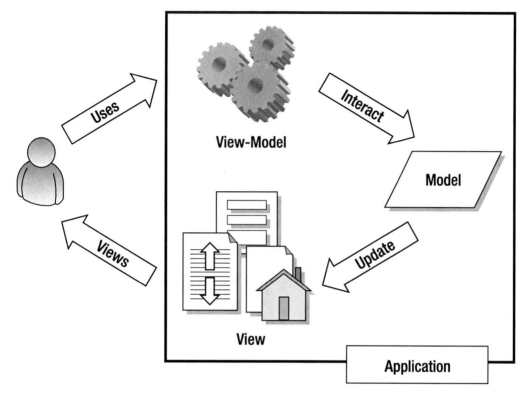

Figure 3–3. The MVVM pattern

Introducing Microsoft Azure and SQL Azure

Azure is the name of Microsoft's cloud services, which developers can use to deliver applications at scale for various workloads and devices. Microsoft Azure provides a runtime framework for applications that currently supports .NET 3.5 and .NET 4.0, as well as load balancers, operating systems, servers, storage, and networking, leaving you free to build the application.

Microsoft Azure provides three services: Windows Azure, SQL Azure, and Windows Azure AppFabric. For building a consumer-facing Windows Phone application, you will be more interested in Windows Azure, which can host web and web service applications, and SQL Azure for the database. Windows Azure AppFabric is more of an Enterprise solution that provides Enterprise Service Bus patterns typically popular in the business process application.

In the following section, you will start first by learning to work with SQL Azure in order to save the notes in the database.

Creating a Cloud Database

The first step is to create an SQL Azure database to store the notes a user creates with this application. Think of SQL Azure as a hosted database in the cloud where you don't have to worry about the infrastructure. If you're familiar with a Microsoft SQL server, you'll be able to work in SQL Azure. NotepadService, which you will be creating in the next section, will connect to this database by using Entity Framework to create, read, update, and delete records from the database.

The Entity Framework

The Entity Framework is an object-relational mapping (ORM) tool that allows you to generate objects based on the tables in a database, taking care of the interaction to the database that otherwise you have to code yourself; the Entity Framework will save you lots time.

Creating an SQL Azure Database

You will be creating a database in SQL Azure in order perform create, read, update, and delete operations for the Notepad application.

Signing Up for SQL Azure

You will create an SQL Azure account in the following steps:

1. Open a browser of your choice.

2. Go to www.microsoft.com/windowsazure/ to sign up and buy the Windows Azure service account. Follow the direction provided by Microsoft in order to purchase and acquire the service account. You can use Microsoft Azure each month for free (25 hours of computing time, 500MB storage, 10,000 storage transactions, 1GB database, and 500MB data transfer); this promotional offer might end soon, though.

3. Go to http://sql.azure.com/ and sign in using the account you created in Step 1.

4. Once signed in, click the SQL Azure menu tab on the left side. When the Windows Azure page loads, you will see the project that you created during the registration process in Step 1. Figure 3–4 corresponds to this step.

Figure 3–4. SQL Azure main screen

Connecting to the SQL Azure Project

After you register and purchase your Azure service account, you can log in to an SQL Azure portal.

1. Click the project hyperlink NAS-DEV. In your case, you should click the name of the project that corresponds to the one you created in the "Signing up for SQL Azure" section.

2. Click the I Accept button on the Terms of Use page, as shown in Figure 3–5.

Figure 3–5. SQL Azure Terms of Use screen

Creating an SQL Azure Database

Here you will be creating an SQL Azure database with a username and password.

3. On the Create Server page, enter NotepadAdmin as the administrator username and P@ssword as the administrator password. Retype the password, and choose North Central US on the Location drop-down. See Figure 3–6 for the inputs. Note that for the location, you want to choose the region closest to you for optimal performance. If you are planning to deploy the application to a specific region, select the appropriate region here.

Figure 3–6. *SQL Azure Create Server screen*

4. Click the Create Server button and you will see Figure 3–7. Take note of the server name assigned to your SQL Azure database as you will need this information to connect using SQL Server Management Studio.

Figure 3–7. SQL Azure Server Administration screen

5. Click the Create Database button. When the pop-up window appears, enter NotepadDB as the name of your database, choose Web on the Specify an edition drop-down menu, and choose 1GB on the Specify the max size drop-down menu, as shown in Figure 3–8. Then click the Create button.

Figure 3–8. SQL Azure Create Database screen

Configuring the SQL Azure Firewall

In the next steps, you will properly configure the SQL Azure firewall so you can connect to the database. By default, SQL Azure denies all access to the database until you add a specific IP.

1. Notice that NotepadDB now appears in the list of databases on the Databases tab. Click the Firewall Settings tab, where you will add your IP to the firewall in order to access the SQL Azure database that you just created from the Microsoft SQL Management Console application to perform various database-related tasks.

2. Select "Allow Microsoft Services to access to this server" checkbox, which will allow programs like Microsoft SQL Management consoles to connect directly to the SQL Azure database, as shown in Figure 3–9.

Figure 3–9. SQL AzureFirewall settings

3. Click the Add Rule button, and when the pop-up appears, enter MyComputer into the Name text box. The pop-up displays your IP address, which you should now copy and paste into the IP Range text boxes, as shown in Figure 3–10.

Figure 3–10. SQL Azure Add Firewall Rule screen

4. Click the Submit button. Note that firewall rules can take up to five minutes to go into effect.

Testing the SQL Azure Database Connection

In this section, you will test that all the configuration steps are performed properly and that you can connect to the database.

1. Let's test to see if you can properly connect. Click the Databases tab.

2. From the list of databases, select NotepadDB. Click the Test Connectivity button, and the pop-up window in Figure 3-11 will appear.

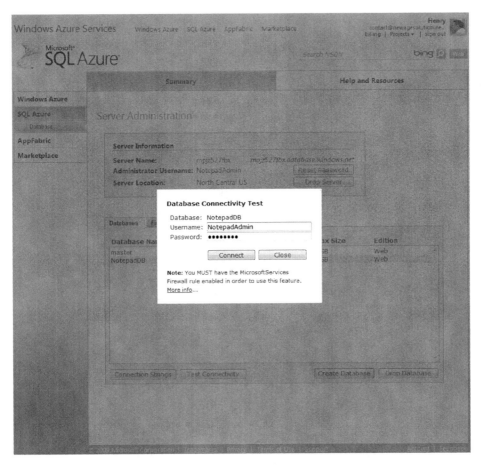

Figure 3–11. SQL Azure Database Connectivity Test

3. Enter NotepadAdmin and P@ssword (or your own versions of these) into the Username and Password boxes and click the Connect button.

4. Click the Connect button and you will see a "Successfully connected to the database" message.

5. Click the Close button to return to the main page.

Creating a Database in SQL Azure

In the following section, you will create database tables in NotepadDB, which is hosted directly in SQL Azure using the Microsoft SQL Server Management application.

Using SQL Server Management Studio to Connect to the Cloud Database

You will be connecting directly to the SQL Azure database NotepadDB you created in the previous steps using the SQL Management application.

1. You want to make sure that you can connect to SQL Azure directly from SQL Management Studio in order to perform various database operations. If you do not have SQL Management Studio installed, you can download the free SQL Server 2008 R2 Express (www.microsoft.com/express/database/). Open SQL Server Management Studio by going to Start ➤ Programs ➤ Microsoft SQL Server 2008 R2, as shown in Figure 3–12.

Figure 3–12. SQL Server Management Studio from the Windows menu

2. In the Connect to Server window, put the server name you obtained previously into the Server name text box, put NotepadAdmin and P@ssword into the Login and Password text box, and click the Connect button, as shown in Figure 3–13.

Figure 3–13. SQL Server Management Studio Connect to Server screen

3. Once you are connected successfully to your SQL Azure database, SQL Server
    Management Studio will display an Object Explorer window on the left side of
    its IDE, as shown in Figure 3–14. Expand the Databases folder and you will find
    NotepadDB, which you just created, listed there (also shown in Figure 3–14).

Figure 3–14. SQL Server Management Studio Object Explorer

Creating SQL Azure Database Tables

Once you are connected to NotepadDB, you can create the tables you'll use to store and manage the
notes your users will create and save. You will be creating the database schema shown in Figure 3–15.

Figure 3–15. NotepadDB database schema

4. Right-click NotepadDB from the Object Explorer window. From the context menu, choose New Query.

5. You will be executing SQL scripts in the query window in order to create tables in NotepadDB.

6. To the newly opened query window, enter or cut and paste the following database script:

```
USE [NotepadDB]
GO

CREATE TABLE [dbo].[User]
(
        [UserId] [uniqueidentifier] NOT NULL,
        [Name] [nvarchar](50) NOT NULL,
    CONSTRAINT [PK_User] PRIMARY KEY ( [UserId] )
)
Go

CREATE TABLE [dbo].[Note]
(
        [NoteId] [int] IDENTITY(1,1) NOT NULL,
        [UserId] [uniqueidentifier] NOT NULL,
        [NoteText] [nvarchar](max) NOT NULL,
        [Description] [nvarchar](50) NOT NULL,
    CONSTRAINT [PK_Note] PRIMARY KEY CLUSTERED ( [NoteId] )
)
GO

ALTER TABLE [dbo].[Note]
        WITH CHECK ADD CONSTRAINT [FK_Note_User] FOREIGN KEY([UserId])
        REFERENCES [dbo].[User] ([UserId])
GO

ALTER TABLE [dbo].[Note] CHECK CONSTRAINT [FK_Note_User]
GO
```

7. Notice that when you expand the tables from NotepadDB in Object Explorer, you will see two tables: Note and User, as shown in Figure 3–16.

Figure 3–16. NotepadDB tables

You now have a live database in SQL Azure! In the next section, you will be creating a web service using Windows Communication Foundation (WCF). The web service layer provides managed APIs the phone application can use to access the database.

Creating a Cloud Service to Access the Cloud Database

You will be creating a WCF service called NotepadService that will be consumed by the Windows Phone Notepad application. Think of NotepadService as the layer that provides managed APIs to the Notepad application. NotepadService will utilize the Entity Framework to generate object models based on the database tables, and it will also generate a persistence layer that performs the database operations, which otherwise you would have to code yourself. The following steps will provide you with instructions on creating and deploying NotepadService to Windows Azure. You will be creating a WCF Azure service and running it from your machine, and then you will package and deploy the project to the Azure cloud, where you will be able to configure it to have multiple services run if your application demand increases.

Creating a Windows Azure Project

You will be creating a Windows Azure NotepadService project in Visual Studio in the following steps. In order to create Azure services, you would need to download Azure tools and SDK from www.microsoft.com/windowsazure/windowsazure/default.aspx.

1. Create a new Windows Phone Application by selecting File ➤ New Project on the Visual Studio command menu. Select the Cloud installed template on the left, and choose Windows Azure Cloud Service from the list on the left (see Figure 3–17). Name the Azure service NotepadService and click OK.

Figure 3–17. *Windows Azure Cloud Service project*

2. You will be prompted to select the type of role. Note here that if you want to host the web project, you need to select ASP.NET Web Role. For Notepad WCF service, select WCF Service Web Role, as shown in Figure 3–18, and click the arrow pointing to the left. In Cloud Service Solution, you will see WCFServiceWebRole; if you hover your mouse over the item, you will see that a little pencil icon appears. Click the pencil icon and change the name to NotepadServiceRole, also shown in Figure 3–18.

51

Figure 3–18. Selecting WCF Service Web Role

Generating an Object Model to Access the Cloud Database

Now that you have the basic plumbing for implementing a WCF service, it's a good time to implement a persistence layer that allows you to interact with the database. The Entity Framework will act as an object-relational mapping tool that will take database tables and create equivalent object models and many of the tedious tasks of coding methods (like add, delete, update, and search).

At the end of this section, you will have created two object models, User and Note, which you can work directly in the code. The Entity Framework provides the ability to save these models directly back to the database.

In the following steps, you will add an Entity Framework item to the project and then connect to NotepadDB in SQL Azure and generate object models.

3. Right-click the NotepadServiceRole project found in Solution Explorer and choose Add ➤ New Item.

4. Click the Data from Installed Templates list, choose ADO.NET Entity Data Model, and name the model NotepadService.edmx (see Figure 3–19).

Figure 3–19. Adding Entity Framework

> 5.   You will be prompted with the Entity Data Model Wizard, as shown in Figure
>   3–20. Click the Next button.

Figure 3–20. Entity Data Model wizard

6. Click the New Connection button. When Choose Data Source appears, select Microsoft SQL Server from the list, as shown in Figure 3–21. Click the Continue button.

Figure 3–21. Choose Data Source window

7. You will be prompted with a Connection Properties window. In the service name, put the SQL Azure server name that you acquired from the previous steps and enter NotepadAdmin and P@ssword as your username and password. From the Select or enter database name drop-down, select NotepadDB, as shown in Figure 3–22.

Figure 3–22. Connection Properties window

8. Click the OK button, and you will return to the Entity Data Model wizard window. Select Yes, include the sensitive data in the connection string radio button, and click the Next button.

9. If you expand the tables, you will see the two tables (Note and User) that you created previously. Select both of the tables, as shown in Figure 3–23.

Figure 3–23. Choosing the database objects

10. Take the default option for everything else and click the Finish button. You will return to the Visual Studio project and see Notepad.edmx, which contains two object models: User and Note, as shown in Figure 3–24.

Figure 3–24. Entity model Notepad.edmx

You now have User and Note object models that you can work with in your NotepadService. In the next section, you will be preparing NotepadService, which will implement simple create, read, update, and delete operations using the entity model that you generated in this section.

Implementing a WCF Service to Access the SQL Azure Database

Now that you have an entity model of User and Note, you can implement NotepadService, which will add, update, delete, and search notes. In this section, you will learn to implement a WCF service; you'll also learn to use Entity Framework to interact with the SQL Azure database.

Coding the WCF Contract

In order to create a WCF service, you must first define a WCF service contract. If everything was done successfully, you'll see a Solution Explorer in Visual Studio that resembles Figure 3–25.

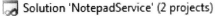

Figure 3–25. *NotepadService project in Solution Explorer*

Open IService.cs and replace the content with the following code. The WCF contract will contain a way to add, delete, update, and search the note in NotepadDB. The namespace System.ServiceModel allows you to add attributes ServiceContract and OperationContract, which must be defined in order to create a WCF service.

```
using System.ServiceModel;
using System.Collections.Generic;
using System;

namespace NotepadServiceRole
{
    [ServiceContract]
    public interface IService
    {
        [OperationContract]
        Guid AddUser(Guid userId, string userName);

        [OperationContract]
        NoteDto AddNote(Guid userId, string notedescription, string noteText);

        [OperationContract]
        void UpdateNote(int noteId, string noteText);
```

```
        [OperationContract]
        void DeleteNote(Guid userId, int noteId);

[OperationContract]
        List<NoteDto> GetNotes(Guid userId);

        [OperationContract]
        NoteDto GetNote(Guid userId, int noteId);

    }
}
```

In the next section, you will create a data contract that will be sent to the client through the service.

Coding the DataContract

Before you implement the service contract, you will need to define two data transfer objects to map to the entity object. Although you can expose the entity generated by the Entity Framework directly to the WCF service, it is not a recommended practice because the Entity Framework exposes information not necessary for the client. For example, information like foreign key, primary key, and any Entity Framework–related information that is in the Note and User objects has no meaning to the client. Also, when the Entity Framework object is serialized, it will include all this unnecessary information, causing the serialized objects coming through the Internet to get huge; since you are working with the Windows Phone over wireless or Wi-Fi transmission, you will want information sent over the wireless to be small.

11. To NotepadServiceRole add the UserDto.cs class with the following code. The namespace you will be using, System.Runtime.Serialization, lets you add DataContract and DataMember attributes that allow the WCF service to serialize this object to be sent over the service to the client.

```
using System.Runtime.Serialization;

namespace NotepadServiceRole
{
    [DataContract]
    public class UserDto
    {
        [DataMember]
        public int UserId { get; set; }

        [DataMember]
        public string Name { get; set; }
    }
}
```

12. Add the NoteDto.cs class to NotepadServiceRole with the following code:

```
using System.Runtime.Serialization;

namespace NotepadServiceRole
{
```

```
[DataContract]
public class NoteDto
{
    [DataMember]
    public int NoteId { get; set; }

    [DataMember]
    public string Description { get; set; }

    [DataMember]
    public string NoteText { get; set; }

}
}
```

Coding the Service

In the following steps, you will implement the NotepadService WCF contract defined in the previous section. You will be using the Entity Framework to access the SQL Azure database.

Open Service1.svc.cs in the NotepadServiceRole project and add the code blocks spelled out in the following sections.

Coding AddUser Method

AddUser will add a new user to the database. Note that you are instantiating NotepadDBEntities, which is the Entity Framework–generated context that connects to the SQL Azure NotepadDB.

```
public Guid AddUser(Guid userId, string userName)
{
    using (var context = new NotepadDBEntities())
    {
        context.AddToUsers(new User()
            {
                UserId = userId,
                Name = userName,
            });
        context.SaveChanges();

        return userId;
    }
}
```

Coding AddNote Method

Note in AddNote method, after instantiating NotepadDBEntities, you are creating the Note entity that you generated in the previous steps using the Entity Framework wizard. Once the note is saved, you are mapping to NoteDto to be sent to the client.

```
public NoteDto AddNote(Guid userId, string notedescription, string noteText)
{
```

```
using (var context = new NotepadDBEntities())
{
    Note note = new Note()
        {
            Description = notedescription,
            UserId = userId,
            NoteText = noteText,
        };
    context.AddToNotes(note);
    context.SaveChanges();

    return new NoteDto()
        {
            NoteId = note.NoteId,
            Description = note.Description,
            NoteText = note.NoteText,
        };
}
}
```

Coding UpdateNote Method

In order to update the note, first you need to instantiate the entity context that connects to NotepadDB, and then you must query for the note that you are going to update. Once the note is retrieved, you will then update the properties and save changes.

```
public void UpdateNote(int noteId, string noteText)
{
    using (var context = new NotepadDBEntities())
    {
        var note = context
                        .Notes
                        .Where(n => n.NoteId.Equals(noteId)
                                ).Single();
        note.NoteText = noteText;
        context.SaveChanges();
    }
}
```

Coding DeleteNote Method

When deleting the note, the note must be retrieved first and then the retrieved note will be added to the DeleteObject of the Notes collection. Then you save the changes where the delete will be performed by the Entity Framework.

```
public void DeleteNote(Guid userId, int noteId)
{
    using (var context = new NotepadDBEntities())
    {
        var note = context
                        .Notes
```

```
                               .Where(n => n.NoteId.Equals(noteId)).Single();
               context.Notes.DeleteObject(note);
               context.SaveChanges();
           }
       }
```

Coding GetNotes Method

GetNotes will bring all the notes associated with the specific userId. You will be using a technique called Linq to Entity that closely resembles the SQL statement. And inside the Linq to Entity, you will be performing translation of the Note entity to NoteDto. This is a very useful technique for mapping an entity object to a data transfer object.

```
       public List<NoteDto> GetNotes(Guid userId)
       {
           using (var context = new NotepadDBEntities())
           {
               var notes = (
                            from eachNote in context.Notes
                            where eachNote.UserId == userId
                            orderby eachNote.Description ascending
                            select new NoteDto
                            {
                                NoteId = eachNote.NoteId,
                                Description = eachNote.Description,
                                NoteText = eachNote.NoteText,
                            }
                        ).ToList();

               return notes;
           }
       }
```

Coding GetNote Method

GetNote will query a single user note from the database.

```
       public NoteDto GetNote(Guid userId, int noteId)
       {
           using (var context = new NotepadDBEntities())
           {
               var notes = (
                            from eachNote in context.Notes
                            where eachNote.NoteId == noteId
                                  && eachNote.UserId == userId
                            select new NoteDto
                            {
                                NoteId = eachNote.NoteId,
                                Description = eachNote.Description,
                                NoteText = eachNote.NoteText,
```

```
                        }
            ).SingleOrDefault();

        return notes;
    }
}
```

Testing Azure WCF NotepadService on Your Machine

You will be testing NotepadService on your machine so that when you connect to NotepadService from the Windows Phone Notepad application, you will be able to debug and step through NotepadService when the service call is made from the Notepad application.

Press F5 and you will notice that the Development Fabric window appears in Internet Explorer. Development Fabric simulates the Azure service environment in your machine. Note that when you expand NotepadService you see NotepadServiceRole, which is the WCF service that you coded in the previous steps. When NotepadService is deployed, you will see one instance of the service deployed, as shown in Figure 3–26. Don't stop the service, as you will be referencing the service from the Notepad application.

Figure 3–26. Development Fabric simulating the Azure Service environment

In the previous steps, you created the NotepadDB database in SQL Azure and the NotepadService hosted locally using Development AppFabric to simulate Windows Azure. In the following section, you will be consuming NotepadService from the Notepad application; when the service works properly, you will be deploying NotepadService to Windows Azure.

Building a Phone Client to Access a Cloud Service

The Notepad application will allow you to add notes and retrieve the notes that will be saved to the cloud database NotepadDB. You will be building the Notepad application that will consume NotepadService, the WCF Azure service that you created previously, and you will verify at the end that the notes are properly saved to SQL Azure NotepadDB. When it's finished, the UI for the Notepad application will resemble Figure 3–27.

Figure 3–27. Notepad application

Creating a Windows Phone Project

To set up the Notepad project, follow the steps you've used in previous examples in this book.

1. Open Microsoft Visual Studio 2010 on your workstation.

2. Create a new Windows Phone Application by selecting File ➤ New Project on the Visual Studio command menu. Select Silverlight for Windows Phone from Installed Templates, and then select the Windows Phone Application template on the right when the list appears, as shown in Figure 3–28. Name the application Notepad and click OK.

Figure 3–28. Creating a Windows Phone Application project

Building the User Interface

You will be building the user interface using XAML in Visual Studio. For building simple controls, it's faster to work with XAML code. First, you'll build two user controls, NoteListUsercontrol, which will display the list of the notes that the user can select to display and edit, and UserRegistrationUserControl, where the user can register so that the notes can be saved to NotepadDb in the cloud.

Building UserRegistrationUserControl

UserRegistrationUserControl is displayed the first time when the user starts the Notepad application; thereafter, the user registration information will be saved to the isolated storage application settings (isolated storage will be covered in detail in Chapter 13).

3. Right-click the Notepad project and choose Add ➤ New Item.

4. From the Add New Item window, choose Windows Phone User Control and name the control UserRegistrationUserControl.xaml, as shown in Figure 3–29. Click the Add button.

Figure 3–29. Creating UserRegistrationUserControl

5.   Open `UserRegistrationUserControl.xaml`, which you just added from Solution Explorer. Replace the content with the following XAML code, and you will see a control that will resemble Figure 3–30 in Visual Studio design view.

Figure 3–30. UserRegistrationUserControl design view

Declaring the UI Resources

Take the default namespaces as shown in the following code:

```
<UserControl x:Class="Notepad.NoteListUserControl"
    xmlns="http://schemas.microsoft.com/winfx/2006/xaml/presentation"
    xmlns:x="http://schemas.microsoft.com/winfx/2006/xaml"
    xmlns:d="http://schemas.microsoft.com/expression/blend/2008"
    xmlns:mc="http://schemas.openxmlformats.org/markup-compatibility/2006"
    mc:Ignorable="d"
    FontFamily="{StaticResource PhoneFontFamilyNormal}"
    FontSize="{StaticResource PhoneFontSizeNormal}"
    Foreground="{StaticResource PhoneForegroundBrush}"
    d:DesignHeight="480" d:DesignWidth="480">
```

Adding Components for UserRegistrationUserControl

You will be adding a Register button, a UserName label, and a TextBlock to capture the username.

```
<Grid x:Name="LayoutRoot" Background="{StaticResource PhoneChromeBrush}">
        <Button Content="Register" Height="72" HorizontalAlignment="Left"
                Margin="118,260,0,0" Name="btnSave" VerticalAlignment="Top"
                Width="160" Click="btnSave_Click" />
        <TextBox Height="72" HorizontalAlignment="Left"
                Margin="118,154,0,0" Name="txtUserName" Text=""
                VerticalAlignment="Top" Width="337" />
        <TextBlock Height="30" HorizontalAlignment="Left"
                Margin="17,177,0,0" Name="textBlock1"
                Text="UserName: " VerticalAlignment="Top" />
</Grid>
```

Building NoteListUserControl

NoteListUserControl displays the list of notes that the user created. The control will be prompted when the user clicks the View/Edit button from the MainPage.

6. Right-click the Notepad project and choose Add ➤ New Item.

7. From the Add New Item window, choose Windows Phone User Control and name the control NoteListUserControl.xaml. Click the Add button.

8. Open NoteListUserControl.xaml, which you just added from Solution Explorer, replace the content with the following XAML code, and you will see a control that will resemble Figure 3–31 in Visual Studio design view.

Figure 3–31. NoteListUserControl design view

Declaring the UI Resources

Take the default namespaces shown in the following code:

```
<UserControl x:Class="Notepad.NoteListUserControl"
    xmlns="http://schemas.microsoft.com/winfx/2006/xaml/presentation"
    xmlns:x="http://schemas.microsoft.com/winfx/2006/xaml"
    xmlns:d="http://schemas.microsoft.com/expression/blend/2008"
    xmlns:mc="http://schemas.openxmlformats.org/markup-compatibility/2006"
    mc:Ignorable="d"
    FontFamily="{StaticResource PhoneFontFamilyNormal}"
    FontSize="{StaticResource PhoneFontSizeNormal}"
    Foreground="{StaticResource PhoneForegroundBrush}"
    d:DesignHeight="480" d:DesignWidth="480">
```

Adding Components for NoteListUserControl

You will be adding a ListBox control that will be bound to the Notes, which is a collection of NoteDto coming from the NotepadViewModel object you will be implementing later. Each ListBoxItem will contain a TextBlock that is bound to NoteDto's Description property.

```
<Grid x:Name="LayoutRoot" Background="{StaticResource PhoneChromeBrush}">
    <ListBox Height="458" HorizontalAlignment="Left" Margin="10,10,0,0" Name="lstNotes"
            VerticalAlignment="Top" Width="460"
SelectionChanged="lstNotes_SelectionChanged"
            ItemsSource="{Binding Notes}">
        <ListBox.ItemTemplate>
            <DataTemplate>
                <StackPanel>
                    <TextBlock Text="{Binding Description}" />
                </StackPanel>
            </DataTemplate>
        </ListBox.ItemTemplate>
```

```
            </ListBox>
        </Grid>
</UserControl>
```

Building MainPage

MainPage will contain the user controls NoteListUserControl and UserRegistrationUserControl (which you just created) and the buttons Add, AddNew, Delete, and View/Edit, which will allow the user to add, insert, and delete the notes.

Declaring the UI Resources

The namespaces you see in the following code snippet are typically declared by default when you first create a Windows Phone project. In particular, the namespaces xmlns:phone="clr-namespace:Microsoft.Phone.Controls; assembly=Microsoft.Phone" allow you to add common Windows Phone controls to the application main page.

You will also be adding xmlns:uc="clr-namespace:Notepad"; it allows you to add BooleanToVisibilityConverter, which implements converting value from the Boolean to Visibility that is set on the controls.

```
<phone:PhoneApplicationPage
    x:Class="Notepad.MainPage"
    xmlns="http://schemas.microsoft.com/winfx/2006/xaml/presentation"
    xmlns:x="http://schemas.microsoft.com/winfx/2006/xaml"
    xmlns:phone="clr-namespace:Microsoft.Phone.Controls;assembly=Microsoft.Phone"
    xmlns:shell="clr-namespace:Microsoft.Phone.Shell;assembly=Microsoft.Phone"
    xmlns:d="http://schemas.microsoft.com/expression/blend/2008"
    xmlns:mc="http://schemas.openxmlformats.org/markup-compatibility/2006"
    xmlns:uc="clr-namespace:Notepad"
    mc:Ignorable="d" d:DesignWidth="480" d:DesignHeight="768"
    FontFamily="{StaticResource PhoneFontFamilyNormal}"
    FontSize="{StaticResource PhoneFontSizeNormal}"
    Foreground="{StaticResource PhoneForegroundBrush}"
    SupportedOrientations="Portrait" Orientation="Portrait"
    shell:SystemTray.IsVisible="True">
```

Building the Main Page and Adding Components

In MainPage, you will be adding Add, Delete, AddNew, and View/Edit buttons to work with the notes. Two TextBlocks, txtNotes, and txtNoteName, are added to display the note name and the note content. txtNote and txtNoteName are bound to SelectedNote.NoteText and SelectedNote.Description. The SelectedNote property comes from the NotepadViewModel object, which gets bound to the context of MainPage so that any control in MainPage can bind to any properties of the NotepadViewModel object.

There are two user controls that you will be adding: Visibility of these user controls is controlled by the ShowNoteList and NeedUserId properties found in NotepadViewModel. When the user clicks the View/Edit button, ShowNoteList will be set to true, causing NoteListUserControl, bound to the ShowNoteList property, to appear to the user.

When the user first starts the application and doesn't have the user ID stored in the application settings, NeedUserId will be set to true in NotepadViewModel, causing the UserRegistrationUserControl to appear.

Adding BoolToVisibilityConvert

Note that you will be adding a custom converter that will convert the Boolean value received from NotepadViewModel to Visibility enumeration in order to hide and unhide the controls. You will be coding BoolToVisibilityConvert in later.

```
<UserControl.Resources>
    <uc:BoolToVisibilityConverter x:Key="BoolToVisibilityConverter" />
</UserControl.Resources>

<Grid x:Name="LayoutRoot" Background="Transparent">
    <Grid.RowDefinitions>
        <RowDefinition Height="Auto"/>
        <RowDefinition Height="*"/>
    </Grid.RowDefinitions>

    <StackPanel x:Name="TitlePanel" Grid.Row="0" Margin="12,17,0,28">
        <TextBlock x:Name="ApplicationTitle" Text="Notepad"
                   Style="{StaticResource PhoneTextNormalStyle}"
                   HorizontalAlignment="Left" Margin="12,0,0,0" Width="89"/>
    </StackPanel>

    <Grid x:Name="ContentPanel" Grid.Row="1" Margin="12,0,12,0">
        <Button Content="Add" Height="72" HorizontalAlignment="Left"
                Margin="-8,10,0,0" x:Name="btnSave" VerticalAlignment="Top" Width="99"
                Click="btnSave_Click" />
        <Button Content="Delete" Height="72" HorizontalAlignment="Left"
                Margin="71,10,0,0" x:Name="btnDelete" VerticalAlignment="Top" Width="125"
                Click="btnDelete_Click" />
        <Button Content="AddNew" Height="72"
                Margin="176,10,128,0" x:Name="btnAddNew" VerticalAlignment="Top"
                Click="btnAddNew_Click" />
        <Button Content="View/Edit" Height="72" HorizontalAlignment="Left"
                Margin="306,10,0,0" Name="btnEdit" VerticalAlignment="Top" Width="160"
                Click="btnViewEdit_Click" />
        <TextBox x:Name="txtNote" TextWrapping="Wrap"
                 Margin="10,163,8,8" AcceptsReturn="True"
                 Text="{Binding Path=SelectedNote.NoteText}"/>
        <TextBlock x:Name="lblNoteName" HorizontalAlignment="Left" TextWrapping="Wrap"
                   Text="Note Name:" VerticalAlignment="Top" Margin="32,114,0,0"/>
        <TextBox x:Name="txtNoteName" TextWrapping="Wrap"
                 VerticalAlignment="Top" Margin="143,91,8,0"
                 Text="{Binding Path=SelectedNote.Description}"/>
        <uc:NoteListUserControl x:Name="ucNoteList"
                 Visibility="{Binding ShowNoteList, Converter={StaticResource
BoolToVisibilityConverter}}" d:IsHidden="True" />
        <uc:UserRegistrationUserControl x:Name="ucUserRegistration"
```

```
                    Visibility="{Binding NeedUserId, Converter={StaticResource
BoolToVisibilityConverter}}" d:IsHidden="True"  />
        </Grid>
    </Grid>
```

In the next section, you will be adding events for the controls that you built in previous steps.

Coding MainPage

In Solution Explorer, open MainPage.xaml.cs and replace the code there with the following C# code blocks to implement the UI interacting with the user to add, delete, view, and edit notes, and to register the user for the first time.

Specifying the Namespaces

Begin by listing the namespaces the application will use.

```
using System.Windows;
using Microsoft.Phone.Controls;
```

Code Constructor

In the constructor of MainPage, you will be setting DataContext of the user controls to the NotepadViewModel instance. When DataContext of ucNoteList and ucUserRegistraton is set to NotepadViewModel, the controls within the user controls' values will be controlled by the properties of NotepadViewModel.

```
        public MainPage()
        {
            InitializeComponent();

            this.DataContext = NotepadViewModel.Instance;
            ucNoteList.DataContext = NotepadViewModel.Instance;
            ucUserRegistration.DataContext = NotepadViewModel.Instance;
        }
```

Coding the Save Button Event

When the user clicks the Add button, the SaveNote method from the NotepadViewModel instance will be called. Any direct calls to NotepadService will be handled from NotepadViewModel, leaving the handling of the web service call complexity centralized to NotepadViewModel. This is a great abstraction technique, allowing you to easily maintain the application.

```
        private void btnSave_Click(object sender, RoutedEventArgs e)
        {
            if (!string.IsNullOrEmpty(txtNote.Text))
            {
                NotepadViewModel.Instance.SaveNote(txtNoteName.Text, txtNote.Text);
```

```
        }
    }
```

Coding the ViewEdit Button Event

When the ViewEdit button is clicked, the ShowNoteList property in `NotepadViewModel` will be set to true, which will trigger `NoteListUserControl` to appear. ShowNoteList will be set to true only if there are Notes to be selected.

```
private void btnViewEdit_Click(object sender, RoutedEventArgs e)
{
    if (!string.IsNullOrEmpty(txtNote.Text))
    {
        NotepadViewModel.Instance.SaveNote(txtNoteName.Text, txtNote.Text);
    }
}
```

Coding the AddNew Button Event

When the AddNew button is clicked, SelectedNode in `NotepadViewModel` will be set to null, triggering the txtNote and txtNoteName contents to be set to empty because they are bound to SelectedNote. Although you can directly set the text fields of txtNote and txtNoteName to an empty string, you are abstracting this particular task to `NotepadViewModel` because when the user selects the specific user note from NoteListUserControl, the txtNote and txtNoteName content will be automatically changed because they are bound to SelectedNote.

```
private void btnAddNew_Click(object sender, System.Windows.RoutedEventArgs e)
{
    NotepadViewModel.Instance.SelectedNote = null;
}
```

Coding the Delete Button Event

When the Delete button is clicked, the `DeleteNote` method from the `NotepadViewModel` instance will be invoked, SelectedNode will be set to null, and txtNote and txtNoteName will be set to an empty string automatically because they are bound to SelectedNode.

```
private void btnDelete_Click(object sender, System.Windows.RoutedEventArgs e)
{
    NotepadViewModel.Instance.DeleteNote();
}
```

Coding the BoolToVisibilityConvert

You will create a custom converter that implements `IValueConverter`, which can be used during the binding in the control where the bound value can be converted to any value that the control will understand. `BoolToVisibilityConvert` will convert Boolean value bound to the control Visibility to Visibility enumeration so that the controls can hide and unhide.

9. Right-click the Notepad project and choose Add ➤ Add New Item.

10. When the Add New Item window pops up, choose Class and name the class BoolToVisibilityConvert, as shown in Figure 3–32. Click the Add button.

Figure 3–32. Adding BoolToVisibility class to the project

11. Open BoolToVisibilityConvert.cs and paste the code blocks spelled out in the following sections.

Specifying the Namespaces and Applying IValueConverter Interface

The namespace System.Windows.Data will allow you to declare the IValueConverted interface for the BoolToVisibilityConverter class.

```
using System;
using System.Windows;
using System.Windows.Data;

namespace Notepad
{
    public class BoolToVisibilityConverter : IValueConverter
    {
```

Implementing IValueConvert

In order to convert bound value to the control property or transform to other value, you need to implement the Convert and ConvertBack methods.

```
public object Convert(object value, Type targetType,
object parameter, System.Globalization.CultureInfo culture)
    {
        bool boolValue;

        if (bool.TryParse(value.ToString(), out boolValue))
        {
            return boolValue ? Visibility.Visible : Visibility.Collapsed;
        }
        else
        {
            // By default it will always return Visibility.Collapsed
            // even for the case where the value is not bool
            return Visibility.Collapsed;
        }

    }

public object ConvertBack(object value, Type targetType,
object parameter, System.Globalization.CultureInfo culture)
    {
        Visibility visibilityValue = Visibility.Collapsed;

        try
        {
            visibilityValue = (Visibility)Enum.Parse(typeof(Visibility),
(string)value, true);
            return visibilityValue;
        }
        catch (Exception)
        {
            // if fails to conver the value to Visibility
            // it will return Collapsed as default value
            return visibilityValue;
        }

    }
}
```

Adding Reference to NotepadService

Before you code NotepadViewModel, add a web service reference to the NotepadService WCF service that will be hosted in Azure.

12. Right-click the References folder found under the Notepad project in Solution Explorer, and choose Add Service Reference.

13. You will be prompted with the Add Service Reference window. In Address, enter http://127.0.0.1/Service.svc, and enter NotepadServiceProxy in the Namespace text box. Click the Go button and NotepadService information is retrieved. You will see Service1 in the Services box.

14. When you expand Service1, you will see IService. Click IService and the Operations box will be populated with NotepadService, as shown in Figure 3–33. Click the OK button.

Figure 3–33. Adding service reference to NotepadService

Coding NotepadViewModel

NotepadViewModel is considered the controller of this application, and it controls the events and the data that will manipulate the UI. You can think of it as the brain of the application.

15. Right-click the Notepad project and choose Add ➤ Add New Item.

16. When the Add New Item window pops up, choose Class; name the class NotepadViewModel. Click the Add button. Your Solution Explorer should resemble Figure 3–34.

Solution 'Notepad' (1 project)
- ▲ Notepad
  - ▷ Properties
  - ▷ References
  - ▲ Service References
    - ▷ NotepadServiceProxy
  - ▷ Bin
  - ▷ obj
  - ▷ App.xaml
    - ApplicationIcon.png
    - Background.png
    - BoolToVisibilityConverter.cs
  - ▷ MainPage.xaml
  - ▷ NoteListUserControl.xaml
    - NotepadViewModel.cs
    - ServiceReferences.ClientConfig
    - SplashScreenImage.jpg
  - ▷ UserRegistrationUserControl.xaml

Figure 3–34. Notepad project items in Solution Explorer

17. Open NotepadViewModel.cs, found under the Notepad project, and enter the following C# code.

Specifying the Namespaces and Applying INotifyPropertyChanged

The namespace Notepad.NotepadServiceProxy allows you to work with the web service NotepadService you referenced. System.IO.IsolatedStorage allows you to save the registered user ID so that the application will know what notes to work within the database. System.ComponentModel allows you to implement the INotifyChanged interface that can raise the property changed events, allowing the controls that are bound to properties like Notes, SelectedNotes, ShowNoteList, and NeedUserId to respond to the changes. System.Linq allows you to query to objects with syntax that resembles the SQL statement.

```
using System;
using System.Windows;
using System.IO.IsolatedStorage;
using System.ComponentModel;
using Notepad.NotepadServiceProxy;
using System.Collections.ObjectModel;
using System.Linq;

namespace Notepad
```

```
{
    /// <summary>
    /// Settings class is singleton instance that will contain various application
    /// configuration that will be used by all the controls of the application.
    /// </summary>
    public sealed class NotepadViewModel : INotifyPropertyChanged
    {
```

Initializing the Variables

There are many variables that will be added to NotepadViewModel that will control the behavior of the UI controls. Please refer to the comments in the following code for an explanation of what significance the properties have for the UI controls.

```
        // For creating Singleton instance
        public static NotepadViewModel Instance = new NotepadViewModel();

// For calling Notepad web service
        private ServiceClient _svc;

        // Populated when the user registers firstime
        // and the value is saved to the isolated storage
        public Guid UserId
        {
            get
            {
                if (IsolatedStorageSettings.ApplicationSettings.Contains("UserId"))
                {
                    return (Guid)IsolatedStorageSettings.ApplicationSettings["UserId"];
                }
                else
                {
                    return Guid.Empty;
                }
            }
            set
            {
                if (IsolatedStorageSettings.ApplicationSettings.Contains("UserId"))
                {
                    IsolatedStorageSettings.ApplicationSettings["UserId"] = value;
                }
                else
                {
                    IsolatedStorageSettings.ApplicationSettings.Add("UserId", value);
                }

                // Raise property changed event to alert user registration control
                // so that if the UserId is empty user registration screen
                // will be prompted for the user to register.
                //
                // To see how raise property changed event works with control Binding
```

```csharp
                // see Binding attributes on ucUserRegistration control in MainPage.xaml
                this.RaisePropertyChanged("UserId");
                this.RaisePropertyChanged("NeedUserId");
            }
        }
// Checks to see if the UserId exist in the isolated storage
        // and make sure UserId is not an empty Guid
        public bool NeedUserId
        {
            get
            {
                return !IsolatedStorageSettings.ApplicationSettings.Contains("UserId")
                    || (Guid)IsolatedStorageSettings.ApplicationSettings["UserId"]
== Guid.Empty;
            }
        }

        // ShowNoteList is bound to NoteListUserControl in the MainPage
        // and it will hide if false and else unhide if true.
        private bool _showNoteList = false;
        public bool ShowNoteList
        {
            get
            {
                return _showNoteList;
            }

            set
            {
                _showNoteList = value;
                this.RaisePropertyChanged("ShowNoteList");
            }
        }

        // SelectedNote is populated from NoteListUserControl
        // when the user selects the note from the list box.
// SelectedNote is then used in MainPage by txtNote and
// txtNoteName to populate to textbox content.
        private NoteDto _note;
        public NoteDto SelectedNote
        {
            get
            {
                return _note;
            }

            set
            {
                _note = value;
                this.RaisePropertyChanged("SelectedNote");
            }
        }
```

```
        // Collection of NoteDto is populated by calling GetNotes service call
// and all user notes will be contained in this collection.
        private ObservableCollection<NoteDto> _notes;
        public ObservableCollection<NoteDto> Notes
        {
            get
            {
                return _notes;
            }

            set
            {
                _notes = value;
                this.RaisePropertyChanged("Notes");
            }
        }
```

Adding the Constructor

In the constructor, you will be adding event handlers for the service calls. GetNotesCompleted will
return all the user notes. AddNote, UpdateNote, and DeleteNote will add, update, and delete the note
and return successfully if no error occurs, otherwise the error will be reported back to the callbacks. In
the constructor ServiceClient, the web service proxy will be initialized and the RebindData method that
makes the call to the GetNotes method will populate the Notes property.

```
        private NotepadViewModel()
        {
            _svc = new ServiceClient();
            _svc.GetNotesCompleted += new
EventHandler<GetNotesCompletedEventArgs>(_svc_GetNotesCompleted);
            _svc.AddNoteCompleted += new
EventHandler<AddNoteCompletedEventArgs>(_svc_AddNoteCompleted);
            _svc.UpdateNoteCompleted += new
EventHandler<AsyncCompletedEventArgs>(_svc_UpdateNoteCompleted);
            _svc.AddUserCompleted += new
EventHandler<AddUserCompletedEventArgs>(_svc_AddUserCompleted);
            _svc.DeleteNoteCompleted += new
EventHandler<AsyncCompletedEventArgs>(_svc_DeleteNoteCompleted);

            if (this.NeedUserId)
            {
                this.Notes = new ObservableCollection<NoteDto>();
            }
            else
            {
                this.RebindData();
            }
        }

        // To rebind the data GetNotes will be called to retrieve
```

```
        // all the user notes and resetting Notes value.
        public void RebindData()
        {
            _svc.GetNotesAsync(this.UserId);
        }
```

Adding SaveNote, AddUser, DeleteNote

Here you will be using the Linq to Object technique to query the Notes property to check if noteName exists. If the note exists, UpdateNote will be called; otherwise AddNote will be called. The AddUser method will make a service call to add the user. DeleteNote will call the DeleteNote service.

```
        public void SaveNote(string noteName, string noteText)
        {
            // Search the user notes and see if the note already exist
            var note = (from eachNote in this.Notes
                        where eachNote.NoteText.Equals(noteText,
StringComparison.InvariantCultureIgnoreCase)
                        select eachNote).SingleOrDefault();

            if (note == null)
            {
                _svc.AddNoteAsync(this.UserId, noteName, noteText);
            }
            else
            {
                _svc.UpdateNoteAsync(note.NoteId, noteText);
            }

            this.SelectedNote = note;
        }

        public void AddUser(Guid userId, string userName)
        {
            if (this.NeedUserId)
            {
                _svc.AddUserAsync(userId, userName);
            }
        }

        public void DeleteNote()
        {
            _svc.DeleteNoteAsync(this.UserId, this.SelectedNote.NoteId);
        }
```

Adding NotepadService Eventhandlers

The following code will handle callbacks for NotepadService calls.

AddNoteCompleted

When the note is added successfully, SelectedNote will be set with the result returned from the call.

```
private void _svc_AddNoteCompleted(object sender, AddNoteCompletedEventArgs e)
{
    if (e.Error == null)
    {
        this.SelectedNote = e.Result;
        this.RebindData();
    }
    else
    {
        MessageBox.Show("Failed to add the note. Please try again!");
    }
}
```

GetNotesCompleted

The returned result will contain all the user notes and will be set to the Notes property.

```
private void _svc_GetNotesCompleted(object sender, GetNotesCompletedEventArgs e)
{
    if (e.Error == null)
    {
        this.Notes = e.Result;
    }
    else
    {
        MessageBox.Show("Failed to get the notes. Please try again!");
    }
}
```

UpdateCompleted

When the updated note is completed, RebindData is called, which will trigger the UI element txtNote, txtNoteName, to be updated in MainPage.

```
private void _svc_UpdateNoteCompleted(object sender, AsyncCompletedEventArgs e)
{
    if (e.Error == null)
    {
        this.RebindData();
    }
    else
    {
        MessageBox.Show("Failed to update the note. Please try again!");
    }
}
```

AddUserCompleted

If the user registration is successful, the UserId property will be set with the return result, saving it to the isolated storage.

```
private void _svc_AddUserCompleted(object sender, AddUserCompletedEventArgs e)
{
    if (e.Error == null)
    {
        // Set the UserId only when AddUser service call
        // was made successfully
        this.UserId = e.Result;
    }
    else
    {
        this.UserId = Guid.Empty;
        MessageBox.Show("Failed to add user please try again!");
    }
}
```

DeleteNoteCompleted

When the delete note call is successful, SelectedNote will be set to null so that txtNote and txtNoteName will be set with an empty string in MainPage, and RebindData is called to update the properties.

```
private void _svc_DeleteNoteCompleted(object sender, AsyncCompletedEventArgs e)
{
    if (e.Error == null)
    {
        this.SelectedNote = null;
        this.RebindData();
    }
    else
    {
        MessageBox.Show("Failed to delete note please try again!");
    }
}
```

Coding INotifyPropertyChanged Interface

Here you will be coding the implementation of the INotifyPropertyChanged event that will be called whenever the Notes, ShowNoteList, NeedUserId, and SelectedNote properties are changed.

```
// Implement INotifyPropertyChanged interface
public event PropertyChangedEventHandler PropertyChanged;
private void RaisePropertyChanged(string propertyName)
{
    PropertyChangedEventHandler propertyChanged = this.PropertyChanged;
    if ((propertyChanged != null))
    {
        propertyChanged(this, new PropertyChangedEventArgs(propertyName));
```

```
            }
        }
    }
}
```

Testing the Application Against NotepadService Deployed Locally

Before you begin, make sure that NotepadService is running Development App Fabric; otherwise press
F5 to start NotepadService as shown in the previous steps. Then press F5 on the Notepad Windows
Phone project. You will see the application shown in Figure 3–27. Enter the username and register, and
add some notes so that you can confirm that the notes are saved to NotepadDB in SQL Azure.

Open up your SQL Server Management Studio by following the steps provided in the previous
sections, type in the following SQL statement, press F5, and you will see the notes and the user data
saved to NotepadDB.

```
select * from [User]
select * from Note
```

When the SQL statement is executed, you should see the data you added in the Results window, as
shown in Figure 3–35.

Figure 3–35. *Querying NotepadDB*

In the next section, you will deploy NotepadService directly to Windows Azure and modifying the Notepad application to consume the web service located in Windows Azure instead of from the local machine.

Deploying the Service to Windows Azure

By deploying to Windows Azure, you will have a redundant, fault-tolerant service that you can scale out if you need to meet the demands of heavy usage. You will see how simple it is to configure the service and deploy.

Preparing for Windows Azure NotepadService

You will be creating a Windows Azure service host in order to deploy WCF NotepadService to a Windows Azure platform.

Signing Up for Windows Azure and Creating a Project

1. Open the browser of your choice.

2. Go to www.microsoft.com/windowsazure/ to sign up and buy the Windows Azure service account. Follow the directions provided by Microsoft in order to purchase and acquire the service account.

3. Go to https://windows.azure.com/ and sign in using the account you created in Step 1.

Connecting to the Windows Azure Project

4. Once you've signed in, click the Windows Azure menu tab on the left side. When the Windows Azure page loads, you will see the project that you created during the registration process (see step 1). See Figure 3–36, which will correspond to this step.

Figure 3–36. Windows Azure project list

5. Click the project hyperlink NAS-DEV. In your case, you should click the name of the project that corresponds to the one you created in Step 1.

Create and Configuring Windows Azure NotepadService

Now you're ready to create and configure the service.

6. Create a new service that will host your WCF service by clicking the New Hosted Service icon on the top left side of the page. You will see the form in Figure 3-37

85

Figure 3–37. Adding a new Azure service to the project

7. In the "Enter a name for your service" box, enter NotepadService; in the "Enter a URL prefix for your service" textbox, type NotepadServiceDemo. Note here that NotepadServiceDemo.cloudapp.net will become your production WCF endpoint that you will be using later in your Windows Phone application.

8. In the "Choose a region or affinity group" section, you have two options. Typically, relating the affinity among other services allows you to run the services in the same region in order to optimize performance.

9. If you are creating multiple services that will interact with other services in the same region, select "Create a new affinity group" or choose the existing Affinity Group from the "Create or choose an affinity group" drop-down.

10. If you won't be creating multiple services that require the services to be in the same region, then select the Anywhere US option from the Choose a Region drop-down.

11. In the Deployment options section, select "Deploy to production environment" and make sure the "Start after successful deployment" checkbox is checked.

12. For Deployment name, I recommend using the version number of your NotepadService, which would be 1.0.0.0.

See Figure 3–38 for appropriately filled information. Keep this browser open as you will be coming back and deploying the packages.

Figure 3–38. Configuring the WCF Azure service

Deploying NotepadService to Windows Azure

In the previous steps, you prepared the NotepadService host; now it's time for you to deploy NotepadService so that you can consume the Azure service from the phone. You will be deploying the service to staging first. Staging is where you test your service before going to production. This is a very convenient way of making sure your service works before going live.

Compiling and Publishing NotepadService

You will need a compiled binary so you can deploy to the Windows Azure host.

1. Go to your NotepadService project, stop the project if it is running, right-click the NotepadService project, and choose Publish.

2. The Publish Cloud Service window will appear. Choose "Create Service Package Only," as shown in Figure 3–39.

Figure 3–39. Create a NotepadService package for Windows Azure

3. Click the OK button. Windows Explorer will open with a directory where you will see two files: NotepadService.cspkg is the compiled binary of NotepadService and ServiceConfiguration.cscfg is the configuration file used by Windows Azure. Take note of the directory path as you will be uploading these files to Windows Azure.

Deploying NotepadService.cspkg and ServiceConfiguration.cscfg to Windows Azure

You will be deploying the packages created in the previous steps to Windows Azure.

4. Go to your browser where the Create a New Hosted Service screen is, as shown in Figure 3–38.

5. Click Browse Locally in the Package location section; browse to where you published compiled NotepadService in the previous section and choose NotepadService.cspkg.

6. In the Configuration file section, click the Browse Locally button; browse to where you published NotepadService and choose ServiceConfiguration.cscfg. You should see a screen that resembles Figure 3–40.

Figure 3–40. Staging Deployment screen

7. Click OK to deploy. You will see Warning screen as shown in Figure 3-41. Click Yes to ignore this warning.

Figure 3–41. Warning screen when creating a new hosted service

8. You will be returned to the main screen of Hosted Service. Note that NotepadService is being created (see Figure 3-42). You will need to wait until the status changes to Ready.

Figure 3–42. NotepadService being created in Windows Azure Platform

9. When the status changes to Ready, select NotepadService 1.0.0.0 and note the
    DNS name on the right. This is the WCF end URL that you will be using. Simply
    append "/Service.svc" to this DNS name on the browser. (for the demo, see
    (http://ef8c3aa169c04db99fbfb74616a0afd6.cloudapp.net/service1.svc) If
    everything was successful, you should see your NotepadService in the browser
    (see Figure 3-43).

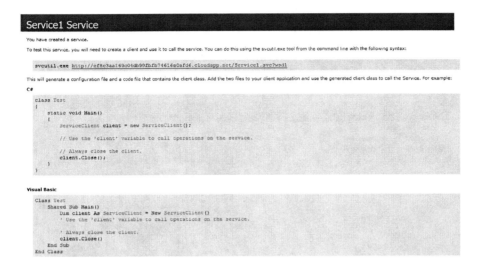

Figure 3–43. NotepadService WCF endpoint when deployed to Windows Azure staging

In following section using you will consume NotepadService deployed to Windows Azure staging.

Testing the Notepad Application Against NotepadService Azure Service

In the previous steps, you deployed NotepadService to the Windows Azure host. You will be changing the Notepad phone configuration to point to the web service that is hosted in Windows Azure and test in the same way you tested when the service was deployed locally to your machine.

10. Go to Visual Studio and open the Notepad project.

11. In Solution Explorer under the Notepad project, open `ServiceReferences.ClientConfig`. Change the endpoint address from 127.0.0.1 to the URL that you received when you deployed to staging in previous steps. See Figure 3–44 with the changed endpoint address.

Figure 3–44. *Changing the service endpoint to the Windows Azure address*

12. Make sure that NotepadService is in Ready status, and then press F5 to run
    your Notepad phone application in the emulator. Follow the previous steps to
    test the Notepad application. It should exhibit exactly the same behavior,
    except that now you are running your Notepad application against the
    Windows Azure service.

Summary

In this chapter, you build a Windows Phone application that makes use of Microsoft's Windows Azure
service to store data to an SQL server in the cloud. Your application is now scalable and fault-tolerant,
and it can accommodate a large number of users. You learned how simple it is to create the service and
the database in the Azure cloud and how Microsoft Azure gives you the power to build an application
without having to worry about creating your own complex IT infrastructure to support it.

In Chapter 4, you will learn to catch exceptions and debug and test Windows Phone applications.
You will learn critical skills that will help you be successful in building a Windows Phone application.

CHAPTER 4

Catching and Debugging Errors

As you develop Windows Phone applications, you must learn how to equip them to handle a number of exceptions that are unique to smartphones. Unlike a desktop computer, a Windows Phone is loaded with devices over which you have little direct control, including GPS, an accelerometer, Wi-Fi, isolated storage, and a radio. A user can decide to turn off an onboard device to save power at any time; isolated storage can run out of space; and a resource such as a cell tower, GPS satellite, or Wi-Fi router might not be available. To identify and fix unexpected exceptions in an application, you need to know how to use the powerful debugging facilities of Visual Studio. To assure yourself that you have dealt with all of the bugs your application is likely to encounter, you need to know how to test your applications on a real device.

In this chapter, you will learn to master critical debugging and troubleshooting skills using Visual Studio IDE, which you can also use to debug any application, including web applications (ASP.NET) and Windows applications.

The following sections are divided into three major topics. We'll walk you through a series of tutorials covering general exception handling in Windows Phone, Visual Studio debugger features, and testing using the emulator and the real device.

Debugging Application Exceptions

In this section, you will learn how to find and deal with two exceptions that are common to Windows Phone applications. The first is the navigation failed exception, which can be thrown when a main page is loaded; the second deals with the web service call that is consumed by the application.

The ErrorHandlingDemo application that you'll use contains two projects: a Windows Phone project and the Calculator web service project, which has an Add method that adds two numbers and returns the result to the caller. Being able to debug and handle web service call exceptions will be critical, especially if you are planning to work with external services like Microsoft Bing Maps services (which are covered in Chapter 14).

When you finally debug and fix all the issues in the application, you will see the result shown in Figure 4–1.

Figure 4–1. ErrorHandlingDemo application

Debugging Page Load Exceptions

The ErrorHandlingDemo application contains bugs that will cause exceptions to be thrown when the application's main page is loaded. In this section, you will learn how to find and fix such problems in Visual Studio.

Catching an Exception

Whenever an application throws an exception, Visual Studio will stop execution at the line where it's thrown. To observe this behavior, let's run the application and take a closer look using the Visual Studio IDE.

Fire up Visual Studio, select File ➤ Open, and browse to the following file, which you can download from the site for this book:

`{unzippeddirectory}\ch04\ErrorHandlingDemo\Start\ErrorHandlingDemo.sln.`

Once the solution file is loaded, press F5 to run it. Notice the raised exception message in Figure 4–2, which points to the code that has caused `ArgumentOutOfRangeException` to be thrown. From DeviceExtendedProperties you can obtain Windows Phone 7 system information, and only the following keys—DeviceManufacturer, DeviceName, DeviceUniqueId, DeviceTotalMemory, ApplicationCurrentMemoryUsage, and ApplicationPeakMemoryUsage—will be available. And when you try to query the system information DName that does not exist, the application throws `ArgumentOutOfException`.

Figure 4–2. *A raised exception in Visual Studio*

Querying Exception Object Values with Immediate Window

Whenever an application running in Visual Studio pauses at a line where an exception has been thrown, you always have an opportunity to observe its variables in Visual Studio's Immediate Window.

Immediate Window is a most useful debugging feature because it allows you to evaluate any statement when the code execution pauses at the breakpoint. If you do not see the immediate window when the breakpoint is hit, you can go to Debug ➤ Windows ➤ Immediate to bring up the Immediate Window, as shown in Figure 4–3.

1. With ErrorHandlingDemo still paused in the debugger, go to the Immediate Window, type in `DeviceExtendedProperties.GetValue("DeviceName")` to query the object value, and press Enter. You will see the result printed in an Immediate Window, as shown in Figure 4–3.

Figure 4–3. *Query object value in Immediate Window*

In next section, you will learn to handle exceptions specific to Windows Phone 7.

Catching an Unhandled Exception in RootFrame_NavigationFailed or Application_UnhandledException

Unhandled exceptions in a Windows Phone application will be caught by one of two main methods: `RootFrame_NavigationFailed` and `Application_UnhandledException`. `RootFrame_NavigationFailed` catches unhandled exceptions thrown while a page is being loaded; `Application_UnhandledException` catches exceptions thrown in all other cases.

2. Press F5 to continue debugging from the breakpoint in the previous section.

The debugger will next break inside `RootFrame_NavigationFailed` in `App.xaml.cs`, as shown in Figure 4–4. Notice that in `App.xaml.cs` you will find various Windows Phone application–related events such as `Application_Launching`, `Application_Activated`, `Application_Deactivated`, `Application_Closing`, `RootFrame_NavigationFailed`, and `Application_UnhandledException`. As far as exceptions are concerned, only two events will be of interest. `RootFrame_NavigationFailed` captures unhandled exceptions when the Windows Phone page fails to load. In ErrorHandlingDemo, unhandled exceptions occur when `MainPage` tries to load and throws `ArgumentOutOfException`.

Figure 4–4. *Breakpoint at RootFrame_NavigationFailed*

3.   With your mouse, hover over NavigationFailedEventArgs e; you will be able to drill into the object value and see the e.Uri that contains the page that caused the error during the load, as shown in Figure 4–5.

Figure 4–5. *NavigationFailedEventArgs.Uri*

4.   Press F5 to continue debugging. You will notice that code execution next breaks in the Application_UnhandledException method. All exceptions that are not handled specifically by a try-catch-finally block will ultimately end up in this method.

Handling an Exception RootFrame_NavigationFailed

When an exception is thrown in the `MainPage` of an application, the exception will be caught by the `RootFrame_NavigationFailed` method, and this is where you want to handle it in order to stop the exception from bubbling up to the `Application_UnhandledException` method.

In `ErrorHandlingDemo`, replace the `RootFrame_NavigationFailed` method with following code. Notice the use of MessageBox in the code to display the proper error with stack trace and set e.Handled to true, which will stop the breakpoint to move to the `Application_UnhandledException` method.

```
// Code to execute if a navigation fails
private void RootFrame_NavigationFailed(object sender, NavigationFailedEventArgs e)
{
    if (System.Diagnostics.Debugger.IsAttached)
    {
        // A navigation has failed; break into the debugger
        System.Diagnostics.Debugger.Break();
    }

    MessageBox.Show(
string.Format("Page {0} failed to load because of with error: {1}",
e.Uri.ToString(), e.Exception.StackTrace));
        e.Handled = true;
    }
```

Fixing the Error in the Code

In the previous section, you added a MessageBox display in case any other page fails to load. In the following steps, you will be fixing the actual cause of the exception in `MainPage`. But first, let's fix the error in `MainPage.xaml.cs`.

Fix the error in `MainPage.xaml.cs` by replacing

```
txtDeviceName.Text = DeviceExtendedProperties.GetValue("DName").ToString()
```

with

```
txtDeviceName.Text = DeviceExtendedProperties.GetValue("DeviceName").ToString().
```

Debugging a Web Service Exception

`ErrorHandlingDemo` contains the `CalculatorService` web service project where the service will be hosted locally and consumed by the demo application. The code is written so that the application will throw the exceptions that you will be fixing.

Catching a Web Service Exception

You will be stepping through the breakpoints in order to understand the behavior of the thrown exception. Before you begin, make sure that both the Windows Phone project and the web service project start simultaneously when you Press F5.

5. Right-click the ErrorHandlingDemo solution in Solution Explorer and choose the property. The solution property page window shown in Figure 4–6 will display.

6. Select the Multiple startup projects option, and CalculatorService and ErrorHandlingDemo projects' Actions are set to Start.

7. Also, put two breakpoints in MainPage.xaml.cs at the line txtAnswer.Text = e.Result.ToString() and _svc.AddAsync(txtX.Text, txtY.Text), as shown in Figure 4–6.

Figure 4–6. *Breaking point to debug CalculatorService web service*

8. Press F5. You will see the application shown in Figure 4–1 in the emulator, and you will notice the WCF Test Client starts as well, as shown in Figure 4–7. The WCF Test Client will host the CalculatorService, allowing you to step into the web service call.

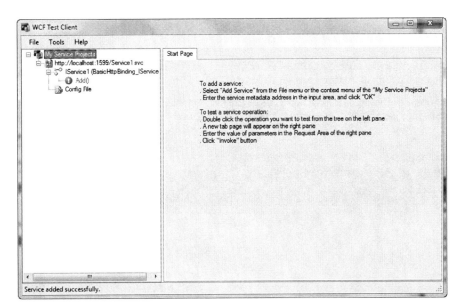

Figure 4–7. *WCF test client*

9. From the emulator, press the Call Calculator Service button.

Notice that the Visual Studio catches `InvalidCastException` thrown from the `CalculatorService` project, as shown in Figure 4–8.

Figure 4–8. InvalidCastException in CalculatorService

10. When you hover over x value you will notice that it contains Test, which can't be converted to integer, thus causing InvalidCastException.

11. Press F5 to continue. Visual Studio breaks at Reference.cs, which is the web service proxy class that was generated against WSDL from Visual Studio (see Chapter 3 for more detail on how to consume web services).

12. Press F5 again. The execution will break on the line txtAnswer.Text = e.Result.ToString() found in MainPage.xaml.cs.

13. In Immediate Window, type in e.Error. You will notice that e.Error is not empty. When the web service returns any kind of error, e.Error will not be empty, and when you try to access e.Result that contains web service call, the result will throw an exception.

14. Press F5 again. Note the exception thrown in the e.Result property, as shown in Figure 4–9.

Figure 4–9. Exception thrown in e.Result when the web service has an error

15. Press F5. The exception will be finally caught in
`Application_UnhandledException`.

Fixing the CalculatorService Exception

After stepping through the breakpoints, you now have enough information to fix the exception.

First, let's check the values received from the caller in `CalculatorService`. Replace `Service1.svc.cs` codes with the following snippet. The `CheckValue` method will make sure that the received value is not null and convert the value to the integer.

```
public int Add(object x, object y)
{
    int xValue = CheckValue(x);
    int yValue = CheckValue(y);

    return xValue + yValue;
```

```
        }

        private int CheckValue(object value)
        {
            int convertedValue = -1;
            if (value == null)
            {
                throw new ArgumentNullException("value");
            }
            else if (!int.TryParse(value.ToString(), out convertedValue))
            {
                throw new ArgumentException(
string.Format("The value '{0}' is not an integer.", value));
            }

            return convertedValue;
        }
```

In `MainPage.xaml.cs`, replace the AddCompleted event delegate with following code. You will be checking to make sure e.Error is empty before retrieving e.Result; if e.Error is not empty, you will be throwing the proper error message.

```
_svc.AddCompleted += (s, e) =>
        {
            if (e.Error == null)
            {
                txtAnswer.Text = e.Result.ToString();
            }
            else
            {
                MessageBox.Show(
string.Format("CalculatorService return an error {0}",
e.Error.Message));
            }
        };
```

Testing the Application

You've finished debugging and fixing the application exceptions, and now you'll be able to properly run the application and handle exceptions.

Press F5 and you will see Figure 4–1; notice now that txtDeviceManufacturer and txtDeviceName are properly populated during the `MainPage` load. When you change txtX to an integer and click the Call Calculator Service button, txtAnswer will be populated with the result received from the web service.

Registering a Windows Phone Device for Debugging

Testing an application on a Windows Phone device is a lot more work than using the Windows Phone emulator because it involves registering your device, physically connecting it to your computer via a USB cable, and running Zune software in the background on your workstation. Here are the steps you need to follow to set up a phone as your debugging platform.

First, you must apply for a Windows Phone Marketplace account at the Windows Phone developer portal.

1. If you don't yet have a Windows Phone account, go to
    `http://create.msdn.com/` and sign up.

Microsoft will review your application and activate your account. If you have not
yet installed Zune software, you can download the latest Zune software from
`www.zune.net/en-us/products/software/download/default.htm`.

2. Once you're approved, click the Windows Start menu on your workstation and
    select All Programs ➤ Zune to start the Zune software. The Welcome page is
    shown in Figure 4–10.

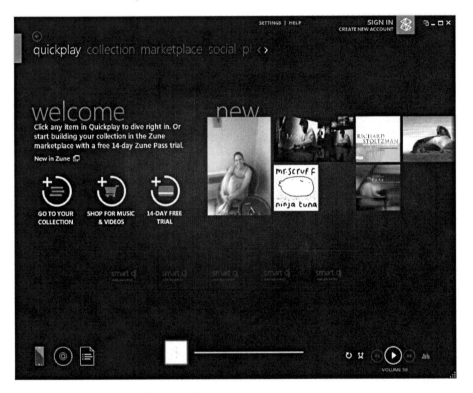

Figure 4–10. The Zune software welcome page

■ **Note** The Windows Phone 7 device is based on the Zune, which is a Microsoft product and iPod competitor for
playing video and audio. A Windows Phone uses Zune software to update a Windows Phone 7 system, and Zune
must be running in order to deploy an application to a device. You can also use Zune software to back up your
device.

---

3. Connect your Windows Phone device to your developer workstation using a USB cable.

4. To confirm that your device is properly connected and recognized by the Zune software, click the phone icon at the bottom left corner of the Zune Welcome screen, as indicated by the arrow in Figure 4–11.

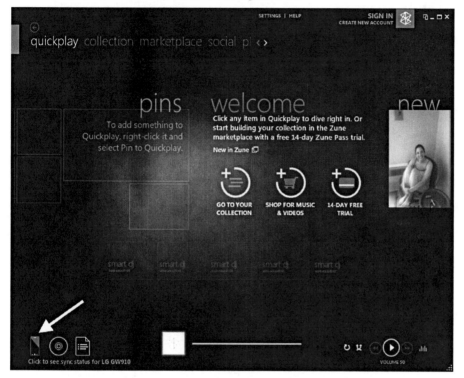

Figure 4–11. Clicking the phone icon in Zune software

5. When you click the phone icon, the Zune software will display detailed information about your device, as shown in Figure 4–12.

Figure 4–12. Windows Phone device detail page in Zune

Now you are ready to actually register your device.

6. Go to the Windows Start menu, select All Programs ➤ Windows Phone Developer Tools, and select Windows Phone Developer Registration, as shown in Figure 4–13.

Figure 4–13. Windows Phone developer registration

A Windows Phone developer registration form will display, as shown in Figure 4–14.

7. Enter the ID and password you used to register for a Windows Phone Marketplace account in step 1.

Figure 4–14. *Windows Phone developer registration*

To confirm that your phone is properly registered, go to `http://create.msdn.com/` and log in.

Once logged in, click My Dashboard ➤ Windows Phone and then click my devices from the left menu, as shown in Figure 4–15.

Figure 4–15. My Windows Phone page

Then click on from the left menu My Account ➤ Devices, as shown in Figure 4-16.

Figure 4–16. Windows Phone registered devices page

In the following section, you will learn tips and tricks to make your life easier when you begin to debug and test using a real device.

TIPS AND TRICKS: DEBUGGING ON A DEVICE

Here are a few things that you should keep in mind to make your life easier and save you time when you're debugging an application on a live Windows Phone.

- When debugging, it's best to disable screen time-out, especially if you are debugging through a complex program that takes a long time. On the Windows Phone device, go to Settings ➤ Lock & Wallpaper, and set the screen time-out to never. After debugging, remember to come back to reset the screen time-out to other so you don't waste your battery.

- When you try to debug in the Windows Phone 7 device, you will get the error message shown here. And when you click No, you will see an "Access Denied" message in your Error List window. This is because your device is locked due to time-out. To avoid this problem during the debugging, disable time-out on the device by following step 1. To resolve this issue, simply unlock your device and restart in debug mode in Visual Studio.

Microsoft Visual Studio ⬛ X

ⓘ There were deployment errors. Continue?

                                                   Yes   No

☐ Do not show this dialog again

Error List

  ❌ 1 Error   ⚠ 0 Warnings   ⓘ 0 Messages

      Description

❌ 1   Access is denied.

🗖 Error List 📟 Immediate Window 📄 Output 🔍 Find Symbol Results

          o   When the Zune application is not started, you will receive the error "Zune
               software is not launched. Retry after making sure that Zune software is
               launched" in the Visual Studio Error List Window.

Handling Device Exceptions

In the following section, you will learn to capture device-specific exceptions. You will be using the
accelerometer device as an example to properly handle unexpected exceptions by catching
AccelerometerFailedException. AccelerometerFailedException can occur if the accelerometer device on
the phone is broken. The exception can also occur if the device throws an unexpected error caused
internally by Microsoft Window Phone framework. Figure 4–17 displays the basic UI of the
CatchDeviceExceptionDemo project that you will be building.

Figure 4–17. CatchDeviceException UI

Creating the CatchDeviceExceptionDemo Project

To set up the CatchDeviceExceptionDemo project, follow the steps you've used for previous examples in this book.

1. Open Microsoft Visual Studio 2010 Express for Windows Phone on your workstation.

2. Create a new Windows Phone Application by selecting File ➤ New Project on the Visual Studio command menu. Select the Windows Phone Application template, name the application CaptureAccelerometerData, and click OK.

3. In order to use the accelerometer, add an assembly reference to
    Microsoft.Devices.Sensors by right-clicking the References folder in Solution
    Explorer, and choose Microsoft.Devices.Sensors from the Add Reference
    window, as shown in Figure 4–18.

Figure 4–18. Adding reference to Microsoft.Devices.Sensors

Building the User Interface

You will be building the user interface using the XAML in the Visual Studio. For building simple controls,
it's faster to work with the XAML code. Go to Solution Explorer, open MainPage.xaml, and replace the
XAML you find there with the code in the next section.

Declaring the UI Resources

The namespaces you see in the following code snippet are typically declared by default when you first
create a Windows Phone project. In particular, namespaces xmlns:phone="clr-
namespace:Microsoft.Phone.Controls; assembly=Microsoft.Phone" allow you to add common
Windows Phone controls to the application main page.

```
<phone:PhoneApplicationPage
    x:Class="CatchingDeviceExceptionsDemo.MainPage"
    xmlns="http://schemas.microsoft.com/winfx/2006/xaml/presentation"
    xmlns:x="http://schemas.microsoft.com/winfx/2006/xaml"
    xmlns:phone="clr-namespace:Microsoft.Phone.Controls;assembly=Microsoft.Phone"
```

```
xmlns:shell="clr-namespace:Microsoft.Phone.Shell;assembly=Microsoft.Phone"
xmlns:d="http://schemas.microsoft.com/expression/blend/2008"
xmlns:mc="http://schemas.openxmlformats.org/markup-compatibility/2006"
mc:Ignorable="d" d:DesignWidth="480" d:DesignHeight="768"
FontFamily="{StaticResource PhoneFontFamilyNormal}"
FontSize="{StaticResource PhoneFontSizeNormal}"
Foreground="{StaticResource PhoneForegroundBrush}"
SupportedOrientations="Portrait" Orientation="Portrait"
shell:SystemTray.IsVisible="True">
```

Building the Main Page and Adding Components

Create two buttons to start and stop the accelerometer.

```
<!--LayoutRoot is the root grid where all page content is placed-->
<Grid x:Name="LayoutRoot" Background="Transparent">
    <Grid.RowDefinitions>
        <RowDefinition Height="Auto"/>
        <RowDefinition Height="*"/>
    </Grid.RowDefinitions>

    <!--TitlePanel contains the name of the application and page title-->
    <StackPanel x:Name="TitlePanel" Grid.Row="0" Margin="12,17,0,28">
        <TextBlock x:Name="ApplicationTitle" Text="CatchingDeviceExceptionsDemo"
Style="{StaticResource PhoneTextNormalStyle}"/>
    </StackPanel>

    <!--ContentPanel - place additional content here-->
    <Grid x:Name="ContentPanel" Grid.Row="1" Margin="12,0,12,0">
        <Button Content="Start Accelerometer" Height="72" HorizontalAlignment="Left"
Margin="84,45,0,0" Name="btnStartAcc" VerticalAlignment="Top"
Width="284" Click="btnStartAcc_Click" />
        <Button Content="Stop Accelerometer" Height="72" HorizontalAlignment="Left"
Margin="84,123,0,0" Name="btnStopAcc" VerticalAlignment="Top"
Width="284" Click="btnStopAcc_Click" />
    </Grid>
</Grid>

</phone:PhoneApplicationPage>
```

Once you have loaded the XAML code, you should see the layout shown in Figure 4–19. In the next section, you will be coding the application.

Figure 4–19. CatchDeviceExceptionDemo design view

Coding the Application

In Solution Explorer, open `MainPage.xaml.cs` and replace the code there with the following C# code blocks.

Specifying the Namespaces

Begin by listing the namespaces the application will use. Note that the inclusion of `Microsoft.Devices.Sensors` will allow you to start and stop Windows Phone's accelerometer.

```
using System.Windows;
using Microsoft.Phone.Controls;
using Microsoft.Devices.Sensors;
```

Initializing Variables

The variable _acc, Accelerometer object, will be used to start and stop.

```
Accelerometer _acc;

        public MainPage()
        {
            InitializeComponent();
            _acc = new Accelerometer();
        }
```

Implementing Accelerometer Start and Stop Behavior

Implement a button event for stopping and starting the accelerometer. Note that you are catching
AccelerometerFailedException, which can be raised during the start and stop of the accelerometer. In
the exception property, you will find ErrorId and Message that contains specific error code and a
description that could explain why the error was raised

```
private void btnStartAcc_Click(object sender, RoutedEventArgs e)
    {
        try
        {
            _acc.Start();

            _acc.ReadingChanged += (s1, e1) =>
                {
                    // Do something with captured accelerometer data
                };
        }
        catch (AccelerometerFailedException ex)
        {
            string errorMessage = string.Format(@"
                    Accelerometer threw an error with ErrorId {0}
    during the start operation
                    with error message {1}
                    ", ex.ErrorId, ex.Message);
            MessageBox.Show(errorMessage);
        }
    }

    private void btnStopAcc_Click(object sender, RoutedEventArgs e)
    {
        try
        {
            _acc.Stop();
        }
        catch (AccelerometerFailedException ex)
        {
            string errorMessage = string.Format(@"
```

```
                        Accelerometer threw an error with ErrorId {0}
        during the stop operation
                        with error message {1}
                        ", ex.ErrorId, ex.Message);
            MessageBox.Show(errorMessage);
        }
    }
```

Testing the Finished Application

To test the finished application, press F5. The result should resemble the screenshot shown in Figure 4–16. The only thing you will not be able to test is being able to raise `AccelerometerFailedException`, which can be raised only if the accelerometer device fails. But the demo will give you a good idea of how you should be handling the device-related exception if it ever occurs.

Summary

In this chapter, you learned how catch and handle errors in an application and how to handle unexpected errors thrown by a Windows Phone. You also learned how to use Visual Studio's powerful debugging features to troubleshoot and fix defects, regardless of whether you're running an application in the emulator or on a real device.

In Chapter 5, you will learn to package, publish, and manage a Windows Phone application for distribution through the Windows Phone Marketplace.

CHAPTER 5

Packaging, Publishing, and Managing Applications

Every developer dreams of becoming an instant millionaire by creating an application that everyone loves to use. You will have that chance when you develop your own application and then package, distribute, and sell it to millions of Windows Phone users worldwide through the Windows Marketplace.

There are three options for distributing your application through the Windows Phone Marketplace.

- You can sell your application at fixed cost that you specify and earn 70% on each sale.

- You can distribute your application for free (up to 100 free applications). If you decide to distribute your application for free, consider incorporating Windows Phone 7 Ad SDK so you can earn money from advertising. Using Microsoft Advertising service, you can produce targeted advertising for your application to display. For example, if you're creating a health related application, you might choose advertising categories from sports, lifestyle, and/or health categories. Note that you are limited to three categories.

- You can distribute your application as a trial application using the Market Trial API so that users can download the application and try it first before making a purchase. A trial application usually only includes a subset of features.

To package and publish your application to the Windows Phone Marketplace, you must pay a yearly fee of US$99 and your application must abide by the rules of the Windows Phone Marketplace. In following sections, you will learn in great detail what you need to do in order to successfully deliver your application to the Windows Phone Marketplace.

Windows Phone Application Publishing Lifecycle

When you develop a Windows Phone application, you distribute it to Windows Phone Marketplace through the Windows Phone developer portal. Figure 5–1 shows the application publishing lifecycle from the developer to the developer portal to the Windows Phone Marketplace to the consumers.

Figure 5–1. Windows Phone application publishing lifecycle

First (1) you must register as a developer with the Windows Phone portal and pay the US$99 fee. Your identity will be verified and you will be issued a certificate that the Windows Marketplace will use to sign your application. In addition, your bank account will be verified so that your earnings can be deposited there. Next (2), if you haven't already done so, you'll need to download the SDK tools for Visual Studio. After you've created your application (3), you will submit it to the portal for validation and certification (4) so Microsoft can assure the application abides by the Windows Phone Marketplace rules. Once your application becomes eligible, it will be signed using the certificate you received during registration (5), and then published to the Windows Phone Marketplace (6).

Once the application is published, users will be able to buy, download, and install it from the Widows Phone Marketplace portal. There, users can also rate it and comment on its virtues and flaws, providing you with feedback that you can use for improvements. The Marketplace will provide you with downloads and sales information as well.

In the followings sections, you will learn a great deal about the certification requirements and the process so that your application can pass through and be submitted to the Windows Phone Marketplace.

Windows Phone Application Certification Requirements

In the battle between iPhone, Android, and Windows Phone, the applications available on each smartphone play a critical role in winning over consumers. Windows Phone Marketplace puts in place the rules and process to ensure that the published applications are of a high quality. You can download Windows Phone 7 application certification requirements from `http://go.microsoft.com/?linkid=9730558`. The following list describes the ideas behind the rules and the process imposed on publishing an application to Windows Phone Marketplace:

1. **Applications are reliable.** You will be dealing with the consumer, who will be picky. Any hint of instability in the application will reflect negatively on the application and the brand behind the phone. So Microsoft will enforce the best practices for creating reliable application.

2. **Applications make efficient use of resources.** Your application must make efficient use of the phone resources while not adversely effecting performance. For example, the battery life can be drained quickly if the location service continues to run even after the user has left your application; your code needs to plan for such events.

3. **Applications do not interfere with the phone functionality.** The user must be notified before modifying any phone settings or preferences.

4. **Applications are free of malicious software.** The application must be safe to install and use.

In following sections, the summary of main points will be presented so that you will be aware of the content of the certification documents. Remember that the following sections describing the certification requirements are based on version 1.3, and Microsoft could modify it or release a newer version, so check the developer portal frequently at `http://create.msdn.com/`.

Application Policies

This section covers the policies that protect the Windows Phone Marketplace and the consumers using any Windows Phone application bought from the marketplace.

Windows Phone Application Binary (XAP File)

You must compile your application in release mode from Visual Studio; this will produce a file with a `.xap` file extension. A XAP file is nothing more than a ZIP file with a different extension name. In fact, if you change the extension name of your XAP file from `.xap` to `.zip`, you will be able to extract its file content. You should be aware of following facts:

1. For installation over the air, the XAP file must be no larger than 20MB.

121

2. You must notify the user that there might be additional charges depending on how the data package is downloaded. Must disclose additional data package to be downloaded if greater than 50.

3. The maximum size of a XAP is 400MB; a XAP greater than 20MB can only be installed through Zune or over Wi-Fi.

Things Your Application Must Not Do

Your application can't do this following:

1. Your application can't sell, link, or promote mobile voice plans.

2. It can't distribute, link, or direct the users to an alternate marketplace.

3. Your application can't taint the security or functionality of Windows Phone devices or Windows Phone Marketplace.

Things Your Application Must Do

Your application must do the following things:

1. Your application must be functional.

2. If submitted as a trial application, it must include a reasonable feature subset of the fully functional application.

3. If your application includes or displays advertising, the advertising must abide by the rules at `http://advertising.microsoft.com/creative-specs`.

4. If your application enables chat, instant messaging, or person-to-person communication and allows the user to create account, the user must be verified of at least 13 years old.

5. If your application sells music, the application must include Windows Phone music Marketplace (if available). If the content of the music is purchased elsewhere, the application must include its own playback media player.

Location Service (GPS)

The following requirements concern the location service (GPS):

1. The location must be obtained using Microsoft Location Service API. (Notifications are the subject of Chapter 17).

2. It can't override, ignore, and circumvent Microsoft toast or prompts related to the Location Service API. (Location Services are covered in Chapter 14).

3. It can't override a user's choice to disable location services on the phone.

4. The application must have enable and disable options for the location service.

5. If the location data is published to other services or other people, the application must fully disclose how the location service information will be used, obtain permission to use the location information, must provide the user with the option to opt in and out, and there must be a visual indicator whenever the information is transmitted. It must also provide a privacy policy statement regarding the location service information usage.

6. Security must be in place to protect the location data obtained.

Push Notification Service (PNS)

The following points summarize the policies relating to the push notification:

1. The application must provide opt in and out options to use the service.

2. It can't excessively use PNS, thereby causing a burden to the Microsoft network or the Windows Phone device.

3. PNS can't be used to send critical, life-or-death information.

Content Policies

Your application must conform to the content restrictions of the Windows Phone Marketplace. If your application already has ratings from ESRB, PEGI and USK, you need to submit the certificates of these ratings. Be mindful of licensed materials, logos, names, and trademarks. The content must not be illegal or suggest harm. Promotion of items that are illegal under local or federal laws (such as alcohol, tobacco, weapons and drugs) is not allowed. X-rated content, hate-related content, realistic violent content, and excessive use of profanity are not allowed.

Keep in mind that these restrictions are highly subjective and Microsoft will have final ruling on any such content. We suggest that you take a practical approach: ask yourself if your application can safely be used and viewed by a minor.

Application Submission Validation Requirements

In order to package and submit an application for certification, you must make sure the requirements in the following sections are met.

Packaging Requirements

When you are getting ready to create a XAP, it's best to use Visual Studio and compile the binaries in Release Mode, which will produce the XAP file and take care of the many requirements identified in the certification document. The following requirements are mentioned because they are easy to overlook:

1. The XAP file can't be greater 400MB.

2. The application icon must be 62 x 62 of PNG file type.

3. The application tile image must be 173 x 173 of PNG file type.

4. Submitted application must have the application title.

Code Requirements

Your application will be subjected to coding requirements. The application must use the documented APIs found only at http://msdn.microsoft.com/en-us/library/ff626516(VS.92).aspx. The following list described those requirements:

1. PInvoker and COM interoperability is not allowed.

2. The application must be compiled in release mode.

3. Windows Phone assemblies can't be redistributed.

4. When using a method from System.Windows.Controls, APIs in Microsoft.Xna.Framework.Game or Microsoft.Xna.Framework.Graphics can't be called.

Using the Application Manifest File to Disclose Phone Features

When the user purchases an application from the Windows Phone Marketplace, the Marketplace will display what phone features the application will use. This is done through submission of the application manifest file for Windows Phone (http://msdn.microsoft.com/en-us/library/ff769509(VS.92).aspx). The phone features added to application manifest are typically added and removed automatically by Visual Studio, so this is not something you would normally be concerned with. However, during your packaging process, you must make sure that the features listed in the application manifest are correctly represented.

Language Validation

The languages supported are English, French, Italian, German, and Spanish. Depending on where you are submitting your application, you must properly localize your application for at least one of the supported languages.

Images for Windows Phone Marketplace

Your application must be submitted with the images and screenshots that will be displayed in the Windows Phone Marketplace.

1. Microsoft recommends that you use 262 DPI.
2. The required small mobile application tile should be 99 x 99 (PNG); the large mobile application tile should be 173 x 173 (PNG).

3. The required large PC application tile should be 200 x 200 (PNG).

4. The optional background art should be 1000 x 800 (PNG).

5. The required screenshot should be 400 x 800 (PNG).

Application Certification Requirements

Once the application is submitted for the certification process, it will be tested against series of certification requirements. The following sections summarize these requirements.

Application Reliability

This section lists the certification requirements for application reliability.

1. The application must run on all Windows Phone 7 devices.

2. The application must handle all raised exceptions and must not crash the application unexpectedly.

3. The application must not hang and become unresponsive to user input. If the application is processing, it must show a visual element (such as a progress bar) plus the ability to cancel the operation.

Performance and Resource Management

This section describes the requirements that deal with performance and resource management issues.

1. The application must launch the first screen within 5 seconds of the application being launched. The 5 second rule also applies even after the application is closed or deactivated and then restarted.

2. The application must respond to user input within 20 seconds after launch. The 20 second rule also applies even after the application is closed or deactivated and then restarted.

3. When the Windows Phone Back button is pressed from first screen, it will exit the application. If the Back button is pressed from other then the first screen, it must return to the previous page. In games, if the Back button is pressed, it should pause the game with context menu displayed; if the Back button is pressed again, it will exit the pause.

4. The application can't use more than 90MB of RAM. If the device has more than 256MB, then the application can use more than 90MB.

Phone Functionality

The application can't prevent the use of the phone's functionalities or hang when making a call, answering an incoming call, ending a call, or sending and receiving SMS or MMS messages.

Security

The application must not contain any viruses and malware. The application must implement type-safe code as described in "Unsafe Code and Pointers" (http://msdn.microsoft.com/en-us/library/

t2yzs44b(v=VS.80).aspx). And finally the application must not run security critical code as described in "Security Changes in the .Net Framework 4" (http://msdn.microsoft.com/en-us/library/dd233103(v=VS.100).aspx). Security is covered in greater detail in Chapter 19.

Technical Support Information

The application must include the application name, version, and technical support information.

Submitting Your First Windows Phone Application to the Windows Phone Marketplace

In the previous sections, you learned how to pass through the Windows Phone Marketplace's validation and certification process by understanding the rules and process set forth to protect the consumer and the Marketplace. Now you will learn to deploy your first Windows Phone application to the Marketplace so you can start making millions. First, let's learn how to package the application for submission.

Packaging the Application

To package the application, you will use Visual Studio. For this demo, you will use the Notepad project that you created in Chapter 3.

1. Open the Notepad solution found in the directory where you unzipped the source code that accompanies this book; the solution is found at [unzipped directory]\Codes\ch03\Notepad\Notepad.sln. Double-click on the solution to open it.

2. Click on Notepad solution found in the Solution Explorer and then select Release mode from the drop-down (see Figure 5-2).

Figure 5–2. Compiling the phone application in Release mode

3. Press F6 to build the solution in Release mode.

4. When the build is done, you'll find the binaries under bin\release directory where the project file is located. To find out where the project file is, click on the Notepad project from the Solution Explorer. In the Properties window, you will see the project path (see Figure 5–3).

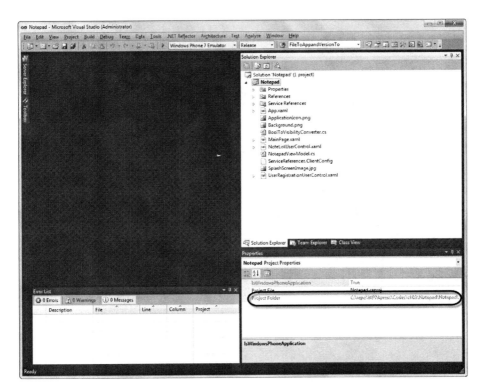

Figure 5–3. Project Folder property

5. Inside of [your project folder]\bin\release, you will find Notepad.xap, which you will be using in next section to submit to the Windows Phone Marketplace.

Submitting the Application

In the previous sections, you compiled a Notepad application and created the Notepad.xap file. In this section you will be deploying the application. Open your browser of choice, go to http://developer.windowsphone.com, and sign into the portal.

1. From the my dashboard menu, choose Windows Phone. If this is your first time submitting an application, you will see the page shown in Figure 5–4.

Figure 5–4. *The my apps page*

2. Click the submit new app button to get to the upload page shown in Figure 5–5.

***Figure 5–5.** The upload page*

3. From the upload page, enter the application name, choose Windows Phone 7 as
    the application platform, English as the default language, and the initial
    version. Then click on application package and browse to where `Notepad.xap` is
    and select the XAP file. Put a Developer note for yourself and a Tester note to
    provide special instructions. Click the Next button.

4. The description page shown in Figure 5–6 will load. Fill out the description dialogue by completing the following steps:

- From the Category drop-down, choose a category that is appropriate for your application.

- Choose a sub-category.

- Add a detailed description and a featured app description (a single sentence that will catch a user's eye at the Marketplace).

- Add keywords that will be used during a search by the user in the Marketplace.

- Add a legal URL, if you have one, and a contact e-mail.

Figure 5–6. The description page

5. The artwork page will load. You will be uploading a large and small application tile, a large PC application tile, and screenshots. The screen resolution is defined in the certification requirements document. Your screen should resemble Figure 5–7. The images for this step can be found in [directory where source code is unzipped]\Codes\ch05. Click the Next button to continue.

Figure 5–7. *The artwork page*

6. The pricing page shown in Figure 5–8 will load. Choose a currency and select the application price. If you are targeting the worldwide market, select Worldwide distribution. If the application is trial application, select Trial supported. Click the Next button to continue.

Figure 5–8. The pricing page

7. The submit page shown in Figure 5–9 will load. Check the checkbox labeled "Automatically publish to Marketplace after passing certification" and click the Submit for certification button.

windows phone: submit new app

step 1 upload

step 2 description

step 3 artwork

step 4 pricing

step 5 submit

___

⊕ back to dashboard

Ready to submit for certification.

Your app is ready to submit for certification. The app will be evaluated against the Windows Phone 7 Technical Certification Requirements.

Review my application details before submitting

☑ Automatically publish to Marketplace after passing certification.

Review the relevant legal terms in the Windows Phone Application Provider Agreement.

Previous   Submit for certification   Save & Quit

Figure 5–9. The submit page

8. You will be returning to the my apps page where you will see the application that you just submitted with a status of testing in progress, as show in Figure 5–10.

Figure 5–10. *Submitted application with Testing in progress status*

Congratulations! You have successfully submitted your Windows Phone application to the worldwide market of Windows Phone users for the price of 99 cents. If your application successfully passes through the certification process, you will be notified by e-mail. If your application fails the certification process, you will be able to see the report of why your application failed and you will have the option to resubmit.

Updating Your Application

In this section, you will learn to redeploy your application with a newer version that might contain new features or fixes to the bugs users have reported.

When you log in to App Hub and go to the my apps page, you will see your published application, similar to that in Figure 5–11.

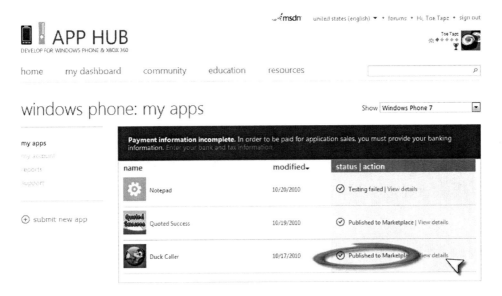

Figure 5–11. Updating an application published to the Marketplace

1. Click on the View Details link, as show in Figure 5–11. You will find this link next to the application that you want to redeploy.

2. On the next screen, you will see the Action drop-down; from it, select Submit application update, as show in Figure 5–12. Note the other Action drop-down options, like being able to change the price, removing the application from the Marketplace, and adding completely different version of the same application (which the consumers must buy—unlike with an update, which they get for free).

Figure 5–12. *Submit application update*

3. The remaining steps are exactly the same as those for submitting a new application to the Marketplace, as described in the previous section. An update must go through the certification process again.

Finding Your Application in the Marketplace

In this section, you will learn to find your application and view ratings and comments. You will be using the Zune software that you downloaded from http://www.zune.net/en-US/products/software/download/downloadsoftware.htm.

1. Install your downloaded Zune software.

2. Open up your Zune software (found at Start ➤ All Programs ➤ Zune). Follow the steps to configure Zune if it's the first time you're using it.

3. Once you are on the main page of Zune, click on the Marketplace link and then click on the APPS link, as shown in Figure 5–13.

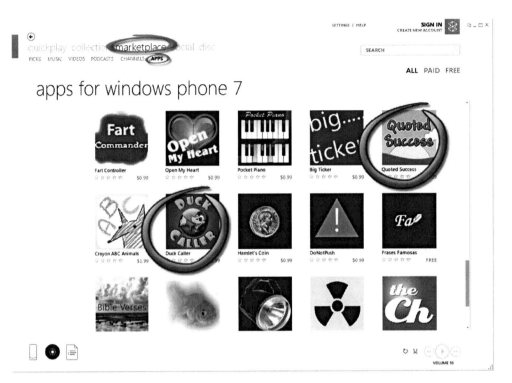

Figure 5–13. Finding your application in the Marketplace using Zune

4. You can either search for your application or navigate to a category to look for your application.

Summary

In this chapter, you learned a great deal about the Windows Phone Marketplace's certification requirements. Then you learned how to package the application in Visual Studio to produce the XAP file and how to submit the application through the Windows Phone development portal for the certification process.

In the following chapters, you will learn about the specific features of the Windows Phone. Chapter 6 covers the accelerometer, which can be used in games to use the phone like steering wheel. You will use the accelerometer to detect the orientation of the phone and capture phone shakes.

Working with the Accelerometer

An accelerometer has many practical uses for applications that depend on the movements of a Windows Phone in three-dimensional space. With data from an accelerometer, you can steer a simulated car in a driving game or fly a plane in a flight simulator. Capturing a motion such as a shake, a punch, a swing, or a slash and mixing this accelerometer data with a physics engine can be used to create Wii-like games. Just for fun, you can build novelty applications to amaze your friends, such as a light saber simulation that makes Star Wars–like sounds as you swing your phone in the air. An accelerometer can even be used for business applications, like a level to use when you hang a picture frame. Under the covers, the controllers for games that run on consoles like the Wii remotes are nothing more than accelerometers wrapped in buttons and plastic.

The accelerometer in a Windows Phone measures the device's movements in space, or more precisely its acceleration along three axes (x, y, and z)relative to the Earth's gravitational pull, which is perpendicular to the ground (9.8 m/sec^2). Think of Newton's apple. When you drop an apple, it will fall toward the earth, and the force that pulls it can be calculated using that well-known high school science formula, force = mass × acceleration. In a Windows Phone, the accelerometer can tell you the orientation of the phone with respect to the earth's gravitational force.

In this chapter, you will learn how to use the Windows Phone accelerometer to write applications that respond to the phone's orientation and movement. In the first example, you will capture data from the accelerometer and interpret the x, y, and z values. In a second demo, you will use readings from the accelerometer to move a ball in a 2D space.

Understanding Orientation and Movement

When you hold a Windows Phone in your hand with its display facing you, think of it as occupying the origin of a three-dimensional graph with its z axis pointing toward you (a positive direction), its y axis pointing down (a negative direction), and its x axis pointing toward the right (a positive direction). Figure 6–1 shows how these three axes are positioned relative to the device as you hold it facing toward you in your hand.

Figure 6–1. Accelerometer axis directions when you hold it in your hand facing toward you

To illustrate the accelerometer reading of the (x, y, z) = (0, -1, 0) means standing the phone up on the table with the front of the phone facing toward you and the phone buttons facing downwards, as shown in Figure 6–2.

If you were to rotate the phone in Figure 6–2 to the right 90 degrees, so that the Windows Phone control buttons are to the right, as shown in Figure 6–3, the expected accelerometer readings would be (x, y, z) = (-1, 0, 0).

If you took the phone in Figure 6–2 and rotated it 180 degrees, (x, y, z) would be (0, 1, 0), as shown in Figure 6–4.

If you were to rotate the phone in Figure 6–4 to the left 90 degrees, as shown in Figure 6–5, (x, y, z) would be (1, 0, 0).

If you were to put the phone flat on the table with the phone facing up, as shown in Figure 6–6, (x, y, z) would be (0, 0, -1).

If you put the phone facing down on the table, as shown in Figure 6–7, (x, y, z) would be (0, 0, 1).

Figure 6–2. *(x, y, z) = (0, -1, 0)*   **Figure 6–3.** *(x, y, z) = (-1, 0, 0)*   **Figure 6–4.** *(x, y, z) = (0, 1, 0)*

Figure 6–5. *(x, y, z) = (1, 0, 0)*   **Figure 6–6.** *(x, y, z) = (0, 0, -1)*   **Figure 6–7.** *(x, y, z) = (0, 0, 1)*

Calculating Distance

The Euclidean distance algorithm is a useful way to calculate a distance between two points in three-dimensional space. This equation allows you to detect sudden movements such as the shaking of the phone.

If (Ox, Oy, Oz) is a previous accelerometer value and (Nx, Ny, Nz) is a new one, you can calculate Euclidean distance as follows:

$$EuclideanDistance = \sqrt{(Nx - Ox)^2 + (Ny - Oy)^2 + (Nz - Oz)^2}$$

Calculating Pitch, Roll, and Yaw

With obtained accelerometer readings you will have a pretty good understanding of the current orientation of the phone, but using the accelerometer data will tell you how far the phone is tilted on the x, y, and z axes. This information can be very useful if you are planning to create airplane simulation games or racing games that use the accelerometer to control the direction of moving objects. Think of it as using a phone like joystick by detecting the tilt motions known as pitch, roll and yaw.

When you hold the phone vertically, with the screen facing you, both the pitch and roll angles are 0 degrees, as shown in Figure 6–8.

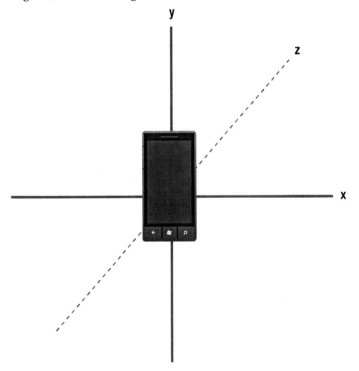

Figure 6–8. *Pitch and roll angles of 0 degrees*

Now if you tilt the phone slightly to the right, you will be able to calculate the pitch (ρ) and roll (φ) angles shown in Figure 6–9. There's another angle of interest, yaw, which is the angle respective to the z axis (not shown in Figure 6–9); think of yaw as phone being tilted towards you or away from you into the page.

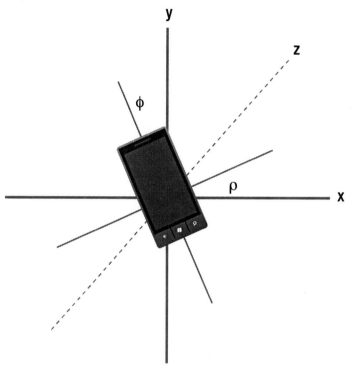

Figure 6–9. *Pitch and roll angles*

In order to calculate pitch (ρ), roll (φ), and yaw (theta) angles you will need the following equations, where Ax, Ay, and Az are the accelerometer values for x, y, and z.

$$\rho = arctan\left(\frac{Ax}{\sqrt{Ay^2 + Az^2}}\right)$$

$$\varphi = arctan\left(\frac{Ay}{\sqrt{Ax^2 + Az^2}}\right)$$

$$\theta = arctan\left(\frac{\sqrt{Ax^2 + Ay^2}}{Az}\right)$$

You'll use Euclidean distance and pitch, roll, and yaw calculations in the examples that follow.

Introducing SDK Support for Accelerometers

In order to use the Windows Phone accelerometer, you'll need to reference the
`Microsoft.Devices.Sensors` namespace, which contains the `Accelerometer` class. Among its members
is the ReadingChanged event, which constantly updates the x, y, and z coordinates of the device as event
arguments e.X, e.Y, and e.Z, with a Timestamp that can be used to calculate velocity, acceleration, and
other values.

There are two things that you must remember about the accelerometer device. First is that heavy
use of the accelerometer will use up the battery of the phone, and thus you must remember to turn it on
only when it's needed and turn it off when done. Second, the accelerometer runs on a thread that is
completely separate from the thread on which the current UI runs. This means that you must use
`Deployment.Current.Dispatcher.BeginInvoke` to update the UI; otherwise you will receive an invalid
cross thread exception.

Retrieving Accelerometer Data

You will begin by building a simple application that captures the accelerometer data. The accelerometer
data consist of acceleration data in x, y, and z directions plus the time in which the acceleration data was
captured. Figure 6–10 displays the basic UI of the accelerometer data. In order for this demo to work,
you must deploy the project to an actual Windows Phone device (please refer to Chapter 4 for deploying
to the device). If you don't have a Windows Phone device, you might consider using Reactive Extension
to simulate the accelerometer behavior. Reactive Extension will not be covered in this chapter, but you
can refer to Chapter 18 for more detail on how to create simulation in order to work with the
accelerometer in the emulator.

Figure 6–10. CaptureAccelerometerData demo

You will build the demo in three steps. First, you'll create a Visual Studio project. Next, you'll build the project's user interface, and then you'll finish up by adding the code the application needs to retrieve and display data from the accelerometer.

Creating the CaptureAccelerometerData Project

To set up the CaptureAccelerometerData project, follow the steps you've used for previous examples in this book.

1. Open Microsoft Visual Studio 2010 Express for Windows Phone on your workstation.

2. Create a new Windows Phone Application by selecting File ➤ New Project on the Visual Studio command menu. Select the Windows Phone Application template, name the application CaptureAccelerometerData, and click OK.

3. In order to use the accelerometer, add an assembly reference to `Microsoft.Devices.Sensors` by right-clicking the References folder in Solution Explorer and choose `Microsoft.Devices.Sensors` from the Add Reference window, as shown in Figure 6–11.

Figure 6–11. Adding a reference to Microsoft.Devices.Sensors

Building the User Interface

You will be building the user interface using the XAML in the Visual Studio (for building simple controls, it's faster to work with the XAML code). Go to Solution Explorer, open `MainPage.xaml,` and replace the XAML you find there with the code in the following sections.

Declaring the UI Resources

The namespaces you see in the following code snippet are typically declared by default when you first create a Windows Phone project. In particular, the namespace xmlns:phone="clr-namespace:Microsoft.Phone.Controls; assembly=Microsoft.Phone" allows you to add common Windows Phone controls to the application main page.

```
<phone:PhoneApplicationPage
    x:Class="CaptureAccelerometerData.MainPage"
    xmlns="http://schemas.microsoft.com/winfx/2006/xaml/presentation"
    xmlns:x="http://schemas.microsoft.com/winfx/2006/xaml"
    xmlns:phone="clr-namespace:Microsoft.Phone.Controls;assembly=Microsoft.Phone"
    xmlns:shell="clr-namespace:Microsoft.Phone.Shell;assembly=Microsoft.Phone"
    xmlns:d="http://schemas.microsoft.com/expression/blend/2008"
    xmlns:mc="http://schemas.openxmlformats.org/markup-compatibility/2006"
    FontFamily="{StaticResource PhoneFontFamilyNormal}"
    FontSize="{StaticResource PhoneFontSizeNormal}"
    Foreground="{StaticResource PhoneForegroundBrush}"
    SupportedOrientations="Portrait" Orientation="Portrait"
    mc:Ignorable="d" d:DesignWidth="480" d:DesignHeight="768"
    shell:SystemTray.IsVisible="True">
```

Building the Main Page and Adding Components

Now, create the components you need to display the x, y, and z values plus the time reading that your application captures from the accelerometer. You'll also want to add components to display the pitch, roll, and yaw values of the device, which you will calculate and use to understand how the phone is oriented. Finally, you also need buttons to start and stop the accelerometer, which are also specified

```
<Grid x:Name="LayoutRoot" Background="Transparent">
    <Grid.RowDefinitions>
        <RowDefinition Height="Auto"/>
        <RowDefinition Height="*"/>
    </Grid.RowDefinitions>

    <StackPanel x:Name="TitlePanel" Grid.Row="0" Margin="24,24,0,12">
        <TextBlock x:Name="ApplicationTitle" Text="CaptureAccelerometer Data"
Style="{StaticResource PhoneTextNormalStyle}"/>
    </StackPanel>

    <Grid x:Name="ContentGrid" Grid.Row="1">
        <TextBlock Name="txtX" Text="TextBlock"
                   Margin="160,56,12,0" FontSize="20"
                   Height="31" VerticalAlignment="Top" />
        <TextBlock Name="txtY" Text="TextBlock"
                   Margin="160,119,12,556" FontSize="20" />
        <TextBlock Name="txtZ" Text="TextBlock"
                   Margin="155,181,12,490" FontSize="20" />
        <TextBlock Name="txtTime" Text="TextBlock"
                   Margin="155,244,12,427" FontSize="20" />
```

```xml
        <Button Content="Start" Height="72"
               Name="btnStart" Width="160"
               Margin="36,514,284,119" Click="btnStart_Click" />
        <Button Content="Stop" Height="72"
               Name="btnStop" Width="160"
               Margin="207,514,113,119" Click="btnStop_Click" />
        <TextBlock FontSize="40" Margin="66,34,331,614"
                  Name="lblX" Text="X" />
        <TextBlock FontSize="40" Margin="66,97,331,552"
                  Name="lblY" Text="Y" />
        <TextBlock FontSize="40" Margin="66,159,346,489"
                  Name="lblZ" Text="Z" />
        <TextBlock FontSize="40" Margin="12,222,331,422"
                  Name="lblTime" Text="Time" />
        <TextBlock FontSize="20" Margin="160,285,7,386"
                  Name="txtPitch" Text="TextBlock" />
        <TextBlock FontSize="22" Margin="0,283,370,365"
                  Name="lblPitch" Text="Pitch" TextAlignment="Right" />
        <TextBlock FontSize="20" Margin="160,345,7,326"
                  Name="txtRoll" Text="TextBlock" />
        <TextBlock FontSize="22" Margin="0,343,370,305"
                  Name="lblRoll" Text="Roll" TextAlignment="Right" />
        <TextBlock FontSize="20" Margin="160,408,7,263"
                  Name="txtYaw" Text="TextBlock" />
        <TextBlock FontSize="22" Margin="0,406,370,242"
                  Name="lblYaw" Text="Yaw" TextAlignment="Right" />
    </Grid>

</phone:PhoneApplicationPage>
```

Once you have loaded the XAML code, you should see the layout shown in Figure 6–12. In the next section, you will be adding events to the updating of the UI with captured accelerometer data.

Figure 6–12. CaptureAccelerometerData demo design view

Coding the Application

In Solution Explorer, open `MainPage.xaml.cs` and replace the code there with the following C# code blocks that will implement the UI updates using accelerometer data.

Specifying the Namespaces

Begin by listing the namespaces the application will use. The inclusion of `Microsoft.Devices.Sensors` will allow you to start and stop Windows Phone's accelerometer.

```csharp
using System;
using System.Windows;
using Microsoft.Phone.Controls;
using Microsoft.Devices.Sensors;
namespace CaptureAccelerometerData
{
    public partial class MainPage : PhoneApplicationPage
    {
```

Initializing Variables

The variable _ac, an Accelerometer object, will be used to start and stop the accelerometer and to retrieve x, y, z, and time. Also notice the inclusion of the ReadingChanged event, which you'll draw on to send captured accelerometer data to your UI.

```
Accelerometer _ac;

        public MainPage()
        {
            InitializeComponent();

            _ac = new Accelerometer();
            _ac.ReadingChanged += new
EventHandler<AccelerometerReadingEventArgs>(_ac_ReadingChanged);
        }
```

Capturing and Displaying Accelerometer Data

Note here that you can't directly change the UI elements upon receiving the accelerometer data because the accelerometer data comes from a different thread than the current UI thread. If you try to change the UI elements directly here, you'll get an invalid cross-thread access error, as shown in Figure 6–13. In order to overcome this problem, you must use the Dispatcher in the current UI thread, as shown in the following code.

Figure 6–13. Invalid cross-thread access error

```
        private void ProcessAccelerometerReading(AccelerometerReadingEventArgs e)
        {
            txtTime.Text = e.Timestamp.ToString();
            txtX.Text = e.X.ToString();
            txtY.Text = e.Y.ToString();
```

```
                    txtZ.Text = e.Z.ToString();
                    txtPitch.Text = RadianToDegree((Math.Atan(e.X / Math.Sqrt(Math.Pow(e.Y, 2) +
Math.Pow(e.Z, 2))))).ToString();
                    txtRoll.Text = RadianToDegree((Math.Atan(e.Y / Math.Sqrt(Math.Pow(e.X, 2) +
Math.Pow(e.Z, 2))))).ToString();
                    txtYaw.Text = RadianToDegree((Math.Atan(Math.Sqrt(Math.Pow(e.X, 2) + Math.Pow(e.Y,
2))/ e.Z))).ToString();
                }
```

Implementing Start and Stop of Accelerometer

Implement the button event for stopping and starting the accelerometer. Note here that you must
anticipate the possible error that might occur when you are trying to start or stop the accelerometer.

```
private void btnStart_Click(object sender, RoutedEventArgs e)
        {
            try
            {
                _ac.Start();
            }
            catch (AccelerometerFailedException)
            {
                MessageBox.Show("Acceleromter failed to start.");
            }
        }

        private void btnStop_Click(object sender, RoutedEventArgs e)
        {
            try
            {
                _ac.Stop();
            }
            catch (AccelerometerFailedException)
            {
                MessageBox.Show("Acceleromter failed to stop.");
            }
        }
    }
}
```

Testing the Finished Application

To test the finished application, press F5. The result should resemble the screenshot in Figure 6–10; you
will see that the x, y, z, and time text blocks are constantly being updated each time you click the Start
button. Remember that to run the application on a Windows Phone 7 device, you must choose the
Windows Phone 7 Device option shown in Figure 6–14.

Figure 6–14. *Choose a Windows Phone 7 device before running the application.*

Using Accelerometer Data to Move a Ball

In this demo, you will use the captured accelerometer data to do something more useful: move the image of a ball as you tilt the phone left, right, forward, and back. This demo will help you understand how to translate the user input of the accelerometer data and apply it to UI elements. Figure 6–15 displays the basic UI of the MoveBallDemo.

Figure 6–15. MoveBallDemo UI

Creating the MoveBall Project

To set up the CaptureAccelerometerData project, follow the steps you've used for previous examples in this book.

1. Open Microsoft Visual Studio 2010 Express for Windows Phone on your workstation.

2. Create a new Windows Phone Application by selecting File ➤ New Project in the Visual Studio command menu. Select the Windows Phone Application template, name the application MoveBallDemo, and click OK.

3. In order to use the accelerometer, add an assembly reference to Microsoft.Devices.Sensors by right-clicking the References folder in Solution Explorer and choose Microsoft.Devices.Sensors from the Add Reference window, as shown previously in Figure 6–11.

Building the User Interface

You will be building the user interface using the XAML in Visual Studio (for building simple controls, it's faster to work with the XAML code). Go to Solution Explorer, open `MainPage.xaml`, and replace the XAML you find there with the code in the following sections.

Declaring the UI Resources

The namespaces you see here are typically declared by default when you first create the Windows Phone project, and the namespaces like `xmlns:phone="clr-namespace:Microsoft.Phone.Controls;assembly=Microsoft.Phone"` will allow you to add common Windows Phone controls.

```
<phone:PhoneApplicationPage
    x:Class="MoveBallDemo.MainPage"
    xmlns="http://schemas.microsoft.com/winfx/2006/xaml/presentation"
    xmlns:x="http://schemas.microsoft.com/winfx/2006/xaml"
    xmlns:phone="clr-namespace:Microsoft.Phone.Controls;assembly=Microsoft.Phone"
    xmlns:shell="clr-namespace:Microsoft.Phone.Shell;assembly=Microsoft.Phone"
    xmlns:d="http://schemas.microsoft.com/expression/blend/2008"
    xmlns:mc="http://schemas.openxmlformats.org/markup-compatibility/2006"
    FontFamily="{StaticResource PhoneFontFamilyNormal}"
    FontSize="{StaticResource PhoneFontSizeNormal}"
    Foreground="{StaticResource PhoneForegroundBrush}"
    SupportedOrientations="Portrait" Orientation="Portrait"
    mc:Ignorable="d" d:DesignWidth="480" d:DesignHeight="768"
    shell:SystemTray.IsVisible="True">
```

Building the Main Page and Adding Components

The UI consists of Start and Stop buttons for stopping and starting the accelerometer and a ball that moves as the Windows Phone is tilted left, right, forward, and backward.

```
<Grid x:Name="LayoutRoot" Background="Transparent">
    <Grid.RowDefinitions>
        <RowDefinition Height="Auto"/>
        <RowDefinition Height="*"/>
    </Grid.RowDefinitions>

    <StackPanel x:Name="TitlePanel" Grid.Row="0" Margin="24,24,0,12">
        <TextBlock x:Name="ApplicationTitle" Text="MoveBallDemo"
Style="{StaticResource PhoneTextNormalStyle}"/>
    </StackPanel>
    <Button Content="Start" Height="72"
            HorizontalAlignment="Left" x:Name="btnStart"
            VerticalAlignment="Top" Width="160"
            Click="btnStart_Click" Margin="8,537,0,0"
            Grid.Row="1" d:LayoutOverrides="HorizontalAlignment" />
    <Button Content="Stop" Height="72"
```

```
                HorizontalAlignment="Left" x:Name="btnStop"
                VerticalAlignment="Top" Width="160"
                Click="btnStop_Click" Margin="168,537,0,0"
                Grid.Row="1" />

        <Canvas x:Name="ContentGrid" Margin="0,8,8,0"
                Grid.Row="1" HorizontalAlignment="Right"
                Width="472" Height="479" VerticalAlignment="Top">
            <Ellipse x:Name="ball" Canvas.Left="126"
                    Fill="#FF963C3C" HorizontalAlignment="Left"
                    Height="47" Stroke="Black" StrokeThickness="1"
                    VerticalAlignment="Top" Width="46"
                    Canvas.Top="222"/>
        </Canvas>
    </Grid>

</phone:PhoneApplicationPage>
```

Once you've loaded the XAML code, you should see the layout shown in Figure 6–16. Now it's time to animate the ball and add the sound effect by wiring up some events.

Figure 6–16. MoveBall demo design view

Coding the Application

In Solution Explorer, open `MainPage.xaml.cs` and replace the code there with the following C# code blocks.

Specifying the Namespaces

Begin by listing the namespaces the application will use. The inclusion of `Microsoft.Devices.Sensors` will allow you to start and stop Windows Phone's accelerometer.

```
using System;
using System.Windows;
using System.Windows.Controls;
using Microsoft.Phone.Controls;
using Microsoft.Devices.Sensors;

namespace MoveBallDemo
{
    public partial class MainPage : PhoneApplicationPage
    {
```

Initializing Variables

The variable _ac, an Accelerometer object, will be used to start and stop the sensor and retrieve the x, y, z, and time values. The ReadingChanged event sends the captured accelerometer data to be displayed in the UI. Finally, the starting position of the ball is set to the center of the canvas where the ball is placed.

```
        private Accelerometer _ac;

        public MainPage()
        {
            InitializeComponent();

            SupportedOrientations = SupportedPageOrientation.Portrait;

            ball.SetValue(Canvas.LeftProperty, ContentGrid.Width / 2);
            ball.SetValue(Canvas.TopProperty, ContentGrid.Height / 2);

            _ac = new Accelerometer();
            _ac.ReadingChanged += new
EventHandler<AccelerometerReadingEventArgs>(ac_ReadingChanged);
        }
```

Handling Captured Accelerometer Data

Here, as in the previous demo, you can't directly change the UI elements upon receiving the accelerometer data because the accelerometer data comes from a different thread than the current UI thread. If you try to change the UI elements directly here, you will get an invalid cross-thread access error, as shown previously in Figure 6–13. In order to overcome this problem, you must use the Dispatcher in the current UI thread, as shown in the following code:

```
private void ac_ReadingChanged(object sender, AccelerometerReadingEventArgs e)
{
    Deployment.Current.Dispatcher.BeginInvoke(() => MyReadingChanged(e));
}
```

Applying Captured Accelerometer Data to the Ball

The following code achieves the behavior where if the phone is tilted vertically with the display facing toward you, based on the algorithm specified in the method, the ball will fall straight very fast. But if you tilt the phone slightly while the display is facing up, the ball will slowly slide to the direction in which the phone is tilted.

```
private void MyReadingChanged(AccelerometerReadingEventArgs e)
{
    double distanceToTravel = 2;
    double accelerationFactor = Math.Abs(e.Z) == 0 ? 0.1 : Math.Abs(e.Z);
    double ballX = (double)ball.GetValue(Canvas.LeftProperty) +
distanceToTravel * e.X / accelerationFactor;
    double ballY = (double)ball.GetValue(Canvas.TopProperty) -
distanceToTravel * e.Y / accelerationFactor;

    if (ballX < 0)
    {
        ballX = 0;
    }
    else if (ballX > ContentGrid.Width)
    {
        ballX = ContentGrid.Width;
    }

    if (ballY < 0)
    {
        ballY = 0;
    }
    else if (ballY > ContentGrid.Height)
    {
        ballY = ContentGrid.Height;
    }

    ball.SetValue(Canvas.LeftProperty, ballX);
    ball.SetValue(Canvas.TopProperty, ballY);
}
```

Adding Start and Stop Button Events

Implement the button event for stopping and starting the accelerometer.

```
        private void btnStart_Click(object sender, RoutedEventArgs e)
        {
            if (_ac == null)
            {
                _ac = new Accelerometer();
            }
            _ac.Start();
        }

        private void btnStop_Click(object sender, RoutedEventArgs e)
        {
            if (_ac == null)
            {
                _ac = new Accelerometer();
            }
            _ac.Stop();
        }
    }
}
```

Testing the Finished Application

To test the finished application, press F5 (remember to choose to run the application on a Windows Phone 7 device, as shown previously in Figure 6–15). Once the application runs on the Windows Phone, click the Start button. Tilt the phone and watch the ball move in the direction the phone is being tilted.

Summary

In this chapter, you learned about the fundamentals of the accelerometer. In the first demo, you captured the accelerometer data and displayed it by updating UI elements on the currently executing UI thread. In the second demo, you moved a ball on the phone screen by using captured accelerometer data to calculate its speed and position.

In Chapter 7, you will create an application bar to display shortcuts for the most commonly used tasks in the application and design it to be a compelling application.

CHAPTER 7

Application Bar

When you're ready to program your Windows Phone 7 application in Visual Studio, you'll know what general features your application will provide. Each of the major application features will need to be accessible via a shortcut or some form of a navigation menu. For Windows Phone 7 applications, Microsoft recommends that you use a standard Windows Phone 7 Application Bar to provide shortcuts for most common tasks within the application. Metro UI design concepts for Windows Phone 7 were covered in Part 1 of this book. The use of an Application Bar within the application helps ensure that these guidelines are properly observed.

An Application Bar is essentially a Windows Phone 7 menu system with clickable icons that conform to the general Metro UI guidelines provided by Microsoft. For example, take a look at the Windows Phone 7 version of the popular social networking application Foursquare (one place you can find its screenshots is http://4square.codeplex.com). At the bottom of the screen, you will see an Application Bar with shortcuts to most common features of the application. Another example is Graphic.ly (www.pcworld.com/article/191549/graphicly.html), an application that uses Deep Zoom capabilities of Silverlight to provide an immersive comic book reading experience. On its Application Bar, Graphic.ly naturally has shortcuts to zoom into and zoom out of the comic book contents, since those features are the most important ones for that application.

In this chapter, you will learn how to create an Application Bar in your programs and the specifications for various elements within the Application Bar. You will also learn about the two types of Application Bars and you will program them both. Within each Windows Phone 7 application, two types of Application Bars can be present: a global Application Bar and a local one. If a global Application Bar is defined, it can be added to any .xaml page within the application via a single XAML statement. Alternately, a local Application Bar would be local to a single application page and must be defined for each .xaml page separately. You will create both global and local Application Bars in this chapter.

The position of the Application Bar on the screen varies with the phone orientation. When the phone is in default portrait orientation, an Application Bar is displayed as a single row of icons at the bottom of the screen. Figure 7–1 shows an example of an Application Bar with three icons for Add, Save, and Delete. The ellipsis to the right of the Delete button signifies the presence of additional shortcuts in the Application Bar (called menu items) that will become visible to you when you click that ellipsis button. In this chapter, you'll learn how to create visually appealing Application Bars that conform to the best practices published by Microsoft.

Figure 7–1. An Application Bar with Add (+ icon), Save (disk icon), and Delete (trash can icon) on Windows Phone 7

Introducing the Application Bar

The contents of an Application Bar are limited to a maximum of four elements. The elements are added and automatically centered in the Application Bar from left to right. Additional application shortcuts can be added to the Application Bar via text-based menu items and are hidden from view by default. The presence of an ellipsis to the right of the main Application Bar icons hints that, in addition to the main icons, there are text-based menu items in the Application Bar. These items serve as additional shortcuts and slide up as a list when the user clicks the ellipsis or the empty space right underneath the ellipsis. An example of what the phone screen looks like when there are menu items present in the application and the ellipsis is pressed is shown in Figure 7–2.

Figure 7–2. *Application Bar with menu items shown. Note how menu items appear in lowercase, regardless of the letter casing when they were created.*

There is good news and bad news when it comes to working with the Application Bar. The good news is that an Application Bar is easy to create and comes with a lot of built-in functionality. For example, when the phone changes orientation from portrait to landscape, the Application Bar automatically moves to the left side of the phone screen. In addition, there is a default animation for showing text-based menu items (shown in Figure 7–2) that didn't fit in the four main icon slots on the Application Bar. Finally, a minor but handy feature that ensures consistent user experience is the automatic addition of a circle around each Application Bar icon (i.e., you as the developer do not have to draw it) and the conversion of textual menu items to lowercase text.

The bad news is that there is little flexibility in creating icons and menus for the Application Bar. The height of the Application Bar is fixed and can't be changed. The size of the icons in the Application Bar is 48 pixels wide and 48 pixels high (generally expressed as 48x48); icons of other sizes will be scaled to fit that size, which results in distortion and thus is not recommended. The actual graphic within the icon has to be 26x26 pixels to properly fit within the circle that the Application Bar automatically draws for each icon. In addition, Microsoft recommends that you always try to use default system theme colors for the Application Bar because the use of custom colors can lead to unpredictable and potentially unfavorable effects on display quality, menu animations, and power consumption.

In the following section, you will create an Application Bar that looks like the one in Figure 7–2. Later in this chapter, you will write code to react to Application Bar events and access different features of your application.

Adding an Application Bar to a Windows Phone 7 Application

Windows Phone 7 provides two types of Application Bars for use with phones apps: a global bar and a local bar. The only way to define a global Application Bar is inside the App.xaml; once defined, it can be added to any page within the Windows Phone 7 application with a single line of XAML code. On the other hand, there are two ways to define a local Application Bar and add it to a particular application page.

1. Using XAML

2. Using Managed Code (i.e., C#, or Visual Basic)

You'll get to try both methods in this chapter when you'll build an Application Bar that provides simple functionality and asks for a person's name, then acts like that name has been saved to the database or the cloud storage. Regardless of the approach you choose and regardless of whether you are building a local or a global Application Bar, there is a preparatory step you should take before you can properly display and use it. That step involves adding images for your Application Bar buttons to project resources.

Adding Images for Use with Application Bar Buttons

Because the maximum size of each Application Bar icon is 48x48 pixels, the size of each image you add to the Application Bar is limited to 26x26 pixels so that a circle can be also properly drawn around it. Since Windows Phone 7 supports the concept of themes, the background of an icon has to match the rest of the theme, and therefore should be made transparent (for more information on working with different themes, please refer to Chapter 9). On this transparent background, the actual graphic should have white foreground color using an alpha channel. You will walk through creating images for the Application Bar using Microsoft Expression Design later in this chapter. Fortunately, in many cases, you won't have to create icons yourself, since Microsoft has released a set of commonly used images for Windows Phone 7 Application Bar, all properly sized and formatted in Microsoft's approved style. These icons are automatically installed for you as part of Windows Phone Developer Tools installation and their default location is in the %Program Files\Microsoft SDKs\Windows Phone\v7.0\Icons folder.

1. Start off by creating a new Visual Studio Project and naming it ApplicationBarSample.

2. Next, organize the project for easier readability by creating a folder for the icon images you'll use in the ApplicationBarSample project. Right-click the project name in the Solution Explorer, select Add ➤ New Folder. Name it Images.

3. Next, copy the icon images to the newly created folder within your project. Using Windows Explorer, copy the image files you need from there to the Images folder of your project. In the example that follows, you will be using the images located in the dark subfolder of the icon archive. Make sure to copy the *.png files only, without any folder structure.

4. Now the images are copied, but Visual Studio still needs to make them a part of the project. Right-click Solution Explorer, then select Add ➤ Existing Item. Select all images by clicking each one while holding the Ctrl key down, or (quicker) by clicking the first image, holding down the Shift key, and then clicking the last image in the set.

5. Finally, you need to instruct Visual Studio to include new images in every build of an application. For each image, right-click the image in the Solution Explorer and choose Properties (you can also press F4 to bring up the Properties dialog). In the Properties dialog box, set the Build action to Content and set the Copy to Output property to Copy Always, as shown in Figure 7–3.

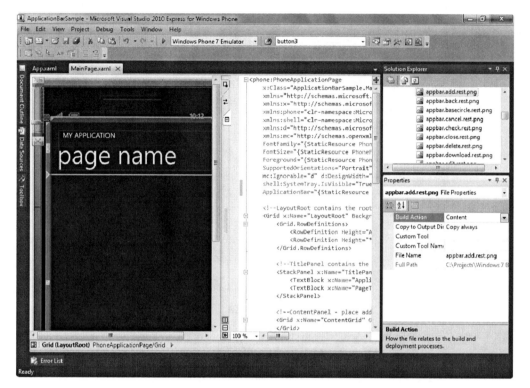

Figure 7–3. *For each image, set Build Action to Content and Copy to Output Directory to Copy Always.*

Now that the project knows where to find the icon images for an Application Bar, it's time to add code to showcase the Application Bar's features.

Adding a Global Application Bar Using XAML

A global Application Bar is created as an application resource in the section of an App.xaml configuration file. Follow these steps to create and add a global Application Bar:

1. In Solution Explorer, right-click the App.xaml file for the ApplicationBarSample project and select Open. This action causes Visual Studio to display the XAML code for the application's resource and configuration page.

2. Next, paste the complete XAML definition of the Application Bar with three icons and two menu items into the Application Resources section. Locate the <Application.Resources> section of the App.xaml and paste the following code

within that section. Note that setting the Text property for each control is required.

```
<shell:ApplicationBar x:Key="GlobalAppMenuBar" Opacity="1" IsVisible="True"
IsMenuEnabled="True">
        <shell:ApplicationBar.Buttons>
            <shell:ApplicationBarIconButton IconUri="/Images/appbar.add.rest.png"
Text="add">
            </shell:ApplicationBarIconButton>
            <shell:ApplicationBarIconButton IconUri="/Images/appbar.save.rest.png"
Text="save">
            </shell:ApplicationBarIconButton>
            <shell:ApplicationBarIconButton IconUri="/Images/appbar.delete.rest.png"
Text="delete">
            </shell:ApplicationBarIconButton>
        </shell:ApplicationBar.Buttons>
        <shell:ApplicationBar.MenuItems>
            <shell:ApplicationBarMenuItem Text="Menu Item 1" IsEnabled="True">
            </shell:ApplicationBarMenuItem>
            <shell:ApplicationBarMenuItem Text="Menu Item 2" IsEnabled="True">
            </shell:ApplicationBarMenuItem>
        </shell:ApplicationBar.MenuItems>
    </shell:ApplicationBar>
```

3. With the global Application Bar defined, you are ready to add it to the pages within your application. Open MainPage.xaml and add the following attribute within the <phone:PhoneApplicationPage> node:

```
ApplicationBar="{StaticResource GlobalAppMenuBar}"
```

4. Press F5 to run the application. You should see an Application Bar identical to the one shown in Figure 7–2. Note that if you see grey "x" symbols instead of expected Application Bar icons, the application can't locate the image files to use inside its Application Bar. Make sure the names and paths to those files are spelled correctly and that the Build action of the images is set to Content and the Copy to Output property is set to Copy Always, as shown in Figure 7–3.

Before moving onto the next section and taking a look at a local Application Bar, let's clean up the MainPage.xaml code by removing the ApplicationBar="{StaticResource GlobalAppMenuBar}" XAML. If you don't do that, you will get an application exception in the next section after you add a local Application Bar.

Adding a Local Application Bar Using XAML

Creating a global Application Bar provides an easy way to add the same exact Application Bar to all pages or screens within your program. In cases where you want to make an Application Bar different for a given page, you would need to create a local Application Bar. One of the two ways to add a local Application Bar to a Windows Phone 7 application is to use XAML markup. Using XAML markup wherever possible is considered best practice since it allows for the separation of design (XAML) and logic (C#) of an application. The following steps show the XAML you need to add to ApplicationBarSample to construct a local Application Bar for the app:

5. In Solution Explorer, right-click the `MainPage.xaml` and select Open. This action causes Visual Studio to display the XAML code for the application's main page. Make sure you have removed the global Application Bar reference from the `MainPage.xaml`, as mentioned at the end of the previous section.

6. You must define a PhoneNavigation element within XAML before adding a local Application Bar. To accomplish that, inside the phone:PhoneApplicationPage, add a phone:PhoneApplicationPage.ApplicationBar element. Notice how this element is automatically available for selection via Visual Studio IntelliSense once you start typing the first few characters—an excellent way to ensure that there are no spelling errors.

```
<phone:PhoneApplicationPage.ApplicationBar>
</phone:PhoneApplicationPage.ApplicationBar>
```

7. It is now time to add the Application Bar XAML to the page. Inside the phone:PhoneApplicationPage.ApplicationBar element, add a shell:ApplicationBar element. Set the IsVisible and the IsMenuEnabled properties to True, and set the Opacity property to 1, like so:

```
<shell:ApplicationBar Opacity="1" IsVisible="True" IsMenuEnabled="True">
    </shell:ApplicationBar>
```

8. Now that you have defined an Application Bar in XAML, you are ready to create buttons for it. The buttons you add are a part of the shell:ApplicationBar.Buttons element, so go ahead and add that element now inside the shell:ApplicationBar element.

```
<shell:ApplicationBar.Buttons>
</shell:ApplicationBar.Buttons>
```

9. Inside the shell:ApplicationBar element, you will create three shell:ApplicationBarIconButton XAML elements to add three button definitions: one each for Add, Save, and Delete. These buttons will show up with images you will define for them. If you had any text-based menu items to add to the Application Bar, the ellipsis in the right corner of the Application Bar would be created automatically for you by Windows Phone 7. The ellipsis is not counted as one of the buttons on the Application Bar; therefore you could have a maximum of four buttons plus an ellipsis. The XAML markup to add three buttons is shown here:

```
<shell:ApplicationBarIconButton IconUri="/Images/appbar.add.rest.png" Text="add">
</shell:ApplicationBarIconButton>
<shell:ApplicationBarIconButton IconUri="/Images/appbar.save.rest.png" Text="save">
</shell:ApplicationBarIconButton>
<shell:ApplicationBarIconButton IconUri="/Images/appbar.delete.rest.png"
Text="delete">
</shell:ApplicationBarIconButton>
```

10. Note that the IconUri properties in this code snippet refer to the default names of the images that come as part of the Windows Phone 7 Tools installation. If you have changed default names of those images, make sure to properly edit the reference used in IconUri as well. Also note the Text element—it's a required element and it can't be an empty string. This text will be visible if you

click the ellipsis in the right corner of the Application Bar, as shown in Figure 7–2.

11. At this point, you are done creating Icon buttons and should make sure that the shell:ApplicationBar.Buttons element is properly closed. Press F5 to view the results of your work—you should see the Application Bar containing three items at the bottom of the phone screen.

The full XAML for a local Application Bar is shown in Listing 7-1, together with text-based menu items for the Application Bar, which you will be adding in the next section. Since menu items are text-based, they are useful in cases where text conveys a better meaning of the shortcut than an icon in the Application Bar. Of course, if you need more than four items to be present in the Application Bar, your only choice is to resort to menu items. In the next section, you will enhance an Application Bar with menu items.

Adding Menu Items

Let's add two menu items, Menu Item 1 and Menu Item 2, to the ApplicationBarSample app.

1. All menu items are a part of shell:ApplicationBar.MenuItems element, so add that element now inside the shell:ApplicationBar element.

```
<shell:ApplicationBar.MenuItems>
</shell:ApplicationBar.MenuItems>
```

2. Finally, you will define MenuItems themselves by adding shell:ApplicationBarMenuItems inside the shell:ApplicationBar.MenuItems element.

```
<shell:ApplicationBarMenuItem Text="Menu Item 1" IsEnabled="True">
</shell:ApplicationBarMenuItem>
<shell:ApplicationBarMenuItem Text="Menu Item 2" IsEnabled="True">
</shell:ApplicationBarMenuItem>
```

If you run the application now, you will now see an Application Bar displayed by the Windows Phone emulator that is identical to the one shown in Figure 7–1. If you click the ellipsis to the right of the icons, the application bar slides up, revealing the two menu items, identical to Figure 7–2. Try it by pressing F5.

Let's talk briefly about the Opacity property of an Application Bar you used in this example. Even though its values can range from 0 to 1, Microsoft recommends that developers use only three values for this property: 0, 0.5, and 1. If the Opacity is set to anything less than 1, the Application Bar will overlay the displayed page of an application. In other words, the contents of that page will extend to the area underneath the Application Bar, which is seldom desirable. If Opacity is set to 1, however, the Application Bar will have a dedicated region at the bottom of the screen and will not be overlaying any portion of an application.

The full XAML markup for creating an Application Bar with three main icons and two menu items is shown in Listing 7-1.

Listing 7–1. *XAML Code to Implement an Application Bar*

```
<phone:PhoneApplicationPage.ApplicationBar>
<shell:ApplicationBar Opacity="1" IsVisible="True" IsMenuEnabled="True">
        <shell:ApplicationBar.Buttons>
```

```
              <shell:ApplicationBarIconButton IconUri="/Images/appbar.add.rest.png"
Text="add">
              </shell:ApplicationBarIconButton>
              <shell:ApplicationBarIconButton IconUri="/Images/appbar.save.rest.png"
Text="save">
              </shell:ApplicationBarIconButton>
              <shell:ApplicationBarIconButton IconUri="/Images/appbar.delete.rest.png"
Text="delete">
              </shell:ApplicationBarIconButton>
          </shell:ApplicationBar.Buttons>
          <shell:ApplicationBar.MenuItems>
              <shell:ApplicationBarMenuItem Text="Menu Item 1" IsEnabled="True">
              </shell:ApplicationBarMenuItem>
              <shell:ApplicationBarMenuItem Text="Menu Item 2" IsEnabled="True">
              </shell:ApplicationBarMenuItem>
          </shell:ApplicationBar.MenuItems>
      </shell:ApplicationBar>
</phone:PhoneApplicationPage.ApplicationBar>
```

Adding an Application Bar via XAML is pretty straightforward thanks to all the powerful and easy-to-use tooling provided by Visual Studio 2010. Using XAML allows you to separate presentation from logic, which is a very good practice. We recommend you use XAML wherever possible. Sometimes, however, XAML alone is not sufficient for the task. Luckily, it is perhaps even easier to work with the Application Bar from managed code, especially if you have a little bit of programming experience. The next section will show you how to do that.

Adding an Application Bar Using Managed Code

The second way to create an Application Bar for a Windows Phone 7 application is to use one of the .NET languages. Both C# and VB.NET are supported, and there are even templates available online for writing Windows Phone 7 applications with F#! It is simply astounding that we have the power of functional programming with F# available to us on a mobile platform.

The steps necessary to create an Application Bar using C# are described here. But first, be sure to remove all of the Application Bar XAML code you wrote for the previous demos.

1. You will be editing the MainPage code of your application. To accomplish this, locate the `MainPage.xaml.cs` file by expanding the `MainPage.xaml` file in the Solution Explorer. Right-click `MainPage.xaml.cs` and select View Code.

2. For easier reference to an Application Bar component inside the Microsoft.Phone assembly (i.e., to avoid typing Microsoft.Phone.Shell.ApplicationBar before each component name), add the following using directive to the top of the `MainPage.xaml.cs` file:

   ```
   using Microsoft.Phone.Shell;
   ```

3. Inside the constructor for the page (i.e., inside the `public MainPage()` code block), right after `InitializeComponent()`, initialize the Application Bar and set its IsVisible and IsMenuEnabled properties, as shown in the following code:

   ```
   ApplicationBar = new ApplicationBar();
   ApplicationBar.IsVisible = true;
   ApplicationBar.IsMenuEnabled = true;
   ```

4. Initialize Application Bar buttons, providing the relative URI to the image that will be used for each button. Note that you must set the Text property of each button; otherwise you will cause an exception.

```
ApplicationBarIconButton btnAdd = new ApplicationBarIconButton(new
Uri("/Images/appbar.add.rest.png", UriKind.Relative));
btnAdd.Text = "add";
ApplicationBarIconButton btnSave = new ApplicationBarIconButton(new
Uri("/Images/appbar.save.rest.png", UriKind.Relative));
btnSave.Text = "save";
ApplicationBarIconButton btnDelete = new ApplicationBarIconButton(new
        Uri("/Images/appbar.delete.rest.png", UriKind.Relative));
btnDelete.Text = "delete";
```

5. Add the buttons to the Application Bar via the following code:

```
ApplicationBar.Buttons.Add(btnAdd);
ApplicationBar.Buttons.Add(btnSave);
ApplicationBar.Buttons.Add(btnDelete);
```

6. Next, you will create two menu items that will appear as text when the ellipsis button is clicked in the Application Bar. Very similar to adding icons, there are initialization and addition steps for each menu item. The initialization code for the menu items looks like this:

```
ApplicationBarMenuItem menuItem1 = new ApplicationBarMenuItem("Menu Item 1");
ApplicationBarMenuItem menuItem2 = new ApplicationBarMenuItem("Menu Item 2");
```

The strings "Menu Item 1" and "Menu Item 2" are the text for the two menu items; in your application, you will certainly change that text to something much more meaningful and fun.

7. Add menu items to the Application Bar.

```
ApplicationBar.MenuItems.Add(menuItem1);
ApplicationBar.MenuItems.Add(menuItem2);
```

8. Finally, you are ready to test the Application Bar. Save your work and press F5 to start debugging the application using Windows Phone 7 emulator. You should see an Application Bar identical to the one shown in Figure 7–1. If you click the ellipsis to the right of the icons, the Application Bar slides up, revealing two menu items, identical to Figure 7–2.

The full code for adding the Application Bar using managed C# code is in Listing 7-2. Note that the full MainPage() constructor is included for readability purposes.

Listing 7–2. C# Code to Implement an Application Bar

```
public MainPage()
{
        InitializeComponent();
        SupportedOrientations = SupportedPageOrientation.Portrait |
        SupportedPageOrientation.Landscape;

        ApplicationBar = new ApplicationBar();
        ApplicationBar.IsVisible = true;
        ApplicationBar.IsMenuEnabled = true;
```

```
ApplicationBarIconButton btnAdd = new ApplicationBarIconButton(new
        Uri("/Images/appbar.add.rest.png", UriKind.Relative));
btnAdd.Text = "add";
ApplicationBarIconButton btnSave = new ApplicationBarIconButton(new
        Uri("/Images/appbar.save.rest.png", UriKind.Relative));
btnSave.Text = "save";
ApplicationBarIconButton btnDelete = new ApplicationBarIconButton(new
        Uri("/Images/appbar.delete.rest.png", UriKind.Relative));
btnDelete.Text = "delete";

ApplicationBarMenuItem menuItem1 = new ApplicationBarMenuItem("Menu Item 1");
ApplicationBarMenuItem menuItem2 = new ApplicationBarMenuItem("Menu Item 2");

ApplicationBar.Buttons.Add(btnAdd);
ApplicationBar.Buttons.Add(btnSave);
ApplicationBar.Buttons.Add(btnDelete);

ApplicationBar.MenuItems.Add(menuItem1);
ApplicationBar.MenuItems.Add(menuItem2);
}
```

While adding the Application Bar to Windows Phone 7 is cool in itself, you can't do much with that Application Bar right now. You can push buttons a few hundred times, but nothing changes on the phone screen or inside the application. To react to button press events, you need to write some managed (C# in this case) code, also called the event handler code. In the next section, you'll learn how to write code that processes and reacts to the button press events.

Wiring Up Events to an Application Bar

There are two steps to writing code that reacts to Application Bar events.

1. Writing a small snippet of *glue code* that links Application Bar button or menu item click to the function that does all the processing (let's call this function the *worker function*).

2. Writing a worker function that performs all the heavy lifting—i.e., rearranges UI elements on the screen, saves data, prompts the user for input, or anything else that the developer decides to do in response to the button or the menu item click event.

Let's start with the Add button, which you'll wire up in the next section.

Adding Glue Code and a Worker Function to the Add Button

Visual Studio has made adding both glue code and a worker function virtually a two-keystroke procedure. Let's see how easy it is to create an event handler for the Add button on your Application Bar using a couple of Visual Studio shortcuts. This demo assumes that you have already created the Application Bar via managed code (not XAML) by following the steps in the "Adding an Application Bar Using Managed Code" section earlier in the chapter.

1. Once again, you will be editing the code of the MainPage of your application. To accomplish this, locate the `MainPage.xaml.cs` file by expanding the `MainPage.xaml` file in the Solution Explorer. Right-click `MainPage.xaml.cs` and select View Code.

2. At the very end of the `MainPage()` constructor, type the following code:

   ```
   btnAdd.Click+=
   ```

3. Notice the appearance of a small pop-up window to the right of the = sign as you type it. You should see the following message:

   ```
   new EventHandler(btnAdd_Click); (Press TAB to insert)
   ```

4. Press the Tab key and notice how a line of code is automatically added after the = sign. This one line of code is the glue code you need to tie together user interaction with the Add button.

   ```
   btnAdd.Click+=new EventHandler(btnAdd_Click);
   ```

5. Now press the Tab key again, and Visual Studio automatically creates a skeleton for the worker function for you. This may not seem like a big deal at first, but it's usually a challenge to remember exactly what parameter types this worker function must have. This shortcut is just one example of how Visual Studio really enhances developer productivity.

6. The worker code that Visual Studio adds to your application looks like this:

   ```
   void btnAdd_Click(object sender, EventArgs e)
   {
                   throw new NotImplementedException();
   }
   ```

Now you're ready to add a bit of interactivity to your Application Bar, which you'll do in the next section.

▪ **Tip**   You are certainly not required to use the shortcut just described to generate event handler code for the Application Bar or for any other event for that matter. You can write all of the previous code by hand, but be very careful to pass the proper parameter types and the proper number of parameters to the event handler.

Reacting to Add Button Events

With a worker function in place for the Add button, let's expand it to accommodate a simplified real-world scenario: when a user clicks the Add button (the button with the + icon on the Application Bar), you will show a text box on the screen that is ready and waiting for user input. You will also add functionality to the Save button (the button with a floppy disk icon) that will display the thank-you message and hide the text box. Of course, in the real world, you would want to store the values entered by the user and react on the user input in some fashion, but that is slightly beyond the scope of this chapter.

Follow these steps to add interactivity to the Application Bar events:

1. Locate `MainPage.xaml` in the Solution Explorer and double-click that file to bring up XAML designer. Click the View menu ➤ Other Windows ➤ Toolbox. You should see XAML *designer* (not code) and a toolbox side-by-side, as shown in Figure 7–4.

■ **Tip**   If you see the toolbox, Windows Phone 7 design surface, and XAML *code* on the screen side-by-side, as in Figure 7–4, click the Collapse Pane (>> icon) in the area between the design surface and XAML to hide the XAML code, as illustrated in Figure 7–4.

■ **Tip** If you do not see the XAML view, click the Expand Pane (<< icon) to bring that view back, as shown in Figure 7–5.

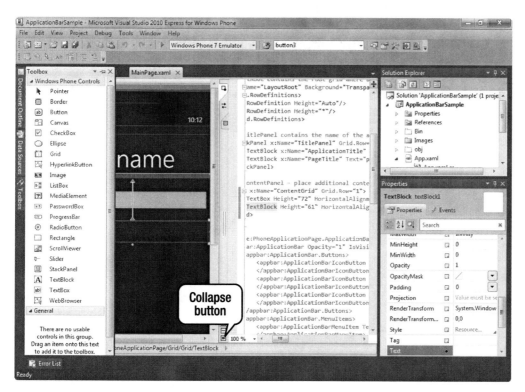

Figure 7–4. Click the Collapse button to hide the XAML.

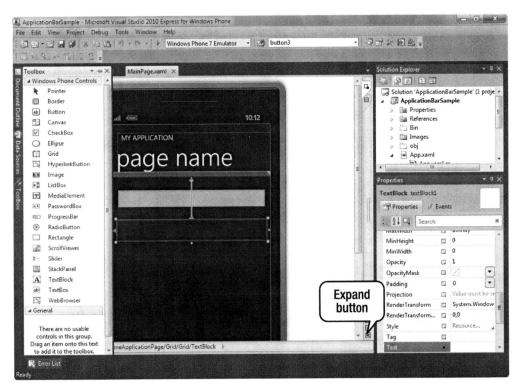

Figure 7–5. Click the Expand button to show the XAML for the current page.

2. From the Toolbox, click and drag the text box to the Windows Phone 7 design surface, as shown in Figure 7–6. Right-click the Text item, and select Properties to show the Properties window in the right corner of the screen.

3. Set the Text property to blank and set the Visibility property to Collapsed.

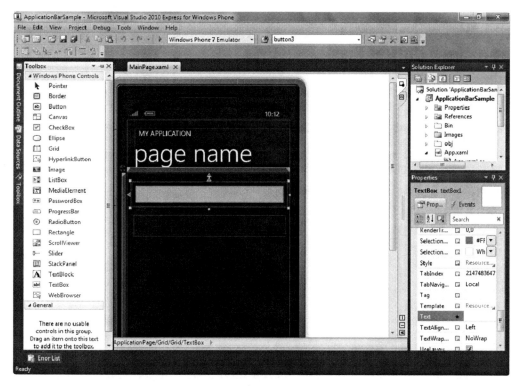

Figure 7–6. Adding a text box to the application

4. In the Toolbox, click and drag the TextBlock to the Windows Phone 7 design surface and place it right underneath the text box. Right-click the TextBlock and select Properties to show the Properties window in the right corner of the screen.

5. Set the Text property to "Please enter your name" and set the Visibility property to Collapsed.

6. Now edit the worker function that was created for you by Visual Studio 2010 in the previous section. Right-click the `MainPage.xaml.cs` file and select View Code. Remove the following line from the `btnAdd_Click` function:

    ```
    throw new NotImplementedException();
    ```

7. Edit the `btnAdd_Click` function to match the following code:

    ```
    void btnAdd_Click (object sender, EventArgs e)
    {
       textBox1.Visibility = Visibility.Visible;
       textBlock1.Visibility = Visibility.Visible;
    }
    ```

8. Press F5 to view the results of your work.

Now, when you click the + icon on the Application Bar, the text box is ready to accept user input.

Reacting to Save Button Events

Continuing the demo, let's now add an event handler to the Save button of the Application Bar. You'll write code so that when the user clicks the Save button, the application will hide the text box and change the text of the textblock to thank the user for entering a name.

1. Locate `MainPage.xaml` in the Solution Explorer, right-click and select View Code. Add the following line of code to the `MainPage()` constructor code. Don't forget to use the Tab+Tab trick to let Visual Studio automatically generate skeleton code for you (described in the previous section).

```
btnSave.Click += new EventHandler(btnSave_Click);
```

2. Add the following code to the `btnSave_Click` function:

```
void btnSave_Click(object sender, EventArgs e)
        {
        textBlock1.Text = "Thank you, "+ textBox1.Text;

        textBox1.Visibility = Visibility.Collapsed;
        }
```

3. Press F5 to see the results of your work. When you click the + icon, you will be prompted to enter your name. Once you enter your name and press the Save button on the Application Bar, the application displays a simple thank-you message. If, for some reason, the full text of the message doesn't fit within the textblock you created, you can increase both the width and the height of the textblock by setting the TextWrapping property of the textblock to Wrap.

Now you're ready to enhance the Application Bar even further by writing code for your menu items to do some meaningful work.

Reacting to Menu Events

The code you write to react to menu click events is almost identical to the code for Application Bar button events, with the glue code attached to the menu item instead of the Application Bar button. The block of code shown next displays a simple text message when the user clicks on the first menu item in the Application Bar that you created previously. Note that only a portion of the `MainPage()` constructor is shown, since the rest of it remains unchanged from the prior demo.

```
        menuItem1.Click+=new EventHandler(menuItem1_Click);
}

void menuItem1_Click(object sender, EventArgs e)
{
        textBlock1.Visibility = Visibility.Visible;
        textBlock1.Text = "You just clicked on Menu Item 1";
}
```

Press F5 to run the application now. You should see an Application Bar with an ellipsis in the right corner. If you press the ellipsis, two menu items become visible. Once clicked, the text on the phone screen changes to reflect the name of the menu item clicked.

In the real application, you will certainly want to do something more meaningful than what you did here. For instance, you may have Help and About menu items. If the user clicks Help, a Web Browser control (discussed in the next chapter) could be programmed to display a set of application help files. If the About menu item is clicked, you can use the Web Browser control to show your company's web page or some basic contact information.

One final thing you need to look at before leaving this chapter is how to use XAML to link event handling code to XAML elements.

Adding Event Handlers with XAML

It is also possible to write the necessary code that attaches (or glues) a certain event to a managed code in XAML. In other words, using this approach, you would define an Application Bar in XAML following the guidelines in the previous section, but write managed C# code to react to events when the user presses Application Bar buttons. For code readability and understandability purposes, this approach may be preferable to the purely managed code approach (where you define Application Bar from managed code) already discussed. Imagine that you are trying to maintain an application that someone else wrote—it would be easier for you to understand and trace application behavior by starting with the XAML design elements and following their glue code into the event handlers. The steps you follow to wire up events in XAML are pretty straightforward, as illustrated here:

1. Locate `MainPage.xaml` in the Solution Explorer and double-click that file to bring up XAML designer.

2. If only the Windows Phone 7 design surface is shown and no XAML *code* is visible, click the Expand Pane (<<) button in the lower right portion of the screen, as shown in Figure 7–5.

3. Paste the following XAML in `MainPage.xaml` (it's identical to XAML from the "Adding a Local Application Bar Using XAML" section of this chapter):

```xml
<phone:PhoneApplicationPage.ApplicationBar>
    <shell:ApplicationBar IsVisible="True" IsMenuEnabled="True">
        <shell:ApplicationBar.Buttons>
            <shell:ApplicationBarIconButton IconUri="/Images/appbar.add.rest.png"
Text="add">
            </shell:ApplicationBarIconButton>
            <shell:ApplicationBarIconButton IconUri="/Images/appbar.save.rest.png"
Text="save">
            </shell:ApplicationBarIconButton>
            <shell:ApplicationBarIconButton IconUri="/Images/appbar.delete.rest.png"
Text="delete">
            </shell:ApplicationBarIconButton>
        </shell:ApplicationBar.Buttons>
        <shell:ApplicationBar.MenuItems>
            <shell:ApplicationBarMenuItem Text="Menu Item 1" IsEnabled="True">
            </shell:ApplicationBarMenuItem>
            <shell:ApplicationBarMenuItem Text="Menu Item 2" IsEnabled="True">
            </shell:ApplicationBarMenuItem>
        </shell:ApplicationBar.MenuItems>
    </shell:ApplicationBar>
</phone:PhoneApplicationPage.ApplicationBar>
```

4. Locate the `<shell:ApplicationBarIconButton IconUri="/Images/appbar.add.rest.png" Text="add">` statement in XAML and add `Click="` to the end of that statement, so that it resembles the code here:

```
<shell:ApplicationBarIconButton IconUri="/Images/appbar.add.rest.png" Text="add"
Click="">
```

Note how Visual Studio automatically shows a choice of New Event Handler right after the double quotes. If you press the Tab key now, the skeleton code for the worker function will be automatically inserted in the `MainPage.xaml.cs` file and it will have a default name of `ApplicationBarMenuItem_Click`. To add functionality to the Application Bar button click event, open `MainPage.xaml.cs` (by right-clicking the `MainPage.xaml` file and selecting View Code) and edit that function in a way similar to what you did in the "Reacting to Button Events" and "Reacting to Menu Click Events" sections. There is also another way to glue XAML code with codebehind by using an ApplicationBar class, as you will see in the next section.

Using the ApplicationBar class to glue XAML and Managed Code

Once you create an Application Bar in XAML, you can use the `ApplicationBar` class and its `Buttons` and `MenuItems` properties to glue managed code to defined XAML elements within that Application Bar. The `Buttons` property provides access to all the buttons created for the application bar, in the order that they were added to the Application Bar. For example, the following code references the Add, Save and Delete buttons created in the previous section and then programmatically disables the Delete button. Notice how since the Add button was added first in your XAML code, it has an index of 0, and the Delete button, which was added third, has an index of 2 within the Buttons list.

```
ApplicationBarIconButton btnAdd = ApplicationBar.Buttons[0] as
ApplicationBarIconButton;
ApplicationBarIconButton btnSave = ApplicationBar.Buttons[1] as
ApplicationBarIconButton;
ApplicationBarIconButton btnDelete = ApplicationBar.Buttons[2] as
ApplicationBarIconButton;

btnDelete.IsEnabled = false;
```

Obtaining programmatic references to Application Bar buttons from code may be desirable where you want to manipulate certain properties of the button, such as its Enabled/Disabled state, in response to some event triggered by the user. As you can see, you can easily obtain those references using properties of the ApplicationBar class.

Summary

In this chapter, you learned how to add an Application Bar with buttons and menu items to your Windows Phone 7 application using either XAML or managed (C#) code. You also learned basic guidelines for Application Bar development and wrote code to react to Application Bar button and menu item events. The presence of an Application Bar is certainly an expected behavior for any mobile application today, and Visual Studio has made the process of adding one easy and straightforward.

In the next chapter, you will learn about the Web Browser control on Windows Phone 7. The Web Browser control helps you provide professional-looking application Help files and aids in navigating the billions of web pages. You will also learn how to dynamically generate HTML content and show it in a web browser.

CHAPTER 8

WebBrowser Control

It felt like false advertising when, just a short ten years ago, cellular phone companies began to promote Internet access as a feature of their devices. As customers quickly learned when they tried to get online, their phones could only properly display web pages written in Wireless Markup Language (WML) and not the traditional HyperText Markup Language (HTML) used by the vast majority of the web sites. Very few sites could afford to build and maintain code in two separate languages—HTML for desktop and WML for mobile phones—and, as a result, web browsing on mobile phones did not take off until fairly recently.

But we live in much more progressive times now. The first release of Windows Phone 7 OS shipped with Internet Explorer 7 installed, which meant that any content that could be viewed in the desktop version of Internet Explorer 7 could be viewed on the phone as well. By the time you read this, Internet Explorer 9 should already have made its way onto Windows Phone 7 devices as part of the OS release codenamed Mango. With IE 9, you can construct very rich user interfaces within the browser with the help of HTML5. The Windows Phone 7 SDK includes a WebBrowser control that you can use to embed one or more instances of a small but fully capable browser inside your applications. In this chapter, you'll learn how and when to use it. But first, let's look at three common scenarios where you would want to use the WebBrowser control.

■ **Note** The WebBrowser control on Windows Phone 7 is very similar to the WebBrowser control you would use if you were creating a full-blown Silverlight application (not the phone version of it)—with few notable differences. Certain features, such as the ability to download and install ActiveX controls, have been disabled to prevent security risks originating from such components. Other differences, such as the ability to access local storage and the absence of cross-domain restrictions in the Windows Phone 7 WebBrowser control, allow for a more flexible behavior of the browser on Windows Phone 7 as compared to Silverlight.

Introducing the WebBrowser Control

The most obvious reason to use the WebBrowser control is to display web content within the page of a Windows Phone 7 application. For instance, if you're developing application that shows Twitter feeds in a portion of the screen, the easiest way to do this would be to create a WebBrowser control in the application and navigate to a given Twitter page from within that control.

Another reason to use the WebBrowser control is to show HTML-formatted content that resides locally on Windows Phone 7. For example, if you decide to include help files with your application, the easiest way to create those files would be in the form of HTML web pages. Then, you can load those web pages in Windows Phone 7 and display them in the WebBrowser control.

Finally, you can use the WebBrowser control to show content that Windows Phone 7 application generates on the fly. That means that you can compose an HTML page dynamically in code and, without first writing that web page out to disk, display it. This is certainly a handy feature that avoids the intermediate steps of first writing an HTML file to local storage and then reading it. This feature is important when the HTML pages you want to show the user are context-sensitive: for instance, if you are developing an application that tracks basketball teams and you want to provide links to information about each individual player on the team, you will want to build your list of players based on the name of the team the user selects. Dynamic content generation allows you to do just that.

In this chapter, you'll learn how to use these capabilities in an application by building a simple car browser application that can search the web for photos of popular car models and display them. To get started, you first must create a main page and add some UI, including a WebBrowser control to display web and HTML content, as illustrated in the next section.

Adding a WebBrowser Control

Before you can use the WebBrowser control to browse for the images of cars online, you need to first add the control to your application. Follow these steps to place the WebBrowser control inside your application:

1. Create a new Windows Phone 7 Application project. Launch Visual Studio 2010 Express and select the Windows Phone Application template, then change the Project name to WebBrowserSample, select OK, and Visual Studio will set up a new project.

2. Click the View menu ➤ Other Windows ➤ Toolbox (alternately, you can also click the Toolbox icon in the Visual Studio application bar) to show the Toolbox with the list of controls available for use.

3. From the Toolbox window on the left, select the WebBrowser control, click it, and drag it onto the Windows Phone 7 design surface, as shown in Figure 8–1.

4. Position and resize the control as needed. In Figure 8–1, the WebBrowser control is positioned to take the upper third of the phone screen.

5. Finally, change the name of the application from My Application to My Car Browser and change the name of the page to Car Explorer. You can do that by double-clicking MainPage.xaml and editing the ApplicationTitle and PageTitle elements accordingly.

■ **Note**   You can set the Height and the Width properties to Auto (this is the default when the control is first dropped on the Windows Phone design surface and is not resized). You can also set the Horizontal Alignment and Vertical Alignment properties to Stretch. All these settings in combination will allow the browser window to expand as much as possible on the phone without covering other visible elements on the phone screen.

With the WebBrowser control in place, you are now ready to look at how to use this control for each of the scenarios previously described.

Figure 8–1. To add the WebBrowser control to the application, drag it from the Toolbox and drop it onto MainPage.xaml on the Windows Phone 7 design surface.

Using a WebBrowser Control to Display Web Content

In the first of the WebBrowser demos, you will use this control to display the contents of the web site—you will show a list of photos of the most beautiful car in the world, the Lamborghini Gallardo.

1. With the WebBrowser control in place, it's time to add code to initialize its content when it loads work. First, right-click MainPage.xaml in Solution Explorer and select View Code (or go directly to the MainPage.xaml.cs file).

2. Whenever the My Car Browser application loads the WebBrowser control, it fires off a Loaded event. By creating a Loaded event handler, you can write code to display a web page with car photos. Add the following code to the MainPage() constructor to create the handler:

```
webBrowser1.Loaded += new RoutedEventHandler(webBrowser1_Loaded);
```

181

Note how the same Visual Studio shortcuts you used for the Application Bar code in the previous chapter apply here as well: namely, right after typing "+=" Visual Studio hints that if you press the Tab key twice, it will create all of the necessary code stubs you need for a handler.

3. Next, let's code the event handler. To the webBrowser1_Loaded() function, add the following code, which will navigate to Microsoft Bing's image search page and pass the phrase "cars Lamborghini Gallardo" to it:

```
webBrowser1.Navigate(new
  Uri("http://www.bing.com/images/search?q=cars+Lamborghini+Gallardo""",
UriKind.Absolute));
```

4. This code creates a new Uri object and specifies that the Uri is not local to your application (that would be UriKind.Relative), but rather a location on the Internet (UriKind.Absolute).

Press F5 to debug your application and see the results so far. You should now see Lamborghini photos, courtesy of the Microsoft Bing engine. You can easily extend this example to respond to user input. For example, you could use the Bing image search to show photos of any car whose name a user enters. Here's how:

5. Add a text box to the page so the user can change the name of the car for which Bing searches. To do that, go to MainPage.xaml and display the page in the Designer (either by double-clicking MainPage.xaml or by right-clicking MainPage.xaml and selecting View Designer). If the Toolbox is not visible, go to View menu ➤ Other Windows ➤ Toolbox or click the Toolbox icon in the Visual Studio application bar. Click and drag the Textbox from the Toolbox, and position it below the WebBrowser control. Next, click and drag the Button, and position it next to the text box.

6. Right-click the text box and select Properties. Delete everything from the Text property. Next, right-click the button and change the value of its Content property to "Show It!" (without the double quotes). The end result should resemble Figure 8–2.

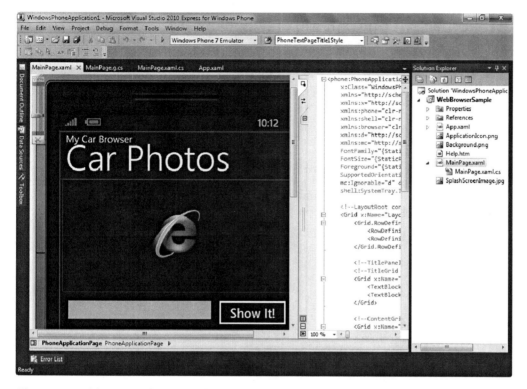

Figure 8–2. *Adding a text box and a button to interact with the WebBrowser control*

7. It's time to add some interactivity to your application. With `MainPage.xaml` still open in Designer view, double-click the button. Notice how the method `button1_Click` opens by default when you do that, ready for your code. Place the following code in the body of that method:

```
webBrowser1.Navigate(new Uri
    ("http://www.bing.com/images/search?q=cars " + textBox1.Text,
    UriKind.Absolute));
```

8. Press F5 to run the application. Initially, you should see the photos of the Lamborghini Gallardo added in the first part of this demo. Go ahead and type "Ford Mustang" in the text box, and press the Show It! button. In the WebBrowser control, you should now see a set of photos of this great American muscle car.

But there's more. You can also use a WebBrowser control to display HTML files—and even strings—that have been stored locally. You'll use that capability to add Help functionality to the Car Browser application in the next section.

Using a WebBrowser Control to Display Local HTML Content

Frequently, you will want to include documentation with your application to advertise its features to users and answer their most common questions. Because of its simplicity and ubiquity, HTML, the same language used to create web pages, has become the default format for such documentation. In this section, you'll create a simple HTML page describing how to work with the car photo application that you created in the previous section. Follow these steps to create and show HTML content on Windows Phone 7:

1. Because adding an HTML file is currently not an option in Visual Studio Express for Windows Phone 7, you will need to add a new XML file to the project. XML files support automated syntax verification features, making it harder for you to make accidental mistakes than if you were creating a text file. Right-click the WebBrowserSample project in the Solution Explorer and select Add ➤ New Item. Then, select XML File from the list of available item types.

2. Type the following in the newly created file (you can also copy and paste this code from the files available for download for this book):

```
<html>
<title>Web Browser Help File</title>
<body>
        <h1>Welcome to the Windows Phone 7 Car Browser Application!
   To view the car photos, type the name of the car in the textbox and press "Show
It!"
   <br/><br/>For example, "Ford Mustang"</h1>
</body>
</html>
```

3. Save the file by pressing the Save button in Visual Studio. Next, right-click XMLFile1.xml in the Solution Explorer and click Rename. Change the name of that file to Help.htm and make sure that the Build action for that file is set to Content (by right-clicking and selecting Properties to bring up the Properties window).

4. Now you will need to jump slightly ahead to the material covered in Chapter 13. Here's why: while you would expect the Help.htm file to be automatically available to the application running on Windows Phone 7, it isn't. Before it is available to your application, the Help.htm file created in the previous step needs to be available to your application in Isolated Storage, which you can think of as disk space reserved for use by your application on Windows Phone 7. As your application loads, you'll need to copy Help.htm to an Isolated Storage location first, and then retrieve it from there for display by the WebBrowser control. For the time being, simply add the following using directives to the top of the code page and then copy into your code the SaveHelpFileToIsoStore method shown in Listing 8–1:

```
using System.IO.IsolatedStorage;
using System.Windows.Resources;
using System.IO;
```

Listing 8–1. SaveHelpFiletoIsoStore Method

```
private void SaveHelpFileToIsoStore()
    {
        string strFileName = "Help.htm";
        IsolatedStorageFile isoStore =
IsolatedStorageFile.GetUserStoreForApplication();

            //remove the file if exists to allow each run to independently write to
            // the Isolated Storage
            if (isoStore.FileExists(strFileName) == true)
            {
                isoStore.DeleteFile(strFileName);
            }
            StreamResourceInfo sr = Application.GetResourceStream(new Uri(strFileName,
UriKind.Relative));
            using (BinaryReader br = new BinaryReader(sr.Stream))
            {
                byte[] data = br.ReadBytes((int)sr.Stream.Length);
                //save file to Isolated Storage
                using (BinaryWriter bw = new
BinaryWriter(isoStore.CreateFile(strFileName)))
                {
                    bw.Write(data);
                    bw.Close();
                }
            }
    }
```

5. Finally, you will invoke the SaveHelpFileToIsoStore method to display the
    contents of Help.htm in the web browser when the browser first loads. Add the
    call to SaveHelpFileToIsoStore in the webBrowser1_Loaded method and set the
    webBrowser URL to navigate to the Help.htm file, as shown here:

    ```
    void webBrowser1_Loaded(object sender, RoutedEventArgs e)
    {
        SaveHelpFileToIsoStore();
        webBrowser1.Navigate(new Uri("Help.htm", UriKind.Relative));
    }
    ```

6. Press F5 to run the application. You should see the simple HTML Help page
    displayed in the WebBrowser control.

In your application, you can use the technique shown previously to provide documentation or Help
files, as well as contact information about your company. Sometimes, however, all you want to show is a
short, nicely formatted HTML message, and it's somewhat tedious to write and include all the code to
save HTML files to Isolated Storage and such, as shown in the previous section. Fortunately, the
WebBrowser control has a solution for scenarios like this. In the next section, you will learn how to bypass
Isolated Storage and show HTML generated directly by code.

Using a WebBrowser Control to Display Dynamic Content

Suppose a user enters "Ford" in the text box of your photo browsing application. Unless you query the user, you won't know whether the user meant "Ford Mustang" or "Ford F-150." One way to find out would be to create a page with HTML markup and display it to the user, asking for more information. You could then save the generated file to Isolated Storage, and load it using the technique described in the previous section. But that would certainly be a cumbersome approach for such a simple task. Luckily, there's a much easier way to show a dynamically generated HTML page: using the NavigateToString method of the WebBrowser control. This method takes a single argument—a string— that contains the complete HTML code needed to display the page you have in mind in the WebBrowser control. The next demo shows just how easy it is to use this method.

1. Bring up the MainPage.xaml.cs file in the code editor (either by double-clicking it or clicking the MainPage.xaml file in the Solution Explorer and choosing View Code).

2. Next, you will construct the HTML code to display to the user. Make the button1_Click method look identical to the following code—notice how NavigateToString loads up what amounts to a basic HTML page directly into the WebBrowser control, without your having to save this HTML to the Isolated Storage. Also note that building an HTML string in code becomes a bit ugly very quickly, so NavigateToString should not be abused for large HTML messages/files.

```
webBrowser1.NavigateToString(@"<html>
<body><center><div style='font: Arial 12px;'>
Which Ford model would you like to see?<br><br>
                        <a
href='http://www.bing.com/images/search?q=cars+Ford+Mustang'>Ford
Mustang</a> or <a href='http://www.bing.com/images/search?q=cars+Ford+F150'>Ford F-
150</a></div></center></body></html>");
```

3. Press F5 to run the application. If you type "Ford" in the text box and press the Show It! button, you should see a dynamically generated HTML message with hyperlinks asking you to clarify which Ford model you would like to see, just like Figure 8–3. Note that "Ford" is currently case-sensitive; in other words, you don't get the prompt if you type "ford." Refactoring this code to be case-insensitive is left as an exercise for the reader.

▪ **Note** Of course, users will get this response no matter *what* they type, but delving into more complex search logic is not the purpose of this chapter.

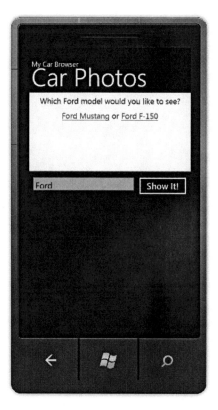

Figure 8–3. Showing dynamically generated HMTL content

Many web-based applications have been built, from translators to elaborate e-commerce systems, and all of them are easily accessible and could even be enhanced with the use of the WebBrowser control on Windows Phone 7. But the WebBrowser control can do even more: in the next section, you will learn how to save the web pages locally so that you can potentially parse certain information or search within them.

Saving Web Pages Locally

You can also save the contents of web sites and web pages to a Windows Phone 7 as strings of HTML code, using Isolated Storage and the SaveToString method of the WebBrowser control. This approach saves only the HTML on a page (of course, you probably already guessed that from the name of the method!) and ignores its images and CSS files. After saving HTML to Isolated Storage, you can load it on demand. Before doing that, however, make sure to read the security considerations at the end of this chapter.

This demo will show you how to save an HTML web page locally and then load it at a later time.

1. Open the WebBrowserSample project and bring up MainPage.xaml in the design window.

2. Add two buttons to the Windows Phone 7 design surface, as shown in Figure 8–4. Change the Content property of the top button to "Save to local storage."Change the Content property of the bottom button to "Load saved content.

Figure 8–4. *Adding the buttons to persist web content to Isolated Storage*

3. Make sure to change the names of both buttons, as shown in Figure 8–4. You can change the name in the Properties window by clicking next to the Button text at the very top of the Properties window. Name the top button btnSave and name the bottom button btnLoad.

4. Next, write the event handler code for the Save button click. Double-click the top button to bring up MainPage.xaml.cs in the code view. Change the btnSave_Click method to be identical to the following:

```
private void btnSave_Click(object sender, RoutedEventArgs e)
{
        string strWebContent = webBrowser1.SaveToString();
        SaveStringToIsoStore(strWebContent);
}
```

5. Next is the event handler code to load the previously saved web page. Double-click the bottom button and make the btnLoad_Click method look like the code block here:

```
private void btnLoad_Click(object sender, RoutedEventArgs e)
{
    webBrowser1.Navigate(new Uri("web.htm", UriKind.Relative));
}
```

6. Jumping ahead again to what will be covered in Chapter 13, you need to add
    the implementation of the SaveStringToIsoStore method that will perform the
    actual save of the HTML string to a file in the local storage.

```
private void SaveStringToIsoStore(string strWebContent)
{
     IsolatedStorageFile isoStore =
IsolatedStorageFile.GetUserStoreForApplication();

     //remove the file if exists to allow each run to independently write to
     // the Isolated Storage
     if (isoStore.FileExists("web.htm") == true)
     {
         isoStore.DeleteFile("web.htm");
     }
     StreamResourceInfo sr = new StreamResourceInfo(new
MemoryStream(System.Text.Encoding.UTF8.GetBytes(strWebContent)), "html/text");
     using (BinaryReader br = new BinaryReader(sr.Stream))
     {
         byte[] data = br.ReadBytes((int)sr.Stream.Length);
         //save file to Isolated Storage
         using (BinaryWriter bw = new
BinaryWriter(isoStore.CreateFile("web.htm")))
         {
             bw.Write(data);
             bw.Close();
         }
     }
}
```

7. Make sure the button1_Click event looks identical to the one here:

```
private void button1_Click(object sender, RoutedEventArgs e)
{
   webBrowser1.Navigate(new Uri
   ("http://www.bing.com/images/search?q=cars " + textBox1.Text,
   UriKind.Absolute));
}
```

8. You are now ready to test the application. Press F5 to run it, type "Ford
    Mustang" in the text box, and press the Show It! button. Photos of the Ford
    Mustang should appear in the browser window. Next, press the "Save Content
    to Isolated Storage" button. Then, erase the word "Mustang" from the text box,
    leaving only "Ford" and press the Show It! button. A friendly reminder that you
    need to provide more information pops up. Finally, press "Load Saved
    Content" to show the (distorted) thumbnails of the Ford Mustang.

The content is distorted because only the HTML of the web page is saved. Many CSS stylesheets that
control positioning of the elements and their look are not persisted as part of the SaveToString method.
Images may be missing as well, since the absolute paths to those images are no longer valid.

Choosing Display and Security Settings

Usually, you can safely assume that web sites and web pages will look the same in both the desktop version of Internet Explorer and the Windows Phone 7 Internet Explorer Mobile browser, on which the WebBrowser control is based. There are a few cases, however, where special considerations apply to the WebBrowser control running on Windows Phone 7. The next few sections will go over those special cases.

Viewport

In Internet Explorer Mobile (which is the version of Internet Explorer running on Windows Phone 7), the viewport is a rectangular region that controls where text will wrap on the page. At the time of this writing, only three properties are supported for the viewport: height, width, and user-scalable. Height and width properties control the height and the width of the viewport accordingly, with values ranging between 480 and 10,000 for the height and between 320 and 10,000 for the width. The user-scalable property controls whether a user can zoom in and out of the content of the viewport. This property has two possible values: yes and no. The default (and recommended) setting for this property is yes. You set the properties of the viewport inside the meta tag, as shown in the example in the next section.

CSS

There is also a CSS property, -ms-text-size-adjust, that controls the size of the text displayed on the screen. When Windows Phone 7 renders text in the browser (and the WebBrowser control), it adjusts the size of that text based on this -ms-text-size-adjust property. If this CSS property is set to auto for a given element, Windows Phone 7 tries to determine the text size that will be most readable on a given screen. If that property is set to none, Windows Phone 7 does not make any adjustments to text. There is also a third option for this property: a numeric percentage value, which will scale the text from its original size according to the percentage specified. Just as any other CSS property, -ms-text-size-adjust can be set for the whole page or any portion of the page. Let's take a look at an example that will help you visualize this property.

1. Refer to the Help.htm file you created for showing static HTML content in the WebBrowser control. Edit that file to make it look like the following HTML block; in essence, you are simply adding a CSS DIV element and introducing -ms-text-size-adjust around one of the elements:

```
<html>
  <head>
    <title>Web Browser Help File</title>
    <meta id="viewport" name="viewport" content="width=900;" />
  </head>
  <body>
      <h1>Welcome to the Windows Phone 7 Car Browser Application!
    To view car photos, type the name of the car in the textbox and press "Show It!"
    <br/><br/>For example, <div style= "-ms-text-size-adjust:250%">"Ford Mustang"</div>
  </h1>
  </body>
</html>
```

2. Press F5 to run the application. You should see the text "Ford Mustang" two and half times (250%) larger than the rest of the text on this page.

Early documentation from Microsoft stated that Internet Explorer Mobile also supports the `-webkit-text-size-adjust` property, used by other mobile browsers to control text size, in place of `-ms-text-size-adjust`. However, support for the `-webkit-text-size-adjust` property has been withdrawn since then.

Security

With phones becoming "smarter and smarter" what seems like every hour, there's always the danger of mobile applications behaving badly, whether intentionally or not. To help protect phone users from the most common types of security problems plaguing desktop computers connected to the Internet, Microsoft introduced a set of security rules for loading web content onto the phone. All Windows Phone 7 applications must observe these rules if they are to run on Windows Phone 7 devices.

As Windows Phone 7 developers, we must be aware of these security restrictions to ensure the smoothest possible performance of our applications. The following list summarizes items that are either disabled or just different in the Internet Explorer Mobile version compared to its desktop counterpart:

1. Script is disabled by default in the WebBrowser control. To enable it, the developer must explicitly set the IsScriptEnabled property of the control.

2. Internet Explorer Mobile does not allow users to download and install third-party plug-ins, such as ActiveX controls and Adobe Flash plug-ins. Sites that rely on such plug-ins for their functionality will not work properly on Windows Phone 7.

3. Within the WebBrowser control, users cannot navigate from `https://` (secure) to `http://` (unsecure) Internet locations.

4. Applications cannot share cookies with Internet Explorer Mobile.

In addition to this list, there are special cross-site considerations applicable just to the WebBrowser control. When a web page loads into the Windows Phone 7 WebBrowser control from the network location (i.e., the Internet), it is prohibited from making web service calls into the domain other than the one from which it has been loaded. This is done to prevent unauthorized access to sensitive information without a user's knowledge. This behavior is identical to the behavior of a standard Silverlight application restricted to web service calls into its own domain unless a special `crossdomain.xml` file is present at the root of another domain, allowing remote calls.

However, on Windows Phone 7, content loaded from Isolated Storage or via the `NavigateToString` method is not subject to cross-domain restrictions. This also includes content previously loaded from the network location and saved to the Isolated Storage via the `SaveToString` method, as you have seen illustrated in this chapter. It is therefore extremely important to consider the possible cross-domain consequences of saving web pages into the local storage and then re-loading them.

Summary

In this chapter, you learned to use the WebBrowser control for Windows Phone 7 to search for and display web content in an application. You created a simple Car Browser application using the WebBrowser control and displayed local static and dynamically generated HTML pages. You also learned how to store and retrieve web and HTML content from local storage on the phone itself. You'll explore local storage in greater depth in Chapter 13. Finally, you should now have a basic understanding of the viewport and custom Internet Explorer Mobile CSS elements, and an appreciation of the security issues you'll encounter when you use the WebBrowser control.

In the next chapter, you'll explore what is perhaps the most important aspect of any modern application: its styling. We will go over general principles of appealing layouts and themes, as well as delve into the specifics of visually engaging controls within applications.

CHAPTER 9

Working with Controls and Themes

Every time you pass through an airport or a train station, you expect to see myriad signs directing you to points of interest, such as connecting gates, luggage pickup, or a taxi line. And while the words on these signs are certainly important, perhaps just as important are the accompanying visual symbols. Our minds become so accustomed to visual elements that often we don't even need to read the words to understand a sign's meaning, and the presence of visual elements certainly helps when we're in another country where we don't speak the local language.

This universal visual language of signs is the main idea behind the user interface system in Windows Phone 7. Microsoft designers want the elements in the Windows Phone 7 UI to direct users to the content that they want, just as airport signs direct people where they need to go. Within Microsoft, this contemporary UI has been code-named Metro and, per the *UI Design and Interaction Guide for Windows Phone 7*, elements of Metro UI are meant to be visually appealing and to encourage exploration of the applications you build.

In this chapter, you will explore the most important design principles at the heart of Metro UI and learn how to ensure that your application conforms to them. You will also gain an understanding of themes on the Windows Phone 7 device and learn how to make your application theme-aware. Finally, you will take a look at the controls that are available to you for use in Windows Phone 7 applications, especially the innovative Panorama and Pivot controls that are unique to Windows Phone 7. You have already used many of the controls within Windows Phone 7 in the previous chapters of this book, so this chapter will recap and introduce you to the less common controls.

Introducing the Metro Design System

The big idea behind the Windows Phone 7 design system (Metro) is to direct users to the content they want using design elements that are both effective in conveying their message and attractive. The *UI Design and Interaction Guide for Windows Phone 7* (available as a PDF download from http://go.microsoft.com/fwlink/?LinkID=183218) specifically states that visual elements within applications "should encourage playful exploration so that the user feels a sense of wonder and excitement" when using your application. Microsoft strongly encourages all application developers to adopt Metro design principles in their applications. Fortunately, to help those who may not be particularly strong in graphic design, Microsoft has ensured that all application controls (i.e., text box, button, etc.) are Metro-compliant by default. The controls that ship with Windows Phone 7 development tools already have the look and feel dictated by Metro UI guidelines, so it's your job as a developer to preserve that look and feel throughout your applications.

▨ **Note** An open source project, Silverlight for Windows Phone Toolkit, contains many additional controls that are ready to use inside your application and that conform to Metro design guidelines as well. This Toolkit is also constantly being updated with new controls and features; make sure to check it out at `http://silverlight.codeplex.com/`. Perhaps it already contains that cool control that you were considering building yourself (Date or Time Picker, for example).

When you first start working with standard controls within Windows Phone 7 applications, you may be surprised by their minimalistic, two-dimensional look. That appearance, however, emphasizes another one of the main principles of Metro UI design: "Delight through content instead of decoration." Microsoft encourages developers to reduce the complexity of visual elements that are not part of content and to communicate with users of their applications as directly as possible. According to the Metro designers, the content and functionality of the application should be the most engaging factor of the Windows Phone 7 application.

Another pillar of Metro UI is the use of a standard contemporary-looking font. Segoe WP is the standard system font on Windows Phone 7 devices and it is a Unicode font. It is available in the following five styles:

- Regular
- Bold
- Semi-bold
- Semi-light
- Black

You can also embed your own fonts in any application you write, but they will be available for use only within your application and not outside of it. To conform to the Metro guidelines, however, it's probably wise to stick with the standard fonts that ship with the tools.

Windows Phone Chrome

The term *Windows Phone Chrome* refers to two areas on the device screen, one at the top and the other at its bottom, as illustrated in Figure 9–1. The *System Tray* is one of two primary components of Windows Phone Chrome; the *Application Bar* is the other.

The System Tray is the top portion of Windows Phone Chrome and contains several indicators that display system-level status information. The System Tray displays the following icons, left to right, in the order listed here:

- Signal strength
- Data connection
- Call forwarding
- Roaming
- Wireless network signal strength

- Bluetooth status

- Ringer mode

- Input status

- Battery power level

- System clock

■ **Note** The screen shown in Figure 9–1 is the emulator screen, and it does not include all of the items mentioned in the preceding list.

Figure 9–1. Windows Phone 7 Chrome

By default, only the system clock is visible at all times. To make other items visible, you need to double-tap (double-click in the emulator) in the System Tray area. These indicators slide into view for approximately eight seconds before sliding out of view. Note that although you can programmatically hide the System Tray, it is not a recommended practice under Metro guidelines.

In Chapter 7, you learned how to work with the Application Bar, the second part of Windows Phone 7 Chrome. To quickly recap, the Application Bar is limited to four icons; if there are more navigational items to display, they should be put inside the menu items. There is a set of default Application Bar icons included with each distribution of Windows Phone 7 tools, and it can be used to build basic Application Bars quickly.

Screen Orientations

Windows Phone 7 supports three screen orientations: portrait, landscape left, and landscape right. In portrait orientation, the page is vertically oriented with hardware buttons appearing at the bottom of the device. Portrait orientation is the default orientation of the device, and the Start screen is always shown in portrait orientation. In landscape left, the System Tray appears on the left of the device, and in landscape right, the System Tray appears on the right.

Your application can't switch the orientation of its screen by itself, since the Orientation property is read-only. You can, however, set a fixed orientation where you disallow application support for certain screen orientations. Some system components can adjust to changes in orientation. For example, application bar icons automatically rotate when the device changes from portrait to landscape mode. Other components with similar orientation-aware behaviors include the System Tray, Application Bar Menu, Volume/Ring/Vibrate Display, Push Notifications, and Dialogs.

Having discussed some of the principles and components of Metro UI, it's time to turn your attention to the support for themes on Windows Phone 7 devices. Themes make the phone more personal, which goes hand in hand with the Metro guideline that the experience of using the phone should be an engaging one.

Themes on Windows Phone 7 Devices

A Windows Phone 7 theme is a combination of a background and an accent color. Users can select from themes that ship with the phone, developers can access them in their code, and companies can alter them to match their own branding colors. Themes are set in the Settings ➤ Themes portion of the Windows Phone 7 device or the emulator.

Themes can also be applied dynamically during the runtime of an application by overwriting or injecting the custom themes into `Resources.MergedDictionaries` found in `Application.Current`, as shown in the following code snippet:

```
ResourceDictionary res = new ResourceDictionary();
res.Source =
    new Uri("/MyApplication;component/Assets/MyStyles.xaml", UriKind.RelativeOrAbsolute);
Application.Current.Resources.MergedDictionaries.Add(res);
```

Currently, there are two possible background settings—Dark (default) and Light. There are ten accent colors to choose from, starting with a Microsoft-ish blue (the default) and ranging all the way to a decidedly 70s lime green.

■ **Note** Microsoft recommends you use as little white color as possible (especially in backgrounds), since excessive use of white color may have a negative impact on battery life.

The combination of two background colors and ten accent colors provides the user with a total of twenty possible themes, delivering on the engagement and personalization promise of Metro design principles. Applications automatically adjust to the selected theme and ensure that all UI elements appear consistently across the platform. A quick walk-through demonstrates theme-awareness of Windows Phone 7 controls and UI elements.

Applying a Theme

In this walk-through, you will add a set of Windows Phone 7 controls to an application, creating some of them with XAML and some through managed code. You will change the theme in the emulator and observe the effect this change has on the controls. Follow these steps to get a better understanding of theming support in Windows Phone 7.

Creating a User Interface

First, you will add a set of standard controls to a Windows Phone 7 application.

1.   Launch Visual Studio 2010 Express and select the Windows Phone Application template. Change the Project Name to Theming, select OK, and Visual Studio will set up a new project.

2.   Open MainPage.xaml in Design mode and add a text box, textblock, check box, button, and a black rectangular shape to the page. Your end goal is a simple interface that resembles the one in Figure 9–2. Here's the XAML:

```
<!--LayoutRoot is the root grid where all page content is placed-->
<Grid x:Name="LayoutRoot" Background="Transparent">
    <Grid.RowDefinitions>
        <RowDefinition Height="Auto"/>
        <RowDefinition Height="*"/>
    </Grid.RowDefinitions>

    <!--TitlePanel contains the name of the application and page title-->
    <StackPanel x:Name="TitlePanel" Grid.Row="0" Margin="12,17,0,28">
        <TextBlock x:Name="ApplicationTitle" Text="THEMES AND COLORS"
    Style="{StaticResource PhoneTextNormalStyle}"/>
    <TextBlock x:Name="PageTitle" Text="THEMES" Margin="9,-7,0,0"
    Style="{StaticResource PhoneTextTitle1Style}"/>
    </StackPanel>

    <!--ContentPanel - place additional content here-->
    <Grid x:Name="ContentPanel" Grid.Row="1" Margin="12,0,12,0">
        <TextBox Height="72" HorizontalAlignment="Left" Margin="-4,6,0,0"
    Name="textBox1" Text="TextBox" VerticalAlignment="Top" Width="454" />
```

```
        <TextBlock Height="30" HorizontalAlignment="Left" Margin="11,80,0,0"
Name="textBlock1" Text="TextBlock" VerticalAlignment="Top" Width="329" />
        <CheckBox Content="CheckBox" Height="72" HorizontalAlignment="Left"
Margin="12,116,0,0" Name="checkBox1" VerticalAlignment="Top" />
        <Button Content="Button" Height="72" HorizontalAlignment="Left"
Margin="9,194,0,0" Name="button1" VerticalAlignment="Top" Width="160" />
        <Rectangle Height="110" HorizontalAlignment="Left" Margin="249,137,0,0"
Name="rectangle1" Stroke="Black" StrokeThickness="1" VerticalAlignment="Top"
Width="156" />
        </Grid>
    </Grid>
```

Adding Code to Draw an Elliptical Shape

In addition to using the powerful Visual Designer to add controls to Windows Phone 7 pages, as you just did, you can add controls programmatically. The steps here show you how to do that.

1. Go to the Theming project in Solution Explorer and open MainPage.xaml.cs (right-click MainPage.xaml and choose View Code).

2. To add a white ellipse to the page, paste the following code inside the MainPage constructor:

    ```
    Ellipse e = new Ellipse();
    e.Width = 100.0;
    e.Height = 120.0;
    e.StrokeThickness = 2.0;

    e.HorizontalAlignment = HorizontalAlignment.Left;
    e.VerticalAlignment = VerticalAlignment.Top;

    Color backgroundColor = Color.FromArgb(255, 255, 255, 255);
    e.Fill = new SolidColorBrush(backgroundColor);
    e.Margin = new Thickness(10, 300, 10, 10);

    ContentPanel.Children.Add(e);
    ```

Figure 9–2. Theming application UI layout

Press F5 to run the application. The application screen should now display all of the controls you've added, including a white ellipse.

Changing the Theme

In this part of the walk-through, you will change the emulator's theme to observe the effect it has on the Theming application.

1. Press the Windows button on the emulator to bring up the Start screen. Then press the ➤ key (the arrow in the upper right corner of the emulator screen) and select Settings ➤ Themes to bring up the Themes dialog.

2. Change the background to Light, and change the accent color to Red (note that you may have to scroll to locate the red accent color).

3. Press the Windows button again to go back to the Start screen. Note that your application is no longer running (it stopped when you pressed the Windows button), so go back to Visual Studio 2010 Express and press F5 to re-launch your application.

4. Note that you can see the same controls as before, except the ellipse that you drew from code is nowhere to be found. Figure 9–3 shows two versions of the same application side by side, each with a different theme.

Figure 9–3. Two themes applied to the same Theming application example

By now, you have probably guessed that the reason the ellipse is not visible is that the application paints it white and then displays it on a white background. But how did the other controls manage to show up on the white background when they originally were white themselves? And how can you make the ellipse behave the same way?

The answers lie in a Windows Phone 7 concept known as *theme awareness*. By default, Windows Phone 7 controls are theme-aware and adjust their appearance based on the theme selected on the device. Problems arise when the color values are hardcoded in the control, as you have done for the ellipse and the rectangle border. In the next few steps, you'll correct the issue of hardcoded colors, first with a designer and the second in code.

5. If it's still running, stop the application. Open MainPage.xaml in the Design view, and select the rectangular shape. Press F4 to bring up the Properties

window, and then click the diamond symbol to the right of the Stroke property.

6. From the pop-up dialog, click Apply Resource. From the next dialog, double-click the PhoneAccentBrush setting to use the currently selected accent color to draw a rectangle.

7. Now, adjust the color of the ellipse to the currently selected accent color. Since you drew the ellipse from code, open the `MainPage.xaml.cs` file and change the following line of code from

```
Color backgroundColor = Color.FromArgb(255, 255, 255, 255);
```
to

```
Color backgroundColor =
(Color)Application.Current.Resources["PhoneAccentColor"];
```

Press F5 to run your application. You should see both the rectangle and ellipse appear in red (or the currently selected accent color).

▧ **Note** Avoid using hardcoded values for color if possible. It's hard to predict what combination of themes a user will choose, so your visual elements may not show up as desired. Instead, use one of the predefined theme resources (a full list of resources is available at http://msdn.microsoft.com/en-us/library/ff769552%28VS.92%29.aspx) to ensure that your application is fully theme-aware in accordance with Metro design principles.

Now that you know how to ensure your application is theme-aware, in the next section you will learn how to approach cases where you absolutely must customize your application based on the currently selected theme.

Detecting the Currently Selected Theme

Sooner or later, you'll want to customize your application depending on whether a dark or a light theme is currently active. For example, you may have a beautiful custom graphic within your application that simply does not render well when the background theme colors are changed; instead, you would like to show a different graphic depending on the currently active theme. The following walk-through shows you how to accomplish just that: it detects the currently selected theme and adjusts the message based on whether the current theme has a light or dark background.

1. Launch Visual Studio 2010 Express and select the Windows Phone Application template. Change the Project Name to DetectTheme, select OK, and Visual Studio will set up a new project.

2. Open `MainPage.xaml` in Design mode, and add a TextBlock to the page. For this walk-through, you will simply modify the message within this TextBlock; for real-world applications, you will probably choose to do something a bit more exotic than this, such as show a different image.

3. Open `MainPage.xaml.cs` (right-click `MainPage.xaml` in Solution Explorer and choose View Code) and add the following code to the `MainPage` constructor, right below the `InitializeComponent()` method:

```
Visibility v = (Visibility)Resources["PhoneLightThemeVisibility"];
        if (v == System.Windows.Visibility.Visible)
        {
                textBlock1.Text = "Let there be light!";
        }
        else
        {
                textBlock1.Text = "It's dark!";
        }
```

Note that you are using the Visibility property to determine whether the light theme is visible and to take action accordingly.

Press F5 to run the application. If you still have a light background selected from the previous walk-through, you will see a "Let there be light!" message. Otherwise, an "It's dark!" message will be displayed.

So far, you've touched on the basics of theming and looked at how to make your application theme-aware and how to customize its behavior based on the theme selected. Next, you'll look at the controls provided as part of Windows Phone 7 Developer tools, since it's these controls that really make the Metro experience complete.

Panorama and Pivot Controls

In earlier chapters, you used of several base controls that ship with the Windows Phone 7 development tools, including text boxes, textblocks, and buttons—the kinds of controls you'd expect within any UI framework. But the Windows Phone developer tools include a number of unique controls as well, including a web browser and a Bing maps control, both of which will be covered in later chapters. Two others are the Panorama and Pivot controls, which are integral to Metro and the Windows Phone user experience.

The Panorama and Pivot controls offer two ways to develop an application that requires page navigation. With a Panorama control, you can present the UI of an application on one horizontal canvas that extends beyond the left and right boundaries of the device screen and can be flicked to the left and right with touch gestures. With a Pivot, you can present the UI of an application as a series of pages, much like tabbed pages, by touching its header or flicking through the pages. A Panorama is like a scroll; a Pivot is more like a series of cards laid down from left to right.

In the following section, you'll learn how to use a Panorama control to create some engaging UI for an airport application that displays arrivals and departures. You'll also take a brief look at the Pivot control, whose outfitting and use is nearly identical to the Panorama control, though its effects are quite different.

Using the Panorama Control

In every video ad for a Windows Phone 7 device, the scrollable UI of the Panorama control is usually the first thing that people notice. The People hub on the Start screen of Windows Phone 7 is implemented using this control. So is the Music + Videos hub. These interactions essentially involve the ability to keep scrolling horizontally far past the end of the screen. The Panorama control allows for a unique experience that is associated with the native Windows Phone 7 look and feel.

A Panorama control can be thought of as a long, horizontal canvas. A secondary control called a PanoramaItem serves as a container that hosts content and other controls such as text blocks, buttons, and links. There are three ways to incorporate Panorama behavior into your application:

1. Create a new Windows Phone project and choose Windows Phone Panorama Application as the template to use for the application. While this is an extremely powerful approach, this type of template creates a Model-View-ViewModel (MVVM)–based project, which has a significant learning curve and is quite different from the way you have developed Windows Phone 7 applications so far in this book (for an example of an MVVM application, see Chapter 3).

2. Add the Panorama control to the Visual Studio Toolbox (via right-clicking the Toolbox and navigating to the assembly containing this control) and then drag and drop it to your application.

3. Add a new page to your application that contains a Panorama control. This is perhaps the easiest way to quickly incorporate the Panorama control inside our application; this is the approach you will pursue in this section.

In the following walk-through, you will create an application to display the arrival and departures of flights at a fictional airport. In addition, you will add a search capability (or just the user interface elements of it) to this application. You will use the Panorama control to implement this functionality where the long background gives you the feeling that you are inside the airport as you navigate left or right to the pages.

Your application will not contain any code, since your primary goal in this chapter is to explore the controls available for Windows Phone 7, and in this section you are exploring the Panorama control. To create Panorama control, you will use Option 3 from the list in the previous section and use XAML to build a new page with a Panorama control.

1. Launch Visual Studio 2010 Express and select the Windows Phone Application template. Change the Project Name to Panorama, select OK, and Visual Studio will set up a new project.

2. Right-click the project name in Solution Explorer and select Add ➤ New Item ➤ Windows Phone Panorama Page. Accept the default name of PanoramaPage1.xaml for the file, and press the OK button.

3. You now have a page with the Panorama control in it within the application, but there is no way to get to it. You could either add navigation from MainPage.xaml or simply make PanoramaPage1.xaml the main page within the application. To implement the second choice, rename the current MainPage.xaml to MainPage1.xaml and then rename PanoramaPage1.xaml to MainPage.xaml. Now the Panorama page should be the default page that comes up when the application is launched.

4. It is time to customize and add content to the Panorama control. Go ahead and change the `<controls:Panorama...` element to the following:

    ```
    <controls:Panorama Title="airport" Foreground="Red">
    ```

5. To add new tabs or containers to the Panorama control, you would use the `<controls:PanoramaItem...` XAML element. Go ahead and add a third PanoramaItem that will contain a text box and a button to search for departures to a specific city right above the closing tag for the Panorama control

`</controls:Panorama>`. Notice that as you add PanoramaItem, your designed view reflects the changes.

```
<!--Panorama item three-->
<controls:PanoramaItem Header="search" Foreground="{StaticResource
PhoneAccentBrush}">
    <Grid>
      <TextBox Height="72" HorizontalAlignment="Left" Margin="-12,-2,0,0"
      Name="textBox1" Text="TextBox" VerticalAlignment="Top" Width="271" />
        <Button Content="Search" Height="72" HorizontalAlignment="Left"
      Margin="242,-4,0,0" Name="button1" VerticalAlignment="Top" Width="160"
/>
      </Grid>
    </controls:PanoramaItem>
```

■ **Note** The use of `Foreground="{StaticResource PhoneAccentBrush}"` binding allows the foreground color of the text to be the current theme's accent color.

---

6. Make some minor adjustments to the first two Panorama items to bring them in line with the rest of the UI layout. Replace the top two `<controls:PanoramaItem…` elements with the following XAML:

```
<!--Panorama item one-->
<controls:PanoramaItem Header="arrivals" Foreground="{StaticResource
PhoneAccentBrush}">
    <Grid>
    </Grid>
  </controls:PanoramaItem>

<!--Panorama item two-->
<controls:PanoramaItem Header="departures" Foreground="{StaticResource
PhoneAccentBrush}">
    <Grid/>
    </controls:PanoramaItem>
```

7. Finally, add a background image to the Panorama control. The recommended size for the background image is 800 pixels high (of course, that's the standard resolution of Windows Phone 7 devices) and 2,000 or fewer pixels wide. To specify the background image, add the following XAML tag right below the `<controls:Panorama …` tag:

```
<controls:Panorama.Background>
      <ImageBrush ImageSource="PanoramaBackground.jpg"></ImageBrush>
    </controls:Panorama.Background>
```

8. Press F5 to run the application. You should see a screen that looks very similar to Figure 9–4 (minus the background image, perhaps). Flicking the Panorama control from right to left should allow you to see Arrivals and Departures plus a separate tab designated for searching airport schedules.

Figure 9–4. *Panorama control example*

As you can see, it is pretty easy to use a Panorama control, and you can place different contents within the PanoramaItem tag. Using the Panorama control, together with the Pivot control discussed next, provides a very easy way to impress your users with cool designs, layouts, and coding techniques. Considering that you didn't have to hire a graphics designer to get here, this is a very powerful weapon in the Windows Phone 7 developer arsenal.

■ **Note**   Microsoft recommends limiting the number of PanoramaItems to a maximum of four to ensure smooth application performance. In addition, it is considered best practice to hide PanoramaItem until it has content to display.

Using the Pivot Control

The Pivot control is a close cousin of the Panorama control. The basic premise of having multiple pages easily accessible is preserved; however, the ability to click the header to show the contents of a new page is not possible with a Panorama control. A screenshot of a simple Pivot control is shown in Figure 9–5. A user can tap (or click in the emulator) the word "departures" and be immediately presented with the portion of the application dealing with airport departures.

Creating a Pivot control is very much like creating a Panorama control; there are still three possible ways of adding it to your application (except you would add a Windows Phone Pivot Page, of course). Within the control itself, you would work with PivotItems, not PanoramaItems, but the rest of the design approaches are almost identical. If you feel uncertain about how to work with Pivot controls on Windows Phone 7, you can download a Pivot project available for this book. In addition, you can visit MSDN instructions on working with the Pivot control located at `http://msdn.microsoft.com/en-us/library/ff941123(v=VS.92).aspx` for a quick reference.

Figure 9–5. *Pivot control example*

Understanding Frame and Page Navigation

To navigate from screen to screen in a Windows Phone 7 application, an understanding of the PhoneApplicationFrame and PhoneApplicationPage controls is important. There is only one PhoneApplicationFrame available to a Windows Phone 7 application; this frame reserves space for the System Tray and the Application Bar, as well as the content area where PhoneApplicationPage controls live. You can create as many different pages as needed and then navigate to those pages from the frame. Refer to Figure 9–6 to see how the controls are placed in the phone.

Figure 9–6. *PhoneApplicationFrame and PhoneApplicationPage*

To navigate from page to page within your application, use the `NavigationService` class. This class exposes methods to navigate to pages given a URI, as well as to go back to the previous page. The following walk-through illustrates the use of the `NavigationService` class.

Creating a User Interface for NavigationTest Project

The NavigationTest project will contain two XAML pages (`MainPage.xaml` and `Page1.xaml`) and will navigate between the two.

1. Launch Visual Studio 2010 Express and select the Windows Phone Application template. Change the Project Name to NavigationTest, select OK, and Visual Studio will set up a new project.

2. Right-click the project name in Solution Explorer and select Add ➤ New Item ➤ Windows Phone Portrait Page. Accept the default name of `Page1.xaml` and press OK.

3. Open `MainPage.xaml` in Design view. From the toolbox, drag and drop the HyperlinkButton control. With that control selected, press F4 to display its properties and change the contents say "Go to Page1."

4. Open Page1.xaml in the Design view, and add a button to that page from the
    toolbox. Edit the contents of the button to say "Go Back to Main Page."

5. Add a TextBlock underneath the button on Page1.xaml. This TextBlock will be
    used to show the parameters passed in to this page.

In the next section, you will use NavigationService to navigate between pages.

Adding Navigation Code

When the user clicks the "Go to Page 1" hyperlink, you will be using NavigationService to move to
Page1.

1. Open MainPage.xaml and double-click the hyperlink on that page. Implement
    the hyperlinkButton1_Click event handler with the following code:

```
private void hyperlinkButton1_Click(object sender, RoutedEventArgs e)
{
 NavigationService.Navigate(new Uri("/Page1.xaml", UriKind.Relative));

}
```

2. Open Page1.xaml and double-click the button on that page. Implement the
    button1_Click event handler with the following code:

```
private void button1_Click(object sender, RoutedEventArgs e)
{
        NavigationService.GoBack();
}
```

3. Press F5 to run the application. Now when you click the hyperlink on
    MainPage.xaml, you are taken to Page1.xaml. When you click the button on
    Page1.xaml, you are taken back to MainPage.xaml. In the next section, you will
    enhance this application slightly to pass parameters between the pages.

Adding Code to Pass Parameters Between Pages

In the previous section, you learned how to successfully navigate from page to page. In this section, you
will see how to pass parameters from one page to another.

1. Open MainPage.xaml.cs and change the hyperlinkButton1_Click event handler
    to the following:

```
private void hyperlinkButton1_Click(object sender, RoutedEventArgs e)
{
        NavigationService.Navigate(new Uri("/Page1.xaml?message=Hello,World",
        UriKind.Relative));
}
```

Here, you are passing the hard-coded string "Hello, world" to Page1.xaml for processing.

2. In Page1.xaml, you will try to read the query string passed from the prior pages
    to see if there are non-empty values. Open Page1.xaml.cs and add the following
    code to that file:

```
protected override void OnNavigatedTo(System.Windows.Navigation.NavigationEventArgs
```

```
e)
    {
        base.OnNavigatedTo(e);
        string msg = "";
        if (NavigationContext.QueryString.TryGetValue("message", out msg))
                textBlock1.Text = msg;
    }
```

3. Press F5 to run the application. Now, if you press the hyperlink from
   MainPage.xaml, you should see the "Hello, world" message displayed on Page1.

Having talked about controls, let's close out this chapter with a neat effect you can add to your
application to increase the buzz about it.

Adding Transition Effects

To spice up your application, you can add what is called a "tilt" effect to the visual elements. The tilt
effect provides visual feedback to the user of the Windows Phone 7 application during manipulation of
visual elements within the application. So, instead of just "pressed" and "unpressed" states, elements
can also have "being pressed" and "being unpressed" states. The integration of tilt is pretty
straightforward, and in the end it will certainly be completely up to you whether you would like to use it
within your application. But if you do decide to give this effect a try, follow this walk-through.

Creating a User Interface

The user interface for the test application will be composed of four controls within the page: ListBox,
Button, Hyperlink, and a Checkbox.

1. Launch Visual Studio 2010 Express and select the Windows Phone Application
   template. Change the Project Name to TiltableTest, select OK, and Visual
   Studio will set up a new project.

2. Open MainPage.xaml in Design mode, and add a ListBox with four items, a
   Button, a Hyperlink, and a Checkbox to the page, with the end goal of creating a
   user interface like the one shown in Figure 9–7.

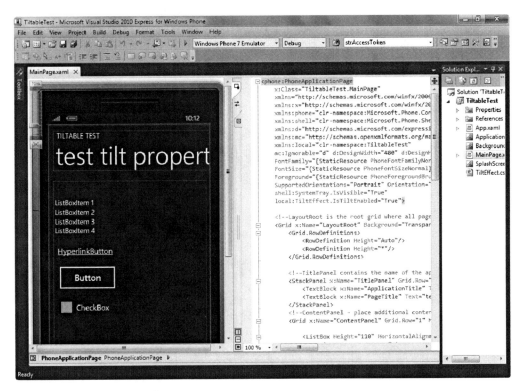

Figure 9–7. *TiltableTest UI layout*

3. You can also paste the following XAML code to get the same interface depicted in Figure 9–7:

```
<!--ContentPanel - place additional content here-->
<Grid x:Name="ContentPanel" Grid.Row="1" Margin="12,0,12,0">

<ListBox Height="110" HorizontalAlignment="Left" Margin="6,47,0,0"
Name="listBox1"
        VerticalAlignment="Top" Width="460" ItemsSource="{Binding}" >
                <ListBoxItem Content="ListBoxItem 1" ></ListBoxItem>
        <ListBoxItem Content="ListBoxItem 2" ></ListBoxItem>
                <ListBoxItem Content="ListBoxItem 3" ></ListBoxItem>
                <ListBoxItem Content="ListBoxItem 4" ></ListBoxItem>
        </ListBox>
        <HyperlinkButton Content="HyperlinkButton" Height="30"
HorizontalAlignment="Left"
        Margin="-109,185,0,0" Name="hyperlinkButton1" VerticalAlignment="Top"
        Width="409" />

<Button Width="186" Height="85" Content="Button" HorizontalAlignment="Left"
VerticalAlignment="Top" Margin="9,234,0,0" />
        <CheckBox Content="CheckBox" Height="72" HorizontalAlignment="Left"
```

```
                       Margin="12,325,0,0" Name="checkBox1" VerticalAlignment="Top" />

        </Grid>
```

Now that you've added controls to the MainPage, you'll add Tilt effects to the controls.

Downloading TiltEffect.cs and Applying Dependency Properties

To integrate the Tilt effect into your application, you will need to download TiltEffect.cs and properly integrate it into your project.

1. Download the Tilt Effect Control Sample from http://go.microsoft.com/fwlink/?LinkId=200720, and extract the contents of the .zip file to a known location.

2. From within the TiltableTest project you created previously, right-click the Add ➤ Existing Item, navigate to the location from Step 1, and find the TiltEffect.cs file.

3. With TitlEffect.cs now a part of your project, double-click that file to open it. Change the following statement

   ```
   namespace ControlTiltEffect
   ```

   to

   ```
   namespace TiltableTest
   ```
   Essentially, you just changed the namespace of this file so that it now belongs to your application.

4. Now you need to add the IsTiltEnabled dependency property to the MainPage.xaml page. Open MainPage.xaml in a XAML view and, at the very top of the page, right below the xmlnss:mc=… add the following statement:

   ```
   xmlns:local="clr-namespace:TiltableTest"
   ```

5. You're almost done! At the top of the page, beneath the statement

   ```
   shell:System Tray.IsVisible="True"
   ```

   add

   ```
   local:TiltEffect.IsTiltEnabled="True">
   ```

6. Right-click the project and select Build. After the project builds, you are ready to run the application.

Press F5 to run the application. Now when you click the button or the items in the ListBox, you should see an animation in which these items first contract and then expand. This is another element of interactivity that you can use to further enhance user experience of your application and add to that Wow factor.

▨ **Note** You can suppress the Tilt effect on any control by adding the local:TiltEffect.SuppressTilt="True" attribute to that control.

Summary

In this chapter, you learned the basic concepts of the Metro design system and theme support on Windows Phone 7 devices. You learned how to detect which theme is being used, how to create theme-aware applications, and how to navigate between the pages within Windows Phone 7 application. You also learned how to work with Panorama, Pivot, PhoneApplicationFrame, and PhoneApplicationPage controls. Finally, you learned how to further enhance user interaction via the introduction of Tilt effects in your applications. The next chapter covers the integration options available on Windows Phone OS 7.0.

CHAPTER 10

Integrating Applications with the Windows Phone OS

When a third-party application runs on a Windows Phone, it runs in an execution environment that is highly restricted. The Windows Phone OS must be restrictive in order to protect unsuspecting users of mobile devices from potential malicious application behavior, which may include stealing personal data stored on the phone, dialing phone numbers without users' knowledge, or corrupting other applications' data stores. One of the major restrictions that Windows Phone OS places on mobile applications is limiting them to their own execution environment, or *sandbox*, and not allowing them access to other applications' space or the internals of the operating system. Sandboxing and other Windows Phone security features are covered in great detail in Chapter 19.

Yet many applications need to access the system features of the phone to play a music file in the media library, for example, or to take a photo, or to send a text message. Windows Phone 7 OS enables such application interactions with the device via a set of Application Programming Interface (API) tasks referred to as launchers and *choosers*. Some launchers and choosers may be invoked via hardware buttons on the phone, such as using a camera button to take photos. It is also relatively easy to use launchers and choosers from within your application, but when one is invoked or when a user presses hardware buttons on the phone while your application is running, managing your application state does get a little tricky.

This chapter covers the launchers and choosers available on the Windows Phone 7 platform, as well as various states an application can enter when you invoke them. You will also learn about integrating your applications with popular external services such as Facebook. Finally, you'll take a quick look at Windows Phone 7 hubs, which bring many applications found on desktop devices and in the cloud to the palm of your hand.

Introducing Windows Phone 7 Launchers and Choosers

When an application executes, the Windows Phone 7 OS confines it to its own space, or sandbox. Both memory and file storage are isolated within that sandbox—one application can't access or alter another's memory or file storage. Neither can one application directly call another or access a shared data store, such as a list of contacts, for example. There are obvious reasons for this behavior; Microsoft must ensure that the Windows Phone 7 platform is as secure and stable as possible, and isolating applications is one giant step toward getting there.

There is a set of built-in APIs that provides access to the most common features of Windows Phone 7. These APIs help you perform tasks, such as saving a contact's e-mail address or phone number or placing a phone call (with the mandatory prior user authorization, of course), that require access to shared resources on the phone.

Launchers and choosers, which can be thought of as system functions provided by the Windows Phone OS, provide you with the means to call into these applications. The difference between a launcher and a chooser is small but important: choosers provide a return value into the calling application, whereas launchers do not. If you think about a task of composing an e-mail message, for example, then it is sufficient to "fire and forget" an e-mail application, allowing users to create and send an e-mail. A launcher is an ideal solution for this task. On the other hand, an application allowing you to select a photo from the photo library on the phone needs to pass the selected photo to your application. Windows Phone 7 provides a chooser to perform such a task.

An important concept to remember is that launchers and choosers are separate applications. Since one of the core design principles behind Windows Phone 7 is to maximize battery life, only one application is allowed to execute on the phone at any time. Therefore, if you invoke a launcher or chooser from within your application, that launcher or chooser will replace your application and become the running application. Depending on the circumstances, your application may enter one of several states when that happens. We will cover these possible states when we cover the application life cycle in depth later in this chapter, but in the meantime, Tables 10–1 and 10–2 list the launchers and choosers available on the Windows Phone 7 platform today. You'll find all of them in the `Microsoft.Phone.Tasks` namespace; therefore, to use any of them, be sure to import that namespace into your application via the following standard directive at the very top of the code page:

```
using Microsoft.Phone.Tasks;
```

Launchers

Table 10–1 lists the launchers offered on the Windows Phone 7 platform with a brief description of functionality offered by each.

Table 10–1. Windows Phone 7 Launchers and Their Functions

Launcher	Function
EmailComposeTask	Launch the e-mail application with a new message displayed.
MarketplaceDetailTask	Launch the Windows Phone Marketplace client application and display the details page for the specified product.
MarketplaceHubTask	Launch the Windows Phone Marketplace client application.
MarketplaceReviewTask	Launch the Windows Phone Marketplace client application and display the review page for the specified product.
MarketplaceSearchTask	Launch the Windows Phone Marketplace client application and display the search results from the specified search terms.

Launcher	Function
MediaPlayerLauncher	Launch the media player.
PhoneCallTask	Launch the Phone application; use this to allow users to make a phone call from your application.
SaveEmailAddressTask	Launch the Contacts application; use this to allow users to save an e-mail address from your application to a new or existing contact.
SavePhoneNumberTask	Launch the Contacts application; use this to allow users to save a phone number from your application to a new or existing contact.
SearchTask	Launch the Web Search application.
SmsComposeTask	Launch the SMS application.
WebBrowserTask	Launch the Web Browser application.

Choosers

Table 10–2 lists and describes the choosers available on the Windows Phone 7 platform.

Table 10–2. *Windows Phone Choosers and Their Functions*

Chooser	Function
EmailAddressChooserTask	Launch the Contacts application and obtain the e-mail address of a contact selected by the user.
CameraCaptureTask	Launch the Camera application and allow users to take a photo from your application (for more information and in-depth examples, please refer to Chapter 16).
PhoneNumberChooserTask	Launch the Contacts application and obtain the phone number of a contact selected by the user.
PhotoChooserTask	Launch the Photo Chooser application and select a photo (refer to Chapter 16 for more information and a detailed demo using this Chooser).

Working with Launchers and Choosers

In this section, you will explore how to work with launchers and choosers from within your application. You will use PhoneNumberChooserTask and SmsComposeTask to create an application that selects a contact from the shared list of contacts on the phone and then composes a text message to that contact's phone number.

Creating the User Interface

The user interface for this sample consists of a single button; when the user clicks this button, a list of contacts will be displayed, allowing the user to pick one.

1. Launch Visual Studio 2010 Express, and select the Windows Phone Application template. Change the project name to Tasks, select OK, and Visual Studio will set up a new project.

2. Open `MainPage.xaml` in design mode, and add a button to the page. Change the button's caption to "Send SMS."

Coding Application Logic

When the user clicks the Send SMS button of your application, she should be presented with a list of contacts available on your device. Conveniently for you, even on the emulator, Microsoft has included a sample list of contacts for you to test an application with.

3. Open `MainPage.xaml.cs` (right-click `MainPage.xaml` and select View Code). At the top of the page, add the following using statement:

```
using Microsoft.Phone.Tasks;
```

4. Declare the following module-level variable for the PhoneNumberChooserTask chooser (insert it right above the `MainPage()` constructor):

```
private PhoneNumberChooserTask _choosePhoneNumberTask;
```

5. Instantiate a new PhoneNumberChooserTask object within the `MainPage()` constructor, and associate a method to invoke when the user selects a contact from the list. The method to call upon the chooser's return will accept the phone number selected as one of the parameters. Use the following two lines of code to accomplish that:

```
_choosePhoneNumberTask = new PhoneNumberChooserTask();
_choosePhoneNumberTask.Completed += new
    EventHandler<PhoneNumberResult>(ChoosePhoneNumberTaskCompleted);
```

6. Code the ChoosePhoneNumberTaskCompleted method that will be invoked upon selection of a contact from the list. Note the use of an SmsComposeTask launcher to create a new text message to the person you have selected from the contact list.

```
private void ChoosePhoneNumberTaskCompleted(object sender,
PhoneNumberResult e)
```

```
=
        {
                new SmsComposeTask() { Body = "SMS using Windows Phone 7 Chooser", To

                e.PhoneNumber }.Show();
        }
```

7. Finally, add code to react to the button-click event by opening the
    PhoneNumberChooser launcher. The easiest way to accomplish this is to
    double-click the button with MainPage.xaml open in design view and make the
    button-click event look like the following:

```
        private void button1_Click(object sender, RoutedEventArgs e)
        {
                _choosePhoneNumberTask.Show();
        }
```

8. Press F5 to run your application. Click the Send SMS button, and select
    Andrew R. (Andy) Hill from the list of contacts that comes up on the emulator.
    Immediately after selecting Andy, you should see a screen similar to Figure 10–
    1, where the SMS message has been composed and is ready to be sent to
    Andrew.

To summarize what you have learned so far, your application integrates with the Windows Phone
OS via a set of API methods referred to as launchers and choosers. Working with launchers and choosers
is fairly straightforward, as illustrated by the previous example. If that was all there was to application
integration, it would have made for a very brief chapter. But there's more.

One major limitation of mobile platforms is their inherently short battery life. This limitation causes
OS designers and phone manufacturers to come up with various techniques to balance short battery life
with positive user experience. One such technique is to allow only one application to run on the phone
at any given time. You may be wondering then, what happens when your application yields execution to
the built-in Windows Phone OS application invoked with the launcher? That brings us to the important
Windows Phone concept of application *tombstoning*, a subject you'll explore along with the Windows
Phone application life cycle in the next section.

Figure 10–1. SMS is composed and ready to go to Andrew.

Working with the Windows Phone 7 Application Life Cycle

To program responsive applications on a Windows Phone 7 device, you must be familiar with the concept of tombstoning on that platform. The simplest way to explain tombstoning is to describe it as an event that happens when your application loses focus on the Windows Phone 7 device, such as when a user invokes a launcher or a chooser, or presses the hardware Start button. When your application loses focus, the Windows Phone OS realizes that there is a good chance that the user will want to come back to or reactivate your application shortly, and he or she will expect to find it in its previous state. Therefore, instead of simply terminating your application as soon as it loses focus, the Windows Phone OS remembers its state and provides developers with a means to save session-related information to a custom State dictionary object. However, with tombstoning, there is always a chance that your application may never be reactivated. So, if there is data that needs to be permanently preserved within your application, you should save it to the isolated storage instead of the transient State object.

You will get to observe tombstoning at work shortly, but before that, you need to examine a typical life cycle of a Windows Phone 7 application. Table 10–3 summarizes the application events that can occur during the execution of a typical Windows Phone 7 application. The table also describes the actions you as a developer should take when each of those events occurs.

Table 10–3. Applications Events, Triggers, and Actions

Application Event	Occurs When	Your Actions
Application_Launching	The user taps the entry for an application on the installed applications screen, and a new instance of an application is created.	Do not read application settings from the isolated storage as this will slow down the loading process; do not attempt to restore transient state. When an application launches, it should always appear as a new instance.
Application_Activated	For this event to occur, two conditions must be met: (1) the user navigates away from your application, either by using a launcher or a chooser, or by starting another application and (2) the user then comes back to your application by either completing the launcher or chooser or using the hardware Back button. This event is *not* raised when an application is first launched.	The application should allow the user to continue interaction as if she had never left the application; transient state information should be restored, but the application should not attempt to read the contents of the isolated storage to avoid potential slowdown.
Application_Deactivated	The user navigates away from your application either by invoking a launcher or a chooser, or by launching another application. This event is not raised when your application is closing.	You should save all transient (i.e., related to the current application session) state into the State dictionary. You should save persistent state to an isolated storage. Applications are given ten seconds to complete this event; after ten seconds, if this event is still not completed, an application will be terminated and not tombstoned.
Application_Closing	The user uses the Back key to navigate past the first page of your application.	Save all of the persistent state into the isolated storage.

In the next section, you will code and observe the conditions under which each of the events in the application life cycle is triggered.

Observing Application Life Cycle Events

To help you better understand the conditions under which tombstoning occurs and the events that are fired, let's enhance the application built previously in this chapter to trace the events raised within the application.

Enhancing the User Interface

You will enhance the application user interface by adding a text box and a button control to the design surface of `MainPage.xaml` to make it look similar to Figure 10–2.

1. Launch Visual Studio 2010 Express, and open the previously created Tasks project.

2. Double-click MainPage.xaml in Solution Explorer, and add a text box and a button to the design surface, as shown in Figure 10–2. Clear the Text property of the text box, and set the button's caption to "Launch Browser."

Adding Application Logic to Invoke WebBrowserTask Launcher and Log Events

Now, you will add logic to invoke a WebBrowserTask launcher and navigate to `www.windowsphone.com`, as well as add messages to print in the Debug window when various application life cycle events occur.

3. Add the following using directive to the top of `MainPage.xaml`:

```
using System.Diagnostics;
```

4. You will launch the web browser when the user clicks the Launch Browser button. Double-click the Launch Browser button on `MainPage.xaml`, and make that button's Click event handler look like the following:

```
private void button2_Click(object sender, RoutedEventArgs e)
{
    WebBrowserTask webTask = new WebBrowserTask();
    webTask.Show();
    webTask.URL = "http://www.windowsphone.com";
}
```

5. The application life cycle events discussed in the previous section are all automatically stubbed out (in other words, they contain basic method signatures without any implementation logic) in the `App.xaml.cs` file. Open that file (one way to do it is to right-click `App.xaml` and select View Code) so that you can modify those events by adding tracing logic to them.

6. Within the Application_Launching event, add the following line of code:

```
Debug.WriteLine("Application Launching");
```

7. Within the Application_Activated event, add the following line of code:

```
Debug.WriteLine("Application Activated");
```

8. Within the Application_Deactivated event, add the following line of code:

```
Debug.WriteLine("Application Deactivated");
```

9. Within the Application_Closing event, add the following line of code:

```
Debug.WriteLine("Application Closing");
```

Figure 10–2. User interface for application lifecycle test application

Running the Application

Before running the application, make sure to bring the Visual Studio Output window to the forefront—in Visual Studio, select Debug ➤ Windows ➤ Output on the menu bar. Press F5 to run the application that you have built in the previous steps and observe the messages displayed in the Output window.

1.   When the application first comes up, observe how an Application Launching message is printed in the Output window, indicating that the Application_Launching event has fired, but the Application_Activated event has not fired upon the initial launch of an application.

2.   Click the Launch Browser button to bring up Internet Explorer with the Windows Phone web site open. In the Visual Studio Output window, notice how the Application_Deactivated event fired as soon as the web browser was launched (see Figure 10–3), indicating possible tombstoning of your application.

3.   Click the Back button on the emulator screen. Notice how the Application_Activated event fires and prints a message in the Output window.

221

4. Click the Start button, and observe how Application_Deactivated is fired again. If you click the Back button now, the Application_Activated event is triggered.

5. Finally, click the Back button again. Since you have navigated past the first page of the application, the application is terminated, triggering the Application_Closing event and printing the corresponding message in the Output window.

To summarize the previous experiments, any time your application lost focus, an Application_Deactivated event was triggered. Any time an application gained focus (except for the initial launch), an Application_Activated event was triggered. These concepts are important to keep in mind as we discuss saving and retrieving state information in Windows Phone 7 applications in the next section.

Figure 10–3. Application life cycle illustrated by switching between applications on the phone.

Table 10–4 summarizes the actions you took and the corresponding events raised within your application. You can cross-reference Tables 10-4 and 10–3 for actions to take in order to persist state when a given event is raised within your application.

Table 10–4. Summary of Your Actions and Resulting Application Events

Your Action	Application Event
Pressed F5 to start the application	`Application_Launching`
Pressed Launch Browser button to launch IE on the phone	`Application_Deactivated`
Clicked the Back button to go back to your application	`Application_Activated`
Clicked the Start button	`Application_Deactivated`
Clicked the Back button to return to your application	`Application_Activated`
Clicked the Back button to go past the first page of your application	`Application_Closing`

Managing Application State

Try the following experiment: open the Tasks project if it's not already open within Visual Studio 2010 Express for Windows Phone, and press F5 to run it. In the text box field that comes up, type "Hello, world" (you can press the Page Up key to allow you to type from the keyboard in the emulator). Next, click the Launch Browser button, and then press the Back button to return to your application.

Notice how the text box is blank (the "Hello, world" text is gone) once you come back to the main application screen. Now imagine if your application were a real-world application capturing many different pieces of data and it provided a WebBrowserTask to allow quick lookup of data on the Internet. It would certainly not be acceptable to the end user to have to retype all the information once the WebBrowserTask completes. Hence, you must devise a mechanism to preserve such data when the application is being tombstoned. Enter state management.

If you have done any sort of web development, the concept of state management will already be very familiar to you. And if you haven't been exposed to state management before, it's a fairly easy concept to grasp. Per Microsoft's documentation, when an application like the Tasks application of the previous example is tombstoned, it should save state information in case it is reactivated. The sections that follow will show you how to save and retrieve state information within your application.

Managing State at the PhoneApplicationPage Level

The concept of state management at the page level applies not only to those times when an application is about to be tombstoned and the page needs to persist its state for possible future retrieval. Many times, individual pages within a Windows Phone 7 application must save their session data to allow navigation to other pages within that same application; if the user comes back to the original page, the application should be smart enough to retrieve data previously entered by the user.

To accomplish session persistence for both tombstoning and page navigation scenarios, each page relies on the following three methods within the `PhoneApplicationPage` class:

- `OnNavigatedFrom()`, which is called when the page is no longer an active page in a frame.

- `OnNavigatedTo()`, which is called when the page becomes the active page in a frame.

- OnBackKeyPress(), which is called when the hardware Back key is pressed.

In the following code demo, you will use each one of these methods, as well as the State dictionary object, to persist data from the text box in the Tasks application that you have built in this chapter. Follow these steps to accomplish this task.

You will not be making any changes to the user interface of the Tasks application—it will stay very basic, just as it is shown in Figure 10–2. You will, however, add code to the Tasks application to persist the information that has been entered inside the single text box in that application.

6. Launch Visual Studio 2010 Express, and open the previously created Tasks project, if it's not already open.

7. Open MainPage.xaml.cs (one way is to right-click MainPage.xaml and select View Code). You will add code to save text entered in the text box on MainPage.xaml into the session objects if the page becomes no longer active in a frame—i.e., in that page's OnNavigatedFrom method. Add the following code to the MainPage.xaml.cs file:

```
protected override void
OnNavigatedFrom(System.Windows.Navigation.NavigationEventArgs e)
{
        Debug.WriteLine("Navigated From MainPage");

        if (State.ContainsKey("TextboxText"))
        {
                State.Remove("TextboxText");
        }

        State.Add("TextboxText", textBox1.Text);
        base.OnNavigatedFrom(e);
}
```

Notice the use of the State dictionary object—it is indeed very similar to the Session variable of ASP.NET web-based applications, and in the previous method you add the value from the text box into the State dictionary object.

8. Next, you will add code to retrieve values from the State dictionary object when the user navigates to the current page; you will do that inside the OnNavigatedTo method:

```
protected override void OnNavigatedTo(System.Windows.Navigation.NavigationEventArgs e)
{
        Debug.WriteLine("Navigated To MainPage");

        if (State.ContainsKey("TextboxText"))
        {
                string strTextboxText = State["TextboxText"] as string;

                if (null != strTextboxText)
                        textBox1.Text = strTextboxText;
        }

        base.OnNavigatedTo(e);
}
```

The code you have written thus far is sufficient to save the text from the text box for the duration of the application session; even if an application is tombstoned, and the user later returns to the current page, the text will be properly preserved. Let's test this out really quickly: press F5 to run this application, enter "Hello, world" in the text box, and press the Launch Browser button. Once the browser comes up, press the Back button—you should see "Hello, world" still displayed in the text box, unlike the behavior you saw previously in this chapter, where you did not handle any state information at all.

While saving information for the duration of the session is extremely important, there are many occasions when you would like to save information permanently, so that even if you turn your phone off (or the battery dies), you will still have access to that information. Let's expand the demo to accommodate saving text into the isolated storage on the Windows Phone 7, so that text is available for use as long as the application's isolated storage is intact (and as long as you don't remove this information from the isolated storage, of course). Follow these steps to accomplish this task.

9. Add the following two using directives to the top of the `MainPage.xaml.cs` file:

```
using System.IO.IsolatedStorage;
using System.IO;
```

10. You will add code to save text into the isolated storage area of your application if the user presses the Back button past your application's first page (for example, the user presses the Back button as soon as the application launches). If you would like to get more familiar with isolated storage, see Chapter 13. Add the following method to the `MainPage.xaml.cs` file:

```
protected override void OnBackKeyPress(System.ComponentModel.CancelEventArgs e)
{
        base.OnBackKeyPress(e);
        MessageBoxResult res = MessageBox.Show("Do you want to save your work before
        leaving?", "You are exiting the application",
MessageBoxButton.OKCancel);

        if (res == MessageBoxResult.OK)
        {
                Debug.WriteLine("Ok");
                SaveString(textBox1.Text, "TextboxText.dat");
        }
        else
        {
                Debug.WriteLine("Cancel");
        }
}
```

Notice how the message box is used to ask the user whether to save information to the file inside isolated storage; if the user chooses Yes, the `SaveString` method is called, passing the value to save and the file to save it to.

11. Finally, you need to code the SaveString method that performs all the heavy lifting saving data to the isolated storage. This method accepts the name of the file as one of the parameters, and then it creates a file with that name within the isolated storage. After the file is created, the method saves the data string passed to it inside that file. While persisting string values inside the file is perfectly acceptable for the small application that you are building in this demo, you might consider a different data structure for bigger production applications with lots of data to persist. Serializing data to XML would be a better alternative for such applications, as would be saving data inside a dictionary or key-value collection objects. Here is the full listing of the method to persist data to an isolated storage; make sure it is also present in your code.

```
private void SaveString(string strTextToSave, string fileName)
{
    using (IsolatedStorageFile isf =
IsolatedStorageFile.GetUserStoreForApplication())
    {
        //If user choose to save, create a new file
        using (IsolatedStorageFileStream fs =
isf.CreateFile(fileName))
        {
            using (StreamWriter write = new StreamWriter(fs))
            {
                write.WriteLine(strTextToSave);
            }
        }
    }
}
```

You are now ready to run your application. Press F5 to launch it, type "Hello, world" in the text box shown, and press the Back button. Remember, pressing the Back button past the first page of an application results in termination of that application. Click Yes on the message box prompting you to save your work before leaving. Next, re-launch your application. You should see "Hello, world" displayed in the text box—but you don't. What happened? If you guessed that you still have to retrieve the values previously stored inside the isolated storage, you are correct. You will retrieve those values in the next section, together with looking at the best practices for retrieving this information.

Retrieving Application Initial State

Microsoft guidelines state that within the Application_Launching event there should not be any isolated storage access or web service calls, so that the application comes up and is available for use as quickly as possible. Instead, Microsoft recommends *asynchronously* loading values from the isolated storage of an application once the application is fully loaded. This set of restrictions forces us as developers to code the initialization routines using the following two guidelines:

1. Invoke data initialization and retrieval on a separate thread so as to maximize the responsiveness of an application.

2. Perform application initialization inside the OnNavigatedTo method of the PhoneApplicationPage class.

In this demo, you will add the necessary methods to properly load application data from the isolated storage.

3. You will continue modifying the Tasks project that you have worked with throughout this chapter. At the top of `MainPage.xaml.cs`, add the following using directive:

```
using System.Threading;
```

4. Open `MainPage.xaml.cs` and go to the `OnNavigatedTo` method within that code. You will make adjustments to that method to load data asynchronously (on a separate thread) from the isolated storage, if there is no data in the `State` dictionary. If you recall, the `State` dictionary object is used to hold transient application data, or data that is being saved and retrieved as the user navigates between pages in the application. Therefore, you check the `State` object to determine whether transient or permanently persisted data should be retrieved. Make the `OnNavigatedTo` method look like the following:

```
protected override void
OnNavigatedTo(System.Windows.Navigation.NavigationEventArgs e)
    {
        Debug.WriteLine("Navigated To MainPage");

        if (State.ContainsKey("TextboxText"))
        {
            string strTextboxText = State["TextboxText"] as string;

            if (null != strTextboxText)
            textBox1.Text = strTextboxText;
        }
        else
        {
            LoadAppStateDataAsync();
        }

        base.OnNavigatedTo(e);
    }
```

5. The `LoadAppStateDataAsync` method is responsible for invoking a method that accesses isolated storage data on a separate thread. The full method is shown here:

```
public void LoadAppStateDataAsync
{
    Thread t = new Thread(new ThreadStart(LoadAppStateData));
    t.Start();
}
```

6. Finally, the `LoadAppStateData` method accesses isolated storage data looking for a particular file (hardcoded to be `TextboxText.dat` at the moment) and the settings within that file.

```
public void LoadAppStateData()
{
```

```
                      string strData = String.Empty;

                         //Try to load previously saved data from IsolatedStorage
                         using (IsolatedStorageFile isf =
IsolatedStorageFile.GetUserStoreForApplication())
                             {
                                 //Check if file exits
                                 if (isf.FileExists("TextboxText.dat"))
                                 {
                                         using (IsolatedStorageFileStream fs =
isf.OpenFile("TextboxText.dat",
                                         System.IO.FileMode.Open))
                                         {
                                                 using (StreamReader reader = new
StreamReader(fs))
                                                 {
                                                         strData = reader.ReadToEnd();
                                                 }
                                         }
                                 }
                             }
                         Dispatcher.BeginInvoke(() => { textBox1.Text = strData; });
                 }
```

7. Your application is now complete, and it should handle both transient and persistent states. To test it, press F5 and enter "Hello, world" in the text box presented. Next, press the Back button and answer Yes to save work before leaving. The application is now terminated; if you press F5 again to re-launch the application, the screen should come with "Hello, world" already populated within it.

Best Practices for Managing the Application Life Cycle on the Windows Phone 7 OS

Microsoft provides an important set of application behavior guidelines to follow to ensure a consistent and positive user experience on a Windows Phone 7 platform. Some of the highlights of those best practices are as follows:

1. Ensuring that when the user launches a new instance of an application, it is clear that it's a new instance (in other words, the last example of automatically retrieving settings from the isolated storage upon application launch may not be ideal). At the same time, if an application is being reactivated, the user should feel that the reactivated application has returned in its previous state.

2. Since the user may never return to the application once it becomes tombstoned, any data that needs to be saved to a persistent data store should be saved when either the Closing or Deactivated event fires.

3. Invoking a launcher or a chooser will always deactivate an application and *may* cause it to become tombstoned. An application may not be tombstoned if it launches an experience that feels like it's a part of the original application. Microsoft currently lists the following launchers and choosers as not automatically tombstoning the calling application (it clarifies, however, that an OS *may* still choose to tombstone the calling application if the resources are needed elsewhere):

- PhotoChooserTask

- CameraCaptureTask

- MediaPlayerLauncher

- EmailAddressChooserTask

- PhoneNumberChooserTask

- MultiplayerGameInvite [games]

- GamerYouCard [games]

You can take a look at the full list of best practices for managing the application life cycle (most of which have already been covered in this chapter) at http://msdn.microsoft.com/en-us/library/ff817009(v=VS.92).aspx.

Integrating with Facebook

Applications running on mobile devices, including Windows Phone 7 devices, are ideally suited to take advantage of social networks—these devices are always on and are always with their respective owners, allowing for constant interaction with peers and colleagues. Today, integration of mobile devices into social networks is virtually assumed, so it makes a lot of sense for your application to take advantage of as many social networking features as are applicable. In the next section, you will walk through integrating with (currently) the biggest social network of them all—Facebook. These integration efforts will allow you to practice what you have learned about tombstoning and managing application state so far in this chapter, as well as explore new concepts of tapping vast marketing potential for your application through Facebook. More good news for application developers is that similar integration principles apply to other social networks as well—for example, LinkedIn uses the same protocol (OAuth, which you will learn about shortly) for authorizing applications on behalf of the users to retrieve and manipulate data.

A Few Words about OAuth

Facebook uses OAuth protocol for third-party application authentication and authorization. OAuth is the authorization protocol characterized by separating resource ownership and access to the resource by third parties (referred to as *clients* in the OAuth documentation). In the context of Windows Phone 7 development, the applications that you build that need to post to users' Facebook walls or retrieve resources from the users' social graphs are clients, and Facebook users (they are also users of your application) are the resource owners. Instead of blindly giving away their user name and password to your app, Facebook users will instead grant your application limited time and scope to perform authorized operations on their behalf. These operations may include posting on users' walls or querying users' information. The authorization to perform these operations will come in the form of an OAuth token obtained from Facebook.

Facebook provides an excellent set of step-by-step guidelines for integrating your applications into their vast ecosystem (you can access those at `http://developers.facebook.com/docs/authentication/`). These guidelines state that there are essentially three steps to proper Facebook authorization via OAuth: (1) user authentication, (2) application authorization and (3) application authentication. Let's take a look at how these three steps would happen on a Windows Phone 7 device.

In the next demo, you will enhance the Tasks application that you built so far with the ability to post simple messages to your application users' Facebook wall. In the first step (user authentication), you will need to launch a Web browser on the Windows Phone 7 device and direct it to `www.facebook.com` asking the user to authenticate (note that you cannot simply "post" user name and password to Facebook web page from within a XAML page in your application—that would break the trust chain that OAuth was designed to protect, since your application can easily capture the user name and password values). Once the user is successfully authenticated, she will be presented with a dialog listing all of the action your application intends to take on her behalf—that's the second step in the OAuth implementation. This second step is necessary for the user to make an informed decision about whether to grant your application the necessary rights. Finally, in the third step (application authentication), your application will supply a special unique secret key that identifies your app on Facebook to ensure that the user is giving her information to your app and not someone else's. Let's go ahead and code these three steps.

■ **Note** Before your application is able to interact with Facebook, you must register it on Facebook and obtain the Application ID and a Secret Key. These values are unique to your application; do not share those values with anyone! To register your application, go to `http://developers.facebook.com/setup` and follow the step-by-step guidelines to get the necessary information pieces for your app.

Enhancing the User Interface for Facebook Integration

You will continue working with the Tasks application and add an additional option to post a message to Facebook on the main page of your application plus a separate page containing web browser control for navigating to facebook.com—you'll see why a separate page is needed shortly.

1. Launch Visual Studio 2010 Express, and open the previously created Tasks project.

2. Double-click `MainPage.xaml` in Solution Explorer, and add a button to the design surface, somewhere underneath the other two buttons. Set the name of the button to be btnFacebook and set the button's caption to "Post to Facebook."

3. Right-click on the project name (Tasks) in the Solution Explorer and choose Add ➤ New Item, then choose Windows Phone Portrait Page. Name the page `FBLogin.xaml`.

4.   Double-click the newly added FBLogin.xaml page in Solution Explorer and add
      a web browser control to that page. Make the web browser control occupy the
      whole width and height of the page, since the user will be utilizing this control
      to log in to Facebook.

Adding Application Logic to Post to Facebook

Now, you will add logic to post to Facebook from your application. Remember the brief discussion about
OAuth—posting to Facebook is a multi-step procedure, which includes (1) user authentication, (2) app
authorization and (3) app authentication. Follow the steps below to successfully implement each of
these steps.

1.   First things first—you need to add a couple of references to the project to make
      the code below work. Right-click on the project name in Solution Explorer and
      select Add Reference. Add a reference to Microsoft.Phone.Reactive and
      System.Observable assemblies.

2.   Add the following using directives to the top of the page:

```
using Microsoft.Phone.Reactive;
using System.IO;
using System.Diagnostics;
using System.Text;
```

3.   User authentication will happen inside the newly added FBLogin.xaml page—
      therefore your button click event handler should redirect the user to that page.
      Add the following code to the btnFacebook button click event (notice how you
      pass the MessageToPost parameter to the page):

```
private void btnFacebook_Click(object sender, RoutedEventArgs e)
        {
         NavigationService.Navigate(new
         Uri(String.Format("/FBLogin.xaml?MessageToPost={0}", textBox1.Text),
         UriKind.Relative));
        }
```

4.   In the next step, you will define certain constants, such as permission types
      that an application needs, as well as a standard URL that Facebook gives to
      desktop and mobile developers to use upon successful authentication of an
      application (STR_FB_SuccessUrl constant below). Facebook developer
      documentation gives an in-depth overview of permission types available to
      your application; your sample application simply needs a permission to post
      to users' Facebook wall. Open FBLogin.xaml.cs page (right-click on
      FBLogin.xaml and select View Code) and add the following constant
      declarations to the top of the page (note that you **must** supply your application
      ID and your application secret key for the STR_FB_AppID and FB_AppSecret
      parameters correspondingly):

```
const string STR_FB_Permissions = "publish_stream";
```

```
        const string STR_FB_SuccessUrl =
"http://www.facebook.com/connect/login_success.html";
        const string STR_FB_Login =
        "https://graph.facebook.com/oauth/authorize?display=wap&client_id={0}&redirect
        _uri={1}&scope={2}";
        const string FB_GetAccessToken =
        "https://graph.facebook.com/oauth/access_token?client_id={0}&redirect_uri={1}&
        client_secret={2}&code={3}";

        const string STR_Post = "POST";
        const string STR_Access_token = "access_token";
        const string STR_FB_AppId = "Your App ID";
        const string FB_AppSecret = "Your App Secret";
        const string STR_FormEncoded = "application/x-www-form-urlencoded";
```

5. In this step, you will use Reactive Extensions for .NET (Rx.NET) to subscribe to Webbrowser's control Navigated event. Rx.NET is ideally suited for working with events, such as navigation to and from facebook.com and the like. There is a whole chapter (Chapter 18) in this book devoted to learning and using Rx.NET. For right now, however, a simple understanding that you are reacting to the web browser's Navigated event and then creating a web request to Facebook in the code below is sufficient. Upon receiving the Navigated event, the code below parses out a session ID obtained from Facebook, then uses that session ID to compose a custom message to Facebook requesting an authentication token for the application. The actual posting of the message to the Facebook wall happens in the next step (Step 6). Make the FBLogin() constructor look like the following code:

```
public FBLogin()
{
    InitializeComponent();

    this.Loaded += (sender, args) =>
    {
        var url = string.Format(STR_FB_Login, STR_FB_AppId,
        HttpUtility.UrlEncode(STR_FB_SuccessUrl), STR_FB_Permissions);
        IObservable<IEvent<NavigationEventArgs>> FBResponse;

        //register a subscription to FaceBook navigated event
        FBResponse = Observable.FromEvent<NavigationEventArgs>(webBrowser1,
        "Navigated");
        FBResponse.ObserveOn(Deployment.Current.Dispatcher)
            .Subscribe(evt =>
            {
                //on successful user authentication event only
                if
(evt.EventArgs.Uri.ToString().StartsWith(STR_FB_SuccessUrl))
                {
                    //1. get a session ID from the query string
                    var sessionId =
```

```
                evt.EventArgs.Uri.Query.Substring("?code=".Length);

                                    //get the user and compose an authentication token request
                                    string strTokenId = GetGraphToken(sessionId);
                                    string strMessage = String.Empty;
                                    NavigationContext.QueryString.TryGetValue("MessageToPost",
out
                                strMessage);

                                    //2. get OAuth authentication token and use it to update
user's Facebook wall
                                    UpdateWall("POST", strTokenId, strMessage);
                                    NavigationService.GoBack();
                            }
                        },
                        ex =>
                        {
                            //log/process exceptions here

                        }
                    );

                    //invoke the navigation process
                    webBrowser1.Navigate(new Uri(url, UriKind.Absolute));
                };
            }
```

6. Finally, you will code a couple of helper methods that will create a message to
    Facebook in the format that Facebook can understand, properly parse
    Facebook responses, and redirect. The first one of those methods is the
    GetGraphToken method shown here:

```
        public static string GetGraphToken(string sessionId)
        {
            string strAccessTokenUrl = String.Empty;
            try
            {
                strAccessTokenUrl = string.Format(FB_GetAccessToken, STR_FB_AppId,
                STR_FB_SuccessUrl, FB_AppSecret, sessionId);
            }
            catch (Exception exc)
            {
                System.Diagnostics.Debug.WriteLine("ERROR: " + exc.Message);
                System.Diagnostics.Debug.WriteLine(exc.StackTrace);
            }

            return strAccessTokenUrl;
        }
```

7. The final helper method performs the heavy lifting of posting to Facebook. The gist of it is to use Rx.NET to asynchronously create a POST request to Facebook website, asking for a special OAuth authentication token and, upon successfully getting it, update user's Facebook wall. Don't feel overwhelmed by the length of the method below—you have learned the basic flow of OAuth authorization already, and this method simply implements the details of that flow inside a single function that you could reuse inside the applications that you build. Also, don't forget that you can always download all the code for this book instead of manually typing it in.

```
public static void UpdateWall(string method, string url, string postData)
{
    var webRequest = WebRequest.Create(url) as HttpWebRequest;
    webRequest.Method = method;

    if (method == STR_Post)
    {
        webRequest.ContentType = STR_FormEncoded;
        // request an authentication token
        Observable.FromAsyncPattern<WebResponse>(
                webRequest.BeginGetResponse,
                webRequest.EndGetResponse)()
                .Subscribe(
                wr =>
                {
                    try
                    {
                        // upon completion of request for authentication
token, parse out access
                        // token
                        using (var responseReader = new
                            StreamReader(wr.GetResponseStream()))
                        {
                            string strOutput = responseReader.ReadToEnd();

                            // use access token to compose the request to
post to user's Wall
                            var payload =
                            string.Format("{0}&message={1}&caption={2}&link={3}&name={4}",
                            strOutput, "My WP7 App: \n\n" + postData, "WP7 App",
                            "http://www.windowsphone.com", "WP7 Facebook Integration");

                            var uri = new
                            Uri(string.Format("https://graph.facebook.com/me/feed?{0}",
                            payload));

                            var wc = new WebClient { Encoding =
Encoding.UTF8 };

Observable.FromEvent<UploadStringCompletedEventArgs>(wc,
                            "UploadStringCompleted")
                                                .Subscribe(evt =>
```

```
                                                    {
                                                       try
                                                       {
                                                           if (evt.EventArgs.Result != null)
                                                           {
                                                               //successfully updated wall,
            print SUCCESS message into
                                    // Debug window
                                                               Debug.WriteLine("SUCCESS!");
                                                           }
                                                       }
                                                       catch (WebException ex)
                                                       {
                                                           StreamReader readStream = new
                                    StreamReader(ex.Response.GetResponseStream());

            Debug.WriteLine(readStream.ReadToEnd());
                                                       }
                                                    },
                                                    ex =>
                                                    {

                                                    }
                                               );

                                                       wc.UploadStringAsync(uri, null, payload);
                                                   }

                                           }
                                           catch (WebException ex)
                                           {
                                               StreamReader readStream = new
                                   StreamReader(ex.Response.GetResponseStream());
                                               //Get the error message from Facebook
                                               Debug.WriteLine(readStream.ReadToEnd());
                                           }
                                       });
                        }
                }
```

You are now ready to run the application. Press F5, type "Hello from WP7 and Rx.NET" in the text box that comes up, then press "Post to Facebook" button. You should be prompted to login to Facebook (it's probably a good idea to create a test account on Facebook for testing your application), and, upon successful authentication, your message should appear on your Facebook wall.

This section provided you with the basics of integrating your applications with social networks using OAuth. You should be able to relatively easily modify your applications to talk to LinkedIn and other providers implementing OAuth using the sample code above. The beauty of this implementation is the fact that the whole OAuth flow is embedded inside a single page (FBLogin.xaml), providing for modularized application development.

A final word of caution, however, and it's a very important one: even though in the sample above you have embedded your Facebook application ID and Secret Application Key inside the code, you should never do this in applications that you will distribute to the end users. As you will see in Chapter 19 of this book, it is extremely easy to gain access to application's source code, and you don't want to be sharing your application's secrets with anybody. In the real-world solution, your Windows Phone 7 application will request Facebook ID and a Secret Key from a secure web service that you provide (upon initialization, or right before the user makes a request to post to Facebook wall, for example). We have avoided showing you an implementation of this service here to avoid complicating the example; however, there are good demos on building web services throughout this book, including the one in Chapter 17 where you build a simple WCF service.

░ **Note** Remember to never embed your Facebook Application ID or your Secret Key inside your production code!

Integrating into Windows Phone 7 Hubs

Among the many strengths of the Windows Phone 7 platform is the extent of its integration into the rest of the .NET ecosystem developed by Microsoft over the years, which remains one of its biggest advantages over competing phone platforms. The integrated experience comes in the form of hubs on the phone Start screen, which are essentially menu areas that collect data based on functions. The following hubs are available and are tightly integrated into the Windows Phone 7 OS:

- The **People Hub** integrates feeds from Windows Live and Facebook, and you can also connect other services to Windows Live like LinkedIn, YouTube, Flickr, WordPress, and over 70 more.

- The **Pictures Hub** makes it easy to share pictures and video with your friends via social networks.

- The **Games Hub** with its first and only Xbox Live app, which allows for game, avatar, achievements, and profile integration.

- The **Music and Video Hub** makes the full collection of music and videos available to Zune devices also integrated with Windows Phone 7. In fact, the Zune pass that allows unlimited leasing of music may be one of the best kept secrets of Windows Phone 7 platform!

- The **Marketplace Hub** allows users to find and install certified applications and games on the phone.

- The **Office Hub** with its support of Exchange and Exchange ActiveSync, Outlook (with e-mail, calendar, and contacts all available), PowerPoint, SharePoint, Word, and Excel. You can edit Office documents on your mobile device and have your changes available in real time (i.e., as you change them) to others.

The marketing campaign for Windows Phone 7 is about allowing users to "glance and go," or to get the information or the functionality they need from the phone very quickly (quicker than competing platforms, that is). Hubs play a critical role in providing this "glance and go" experience, and your application can raise that role even further by integrating with hubs directly. When you integrate with one of the hubs, your application becomes visible and available through that hub, and not just through the standard list of applications installed on the device. Of course, the functionality provided by your application must fit with the functionality a user might expect from the hub; for example, a music discovery service that allows you to search and find new music based on what you currently like and own should certainly fit within the Music and Video Hub.

Detailed instructions for integrating with the Pictures Hub are provided in Chapter 16 by using the Extras feature of that hub. The next section of this chapter will briefly cover the Music and Video Hub, giving you a general idea of what it would take for your application to appear there and providing users more of the "glance and go" experience. In addition, we will touch on integration features of Windows Phone 7 platform available to users of SharePoint, a major enterprise collaboration platform from Microsoft.

Integrating your Application with Music and Video Hub

Integrating with Music and Video Hub is simple: once you ensure that your application makes use of the `MediaHistory` and `MediaHistoryItem` classes and provide images to display in the Music and Video Hub tile, the Windows Phone application certification process (discussed in detail in Chapter 5) will take care of the rest. Once the certification process detects that your application uses the `MediaHistory` and `MediaHistoryItem` classes, your application's hub will be set to Music and Video, and your application will show up on the panorama panel titled "Marquee" within that hub. The quickest way to get to Marquee tab is to swipe the panorama from left to right once you are in the Music and Video hub.

Once your application is inside the Music and Video Hub, it can manipulate the tile for that hub, and it can also update the history list of media items played or the list of newly available media items. To update the history and new media items lists, your application will instantiate a new `MediaHistoryItem` object, set its properties, and call WriteRecentPlay and WriteAcquiredItem, correspondingly. To update the Now Playing tile on the phone, you would once again create a new `MediaHistoryItem` object, set its properties, and then assign it to the MediaHistory.Instance.NowPlaying property.

It is certainly inconvenient enough that the emulator does not provide any of the hubs to test integration against, so you have to deploy your application to a real device to test that integration. What could be even more frustrating is the fact that you may need to wait for your application to be certified before it is available for testing as part of the Music and Video Hub. To help prevent potentially lengthy application development procedures for hub integration, Microsoft has come up with a workaround for testing Music and Video Hub integration. Inside the `WMAppManifest.xml` file, located within the Properties folder in your Solution Explorer, make sure to set the HubType value to 1, as illustrated here:

```
<App xmlns="" ProductID="{c98b0a70-e0c1-462f-a756-5d0aff98e066}" Title="Tasks"
RuntimeType="Silverlight" Version="1.0.0.0" Genre="apps.normal" Author="Tasks author"
Description="Sample description" Publisher="Tasks" HubType="1">
```

Microsoft provides a set of guidelines for images that you must submit during the certification step, should you choose to integrate with the Music and Video Hub and decide to update the tile of that hub. These guidelines are summarized in the list below:

1.   Your tile images must be of type JPEG.

2.   You must include your application title or logo on each tile image.

3.   The Now Playing tile must be 358 pixels x 358 pixels in size.

4.   Other tiles must be 173 pixels x 173 pixels in size.

Integration with SharePoint

While Microsoft has been very explicit in their marketing materials that the first release of Windows Phone 7 OS is targeted at everyday consumer and not at enterprise customers, the company has already started creating several critical hooks necessary for enterprises to take notice of the platform. One of such hooks is the fact that you can work within the enterprise SharePoint environment on your Windows Phone 7 device. The SharePoint Workspace Mobile application comes pre-installed on every single Windows Phone 7 device (and is located in the same exact spot on every device—inside the Office hub). Once you log in into SharePoint site, you can browse all Office documents and they will appear in the same exact format as on any other computer capable of connecting to SharePoint. You can modify documents, and your changes, as well as potential conflicts when others modify the same document, will be detected and resolved via the SharePoint integration. Another exciting feature is Offline Documents, which allows you to download and edit documents even if connection to SharePoint site is not available. You can synchronize the documents later, and you will also be guided through resolving potential conflicts within the document due to multiple people working on it.

SharePoint integration is just one example of the powerful platform integration that you have on Windows Phone 7. As the platform continues to evolve, we will see even broader and better integration options available into the vast Microsoft ecosystem out there.

Summary

In this chapter, you learned how applications integrate with the Windows Phone OS. You learned how to use launchers and choosers to accomplish common tasks on the platform. You learned what effects launchers and choosers have on the state of the application that uses them, and you reviewed the application life cycle and managing state within this life cycle. Finally, you got a brief overview of all the major applications already tightly integrated within Windows Phone 7 and grouped in hubs. In the next chapter, you will learn about Trial API and build sample trial applications for submission to the Marketplace.

CHAPTER 11

Creating Trial Applications

Today, many mobile software vendors maintain two versions of their application code, one for the trial version and another for purchase. The code base for the trial version typically includes some—but not all—of the functionality of the full version, as well as code that urges users to upgrade to the full version of the product. The Windows Phone 7 platform, however, eliminates the need for this practice thanks to the handy IsTrial method. The IsTrial method of the Microsoft.Phone.Marketplace.LicenseInformation class provides the functionality you need to create a trial version. Microsoft.Phone.Marketplace.LicenseInformation is a sealed class that contains the methods you'll use to test your applications. You have already learned how to deploy applications to the Windows Phone Marketplace in Chapter 5; in this chapter, you will learn how to add a trial option to applications you deploy so that your potential customers have a chance to try your applications before they buy them. The IsTrial method determines whether an application is running under a trial or a full license, allowing you to limit your application based on the result that IsTrial returns.

Understanding Trial and Full Modes

If you wish to let potential buyers try your application first, you must let Microsoft know that that trial functionality is "allowed"—i.e., available—when you submit your application to the Windows Phone Marketplace. If you specify that trials are allowed, then, in the Marketplace, Microsoft will automatically include a Free Trial button, as shown in Figure 11–1. An important consideration for application developers is that, at present, trials do not expire—they can be replaced by full application versions only if customers decide to purchase applications. Note that while you can certainly simulate time-limited trials (we talk about this in the next paragraph, but basically you would have to do all the plumbing yourself), it's not the recommended way to use Trial API. Time-restricted applications are subject to re-installation, resulting in a mere inconvenience to the end user to continue using your application without paying you a dime.

The implementation of trial functionality is entirely up to the application developer; the developer may choose to limit the functionality of the application and prompt the user to purchase the full version of an application to access all application features. Alternately, the developer may choose to prevent the trial application from running after a certain time period. The way to accomplish these time-limited trials would be to either store the date the application was run for the first time in the Isolated Storage and stop after a certain time period, or to store the number of times the application has been run and disallow its execution after a certain number of runs.

Microsoft recommends that application providers prompt users of their trial software during the trial period to purchase a full version. If a user selects the purchase option, control of the application should be programmatically transferred to Windows Phone Marketplace and the application details page should be displayed. Within the Windows.Phone.Tasks namespace, there is a set of methods that make it quick and easy to complete Marketplace tasks, including searching within the application or music categories and showing the application details page. You have already seen some of those methods in Chapter 10 when you read about launchers and choosers. If, after reviewing application details, the user decides to purchase your application, the trial license is replaced with the full license, and the execution of the IsTrial method should indicate that the application is no longer running in the trial mode.

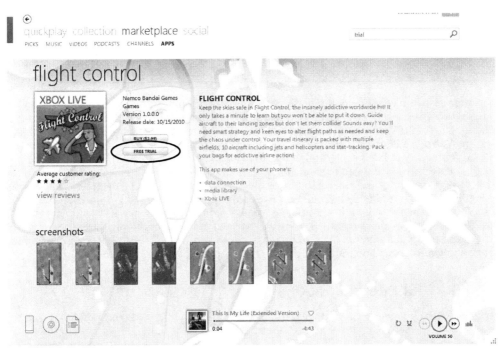

Figure 11–1. A Free Trial button is available in the Marketplace for applications that support Trial mode.

You will now explore in detail both the IsTrial method and the Windows Phone Marketplace API classes that are used to do this work.

Using the IsTrial Method

Using the IsTrial method is straightforward: this method is part of the Microsoft.Phone.Marketplace.LicenseInformation class, and it returns true if an application is being used on a trial basis (i.e., when the user clicks the Free Trial button instead of the Buy button in the Windows Phone Marketplace) and false if an application is running with a full license. Windows Phone Marketplace handles installation of trial and full licenses and determines when each is appropriate. However, when you execute the IsTrial method while you're developing an application or before the application user has acquired a trial or a full application license, its behavior is unpredictable. Microsoft documentation currently says that IsTrial would return true, while our tests show the opposite. Regardless of the outcome during the development stage, you should assume that the IsTrial method will work as designed while an application is in development and make provisions for the application to execute properly when it is running under either a trial license or a full license.

The short example that follows demonstrates the use of the IsTrial method and prints a message onto the screen regardless of whether the current application is running under a trial or a full license.

Creating the User Interface

In this section, you will be creating very simple user interface to test your IsTrial method in Visual Studio 2010 Express.

1. First, launch Visual Studio 2010 Express for Windows Phone and create a new Windows Phone Application project. Name it TrialSample.

2. Now add some user interface elements. From the Toolbox, drag and drop a textblock onto the application design surface. Since you are only getting familiar with the IsTrial method, leave the name of the textblock unchanged (textBlock1) and adjust its width to occupy the entire width of the screen.

Coding Application Logic

Now you will be populating textblock with information about whether or not the current application is in trial mode in the code.

1. Open MainPage.xaml.cs (right-click MainPage.xaml and select View Code), and add the following statement to the top of the page:

```
using Microsoft.Phone.Marketplace;
```

2. In the MainPage() constructor, add the following code right after InitializeComponent():

```
LicenseInformation lic = new LicenseInformation();

if (lic.IsTrial())
{
        textBlock1.Text = "You are running a trial version of our software!";

}
else
{
        textBlock1.Text = "Thank you for using the full version of our
software!";
}
```

3. Press F5 to run the application to see the results of the IsTrial method execution. When the application comes up, you should see a message stating whether you are running a trial version of your application (i.e., the IsTrial method returned true) or the full version.

In the next section, you get to explore options that go beyond simply displaying a text message when the user is executing the trial version of your software. Namely, Windows Phone Marketplace exposes a set of classes to help the user review the details and pay for the full license of your application.

Using the Marketplace APIs

Now that you know how to find out whether an application is running in trial mode, let's add the ability to review an application and buy it. To do that, you'll need two new classes found in the Microsoft.Phone.Tasks namespace: MarketplaceDetailTask and MarketplaceReviewTask. These classes, known as application launchers on the Windows Phone 7 platform and described in Chapter 10, contain all the necessary functionality for your application to switch from trial to full mode.

Both MarketplaceDetailTask and MarketplaceReviewTask classes implement a Show method that launches the Windows Phone Marketplace application and navigates to the specified application page. For the purposes of allowing users to switch from trial license to full license, there is little difference between these two classes. However, for reference purposes, note that MarketplaceDetailTask allows an application developer to specify an ID of the application (in the ContentIdentifier property) to show the Windows Phone Marketplace page for. This application ID is optional—if it's not supplied to the MarketplaceDetailTask class, the details for the current application are shown in the Marketplace. The MarketplaceReviewTask class, on the other hand, does not expose any public properties, and its Show method displays the review page with an option to buy for the current application only.

■ **Note** Navigation to Windows Phone Marketplace must be simulated in your application while you are working on it in the emulator. This is because required licensing and Windows Phone Marketplace ID properties are not created until after your application is complete and submitted (refer to Chapter 5 for submitting your application to the Marketplace). However, Microsoft provides a special "secret" code that signifies that your application can successfully execute the Show method of the MarketplaceDetailTask and MarketplaceReviewTask launchers. Error code 80070057 specifies that the Show call successfully opened the Windows Phone Marketplace application.

Let's enhance the TrialSample application created in the previous walkthrough with an option to review and buy the application from the Windows Phone Marketplace. We will enhance the code so that if an application is executing in the trial mode, it will show two buttons—one with an option to upgrade to the full version and another with an option to cancel and return to the main screen.

Enhancing the User Interface

In this section, you will enhance the user interface to include the option for your application to allow users to upgrade your trial application to full version.

1. Launch Visual Studio 2010 Express for Windows Phone if it is not already open, and open the Windows Phone Application project called TrialSample created during the previous example.

2. From the Toolbox, drag and drop a button onto the design surface directly beneath the textBlock1 control, as shown in Figure 11–2. With that button selected, press F4 to bring up the button properties window, change the button's Content property to Upgrade to Full Version, and set the button's Visibility property to Collapsed. Change the button's name to btnUpgrade.

3. From the Toolbox, drag another button onto the design surface and drop it next to btnUpgrade, as shown in Figure 11–2. With that button selected, press F4 to bring up the button properties window and change the button's Content property to Cancel. Change the button's Visibility property to Collapsed. Change the button's name to btnCancel. You should now end up with a design surface resembling Figure 11–2.

Next, you will add code that responds to the new buttons.

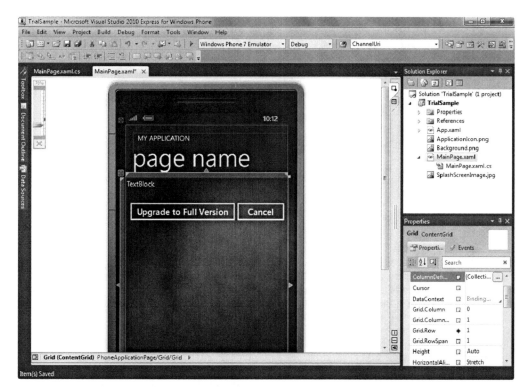

Figure 11–2. TrialSample application layout

Enhancing Application Logic

In this section you will be using MarketplaceReview to give the users option to upgrade to full version in the code.

1. Add the following statement to the top of the page:

    ```
    using Microsoft.Phone.Tasks;
    ```

2. Double-click the Upgrade to Full Version button and change the
    btnUpgrade_Click method to the following:

    ```
    private void btnUpgrade_Click(object sender, RoutedEventArgs e)
    {
        MarketplaceReviewTask marketplaceReviewTask = new
    MarketplaceReviewTask();
        marketplaceReviewTask.Show();
    }
    ```

3. In MainPage.xaml.cs, change the MainPage() constructor to the following:

    ```
    public MainPage()
    {
        InitializeComponent();
        LicenseInformation lic = new LicenseInformation();

        if (lic.IsTrial() == true)
        {
            textBlock1.Text = "You are running a trial version of our
    software!";

            btnUpgrade.Visibility = Visibility.Visible;
            btnCancel.Visibility = Visibility.Visible;
        }
        else
        {
            textBlock1.Text = "Thank you for using the full version of our
    software!";
        }
    }
    ```

When you press F5 to run the application now, two issues will immediately jump out at you. First, the IsTrial method, in its current implementation within Windows Phone 7 Framework, always returns false to the emulator. Because of this, given the logic of the application's current implementation, you will not see the buttons with options to upgrade to the full version of an application. If you try to force those buttons to appear, by incorrectly changing the if (lic.IsTrial() == true) statement to if (lic.IsTrial() == false), for example, then when you click the Upgrade to Full Version button, a second issue surfaces. Since the application has not been approved and is not even registered with Windows Phone Marketplace, you will get an error (as expected) trying to display the application details page (but make sure the error number matches the secret error number mentioned in the Note above!).

For details on the Windows Phone Marketplace registration and application approval process, you should refer to Chapter 5. Here, let's assume that once the proper application registration is in place, Windows Phone Marketplace will properly display the application details page using the MarketplaceReviewTask class and then swap the trial license for the full application license if the user decides to purchase the program. That still leaves you with the need to properly test the application using both trial and full license modes before submitting the application to the Marketplace to ensure that all functionality that belongs to the full mode only is not available to trial users. The process of simulating trial application mode is the subject of the next section.

Simulating Application Trial and Full Modes

While the ability to create both trial and full application versions in the same code base is a boon to the developers who must maintain them, the technique does complicate testing. To properly test the functionality of your application, you must be able to simulate trial and full application modes before you submit it to the Marketplace. There are certainly many ways to do this, from conditional compilation to use of the SimulateTrialMode property within the `Microsoft.Xna.Framework.GamerServices` namespace. Each approach has its merits; however, the best approach is often the one that requires the least amount of changes to your code.

One way to test an application with virtually no changes to its code base is to implement your own mock version of the `LicenseInformation` class. As you have seen, the `LicenseInformation` class can implement the single `IsTrial` method discussed earlier in this chapter. By implementing this class, you can fully control the value returned by the `IsTrial` method and thus the behavior of the application. Then, before going to production, you can swap your implementation of the `LicenseInformation` class for the sealed class provided by Microsoft within the `Microsoft.Phone.Marketplace` namespace.

In this section, you'll create such a class. In the next section, you will build an application that uses this class to test features available to trial and full versions of an application to ensure none of the premium content or features of the applications are leaked to trial users.

To help you create your own implementation of the `LicenseInformation` class, you can (but certainly don't have to) use Reflector.NET, a (formerly free) tool available for download from Red Gate's web site, at `www.red-gate.com/products/reflector/`. Reflector is a great tool and becomes very handy when you would like to peek at the implementation details of common libraries. You can gather a wealth of information not just about the `LicenseInformation` file, but also about the `Microsoft.Phone` assembly in general. Here's how to set up Reflector.NET to help you implement the example that follows:

1. Download and run Reflector.NET, then select File ➤ Open, and navigate to the `Microsoft.Phone.dll` file located by default at `C:\Program Files (x86)\Reference Assemblies\Microsoft\Framework\Silverlight\v4.0\Profile\WindowsPhone`.

2. Drill down into `Microsoft.Phone.dll` ➤ `Microsoft.Phone.Marketplace` ➤ `LicenseInformation`, right-click the `LicenseInformation` class, and click Disassemble. Be sure to also click the Expand Methods link on the right.

You will see a screen similar to the one shown in Figure 11–3, which you will use to speed up your own implementation of the `LicenseInformation` class.

Now follow these steps to implement a version of the `LicenseInformation` class in your code:

1. Launch Visual Studio 2010 Express for Windows Phone if it is not already open, and open the Windows Phone Application project called TrialSample, created during the previous examples.

2. Right-click the project name in Solution Explorer, select Add ➤ New Item, and then select Class from the list of available items. Name the new class `LicenseInformation` and click OK.

3. Now, you can copy the `LicenseInformation` class definition and implementation from Reflector.NET and paste it into your application. Here's a copy of what you'll see:

```
public sealed class LicenseInformation
{
```

```
        // Fields
        private bool m_fIsTrial = true;

        // For testing purpose only!
        public bool IsTrial()
        {
                    return m_fIsTrial;
        }
        // Nested Types
        internal static class NativeMethods
        {
                    // Fields
                    internal const int S_FALSE = 1;
                    internal const int S_OK = 0;

        }
    }
```

Figure 11–3. Using Reflector.NET to peek into the LicenseInformation class

■ **Note** There's no reason not to simplify your own version of the class definition by implementing only the IsTrial method. There is no LicenseClass interface for you to follow. But this exercise gave us a good reason to show the use of a great tool—Reflector—which you may refer to constantly for troubleshooting your own assemblies and learning from the assemblies of others.

4. To eliminate any potential confusion between the fake version of the LicenseInformation class you use for testing your application and the real one provided by Microsoft, you will use the var keyword to create an instance of the LicenseInformation class and then use the fully qualified name to help you visually distinguish between your own implementation of LicenseInformation and the implementation provided by Microsoft. Open MainPage.xaml.cs and change the following line of code at the top of the page from

```
LicenseInformation lic = new LicenseInformation();
```

to

```
var lic = new TrialSample.LicenseInformation();
```

Now you can fully control return values of the IsTrial method by changing the value of the m_fIsTrial variable.

5. Set the m_fIsTrial variable to true and press F5 to run the application.

With these modifications, your TrialSample application will now prompt the user to upgrade to the full version. Changing the value of the m_fIsTrial variable to false and re-running the application results in a message that thanks the user for running an application with the full license.

Once you've verified that the application will behave correctly when you deploy it to the Marketplace, it's time to restore the official version of the LicenseInformation class. Here's how:

6. To switch back to the LicenseInformation class within the Windows Phone 7 Framework, right-click LicenseInformation.cs in Solution Explorer and select Exclude from Project. This action effectively excludes the file from the solution, but does not delete it from the computer system.

7. Finally, you need to change the instance of LicenseInformation to be the instance of the LicenseInformation class provided by Microsoft. Open MainPage.xaml.cs and change the following line of code from

```
var lic = new TrialSample.LicenseInformation();
```

to

```
var lic = new LicenseInformation();
```

Creating trial Windows Phone 7 applications is a relatively straightforward process, as you have seen so far. The biggest challenge is testing these applications to ensure that they behave as expected with both trial and full licenses. Luckily, you have several approaches at your disposal, which we've summarized and one of which we have described in detail.

In the next section, you will create trial and full versions of a more complete application and employ several other Windows Phone 7 development techniques that are covered elsewhere in this book. We hope that this short review will help you further solidify your knowledge of the Windows Phone 7 programming.

Building a Trial Application

The trial software application that you will build in this section is a currency converter. It calls a web service to obtain the current exchange rate for the currencies a user specifies, and then tells users how much of the desired currency they will receive in exchange for the currency they wish to exchange. If the application is running with a trial license, users will be able to convert currencies for free.

However, as we all know, consumers never get the official market exchange rates. Various middlemen take a decent-size cut of foreign exchange transactions, so to calculate the actual amount of foreign currency you can expect to receive, the full application provides another screen, called the More Stuff screen. With More Stuff, users can enter the actual exchange rate quoted by an exchange broker and see how much foreign currency they will receive after they have paid a commission. This More Stuff screen will be available only to those who have paid you $.99 and acquired the full version of the application. Future enhancements to this application could include maps, shared between all users of this application, that show the best places to exchange currency around town, with the commission rates as a percentage of the transaction charged by those places. Power to the consumers at last!

To create this application, you will employ several Windows Phone 7 techniques that are covered in this book. As we introduce such features, we will point to the location in the book where you can find more in-depth coverage of the material. We will also emphasize the functionality that is available and disabled with an application running with a trial license, and we will utilize the approach that we have covered in this book to simulate both trial and full license modes and to ensure that your application functions correctly under both.

Now let's build and test the application.

Building the User Interface

The Currency Converter application includes three pages: one for the main application screen that performs currency conversions; one to prompt the user to upgrade to the full application license when the application is running under a trial license; and one for additional options, such as determining how much money you actually lose on a conversion. In this section, you will create each of these pages. Follow these steps to create a Currency Converter project and add application pages:

1. Launch Visual Studio 2010 Express for Windows Phone, and create a new Windows Phone Application project. Name it CurrencyConversion.

2. Make sure MainPage.xaml is open in Design view. For MainPage.xaml, the end goal is to have a screen with a layout similar to the one shown in Figure 11–4. The screen looks a little busy, so we'll go over each screen element to understand the type of the element and element's name. Element names and types will be referred to from code and, hence, are important to get right. Table 11–1 summarizes field names and types. A portion of the XAML code that creates the Amount to Convert text box, two list boxes, and the corresponding captions are shown here:

```
<TextBlock Height="30" HorizontalAlignment="Left" Margin="24,14,0,0"
Name="textBlock1" Text="Amount to Convert" VerticalAlignment="Top" />
        <TextBox Height="68" HorizontalAlignment="Left" Margin="6,36,0,0"
Name="txtAmountToConvert" Text="" VerticalAlignment="Top" Width="446" />
        <ListBox Height="93" HorizontalAlignment="Left" Margin="24,137,0,0"
Name="lstConvertFrom" VerticalAlignment="Top" Width="220" />
        <TextBlock Height="30" HorizontalAlignment="Left" Margin="24,101,0,0"
Name="textBlock2" Text="Convert from (currency)" VerticalAlignment="Top" Width="220"
/>
        <TextBlock Height="28" HorizontalAlignment="Left" Margin="262,101,0,0"
Name="textBlock3" Text="Convert to (currency)" VerticalAlignment="Top" Width="190"
/>
        <ListBox Height="93" HorizontalAlignment="Left" Margin="263,137,0,0"
Name="lstConvertTo" VerticalAlignment="Top" Width="205" />
```

Figure 11–4. Currency Converter MainPage.xaml page layout

Table 11–1. User Controls for MainPage.xaml

Application Field	Field Name	Field Type
Amount to Convert	txtAmountToConvert	TextBox
Convert from (currency)	lstConvertFrom	ListBox
Convert to (currency)	lstConvertTo	ListBox
Status	txtStatus	TextBlock
Total Converted	txtTotalConverted	TextBlock
Convert Button	btnConvert	Button
More Stuff Button	btnMoreOptions	Button

Next, add the "nag" page, or the page that will try to get users to purchase the full version of our application if the user is executing it under a trial license.

3. To do that, right-click the project name in Solution Explorer and select Add ➤ New Item ➤ Windows Phone Portrait Page. Name the page Upgrade.xaml and select OK.

4. Bring up the design surface of the Upgrade.xaml page, and make it look like Figure 11–5.

The page consists of a message and two buttons. The message prompts the user to upgrade. One of the buttons enables the user to purchase a full license, and the other one simply returns the user to the main application screen. Ensure that the buttons are properly named by verifying their names with Table 11–2.

Table 11–2. User Controls for Upgrade.xaml

Application Field	Field Name	Field Type
Yes, upgrade	btnUpgrade	Button
No, take me back	btnGoBack	Button

Figure 11–5. *The "nag" screen layout*

Finally, add the More Stuff page, or the page that will display features available only to paid users. Sadly, the users of your application will most likely feel cheated at the moment: the only premium feature available to them will be the calculation of the money they do not get as a result of using the currency conversion services.

5. To add the More Stuff page, right-click the project name in Solution Explorer and select Add ➤ New Item ➤ Windows Phone Portrait Page. Name the page `MoreStuff.xaml` and select OK.

6. Bring up the design surface of the `MoreStuff.xaml` page, and make it look like Figure 11–6. Refer to Table 11–3 field names and types.

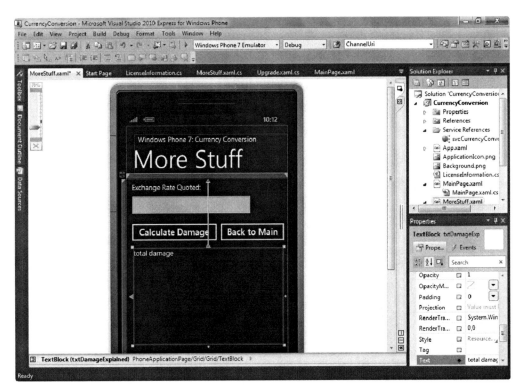

Figure 11–6. The More Stuff screen layout with functionality available to full-license users only

Table 11–3. User Controls for MoreStuff.xaml

Application Field	Field Name	Field Type
Exchange Rate Quoted	txtExchangeRateQuoted TextBox	
Calculate Damage	btnCalculateDamage	Button
Back to Main	btnBackToMain	Button
Total Damage	txtDamageExplained	TextBlock

With the design layout complete, you are now ready to add code to the application. In the next section, you will add code feature-by-feature, starting with a reference to the web service that supplies current exchange rates.

Connecting to a Web Service

To retrieve current currency exchange rates, you will be using a web service located at
www.webservicex.net/CurrencyConvertor.asmx. While there are several ways to connect to a web service
and retrieve data, you will be using the approach discussed in Chapter 18, which draws on the new
Microsoft Reactive Extensions Framework, or Rx.NET. (Note that we use Rx.NET several times
throughout this book, simply because we are convinced that it represents the future of programming on
mobile devices.) Using Rx.NET makes it easier to follow the flow of execution by the program, since it
abstracts—behind a solid Observer pattern—the complexities of invoking of a web service
asynchronously. Follow these steps to add a reference to the Currency Conversion service and to wrap
the results returned by that service within Rx.NET:

1.   With the CurrencyConversion project open, right-click Solution Explorer and select
      Add Service Reference. Paste the following URL into the Address field, as shown in
      Figure 11–7:

      http://www.webservicex.net/CurrencyConvertor.asmx

Figure 11–7. Add Service Reference dialog

Once you click the Go button, Visual Studio should be able to locate the CurrencyConverter service.

2.   Change the namespace in the Add Service Reference Page to svcCurrencyConverter and click OK.

Next, you will need to add reference to the assemblies that contain the Rx.NET modules.

3.   To accomplish this, right-click the project name in Solution Explorer, select Add Reference, and add references to Microsoft.Phone.Reactive and System.Observable assemblies.

4.   Switch to the code view for MainPage.xaml (right-click MainPage.xaml and select View Code) and add the following using directive to the top of the page:

```
using Microsoft.Phone.Reactive;
```

5.   Create a module-level variable referencing the currency converter web service (this would be a local MainPage class variable that should be initialized just above the constructor). Also, declare and initialize a module-level rate variable.

```
svcCurrencyConverter.CurrencyConvertorSoapClient currencyClient = new
        svcCurrencyConverter.CurrencyConvertorSoapClient();
Double dblRate = 0.0;
```

6.   Within the MainPage() constructor, create an Rx.NET subscription to the CurrencyConverter web service by pasting the following code:

```
//create subscription to the web service
var currency =
Observable.FromEvent<svcCurrencyConverter.ConversionRateCompletedEventArgs>(
currencyClient, "ConversionRateCompleted");

currency.ObserveOn(Deployment.Current.Dispatcher).Subscribe(evt =>
{
    dblRate = evt.EventArgs.Result;
        txtStatus.Text = "The current rate is 1 " +
        lstConvertFrom.SelectedItem.ToString()  + " to " +
        evt.EventArgs.Result.ToString() + " " +
    lstConvertTo.SelectedItem.ToString();

        if (txtAmountToConvert.Text.Length>0)
    {
            Double decTotal = evt.EventArgs.Result *
            Convert.ToDouble(txtAmountToConvert.Text);
            txtTotalConverted.Text = txtAmountToConvert.Text + " " +
            lstConvertFrom.SelectedItem.ToString() + " = " +
            decTotal.ToString() + " " +
            lstConvertTo.SelectedItem.ToString();
    }
},
    ex => { txtStatus.Text = "Sorry, we encountered a problem: " + ex.Message; }
);
```

This code creates a subscription to all of the results returned by the currency converter service. It processes the results and shows the conversion rates requested on the screen, including multiplying the total amount to be converted by the conversion rate.

If you would like to understand more about Rx.NET, skip to Chapter 18 right after you finish this chapter. Since the second part of this book is organized as a set of independent tutorials, the chapters in the second part do not have to be read sequentially, but should instead be referred to when needed.

You are almost done establishing a connection and retrieving data from the Currency Converter web service. The one piece that remains to be written is the invocation of this web service, which, in your example, is done via the Convert button.

7. In the design view of MainPage.xaml, double-click the Convert button and change the btnConvert_Click method to look like the following:

```
private void btnConvert_Click(object sender, RoutedEventArgs e)
        {
        currencyClient.ConversionRateAsync((svcCurrencyConverter.Currency)
                lstConvertFrom.SelectedItem, (svcCurrencyConverter.Currency)
                lstConvertTo.SelectedItem);
        }
```

This code invokes the web service asynchronously and passes it the parameters selected by the user (currency names only, in your case). Note how you have to properly cast the parameters to the type expected by the web service (svcCurrencyConverter.Currency type in your case). The results of this asynchronous invocation are returned to the application and are processed within the subscription code just created within the MainPage() constructor code.

With the web service wired up and the data coming back through the Rx.NET subscription to the application, the backbone of your application is complete. Now, you need to introduce navigation between different pages of the application.

Adding Page-to-Page Navigation

In the "Building the User Interface" section, you created three separate pages that make up the application. However, in the application's present state, only a single page (MainPage.xaml) is available during runtime. In this section, you will review navigation between pages in the Windows Phone 7 application. For more in-depth coverage of this material, please refer to Chapter 2.

The envisioned flow of the application is that a separate More Stuff page is available to users with full licenses; users with trial licenses should see an Upgrade page that prompts them to upgrade. Navigating between pages in Windows Phone 7 is similar to navigating between web pages: you can use the NavigationService.Navigate method and pass it the name of the XAML page within the application to navigate to. This is exactly what you'll do in the Currency Converter application.

1. With the Currency Converter application open, double-click the More Stuff button and make the btnMoreOptions_Click method look like the one here:

```
private void btnMoreOptions_Click(object sender, RoutedEventArgs e)
        {
        //use Microsoft implementation of LicenseInformation class
                var lic = new LicenseInformation();

                if (lic.IsTrial() == true)
                {
```

```
                        NavigationService.Navigate(new Uri("/Upgrade.xaml",

                        UriKind.RelativeOrAbsolute));
            }
            else
            {
                        NavigationService.Navigate(new Uri("/MoreStuff.xaml?rate=" +
                        dblRate.ToString() + "&total=" + txtAmountToConvert.Text,
                        UriKind.RelativeOrAbsolute));
            }
        }
```

Notice how this method uses the IsTrial API to check whether an application is executing under a trial or full license, and then it uses the NavigationService.Navigate method to display the Upgrade.xaml page if IsTrial returns true, and it displays the MoreStuff.xaml page if IsTrial returns false. Note that when you navigate to the MoreStuff.xaml page, you also pass two parameters to that page. One way of passing parameters on Windows Phone 7 is identical to parameter passing on the Web—here, you included parameters for currency rate and amount as part of the URL. Parameters start after the name of the page, MoreStuff.xaml, are prefixed by the ? symbol, and are separated from each other by the & symbol.

Passing parameters is not enough in itself; an application must know how to properly process those parameters, which it usually does in the OnNavigatedTo method, as shown next.

2. Open MoreStuff.xaml in the code view and add the following method to receive parameters and assign them to global variables:

```
            protected override void
OnNavigatedTo(System.Windows.Navigation.NavigationEventArgs e)
            {
                        base.OnNavigatedTo(e);
                        string strExchgRate = "";
                        string strTotalToConvert = "";

                        if (NavigationContext.QueryString.TryGetValue("rate", out
strExchgRate))
                                    dblExchgRate = Convert.ToDouble(strExchgRate);

                        if (NavigationContext.QueryString.TryGetValue("total", out
strTotalToConvert))
                                    decTotalToConvert = Convert.ToDecimal(strTotalToConvert);
            }
```

To make the previous code work, you must add the following two module-level variables to the MoreStuff.xaml.cs file:

```
            Double dblExchgRate;
            Decimal decTotalToConvert;
```

What's left is to add navigation to the other pages within the application.

3. Open MoreStuff.xaml in design view, double-click the Back to Main button, and make that button click event handler look like the following:

```
private void btnBackToMain_Click(object sender, RoutedEventArgs e)
{
        NavigationService.Navigate(new Uri("/MainPage.xaml",
        UriKind.RelativeOrAbsolute));
}
```

4. Open Upgrade.xaml in Design view, double-click the Back to Main button, and make that button click event handler look like this:

```
private void btnGoBack_Click(object sender, RoutedEventArgs e)
{
        NavigationService.GoBack();
}
```

Note the different navigation implementation in this case: you are simply using the code to go to the previous page within the application instead of navigating to the specific page.

At this point, application navigation is complete. You are ready to make sure that the trial version of the application does not allow access to the More Stuff page.

Verifying Trial and Full Mode

Creating trial applications is the central theme of this chapter and you have spent the first part of it looking at various issues that may arise as part of trialing an application. When you allow application trials, one of your most important tasks is to ensure that certain application features are accessible to full license holders only; otherwise, there would be no reason to buy an application.

For the Currency Converter application, you must ensure that that the MoreStuff.xaml page is visible only when the application runs with a full license. You have already seen the code that performs this check; in this section, you must verify that the trial mode indeed behaves as expected. You have already learned the technique of writing your own version of the LicenseInformation class just discussed to validate the trial mode of an application. You will use that technique here.

1. With the Currency Converter application open, right-click the project name in Solution Explorer, select Add ➤ New Item, and then select Class from the list of available items. Name the new class LicenseInformation and click OK.

2. Make the LicenseInformation class look like the one here (as you have seen earlier in this chapter, this class definition has been copied from the information generated by Reflector.NET for the LicenseInformation class of the Windows Phone 7 Framework):

```
public sealed class LicenseInformation
{
        // Fields
        private bool m_fIsTrial = true;

        // Methods
        public bool IsTrial()
        {
                    int num = 0;
```

```
                                      if (num != 0)
                                      {
                                              this.m_fIsTrial = true;
                                      }
                                      return this.m_fIsTrial;
                          }

                          // Nested Types
                          internal static class NativeMethods
                          {
                                      // Fields
                                      internal const int S_FALSE = 1;
                                      internal const int S_OK = 0;

                          }
            }
```

You will test the trial mode shortly, right after you put finishing touches on your Currency Converter application.

Adding Finishing Touches

You are nearly ready to test the Currency Converter application—just a few items remain. Before an application is functional, it needs to know what currency to convert to what. Create two list boxes inside the `MainPage.xaml` file to allow the user to make her selection. To keep things simple in the first version, include only three currencies: the US dollar, the euro, and the Russian ruble. When an application loads, you need to load list boxes with these currencies.

7. Open MainPage.xaml.cs and paste the following LoadCurrencies method inside the MainPage() constructor:

```
private void LoadCurrencies()
{
        lstConvertFrom.Items.Add(svcCurrencyConverter.Currency.USD);
        lstConvertFrom.Items.Add(svcCurrencyConverter.Currency.EUR);
        lstConvertFrom.Items.Add(svcCurrencyConverter.Currency.RUB);

        lstConvertTo.Items.Add(svcCurrencyConverter.Currency.USD);
        lstConvertTo.Items.Add(svcCurrencyConverter.Currency.EUR);
        lstConvertTo.Items.Add(svcCurrencyConverter.Currency.RUB);
}
```

`MoreStuff.xaml` needs code to perform calculations on the currency rates passed in and entered into the application. This code belongs inside the btnCalculateDamage_Click event.

8. In Design view, double-click the Calculate Damage button and replace the btnCalculateDamage_Click event code with the following:

```
private void btnCalculateDamage_Click(object sender, RoutedEventArgs e)
{
        decimal decTotalToReceive;
              decimal decTotalAccordingToConversionRate;
```

```
                decTotalToReceive = Convert.ToDecimal(txtExchangeRateQuoted.Text) *
                decTotalToConvert;
                decTotalAccordingToConversionRate = Convert.ToDecimal(dblExchgRate) *
                decTotalToConvert;

                txtDamageExplained.Text = "With exchange rate quoted, you will receive
" +
                decTotalToReceive.ToString() + "\r\n";
            txtDamageExplained.Text = txtDamageExplained.Text +  "Given market exchange
                rate, you should receive " +
                decTotalAccordingToConversionRate.ToString() + "\r\n";

            txtDamageExplained.Text = txtDamageExplained.Text + "You lose " +
                (decTotalAccordingToConversionRate - decTotalToReceive).ToString();
    }
```

Finally, Upgrade.xaml needs code to bring up the Windows Phone Marketplace and load the application review page, which will enable the user to purchase a full version of the application if the user elects to do so. As discussed earlier in this chapter, this is the job for one of the classes within the Microsoft.Phone.Tasks namespace. The Microsoft.Phone.Tasks namespace is covered in much greater detail in the "Launchers and Choosers" section of Chapter 10.

9. Add the following using directive to the top of the Upgrade.xaml.cs file:

    ```
    using Microsoft.Phone.Tasks;
    ```

10. Next, bring up the Upgrade.xaml page in design mode and double-click the Yes, upgrade button. Make that button's click event look like the following:

    ```
            private void btnUpgrade_Click(object sender, RoutedEventArgs e)
            {
                    MarketplaceReviewTask marketplaceReviewTask = new
    MarketplaceReviewTask();
                    marketplaceReviewTask.Show();
            }
    ```

You're done writing code for the Currency Converter application. The application should compile and run if you press F5 now. If, for some reason, there are errors preventing an application from launching, it's best to compare your code to code available for download for this chapter.

Assuming the code runs, the current value of the IsTrial method returned by your own implementation of the LicenseInformation class is true. Therefore, if you run the application and click the More Stuff button, you should see a message prompting you to upgrade to the full version of an application. This is the expected behavior. Go ahead and change the value of m_fIsTrial to false. You should now see the More Stuff screen, as expected for the application with full license.

You can also verify that the program works as expected by entering values and asking it to convert them from one currency to another. For instance, today, as shown in Figure 11–8, $345 is only 267.86 euros. To get that output, type 345 in the Amount to Convert text box, select USD from the Convert From list box and select EUR from the Convert To list box. Then, press the Convert button. Assuming that a connection to the Internet is available, you should get results that are similar.

While the Currency Converter application is functional, it can stand many improvements, particularly in the area of validating user input. For instance, the application throws an error if the user tries to go to the More Stuff screen without entering a value in the Amount to Convert text box.

Addressing this and other similar issues, as well as enhancing the application even further, is left as an exercise for the reader.

Figure 11–8. Currency Converter application converting US$345 to euros

Summary

In this chapter, you learned about Windows Phone 7 trial modes. You learned that there is a single code base for both trial and production versions of an application, and that application developers control which functionality to disable for trial modes using the IsTrial method. You also learned about simulating trial mode, an important technique when creating trial applications. Finally, in this chapter, you created a Currency Converter application that utilized several techniques discussed in this book and perhaps solidified your understanding of several key concepts of Windows Phone 7 development.

In the next chapter, you will learn about internationalizing applications to make them available to many markets whose language and date/time constructs are quite different from those of the American market. That chapter will further help you with your Currency Converter enhancement efforts!

CHAPTER 12

Internationalization

Strong growth in mobile computing propelled by increasingly capable mobile devices is not just a North American phenomenon—people all over the world are increasingly relying on their phones both for business and leisure. This, of course, is wonderful news for Windows Phone 7 developers—the greater the customer base, the more potential revenue or exposure the application gets. There is just one small gotcha when taking mobile application development to the world: the vast majority of customers outside North America speak very little to no English.

So if your goal is to create an application that succeeds globally, you must ensure that it can "speak" many languages. Certainly, one way to make that happen is to create many versions of an application, one for each language market you target. Unfortunately, that approach quickly becomes a nightmare to maintain. Imagine making a small code change to an application, such as rearranging UI controls on its main page—that code change would have to be made to each language version of the application! Fortunately, .NET Framework and the .NET Compact Framework that powers Windows Phone 7 devices provide a set of culture-aware classes and a general approach to implementing multilingual applications. This approach involves creating and editing resource files, which can be developed and distributed independently of your application code

This chapter offers some simple steps that you can take to prepare an app for distribution in more than one language, ones that will save you time later. This topic deserves a book of its own, and indeed a few have been written already (see a list of them on Amazon's web site at www.amazon.com/s/ref=nb_sb_ss_i_0_17?url=search-alias%3Daps&field-keywords=.net+internationalization). We hope that our advice in this chapter will help you avoid extra work when you are ready to share your brilliant creation with non-English speaking population of the world. Let's begin with a closer look at the topic of internationalization and the support for it that the Windows Phone SDK provides.

Understanding Internationalization

Translating your application's interface or its documentation into other languages may be the most important task you'll face when you target your application for a global audience, but it's not the only one. Cultures differ in the ways they display dates, numbers, currencies, and even text. For instance, in the United States, the month is always the first part of the numeric representation of a date. In England, on the other hand, the month comes after the day. This could potentially create confusion—imagine payment due dates being missed because the date was not formatted according to a culture's standards. One way to avoid misinterpretation of numeric dates is to adopt an international standard, such as ISO 8601, that specifies that all dates are to be represented from the most significant to the least significant element: year, month, day, hour, and so on.

Similarly, disagreements over cultural representations of decimal separators have the power to almost stall the development of the programming language (http://en.wikipedia.org/wiki/Decimal_separator). To illustrate how such heated debates can originate, consider the following example: the number "one thousand one and one tenth" would be written in the United States as "1,001.1", with the comma symbol used as the separator for the thousands and the period symbol used for separating the decimals. The same number would be written in Europe as "1.001,1", with the dot used for separating thousands and the comma used to separate the decimals. The Windows Phone 7 operating system, fortunately, automatically makes these locale-aware changes for you. As a developer, however, you must help the framework out a little and ensure that you use appropriate data types and appropriate formatting options for the operations you perform in your applications. For example, you should never represent dates or numbers as strings and hardcode the formatting of those strings in your application if an application is intended for more than one national market.

In addition to these variations in the way different cultures handle numbers and dates, languages also differ in the number of words they require to express an idea, with some more verbose than others. For instance, it is estimated that an average sentence in the German language is 44 percent longer than the same sentence in English. That means that a Windows Phone 7 user interface written in English—its labels, textblocks, text boxes, and so on—may need to reserve additional available white space when designed in the English language and later translated (dynamically, as you'll see shortly) into German or other languages.

Also, if you are targeting international markets, the design of an application should be flexible enough to allow it to "speak" different languages without your having to make extensive changes to the source code. That means that all strings, images, and audio and video content must be placed in separate resource-only files—one for each target culture and language to make it easy to package the application for a new locale. By sticking with Unicode characters (with over 95,000 characters) to encode your strings content, you'll be able to display virtually any language in the world.

Another important consideration in deciding how to prepare to support your application in multiple languages is the amount of material that will need to be translated. Later in this chapter, we recommend you use resource-only files inside Visual Studio. This technique is perfectly acceptable for smaller applications, when there are only a handful of items to translate. However, if the translation requires the use of third-party translation services, you will be better served by looking at more specialized localization tools, such as Alchemy Catalyst, Globalizer.Net, Lingobit Localizer, or Radialix. While the use of such tools is beyond the scope of this chapter, if you ever find that editing resource files in Visual Studio becomes hard to manage, you can refer to the foregoing list to determine whether any of these products makes the task easier.

In MSDN documentation, there are usually two separate sections on internationalizing applications—globalization and localization. Roughly, *globalization* refers to ensuring that all commonly used application concepts, such as dates and currency, are properly represented and used in the system regardless of the locale of the user. *Localization*, on the other hand, refers to translating application resources, such as text of the user interface, into local representation. To muddy these concepts a little more, in the non-Microsoft world, the term internationalization is used to represent what Microsoft refers to as globalization. Since this is already confusing, for the purposes of this chapter, we won't make such a distinction; when we talk about "internationalizing" an application, we refer to ensuring that the application will work without problems in all countries and regions it was intended to work in—i.e., the Microsoft concepts of globalization and localization are blurred.

.NET and the Windows Phone 7 SDK include a number of tools to help you ready an app for international distribution. These tools include the CultureInfo class to properly determine the culture that an application is running in, as well as easy management of resource files that were custom developed for each culture. You will explore these tools next.

Using Culture Settings with ToString to Display Dates, Times, and Text

To see how you can go about preparing an application for the world, you'll build a simple application that announces a new product, in this case a Windows Phone. But first, you will learn how to use the CultureInfo class to ensure dates, numbers, and text appear in the right form regardless of the culture in which the announcement is made. Then you'll see how, by using resource (.resx) files, you can easily add translated content to your app to reach new markets. Figure 12–8 shows how the finished application will look.

Let's jump into code that will set the stage for the discussion of internationalization of Windows Phone 7 applications.

1. Let's start by creating a new project inside Visual Studio and naming it InternationalizationSample.

By default, the MainPage.xaml file is created in the application, with the designer and XAML windows open and ready to program.

2. Double-click MainPage.xaml to bring up the XAML designer window. For convenience and simplicity, you will alter the content of textblocks in the TitleGrid block. Make the XAML of the TitleGrid look identical to the XAML here:

```
<StackPanel x:Name="TitlePanel" Grid.Row="0" Margin="24,24,0,12">
    <TextBlock x:Name="ApplicationTitle" Text="Current Culture Setting"
Style="{StaticResource PhoneTextNormalStyle}"/>
    <TextBlock x:Name="PageTitle" Text="culture" Margin="-3,-8,0,0"
Style="{StaticResource PhoneTextTitle1Style}"/>
</StackPanel>
```

Your project should now look like Figure 12–1. So far you've simply changed the text of the default title textblock in the Windows Phone 7 application.

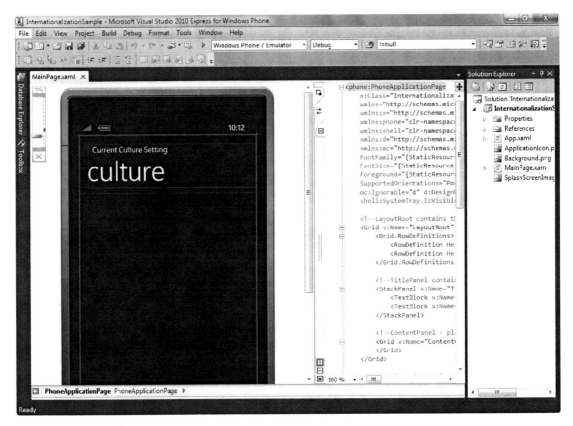

Figure 12–1. Preparing the phone design surface for the internationalization demo

3. Now double-click `MainPage.xaml.cs` to bring up the code view. Alternately, you can right-click the `MainPage.xaml` file and select View Code.

4. Add the following statement to the top of the `MainPage.xaml.cs` file:

    ```
    using System.Globalization;
    ```

5. Paste the following code in the `MainPage()` constructor:

    ```
    PageTitle.Text = CultureInfo.CurrentCulture.ToString();
    ```

6. Press F5 to run the application. You should see a phone emulator screen that looks like the one in Figure 12–2.

Figure 12–2. Running the internationalization demo

Notice how the caption in Figure 12–2 reads "en-US." This caption represents two parts of the current Culture setting on Windows Phone 7. The first part—"en"—states that the English language is the current *language* on this Windows Phone 7 device (or device emulator in your case) and it is a part of an ISO standard to represent culture code associated with the language. The second part—"US"—states that the current *locale* is the United States, and indicates that dates, currency, and other region-specific items should be shown in the format that is native to people in the United States. That part is an ISO standard as well, to represent a subculture code associated with a country or region.

A concept of culture in .NET Framework refers to a set of user preferences specific to the user, such as dates, currency, and calendar format. Besides CurrentCulture, the CultureInfo class contains many properties that may be of interest to you as you internationalize your applications; you can find the full list at http://msdn.microsoft.com/en-us/library/system.globalization.cultureinfo_properties.aspx. For instance, you could have used the DisplayName property to show a friendlier description of the current culture (in your case, you would get "English (United States)." As mentioned, there is a lot of material to cover when it comes to internationalization—a good place to refer to for more information is the MSDN documentation of the System.Global namespace, located at http://msdn.microsoft.com/en-us/library/abeh092z.aspx.

You might think that the locale setting is of minor importance, yet it is extremely important to properly localize your application: in England, for instance, people speak English (certainly!), but, as mentioned, the numeric date format is "dd/mm/yyyy," where the "dd" is the numeric representation of the day, "mm" is the numeric representation of the month, and "yyyy" is the numeric representation of the year. Compare this to the United States, where people speak English as well, but for numerical date representations, the month comes first. In other words, it would be very time-consuming to keep track of all possible localization issues. In the end, you would very likely make mistakes. It's much easier to stand on the shoulders of giants who have thought through many internationalization issues and have made standard libraries and functions available for your use. Your main task is to make sure to use those libraries.

Using the .NET Culture Hierarchy to Ensure Culture Neutrality

Suppose that you have built international support for only a portion of an application. What would happen when a user from a different country accesses features of an application that have not been internationalized? Will the application stop working, display a blank screen, etc.? The answer to this question lies in the concept of the .NET framework called *culture hierarchy*.

There are three types of cultures that you as a developer must be aware of: *invariant, neutral,* and *specific*. These cultures are arranged in a hierarchical manner, with invariant culture being at the top of the hierarchy, neutral in the middle, and specific culture at the bottom, as illustrated in Figure 12–3. When international users access Windows Phone 7 applications, the operating system starts at the bottom of this hierarchy and checks whether an application implements the specific culture of a given user. This check includes whether an application has the resources, such as text for menus and labels, which have been localized for the user's location. If such localized resources are not available, the system then moves up the culture hierarchy and checks whether there are provisions in the application for neutral cultures. Finally, if that check fails, the application defaults to the invariant culture, which is the same as English (US) culture.

For example, if a French-speaking user from Canada accesses Windows Phone 7 applications, the first thing the system checks is whether there are application resources implementing specific "fr-CA" culture. If that specific culture is not supported by an application, the system then performs a check of whether the neutral "fr" culture is supported. If the neutral culture is not supported, then the system defaults to the invariant culture, where none of the resources are localized. In this chapter, you will learn how to create resources for specific cultures, and let the .NET Framework do the heavy lifting of defaulting to neutral or invariant cultures when resources specific to users' culture are not available.

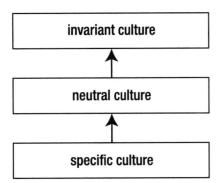

Figure 12–3. Culture hierarchy in Windows Phone 7

Storing and Retrieving Current Culture Settings

On Windows Phone 7, the System.Globalization.CultureInfo class contains all of the necessary information about the phone's current culture settings. In this section, you will write code to retrieve basic properties of the CultureInfo class, as well as code to change the current culture of the phone and to react to those changes. In real-world applications, you are not likely to adjust the current culture in code, since the culture setting should be fully controlled by the user.

In the following example, you will create a simple announcement of an upcoming event, and then, with a click of a button, adjust culture settings to properly display the date, time, and the cost of the event in a different region of the world—Spain. To accomplish that, you will instantiate a new CultureInfo class and set the current thread's CurrentCulture property to this new class. Later in this chapter, you will expand upon this example and make your event advertisement speak different languages without having to change the source code.

■ **Note** You are probably wondering where and how the user would set Windows Phone 7 culture. On both the phone and the emulator, the culture is adjusted in Settings ➤ Region and Language. Region and Language Settings can be accessed by clicking the small arrow to the right of the tiles on the phone screen (next to the Internet Explorer tile in the emulator). Click on Region & Language, and select an international format from the list that you'd like. Notice how both Short and Long Date properties, as well as the First Day of the Week property, adjust to the new format specific to the locale selected. Figure 12–4 illustrates how you can adjust Regional Settings on your phone.

Figure 12–4. Changing the phone's regional settings

1. Start by creating a Visual Studio project and naming it WP7AnniversaryParty.

2. Double-click `MainPage.xaml` in Solution Explorer to bring up the XAML designer window.

For this first example, you will display the contents of just two fields on the screen: the name of the event as well as the event's date and time.

3. Remove one of two default textblocks automatically added to the design surface by Visual Studio. Highlight the textblock with MY APPLICATION text in it (either in XAML or on the design surface) and hit the Delete key.

4. Now let's add the additional six text box controls that you need. If the toolbox is not visible, either click the Toolbox button on the Visual Studio Application Bar or select View ➤ Other Windows ➤ Toolbox. Drag six textblocks to the design surface and position them two per row, one underneath each other, as shown in Figure 12–5.

5. Change the text of the three textblocks on the left to the following: Event Date, Event Time, and Event Cost, as shown in Figure 12–5.

Figure 12–5. Design surface of the WP7AnniversaryParty application

6. Click on each textblock in the right column, press F4, and change the textblock names to txtEventDate, txtEventTime, and txtEventCost correspondingly.

7. Finally, add a button to the design surface and name it Español.

You should now end up with XAML code that matches the XAML shown in Listing 12–1 (you can simply copy and paste XAML code from the source code downloads for this chapter instead of adding elements to the design surface one-by-one, as you've done in the previous steps).

Listing 12–1. WP7 Launch Party UI Code (XAML)

```
<Grid x:Name="LayoutRoot" Background="{StaticResource PhoneBackgroundBrush}">
<Grid.RowDefinitions>
    <RowDefinition Height="Auto"/>
    <RowDefinition Height="*"/>
</Grid.RowDefinitions>

<!--TitleGrid is the name of the application and page title-->
<Grid x:Name="TitleGrid" Grid.Row="0">
    <TextBlock Text="WP7 Party" x:Name="textBlockListTitle" Style="{StaticResource
PhoneTextTitle1Style}"/>
</Grid>

<!--ContentGrid is empty. Place new content here-->
<Grid x:Name="ContentGrid" Grid.Row="1">
    <TextBlock Height="44" HorizontalAlignment="Left" Margin="204,48,0,0"
Name="txtEventDate" Text="TextBlock" VerticalAlignment="Top" Width="276" />
    <TextBlock Height="43" HorizontalAlignment="Left" Margin="5,49,0,0"
Name="textBlock1" Text="Event Date:" VerticalAlignment="Top" Width="193" />
    <TextBlock Height="44" HorizontalAlignment="Left" Margin="204,98,0,0"
Name="txtEventTime" Text="TextBlock" VerticalAlignment="Top" Width="276" />
    <TextBlock Height="43" HorizontalAlignment="Left" Margin="5,99,0,0"
Name="textBlock3" Text="Event Time:" VerticalAlignment="Top" Width="193" />
    <TextBlock Height="44" HorizontalAlignment="Left" Margin="205,146,0,0"
Name="txtEventCost" Text="TextBlock" VerticalAlignment="Top" Width="276" />
    <TextBlock Height="43" HorizontalAlignment="Left" Margin="6,147,0,0"
Name="textBlock4" Text="Event Cost:" VerticalAlignment="Top" Width="193" />
  <Button Content="Español" Height="70" HorizontalAlignment="Left" Margin="6,233,0,0"
Name="button1" VerticalAlignment="Top" Width="160" Click="button1_Click" />
    </Grid>
</Grid>
```

8. Double-click MainPage.xaml.cs to bring up the code view. Alternately, you can right-click the MainPage.xaml file and select View Code.

9. Add the following statements to the very top of the page (right below the last using statement):

```
using System.Globalization;
using System.Threading;
```

10. Next, you will code the function that will populate event details and the function that toggles event locale. You will learn the internationalization

concepts demonstrated in this function shortly, but for now add the code shown in Listing 12–2.

Listing 12–2. ShowEventDetails and ToggleEventLocale functions (C#)

```
private void ShowEventDetails()
{
    textBlockListTitle.Text = "WP7 Party";
    //create the date of October 11, 2011 at 9:00 PM
    DateTime dtLaunchDate = new DateTime(2011, 10, 11, 21, 0, 0);
    //make the cost equal to $5
    decimal decEventCost = 5.0M;

    //ToString() can also return values in specified culture
    //txtEventDate.Text = dtLaunchDate.ToString("D");
    txtEventDate.Text = dtLaunchDate.ToString("D",
        Thread.CurrentThread.CurrentCulture);
    txtEventTime.Text = dtLaunchDate.ToString("T");

    txtEventCost.Text = decEventCost.ToString("C");
}

private void ToggleEventLocale()
{
    //default to English-US culture
    String cul = "en-US";

    if (button1.Content.ToString() == "Español")
    {
        //change the culture to Spanish
        cul = "es-ES";
    }
    else
    {
        cul = "en-US";
    }

    CultureInfo newCulture = new CultureInfo(cul);
    Thread.CurrentThread.CurrentCulture = newCulture;

    ShowEventDetails();
}
```

Now you will call a function to show event details right after the application loads.

11. Paste the call to the ShowEventDetails() function in the MainPage() constructor to show event details in English when the application is launched:

```
ShowEventDetails();
```

Finally, you need to add an event handler to handle the button click, which will toggle the current culture between English and Spanish. The best way to add it is to bring up `MainPage.xaml` in design view and double-click the button.

12. Add the following code:

```
private void button1_Click(object sender, RoutedEventArgs e)
{
    ToggleEventLocale();
}
```

13. Press F5 to run the application. Notice how the date, time, and cost are all shown in the familiar American format. If you press the Español button, you will see the date in Spanish, the time in the 24-hour format, and the cost in euros. The labels with Date, Time, and Cost did not change, however, since you have not made any localization provisions in your code for those. You will localize these resources in the next section of this chapter.

In the preceding example, there are a couple of interesting points worth discussing in more detail. The first one is how you switched from one culture to another in code. To accomplish that, you instantiated a new `CultureInfo` class and set the current thread's CurrentCulture property to this new class. During the instantiation of the `CultureInfo` class, you passed a string to its constructor representing a specific culture ("es-ES" for Spanish and "en-US" for American English). The second important point is the illustration of the use of standard formatting constructs in your code to make internationalizing your application easier. For example, let's put the following line of code at the end of the `ShowEventDetails()` function:

```
txtEventDate.Text = dtLaunchDate.ToString("MM/dd/yyyy");
```

Now when you run the application, notice how the date will be displayed as "11/10/2011" for both Spanish and English versions of your event. This certainly is confusing for residents of Spain, who would think that the Windows Phone 7 anniversary date is actually on November 10, 2011. Remember to use standard formatting options for all UI elements—in the case of the date, the standard formatting you have used with the following line of code to show the "long date representation" is certainly more appropriate:

```
txtEventDate.Text = dtLaunchDate.ToString("D");
```

The third and final important point in the previous example is the ease of switching specific cultures on Windows Phone 7. If you pass "es-MX" instead of "es-ES" into the `CultureInfo()` constructor in the `ToggleEventLocale()` function, you can still see the date translated into the Spanish language, but the currency and time are formatted according to the Mexican standard and not the standard of Spain.

Using Resource Files to Localize Content

Assume now that you have been diligently designing your application for international markets: you have allowed enough space on the user interface for more verbose languages, and you have used only standard formatting options for date, time, and currency values. You still have to perform translation of the application interface and resources to other languages. This could be, certainly, the most labor-intensive part of internationalizing your application.

As mentioned, the application should be flexible enough to function in different locales without the need for code change and recompilation. That means that all resources required for proper functioning of the application need to be located outside the source code of an application and loaded on demand in response to request for culture-specific elements. The location of those resources are the resource-only files, or `*.resx` files. In this section's example, you will enhance your WP7 Anniversary Party announcement application with the use of `.resx` files.

■ **Note** Large resource files may take some time to load on the Windows Phone 7 device. However, according to the Windows Phone 7 Application Certification Requirements document, a Windows Phone 7 application must render its first screen within five seconds of launch. Make sure to always include a splash screen image within the root of your package submitted to the Marketplace (see Chapter 19 for more details about the Marketplace). This splash screen image can be any `.jpg` file of your choosing named `SplashScreenImage.jpg`. Even with the splash screen image, however, be aware that the Microsoft Certification Requirements document further states that an application must be responsive to user input within 20 seconds after its launch—make sure to use resource files diligently so they don't unnecessarily slow down your application.

One benefit of using `.resx` files is that Windows Phone 7 will automatically find and use the resource file appropriate for the user's locale based on the current user's culture settings. Another benefit of resource files comes from the concept of culture hierarchy mentioned previously—.NET Framework provides a default fallback mechanism (i.e., going one level up in the culture hierarchy) for those resources that have not been localized. Also, `.resx` files are easily parseable by external tools, since they are simply XML files. This allows easy editing of those files by third-parties (such as translation services).

■ **Note** Throughout this book, you will see references to .NET Framework on Windows Phone 7. To be completely accurate, however, it is the compact version of .NET Framework (.NETCF) that powers Windows Phone 7. Compact .NET Framework is a portable version of the full .NET Framework, and it has a much smaller size and footprint to accommodate smaller devices. The first version of Windows Phone 7 runs .NETCF version 3.7. So whenever you encounter a reference to .NET Framework in this book, remember that the reference is really to the .NETCF 3.7 or later.

---

1. Unless it's already open, open the WP7AnniversaryParty solution.

2. Right-click the WP7LaunchParty project and select Add ➤ New Item ➤ Resources File.

3. This resource file will contain the values for English-US culture. Name the resource file `AppResources.resx` and click Add.

Remember the discussion of culture hierarchies earlier in this chapter? The fact that your resource file does not contain any locale information in the file name (unlike the Spanish one that you will be creating shortly) makes this an invariant culture resource file—the file that will be shown if no locale-specific resource files are found on the device.

4. Double-click the AppResources.resx file to bring up an empty table. Next, add four entries to that table for Event Title, Event Date, Event Time, and Cost, all in English, as shown in Figure 12–6.

Figure 12–6. Resource file for English -US translation of WP7AnniversaryParty application

Note that the contents of the first and second columns are extremely important: the first one contains the key that the code will use to reference the element, and it must be unique in this resource file. The second column contains the value, or the actual content that will be displayed on the UI at runtime. The third column is useful, but not essential: you can provide descriptive comments about each value in this column.

You will now add a resource file for Spanish translation of the user interface elements.

5. Right-click the WP7LaunchParty project and select Add ➤ New Item ➤ Resources File.

6. Name the resource file AppResources.es-ES.resx and click Add.

Note the "es-ES" portion of the file name—it is extremely important to name resource files in accordance with the specific cultures they represent. In your case, you will provide Spanish (spoken in Spain and not Latin America, for example) translation of the user interface, hence the "es-ES" in the resources file name. If you wanted to add German (spoken in Germany and not Austria, for example) translation as well, your resource file would have the name AppResource.de-DE.resx.

7. Add four entries for Event Title, Event Date, Event Time, and Cost in Spanish, as shown in Figure 12–7.

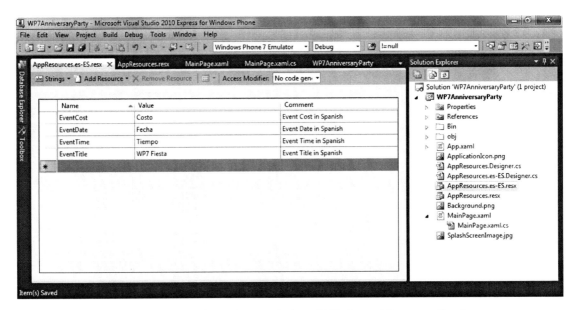

Figure 12–7. Resource file for Spanish-Spain translation of WP7LaunchParty application

---

■ **Note** The translations are approximate and are used for demonstrative purposes only—please forgive the authors if we are not 100 percent accurate.

---

8. You need to rename the textblocks used for captions in your application so that you can easily refer to them in code. Bring up `MainPage.xaml` and change textBlock1 to txtEventDateCaption, textBlock3 to txtEventTimeCaption, and textBlock4 to txtEventCostCaption. You should end up with XAML that matches the following markup:

```
<Grid x:Name="ContentGrid" Grid.Row="1">
    <TextBlock Height="44" HorizontalAlignment="Left" Margin="204,48,0,0"
Name="txtEventDate" Text="TextBlock" VerticalAlignment="Top" Width="276" />
    <TextBlock Height="43" HorizontalAlignment="Left" Margin="5,49,0,0"
Name="txtEventDateCaption" Text="Date:" VerticalAlignment="Top" Width="193" />
    <TextBlock Height="44" HorizontalAlignment="Left" Margin="204,98,0,0"
Name="txtEventTime" Text="TextBlock" VerticalAlignment="Top" Width="276" />
    <TextBlock Height="43" HorizontalAlignment="Left" Margin="5,99,0,0"
Name="txtEventTimeCaption" Text="Time:" VerticalAlignment="Top" Width="193" />
```

```
              <TextBlock Height="44" HorizontalAlignment="Left" Margin="205,146,0,0"
Name="txtEventCost" Text="TextBlock" VerticalAlignment="Top" Width="276" />
              <TextBlock Height="43" HorizontalAlignment="Left" Margin="6,147,0,0"
Name="txtEventCostCaption" Text="Cost:" VerticalAlignment="Top" Width="193" />
              <Button Content="Español" Height="70" HorizontalAlignment="Left"
Margin="6,233,0,0" Name="button1" VerticalAlignment="Top" Width="160" Click="button1_Click" />
         </Grid>
```

9. At the top of the page, add the following two statements:

```
using System.Resources;
using System.Reflection;
```

10. In MainPage.xaml.cs, change the ShowEventDetails() function to match the
    code chunk shown here (note the commented out setting of default (English)
    caption):

```
    private void ShowEventDetails()
    {
        //textBlockListTitle.Text = "WP7 Party";
        ResourceManager rm = new ResourceManager("WP7AnniversaryParty.AppResources",
        Assembly.GetExecutingAssembly());
        textBlockListTitle.Text = rm.GetString("EventTitle");
        txtEventCostCaption.Text = rm.GetString("EventCost");
        txtEventDateCaption.Text = rm.GetString("EventDate");
        txtEventTimeCaption.Text = rm.GetString("EventTime");

        //create the date of November 6, 2010 at 9:00 PM
        DateTime dtLaunchDate = new DateTime(2010, 11, 6, 21, 0, 0);
        //make the cost equal to $5
        decimal decEventCost = 5.0M;

        txtEventDate.Text = dtLaunchDate.ToString("D");
        txtEventTime.Text = dtLaunchDate.ToString("T");

        txtEventCost.Text = decEventCost.ToString("C");
    }
```

11. Press F5 to compile and run the application. Click the button to toggle
    between Spanish and English. Do you see all captions and the event title being
    properly translated? Probably not, since you are missing one critical step: you
    have not indicated that your project must support different locales and which
    locales it must support. You will do that in the next step.

12. It's unfortunate that, at present time, you must edit a project file in the text
    editor (instead of Visual Studio) to indicate which locales your application
    supports. Open Windows Explorer and navigate to the folder where the
    WP7LaunchParty.csproj file is located. Open WP7LaunchParty.csproj in any text
    editor (Notepad is good) and find the <SupportedCultures> node. More than
    likely, that node will not contain any elements. Edit that node to look like the
    two line of text below:

```
<SupportedCultures>es-ES;
</SupportedCultures>
```

Were you supporting more than one culture, you would include all of them in this node with each culture code separated by a semicolon. For example, if you were supporting German and Russian translations as well, you would put es-ES;de-DE;ru-RU; in the <SuportedCultures> element.

13. Save WP7AnniversaryParty.csproj in the text editor. Visual Studio should detect an external change to this file and ask you if you would like to reload the project. Click Yes.

14. Add the following line of code to the ToggleEventLocale method, right below the Thread.CurrentThread.CurrentCulture = newCulture; statement:

    Thread.CurrentThread.CurrentUICulture = newCulture;

15. Press F5 to run the application.

Since you have provided a non-locale specific (invariant) file, AppResources.resx, with English (US) captions for the invitation text in it, you see a US English interface upon launching the application. Once you click the button to toggle the application into Spanish, you should see the event title and captions translated into the Spanish language, as shown in Figure 12–8. The cool part about this translation is that it's completely dynamic—the string values are loaded from the resource file instead of being hardcoded!

Figure 12–8. Spanish application interface

If you examine Figure 12–8 carefully, you will notice a couple of things. First, the date of the event almost ran off the screen in Spanish—a clear mistake on your part for not allowing an extra 40 percent of space (by perhaps allowing text wrapping) inside that date value for languages that are more verbose than English. Second, the caption for Cost did not translate into Spanish—it should be Costo in Spanish, not Cost. What's going on here?

The reason for this is that in AppResources.es-ES.resx, there is no entry named EventCost. There is an entry with the name Cost, but that is not the name you are referring to from code. This mistake is a good demonstration of the application's cultural fallback: there was no entry in the Spanish version for EventCost, so the application "fell back" to the default language (English-US) to represent a given caption—the raison d'être of the resource files!

Correct this typo by double-clicking the AppResources.es-ES.resx file and changing the name of the Cost entry to EventCost. Now re-run the application. You should see the proper caption, Costo, for the Spanish version of your announcement.

■ **Note** The MSDN documentation for internationalizing Windows Phone 7 applications proposes an entirely different approach than the one we've advocated in this example. MSDN examples encourage you to add a separate class to return resources. In this example, however, we have simplified things a bit and used the ResourceManager class to locate resources within the resource files.

The main reason our example differs from the approach advocated by the MSDN documentation is that we are dynamically (i.e., in code) changing the culture of an application. We needed to do this for demonstration purposes, since changing local culture is a bit cumbersome if done in the emulator. Dynamic rebinding of elements (to toggle captions between English and Spanish) would be a bit more involved. The addition of a separate class and references to that class, as illustrated in the MSDN documentation, could have also taken away from the main points illustrated during the example. But we could certainly have used an approach other than using the ResourceManager class to accomplish the localization of the application.

Summary

In this chapter, you learned how to prepared an application to work in parts of the world other than the United States by using stored culture information and the ToString function to determine how to display data; ISO culture codes to reset an app's CulturalInfo object to the user's preferred language and country environment; and resource files to provide translated versions of field names, documentation, and even media. You learned what specific issues to consider when developing applications for international markets, such as dates, numbers, and currency translations between locales; you also learned how to translate application resources via Visual Studio resource files.

In the next chapter, you will take a look at how to persist files and settings on Windows Phone 7 via the use of local storage. You will save images and application settings and then load them on demand from a local store on Windows Phone 7.

CHAPTER 13

Isolated Storage

In Chapter 3, you learned that Microsoft Azure provides a reliable place to store and access data but using it requires Internet access. Sometimes it's more efficient to cache frequently accessed data on the Windows Phone device itself.

Isolated storage is a place on a Windows Phone 7 device where an application can save files, configuration information, and other data. Each application is allocated its own portion of the available space, but can't access file systems used by the operating system itself, a limitation that prevents a rogue application from accessing system data and possibly corrupting it. The amount of storage that can be assigned to any single application depends on the phone's available space.

With isolated storage, a Windows Phone application can create and maintain a virtual file storage system that can contain virtual folders and files; you won't have direct access to the underlying Windows Phone file system but the isolated storage will provide you with API to work with the file system. All input and output operations can be performed only on the application's isolated storage level.

Support for isolated storage on a Windows Phone is provided by the following two namespaces, whose features are depicted by Figure 13–1.

- *Isolated File Storage*: `System.IO.IsolatedStorage.IsolatedStorageFile` allows you to create, use, and remove directories and files in the virtual isolated storage. The files can be added and retrieved through file stream using `System.IO.IsolatedStorage.IsolatedFileStream`, which can also cache images, sounds, and files that are dynamically loaded from the Web. In the first demo, you will learn how use isolated storage to cache an image loaded from the Web.

- *Isolated Local Settings*: `System.IO.IsolatedStorage.IsolatedStorageSettings` provides APIs for storing and working with key-value pairs cached in isolated storage and for storing application settings and user specific settings.

Figure 13–1. Using the Isolated Storage APIs

In this chapter, you will learn how to work with a phone's isolated storage. The first example will show you a technique to cache an image downloaded from the Web into the isolated storage file. The second demo will show you how to save and retrieve name and value pairs using isolated storage settings.

Working with Isolated Directory Storage

You'll begin by building an application to work with the local storage on a phone. The application, named IsolatedStorageStoreImageDemo and shown in Figure 13–2, demonstrates the basic functions available through the isolated storage APIs, including the following:

- Retrieving application-specific isolated storage.

- Getting isolated storage quota.

- Saving and retrieving isolated storage files.

In this demo, when the Get Image button is clicked for the first time, the application checks to see whether there is enough space available in isolated storage. If there is, the image will be downloaded from the web site and then saved to isolated storage via isolated storage file stream. If the button is clicked again, the image will be loaded into an isolated storage file.

Figure 13–2. IsolatedStorageStoreImageDemo

You'll build the demo in three steps. First, you'll create a new Visual Studio project. Next, you'll build the project's user interface and finish up by adding code to respond to commands from the user.

Creating the IsolatedStorageStoreImageDemo Project

To set up the IsolatedStorageStoreImageDemo project, follow the steps you've used for previous examples in this book.

1. Open Microsoft Visual Studio 2010 Express for Windows Phone on your workstation.

2. Create a new Windows Phone Application by selecting File ➤ New Project on the Visual Studio command menu. Select the Windows Phone Application template, name the application IsolatedStorageStoreImageDemo, and click OK, as shown in Figure 13–3.

Figure 13–3. Windows Phone Application template for creating IsolatedStorageStoreImageDemo

Coding the User Interface

You'll first code the user interface, which we've chosen to implement in XAML. Sometimes it's faster to work with XAML than with managed code, especially when you're working with a simple example, like this one, which requires only a few controls. Go to the Solution Explorer, open MainPage.xaml, and replace the XAML you find there with the code that appears in the following sections.

Selecting the UI Resources

Begin by adding the following XAML markup to MainPage.xaml to identify where the resource to build the application's main page will be found:

```
<phone:PhoneApplicationPage

    x:Class="IsolatedStorageStoreImageDemo.MainPage"
    xmlns="http://schemas.microsoft.com/winfx/2006/xaml/presentation"
    xmlns:x="http://schemas.microsoft.com/winfx/2006/xaml"
    xmlns:phone="clr-namespace:Microsoft.Phone.Controls;assembly=Microsoft.Phone"
    xmlns:shell="clr-namespace:Microsoft.Phone.Shell;assembly=Microsoft.Phone"
    xmlns:d="http://schemas.microsoft.com/expression/blend/2008"
    xmlns:mc="http://schemas.openxmlformats.org/markup-compatibility/2006"
    mc:Ignorable="d" d:DesignWidth="480" d:DesignHeight="768"
    FontFamily="{StaticResource PhoneFontFamilyNormal}"
    FontSize="{StaticResource PhoneFontSizeNormal}"
    Foreground="{StaticResource PhoneForegroundBrush}"
    SupportedOrientations="Portrait" Orientation="Portrait"
    shell:SystemTray.IsVisible="True">
```

Referencing the namespace as xmlns="http://schemas.microsoft.com/winfx/2006/xaml/presentation"
allows you to use common Windows Phone controls such as text boxes, buttons, and list boxes to create
the main page. The code snippet also includes a reference to a codebehind class
(x:Class="IsolatedStorageStoreImageDemo.MainPage") that will handle the main page controls' events.

Building the Main Page and Adding Components

Next, to create the main application page and populate it with controls, add the following XAML markup
to the preceding block of code, also in MainPage.xaml:

```
<Grid x:Name="LayoutRoot" Background="{StaticResource PhoneBackgroundBrush}">
    <Grid.RowDefinitions>
        <RowDefinition Height="Auto"/>
        <RowDefinition Height="*"/>
    </Grid.RowDefinitions>

    <!--TitleGrid is the name of the application and page title-->
    <Grid x:Name="TitleGrid" Grid.Row="0">
        <TextBlock Text="IsolatedStorageStoreImageDemo"
                   x:Name="textBlockPageTitle"
                   Style="{StaticResource PhoneTextTitle1Style}"
                   FontSize="28" />
    </Grid>

    <!--ContentGrid is empty. Place new content here-->
    <Grid x:Name="ContentGrid" Grid.Row="1">

<Image Height="458" HorizontalAlignment="Left"
               Margin="20,134,0,0" Name="image1" Stretch="Uniform"
               VerticalAlignment="Top" Width="423" />
        <Button Content="Get Image" Height="70"
                HorizontalAlignment="Left" Margin="0,598,0,0"
```

```
                    Name="btnGetImage" VerticalAlignment="Top"
                    Width="443" Click="btnGetImage_Click" />
            <TextBox Height="72" HorizontalAlignment="Left"
                    Margin="12,29,0,0" Name="txtImageUrl"
                    Text="http://res1.newagesolution.net/Portals/0/twitter2_icon.jpg"
                    VerticalAlignment="Top" Width="460" />
        </Grid>
    </Grid>

</phoneNavigation:PhoneApplicationPage>
```

Once you've loaded the XAML code for the main page, you should see the layout shown in Figure 13–4. Now it's time to use the Isolated Storage APIs to add behavior to the application.

Figure 13–4. IsolatedStorageStoreImageDemo Design view

Coding the Application

In Solution Explorer, open `MainPage.xaml.cs` and replace the code there with the following C# code blocks, in precisely the order in which they are presented.

Specifying the Namespaces

Begin by specifying the namespaces the application will use. `System.IO.IsolatedStorage` and `System.IO` contain the APIs needed to work with the isolated file storage.

```
using System;
using System.Net;
using System.Windows;
using Microsoft.Phone.Controls;
using System.Windows.Media.Imaging;
using System.IO.IsolatedStorage;
using System.IO;

namespace IsolatedStorageStoreImageDemo
{
```

Initializing Variables

Now add the following block of code to `MainPage.xaml.cs` to initialize the application's variables:

```
    public partial class MainPage : PhoneApplicationPage
    {
        private string ImageFileName = null;


        WebClient _webClient; // Used for downloading the image first time from the web site
...
```

Initializing the Application

Now add the application's constructor, which uses the WebClient.OpenReadCompleted event to download its target image. The code contains logic to check whether enough space is available in the phone's isolated storage to save the downloaded image. If space is available, the image gets saved; otherwise it's loaded directly into the image control.

```
        public MainPage()
        {
            InitializeComponent();

            SupportedOrientations = SupportedPageOrientation.Portrait |
                SupportedPageOrientation.Landscape;

            _webClient = new WebClient();
```

```
                // Handles when the image download is completed
                _webClient.OpenReadCompleted += (s1, e1) =>
                    {
                        if (e1.Error == null)
                        {
                            try
                            {
                                bool isSpaceAvailable =
                            IsSpaceIsAvailable(e1.Result.Length);

                                if (isSpaceAvailable)
                                {
                                    // Save Image file to Isolated Storage
                                    using (IsolatedStorageFileStream isfs =
                                new IsolatedStorageFileStream(ImageFileName,
                                            FileMode.Create,
                                    IsolatedStorageFile.GetUserStoreForApplication()))
                                    {
                                        long imgLen = e1.Result.Length;
                                        byte[] b = new byte[imgLen];
                                        e1.Result.Read(b, 0, b.Length);
                                        isfs.Write(b, 0, b.Length);
                                        isfs.Flush();
                                    }

                                    LoadImageFromIsolatedStorage(ImageFileName);
                                }
                                else
                                {
                                    BitmapImage bmpImg = new BitmapImage();
                                    bmpImg.SetSource(e1.Result);
                                    image1.Source = bmpImg;
                                }
                            }
                            catch (Exception ex)
                            {
                                MessageBox.Show(ex.Message);
                            }
                        }
                    };
                }
```

■ **Note** In order to create a sub-directory, you must create a directory path string, such as
"MyDirectory1\SubDirectory1" and pass it to the CreateDirectory method. To add a file to SubDirectory1,
you must create a string that combines the file name with its path, such as
"MyDirectory1\SubDirectory1\MyFileInSubDirectory1.txt", and then use IsolatedStorageFileStream to
create a file. In order to add contents to the file, use StreamWriter.

When you use the Remove method in IsolatedStorageFile, use it with caution as it will delete all directories and files. To avoid accidently deleting everything in the isolated storage, create a warning prompt window to confirm with the user that it will be OK to delete everything in the isolated storage. Another possibility is to use IsolatedStorage.DeleteFile or IsolatedStorage.DeleteDirectory to delete a specific file or directory to avoid removing all files or directories. Please refer to MSDN documentation for more information at http://msdn.microsoft.com/en-us/library/kx3852wf(VS.85).aspx.

■ **Tip** System.IO.Path.Combine provides a great way to combine directory paths and files without worrying if the backslashes (\) are properly added. Also, when searching files or directories, you can use a wild card (*) when building a directory or file path.

Checking Availability of Isolated Storage Space

Now, add code for the isSpaceAvailable helper method that the application uses to determine whether there is enough space available in isolated storage to store the image.

```
// Check to make sure there are enough space available on the phone
        // in order to save the image that we are downloading on to the phone
        private bool IsSpaceIsAvailable(long spaceReq)
        {
            using (IsolatedStorageFile store =
IsolatedStorageFile.GetUserStoreForApplication())
    {
                long spaceAvail = store.AvailableFreeSpace;
                if (spaceReq > spaceAvail)
                {
                    return false;
                }
                return true;
            }
        }
```

Adding a Button Event to Retrieve the Image from Isolated Storage

When the Get Image button is clicked, it checks to see if the image exists in the isolated storage. If the image exists, the image is loaded from the isolated storage; otherwise the image is downloaded from the web site.

```
private void btnGetImage_Click(object sender, RoutedEventArgs e)
{
    using (IsolatedStorageFile isf =
        IsolatedStorageFile.GetUserStoreForApplication())
    {
        bool fileExist = isf.FileExists(ImageFileName);

        if (fileExist)
        {
            LoadImageFromIsolatedStorage(ImageFileName);
        }
        else
        {
                    if (!string.IsNullOrEmpty(txtImageUrl.Text))
            {
        // Use Uri as image file name
                Uri uri = new Uri(txtImageUrl.Text);
                ImageFileName =
uri.AbsolutePath.Substring(uri.AbsolutePath.LastIndexOf('/')+1);
                _webClient.OpenReadAsync(new Uri(txtImageUrl.Text));
            }

        }

    }

}
```

Adding a Method to Retrieve the Image from Isolated Storage

The image is streamed directly from the isolated storage into the image control.

```
private void LoadImageFromIsolatedStorage(string imageFileName)
{
    // Load Image from Isolated storage
    using (IsolatedStorageFile isf =
IsolatedStorageFile.GetUserStoreForApplication())
    {
        using (IsolatedStorageFileStream isoStream =
isf.OpenFile(imageFileName, FileMode.Open))
        {
            BitmapImage bmpImg = new BitmapImage();
            bmpImg.SetSource(isoStream);
            image1.Source = bmpImg;
        }
    }
}
```

Testing the Finished Application

To test the completed application, press F5 on your keyboard and run it.

In this brief demo, you've learned to work with isolated storage files by storing a downloaded image into the isolated storage and then retrieving the image from the isolated storage. In the next demo, you will interact with the name and value dictionary of the isolated storage settings.

Working with Isolated Storage Settings

In this section, you'll build an application, named IsolatedStorageSettingsDemo, that demonstrates CRUD operations (create, read, update, and delete) of System.IO.IsolatedStorage.IsolatedStorageSettings. Figure 13–5 shows how its UI will look on a Windows Phone.

Figure 13–5. IsolatedStorageSettingsDemo

In the IsolatedStorageSettingsDemo application, when the Save button is clicked, the value in the Value text box will be added to the isolated storage settings using the key in the Key text box. Whenever new key-value pair data is added to the isolated storage settings, the key will be added to the list box of keys. When any of the keys in the list box of keys is selected, the Key text box and the Value text box will be populated with the data retrieved from the isolated storage settings. The Delete button will delete the selected key from the isolated storage settings.

To build the demo, create a new project and then add XAML markup to create a new main page and its controls. Finally, you'll add behavior to the application with C# code that makes use of isolated storage APIs to save and retrieve key-value pairs.

Creating a New Project

To create the new IsolatedStorageSettingsDemo project, open Microsoft Visual Studio 2010 Express for Windows Phone. Select File ➤ New Project on the Visual Studio menu, select the Windows Phone Application template on the New Project dialogue, name the application IsolatedStorageSettingsDemo, and click OK, as shown in Figure 13–6.

Now you'll build the application main page.

Figure 13–6. Windows Phone Application template for creating IsolatedStorageSettingsDemo

Building the Application UI (XAML)

To create the UI for IsolatedStorageSettingsDemo, go to Solution Explorer, open `MainPage.xaml`, and replace XAML with the following chunks of XAML markup in the sequence shown.

Selecting the UI Resources

The following code identifies where to find the UI controls that will be used to build this main page for this application. Using the namespace `xmlns="http://schemas.microsoft.com/winfx/2006/xaml/presentation"` will allow you to add common Windows Phone controls like text boxes, buttons, and list boxes, which will be used to create the main page. Also, you are adding a reference to a codebehind class (`x:Class="IsolatedStorageSettingsDemo.MainPage"`) that will handle the main page controls' events.

```
<phone:PhoneApplicationPage
    x:Class="IsolatedStorageSettingsDemo.MainPage"
    xmlns="http://schemas.microsoft.com/winfx/2006/xaml/presentation"
    xmlns:x="http://schemas.microsoft.com/winfx/2006/xaml"
    xmlns:phone="clr-namespace:Microsoft.Phone.Controls;assembly=Microsoft.Phone"
    xmlns:shell="clr-namespace:Microsoft.Phone.Shell;assembly=Microsoft.Phone"
    xmlns:d="http://schemas.microsoft.com/expression/blend/2008"
    xmlns:mc="http://schemas.openxmlformats.org/markup-compatibility/2006"
    FontFamily="{StaticResource PhoneFontFamilyNormal}"
    FontSize="{StaticResource PhoneFontSizeNormal}"
    Foreground="{StaticResource PhoneForegroundBrush}"
    SupportedOrientations="Portrait" Orientation="Portrait"
    mc:Ignorable="d" d:DesignWidth="480" d:DesignHeight="768"
    shell:SystemTray.IsVisible="True">
```

Building the Main Page and Adding Controls

Now add the various controls and layouts you need to create the UI shown in Figure 13–5.

```
<Grid x:Name="LayoutRoot" Background="{StaticResource PhoneBackgroundBrush}">
    <Grid.RowDefinitions>
        <RowDefinition Height="Auto"/>
        <RowDefinition Height="*"/>
    </Grid.RowDefinitions>

    <!--TitleGrid is the name of the application and page title-->
    <Grid x:Name="TitleGrid" Grid.Row="0">
        <TextBlock Text="Isolated Storage Settings Demo"
                x:Name="textBlockListTitle"
                Style="{StaticResource PhoneTextTitle1Style}"
                FontSize="30" />
    </Grid>

    <!--ContentGrid is empty. Place new content here-->
    <Grid x:Name="ContentGrid" Grid.Row="1">
```

```xml
        <TextBox Height="72" HorizontalAlignment="Left"
                Margin="172,46,0,0" Name="txtKey" Text=""
                VerticalAlignment="Top" Width="212" />
        <Button Content="Save" Height="70"
                HorizontalAlignment="Left" Margin="78,228,0,0"
                Name="btnSave" VerticalAlignment="Top" Width="160"
                Click="btnSave_Click" />

    <ListBox Height="301" HorizontalAlignment="Left" Margin="94,392,0,0"
                Name="lstKeys" VerticalAlignment="Top" Width="290" BorderBrush="White"
                BorderThickness="1" SelectionChanged="lstKeys_SelectionChanged" />
        <TextBlock Height="39" HorizontalAlignment="Left" Margin="94,62,0,0"
                Name="lblKey" Text="Key" VerticalAlignment="Top" />
        <TextBox Height="74" HorizontalAlignment="Left" Margin="172,124,0,0"
                Name="txtValue" Text="" VerticalAlignment="Top" Width="212" />
        <TextBlock Height="39" HorizontalAlignment="Left" Margin="94,140,0,0"
                Name="lblValue" Text="Value" VerticalAlignment="Top" />
        <Button Content="Delete" Height="70" HorizontalAlignment="Left"
                Margin="224,228,0,0" Name="btnDelete" VerticalAlignment="Top"
                Width="160" Click="btnDelete_Click" />
        <TextBlock Height="39" HorizontalAlignment="Left" Margin="94,347,0,0"
                Name="lblListOfKeys" Text="List of Keys" VerticalAlignment="Top" />
    </Grid>
  </Grid>

</phoneNavigation:PhoneApplicationPage>
```

Once you've added the XAML markup blocks displayed in this section to `MainPage.xaml`, you should see the UI shown on the Visual Studio Design View tab in Figure 13–7.

Figure 13–7. *IsolatedStorageSettingsDemo design view*

Now it's time to add behavior to the application.

Coding Application Behavior (C#)

From Solution Explorer, open MainPage.xaml.cs and replace the code you find there with the following blocks of C# code.

Specifying the Namespaces

Begin by listing the namespaces the application will use. Note the inclusion of System.IO.IsolatedStorage in order to work with the isolated storage settings.

```
using System;
using System.Windows;
using System.Windows.Controls;
```

```
using Microsoft.Phone.Controls;
using System.IO.IsolatedStorage;
namespace IsolatedStorageSettingsDemo
{
    public partial class MainPage : PhoneApplicationPage
    {
        private IsolatedStorageSettings _appSettings;
```

Initializing the Application

Now add the next code block to the MainPage class. Notice the use of the BindKeyList() method, which will retrieve all keys from the isolated storage settings and bind them to the list box created in the previous section.

```
public MainPage()
    {
        InitializeComponent();
        SupportedOrientations = SupportedPageOrientation.Portrait;
        _appSettings = IsolatedStorageSettings.ApplicationSettings;
    BindKeyList();
    }
```

Adding the Save Button Event Handler

Now add an event handler for the Save button. When the Save button is clicked, the application reads the key and the value from the text boxes into the isolated storage settings.

```
        // Handles Create and Update
// If the key does not exist key-value pair will be added
// ElseIf the key exists the value will be updated
        private void btnSave_Click(object sender, RoutedEventArgs e)
        {
            if (!String.IsNullOrEmpty(txtKey.Text))
            {
                if (_appSettings.Contains(txtKey.Text))
                {
                    _appSettings[txtKey.Text] = txtValue.Text;
                }
                else
                {
                    _appSettings.Add(txtKey.Text, txtValue.Text);
                }
_appSettings.Save();
                BindKeyList();
            }
        }
```

■ **Note** An isolated storage file will perform much better than isolated storage settings because a file can be streamed in and out of the isolated storage file as raw data by using `StreamWriter` and `StreamReader`, whereas the storage and retrieval of data in an isolated storage settings key-value pair dictionary requires serialization. However, there is complexity in using isolated storage files: you need to use the file stream to save and retrieve the data and you must be careful to dispose the stream after each use. In the isolated storage settings, there is inherent simplicity in using the key to save and retrieve the data.

Adding the Delete Button Event Handler

Next, add an event handler for the Delete button. When the Delete button is clicked, it removes the selected key from the isolated storage settings and rebinds the list box.

```
private void btnDelete_Click(object sender, RoutedEventArgs e)
{
    if (lstKeys.SelectedIndex > -1)
    {
        _appSettings.Remove(lstKeys.SelectedItem.ToString());
_appSettings.Save();
        BindKeyList();
    }
}
```

Adding the Listbox Changed Event

Finally, you'll use the Listbox changed event to update the Key and Value text boxes of the application interface. When the user selects a key from the list box, the application will load the key and its associated value from the isolated storage settings using the selected key and then populate the key and value text boxes.

```
// When key is selected value is retrieved from the storage settings
private void lstKeys_SelectionChanged(object sender, SelectionChangedEventArgs e)
{
    if (e.AddedItems.Count > 0)
    {
        string key = e.AddedItems[0].ToString();
        if (_appSettings.Contains(key))
        {
            txtKey.Text = key;
            txtValue.Text = _appSettings[key].ToString();
        }
    }
}
```

```
        private void BindKeyList()
        {
            lstKeys.Items.Clear();
            foreach (string key in _appSettings.Keys)
            {
                lstKeys.Items.Add(key);
            }
            txtKey.Text = "";
            txtValue.Text = "";
        }

    }
}
```

Testing the Finished Application

To test the finished application, press F5. The result should resemble the screenshot shown in Figure 13–5.

Summary

In this chapter, you learned how to save application data on a Windows Phone device using either an isolated storage file or isolated storage settings. From the demo applications, you learned to create, read, update, and delete isolated storage data.

In Chapter 14, you will learn to pinpoint the location of the phone by working with the Windows Phone's global positioning system (GPS), connected networks, and cellular telephone networks. You will also learn to interact with Microsoft's Bing Maps.

CHAPTER 14

Using Location Services

All Windows Phone devices are required to ship with a GPS receiver; as a result, you can develop applications that are *location aware*. The GPS receiver in the Windows Phone gets the data in the form of longitude and latitude.

There are many popular applications available for phones these days that use location data, such as restaurant finder applications, and navigation applications that give driving directions and plot the street address on a map using the services like Yahoo, Google, and Microsoft Bing Maps. With Microsoft Bing Maps service, you can convert the address into a GPS coordinate system and plot it using the Bing Maps Silverlight control of the Windows Phone.

Even search engines take advantage of the phone's GPS by providing relevant search results based on the location of the phone. There is an application that tracks your location while you are running and, based on the distance travelled, gives you total calories burned.

Social networking applications like Twitter and Facebook also take advantage of the GPS tracking system on your phone by tagging your tweets or uploaded photos with the location information. There are applications that even allow you to share your current location with your friends and family. This can be life-saving information: a lost sea kayaker was found out in the ocean because he had a phone in his possession and the Coast Guard was able to locate him by his GPS location.

Understanding Windows Phone Location Services Architecture

A Windows Phone device can determine its current position on the surface of the earth in one of three ways. The first approach is to use the built-in GPS receiver, which uses satellites and is the most accurate but consumes the most power. The second and third approaches are to use Wi-Fi and the triangulation of the cell phone towers, which are much less accurate then GPS receiver but consume less power. Fortunately, the Windows Phone Location Service automatically decides which option is best for the location of a device and presents its best guess of longitude and latitude through the Bing Maps location service. With a longitude and latitude reading in hand, an application can plot it on a Bing Maps Silverlight control map. Another approach is to use the street or civic address returned by the on-board location service to query the Bing Maps web service for its corresponding GPS coordinates (longitude and latitude) and plot them on a Bing Maps map.

In upcoming sections, you will learn how to take advantage of the Windows Phone's GPS receiver to track your movements and how to plot an address on the Bing Maps Silverlight control using the Microsoft Bing Maps service.

Introducing the Windows Phone Location Service and Mapping APIs

In order to use the location service on a device, you need to reference the System.Device assembly and declare System.Device.Location in your code. And before you can take advantage of the location service, you must enable the location service on the phone by going to Settings ➤ Location ➤ Turn on Location Services option. You can detect whether the phone's location service is enabled using the StatusChanged event of GeoCoordinateWatcher, as seen in the following code:

```
GeoCoordinateWatcher geoCoordinateWatcher;
geoCoordinateWatcher = new GeoCoordinateWatcher(GeoPositionAccuracy.High);
geoCoordinateWatcher.MovementThreshold = 100; // in Meters
geoCoordinateWatcher.StatusChanged += (s, e) =>
    {
        if (e.Status == GeoPositionStatus.Disabled)
        {
            MessageBox.Show("Please enable your location service by going to Settings ->
Location -> Turn on Location Services option.");
        }
    };
```

Another way to check if the location service is enabled is to use TryStart to see if the GeoCoordinateWatcher can be started:

```
if (!_geoCoordinateWatcher.TryStart(true, TimeSpan.FromSeconds(5)))
{
        MessageBox.Show("Please enable Location Service on the Phone.",
"Warning", MessageBoxButton.OK);
}
```

Next, you need to set DesiredAccuracy and provide MovementThreshold in GeoCoordinateWatcher, as seen in the previous code.

GeoPositionAccuracy.Default uses Wi-Fi or cell phone towers and thus depends on the availability of these sources while GeoPositionAccuracy.High uses the GPS receiver built into the phone device; Windows Phone will automatically choose one to use. MovementThreshold is a very important property to set because MovementThreshold specifies the change in distance in meters before the PositionChanged event notifies the application that new coordinates are available; the lower the value of MovementThreshold, the more accurately the position will be tracked, but you will pay a price in higher power consumption. Microsoft recommends that you set MovementThreshold to at least 20 meters to filter out this noise.

In the following sections, you will learn how to use the Windows Phone Location Service by simulating the behavior of the GPS receiver. This simulation allows you to test location-aware applications (like the ones you'll build in this chapter) in the emulator, which lacks a real GPS receiver.

Simulating the Location Service

In order to simulate use of the location service, you will be intercepting the GeoCoordinateWatcher's PositionChanged event using an `Observable` object. With an `Observable` object, you can subscribe to an event and then stream the data received to the subscribed event delegates. For the examples in this chapter, you will subscribe to the PositionChanged event to feed GPS data to the parts of your application that consume it. The use of `Observable` objects is covered in more detail in Chapter 18.

Creating the GeoCoordinateWatcherDemo Project

To set up the GeoCoordinateDemo project, follow the steps you used for previous examples in this book. In order to use the .NET Reactive Extension, you will need to add a reference to `Microsoft.Phone.Reactive`. You'll also need to reference `System.Device` in order to use the location service and, most importantly, `System.Observable`, in order to feed GPS data to the location service.

1. Open Microsoft Visual Studio 2010 Express for Windows Phone on your workstation.

2. Create a new Windows Phone Application by selecting File ➤ New Project on the Visual Studio command menu. Select the Windows Phone Application template, and name the application GeoCoodinateWatcherDemo.

3. Add a reference to `Microsoft.Phone.Reactive` in order to use Reactive Extension. Also add a reference to `System.Device` in order to use the location service. In Solution Explorer, you should be able to see the added reference, as shown in Figure 14–1.

Solution 'GeoCoordinateWatcherDemo' (1 |
 ▲   GeoCoordinateWatcherDemo
   ▷   Properties
   ▲   References
      Microsoft.Phone
      Microsoft.Phone.Interop
      Microsoft.Phone.Reactive
      mscorlib
      system
      System.Core
      System.Device
      System.Net
      System.Observable
      System.Windows
      System.Xml
   ▷   App.xaml
     ApplicationIcon.png
     Background.png
   ▲   MainPage.xaml
      MainPage.xaml.cs
     SplashScreenImage.jpg

Figure 14–1. Project references to use the Reactive Extension and the location service

Coding the User Interface

You will be building the user interface using the XAML in the Visual Studio. For building simple controls, it's faster to work with the XAML code. Go to the solution, open MainPage.xaml, and replace the XAML you find there with the following code.

Declaring the UI Resources

The namespaces you see in the following code snippet are typically declared by default when you first create a Windows Phone project. In particular, namespace xmlns:phone="clr-namespace:Microsoft.Phone.Controls;assembly=Microsoft.Phone" allows you to add common Windows Phone controls to the application main page.

```
<phone:PhoneApplicationPage
    x:Class="GeoCoordinateWatcherDemo.MainPage"
    xmlns="http://schemas.microsoft.com/winfx/2006/xaml/presentation"
    xmlns:x="http://schemas.microsoft.com/winfx/2006/xaml"
    xmlns:phone="clr-namespace:Microsoft.Phone.Controls;assembly=Microsoft.Phone"
    xmlns:shell="clr-namespace:Microsoft.Phone.Shell;assembly=Microsoft.Phone"
```

```
xmlns:d="http://schemas.microsoft.com/expression/blend/2008"
xmlns:mc="http://schemas.openxmlformats.org/markup-compatibility/2006"
mc:Ignorable="d" d:DesignWidth="480" d:DesignHeight="768"
FontFamily="{StaticResource PhoneFontFamilyNormal}"
FontSize="{StaticResource PhoneFontSizeNormal}"
Foreground="{StaticResource PhoneForegroundBrush}"
SupportedOrientations="Portrait" Orientation="Portrait"
shell:SystemTray.IsVisible="True">
```

Building the Main Page and Adding Components

Next, add two textblocks, txtLatitude and txtLongitude, to display the longitude and latitude that the phone location service provides.

```
<Grid x:Name="LayoutRoot" Background="Transparent">
    <Grid.RowDefinitions>
        <RowDefinition Height="Auto"/>
        <RowDefinition Height="*"/>
    </Grid.RowDefinitions>

    <StackPanel x:Name="TitlePanel" Grid.Row="0" Margin="12,17,0,28">
        <TextBlock x:Name="ApplicationTitle" Text="GeoCoordinateWatcherDemo"
Style="{StaticResource PhoneTextNormalStyle}"/>
    </StackPanel>

    <Grid x:Name="ContentPanel" Grid.Row="1" Margin="12,0,12,0">
        <TextBox Height="72" Name="txtLongitude" Text=""
                Margin="193,142,41,393" />
        <TextBox Height="72" Name="txtLatitude" Text=""
                Margin="193,236,41,299" />
        <TextBlock Height="30" HorizontalAlignment="Left"
                Margin="78,202,0,0" Name="textBlock1"
                Text="Longitude" VerticalAlignment="Top" />
        <TextBlock Height="30" HorizontalAlignment="Left"
                Margin="78,306,0,0" Name="textBlock2"
                Text="Latitude" VerticalAlignment="Top" />
    </Grid>
</Grid>
</phone:PhoneApplicationPage>
```

Once you have loaded the XAML code, you should see the layout shown in Figure 14–2. In the next section, you will be adding events to handle updating the UI with the received GPS data from the location service.

301

Figure 14–2. GeoCoordinateWatcherDemo Design view

Coding the Application

In Solution Explorer, open `MainPage.xaml.cs` and replace the code there with the following C# code blocks, which will implement the UI updates using the location service with the data received from Reactive Extension.

Specifying the Namespaces

Begin by listing the namespaces the application will use. You will need `System.Device.Location` in order to use the location service. Declare `Microsoft.Phone.Reactive` in order to use the Reactive Extension's Observable. Also note that you will need `System.Threading` in order to feed the GPS data into the location service; you can think of Reactive Extension's Observable as if it were the satellite, Wi-Fi, or communication tower sending the GPS data.

```
using Microsoft.Phone.Controls;
using System.Threading;
using Microsoft.Phone.Reactive;
using System.Device.Location;
using System.Collections.Generic;
using System;
```

Initializing Variables

The variable _geoCoordinateWatcher is an instance of the Windows Phone location class that you'll use to access and retrieve location data. Notice in the constructor you declared the PositionChanged event in order to receive the location service's GPS data. Also, you'll be starting the thread that will simulate the GPS data that is sent to the PositionChanged event delegate.

```
GeoCoordinateWatcher _geoCoordinateWatcher;

public MainPage()
{
    InitializeComponent();

    // initialize GeoCoordinateWatcher
    _geoCoordinateWatcher = new GeoCoordinateWatcher();

    // PositionChanged event will receive GPS data
    _geoCoordinateWatcher.PositionChanged +=
        new EventHandler<GeoPositionChangedEventArgs<GeoCoordinate>>
            (_geoCoordinateWatcher_PositionChanged);

    // simulateGpsThread will start Reactive Extension
    // where EmulatePositionChangedEvents will be feeding
    // the data to PositionChanged event
    Thread simulateGpsThread = new Thread(SimulateGPS);
    simulateGpsThread.Start();
}
```

Simulating GPS Data Using Reactive Extension's Observable

In the previous constructor, you initiated a thread that executes the SimulateGPS method. In the SimulateGPS method, the Reactive Extension's Observable subscribes to the PositionChanged event in order to feed the GPS data. Notice that GPSPositionChangedEvents constantly sends GeoPositionChangedEventArgs every two seconds, which then gets received by GeoCoordinateWatcher's PositionChanged event and the GPS data.

```
// Reactive Extension that intercepts the _geoCoordinateWatcher_PositionChanged
// in order to feed the GPS data.
private void SimulateGPS()
{
    var position = GPSPositionChangedEvents().ToObservable();
```

```
        position.Subscribe(evt => _geoCoordinateWatcher_PositionChanged(null, evt));
    }

    private static IEnumerable<GeoPositionChangedEventArgs<GeoCoordinate>>
GPSPositionChangedEvents()
    {
        Random random = new Random();

        // feed the GPS data
        while (true)
        {
            Thread.Sleep(TimeSpan.FromSeconds(2));

            // randomly generate GPS data, latitude and longitude.
// latitude is between -90 and 90
double latitude = (random.NextDouble() * 180.0) - 90.0;
// longitude is between -180 and 180
double longitude = (random.NextDouble() * 360.0) - 180.0;
            yield return new GeoPositionChangedEventArgs<GeoCoordinate>(
                    new GeoPosition<GeoCoordinate>(DateTimeOffset.Now, new
GeoCoordinate(latitude, longitude)));
        }

    }
```

Displaying GPS Data

In this demo, the received GPS data is displayed directly to the user. Notice here that you are using Dispatcher.BeginInvoke to execute the lambda expression of an anonymous method. Using Dispatcher.BeginInvoke to update the UI with the GPS data is absolutely necessary because the PositionChanged event is executed in a different thread than the UI, and thus you must explicitly use Dispatcher.Invoke to run UI specific codes.

```
    private void _geoCoordinateWatcher_PositionChanged(object sender
        , GeoPositionChangedEventArgs<GeoCoordinate> e)
    {
        this.Dispatcher.BeginInvoke(() =>
        {
            txtLatitude.Text = e.Position.Location.Latitude.ToString();
            txtLongitude.Text = e.Position.Location.Longitude.ToString();
        });
    }
```

Testing the Finished Application

To test the application, press F5. The result should resemble the screenshot in Figure 14–3, and you will see constantly changing longitude and latitude in the textblocks.

Figure 14–3. GeoCoordinateWatcherDemo

Using GeoCoordinateWatcher and the Bing Maps Control to Track Your Movements

You'll begin by building an application to work with the phone's location service, GeoCoordinateWatcher. The application, Bing Map Demo, is shown in Figure 14–4 and demonstrates the basic functions available through GeoCoordinateWatcher, the location service that was introduced in the previous section. The application will display your location with a blinking icon on a map and continuously update your position as you move.

In this demo, when you click the Start button, it will start the location service that will send notification when the position is changed; upon the changed position event, the Bing Maps map will be updated with the new position. You can actually start the application while you are walking and watch the position of the locator (red dot) on the map change as you move.

Figure 14–4. Bing Maps Demo using GeoCoordinateWatcher

You'll build the demo in four steps. First, you need to register with the Bing Maps service portal and create a new Visual Studio project. Next, you'll build the project's user interface and finish up by adding code to respond to commands from the user.

Registering with the Bing Maps Service Portal and Installing the Bing Maps SDK

Before you can use the Bing Maps Silverlight control and its service offerings, you must register with Bing Maps at www.bingmapsportal.com. Go to www.bingmapsportal.com and you should see something similar to Figure 14–5.

Figure 14–5. Bing Maps portal to create new user

1. Click the Create button and follow the instructions provided by Microsoft.

2. Once you create a Bing Maps service user, you must create an application key so that you can use the Bing Maps control and the Bing Maps service from Windows Phone. Sign in to the Bing Maps portal; once you are logged in, click the "Create or view keys" link shown in Figure 14–6.

Figure 14–6. Creating an application key to use Bing Maps service

Once you've created the Bing Maps application key, you must install the Windows Phone SDK found at `http://create.msdn.com/en-us/home/getting_started`.

If you successfully installed the Windows Phone SDK, the binaries (`Microsoft.Phone.Controls.Maps`) can be referenced from the project in order to use the Bing Maps Silverlight control.

Creating the BingMapDemo Project

To set up the BingMapDemo project, follow the steps you've used for previous examples in this book.

1. Open Microsoft Visual Studio 2010 Express for Windows Phone on your workstation.

2. Create a new Windows Phone Application by selecting File ➤ New Project on the Visual Studio command menu. Select the Windows Phone Application template, and name the application BingMapDemo.

3. In order to use Bing Maps control in Windows Phone, you must reference
   Microsoft.Phone.Controls.Maps, and in order to track your movement, you
   need to add reference to System.Device to use the location service. Open
   Solution Explorer and add those references now. Check to ensure that your list
   of references matches the list shown in Figure 14–7.

Figure 14–7. *Referenced assemblies needed for Bing Maps control*

Coding the User Interface

Now it's time to code the user interface. Let's implement it in XAML (sometimes it's faster to work with XAML when working with a simple example that requires only a few controls). Go to Solution Explorer, open MainPage.xaml, and replace the XAML you find there with the following two blocks of code.

Declaring the UI Resources

Most of the namespaces you see in this snippet are typically declared by default when you first create a Windows Phone project. The following namespace is unique to this application and allows you to add the Bing Maps control you will use to plot your location: xmlns:BingMap="clr-namespace:Microsoft.Phone.Controls.Maps;assembly=Microsoft.Phone.Controls.Maps".

```
<phone:PhoneApplicationPage
    x:Class="BingMapDemo.MainPage"
    xmlns="http://schemas.microsoft.com/winfx/2006/xaml/presentation"
    xmlns:x="http://schemas.microsoft.com/winfx/2006/xaml"
    xmlns:phone="clr-namespace:Microsoft.Phone.Controls;assembly=Microsoft.Phone"
    xmlns:shell="clr-namespace:Microsoft.Phone.Shell;assembly=Microsoft.Phone"
    xmlns:d="http://schemas.microsoft.com/expression/blend/2008"
    xmlns:mc="http://schemas.openxmlformats.org/markup-compatibility/2006"
    xmlns:BingMap=
"clr-namespace:Microsoft.Phone.Controls.Maps;assembly=Microsoft.Phone.Controls.Maps "
    FontFamily="{StaticResource PhoneFontFamilyNormal}"
    FontSize="{StaticResource PhoneFontSizeNormal}"
    Foreground="{StaticResource PhoneForegroundBrush}"
    SupportedOrientations="Portrait" Orientation="Portrait"
    mc:Ignorable="d" d:DesignWidth="480" d:DesignHeight="768"
    shell:SystemTray.IsVisible="True">
```

Building the Main Page and Adding a Bing Maps Control

To the main page, you will be adding a Bing Maps control to display your position and a button to start the location service. You'll also add an animation storyboard named BlinkLocator to cause the locator icon to blink by changing its color. Note that inside bingMap control there is a BingMap:Pushpin named bingMapLocator. The map layer bingMapLocator contains an Ellipse control named locator, whose initial map position in latitude and longitude is (0, 0). In this application, the location service will provide changing positions in the latitude and longitude so that the locator position can be properly updated. This is a very simple but very powerful demonstration of using the location service and Bing Maps control. You can use the same technique for Yahoo or Google Maps, as their API is very similar to Bing Maps.

```
    <phone:PhoneApplicationPage.Resources>
        <Storyboard x:Name="BlinkLocator" AutoReverse="True" RepeatBehavior="Forever">
            <ColorAnimationUsingKeyFrames
Storyboard.TargetProperty="(Shape.Fill).(SolidColorBrush.Color)"
Storyboard.TargetName="locator">
                <EasingColorKeyFrame KeyTime="0" Value="Red"/>
```

```
                                <EasingColorKeyFrame KeyTime="0:0:1" Value="#FFCEFF00"/>
                    </ColorAnimationUsingKeyFrames>
        </Storyboard>
    </phone:PhoneApplicationPage.Resources>

    <Grid x:Name="LayoutRoot" Background="Transparent">
        <Grid.RowDefinitions>
            <RowDefinition Height="Auto"/>
            <RowDefinition Height="*"/>
        </Grid.RowDefinitions>

        <StackPanel x:Name="TitlePanel" Grid.Row="0" Margin="24,24,0,12">
            <TextBlock x:Name="ApplicationTitle" Text="Bing Map Demo"
                       Style="{StaticResource PhoneTextNormalStyle}"/>
        </StackPanel>

        <Grid x:Name="ContentGrid" Grid.Row="1">
            <BingMap:Map Name="bingMap" NavigationVisibility="Collapsed"
                         Margin="0,0,0,72">
                <BingMap:Pushpin Name="bingMapLocator">
                  <BingMap:Pushpin.Content>
                    <Ellipse Fill="Red" Width="20" Height="20"
                             BingMap:MapLayer.Position="0,0"
                             Name="locator" />
    <BingMap:Pushpin.Content>
            </BingMap: Pushpin>
              </BingMap:Map>
            <Button Content="Start" Height="72" HorizontalAlignment="Right"
Margin="0,633,0,0" Name="btnStart" VerticalAlignment="Top" Width="160"
Click="btnStart_Click" />
            <TextBlock Height="30" HorizontalAlignment="Left" Margin="6,657,0,0"
Name="txtStatus" Text="Status" VerticalAlignment="Top" Width="308" />
        </Grid>
    </Grid>

</phone:PhoneApplicationPage>
```

■ **Tip**   In this code, you changed the content of the Pushpin, which is the locator that specifies where you are. You can add any type of control and change the appearance of the Pushpin. You can even put a placeholder and dynamically change the content of the Pushpin.

Once you have loaded the XAML code, you should see the layout shown in Figure 14–8. In the next section, you will be adding an event to consume the GPS data and plot the data onto the map layer of the Bing Maps Silverlight control.

Figure 14–8. BingMapDemo Design view

Coding the Application

In Solution Explorer, open `MainPage.xaml.cs` and replace the code there with the following C# code blocks, which will implement the media player's functionalities.

Specifying the Namespaces

Begin by listing the namespaces the application will use. Notice the inclusion of `Microsoft.Maps.Control`, which will allow you to manipulate Bing Maps control, and `System.Device`, which will allow you to work with `geoCoordinateWatcher`, which will retrieve the location data from GPS, Wi-Fi, or cellular towers.

```
using System;
using System.Windows;
using Microsoft.Phone.Controls;
using Microsoft.Maps.MapControl;
using System.Device.Location;
namespace BingMapDemo
{
```

```
public partial class MainPage : PhoneApplicationPage
{
```

Initializing Variables

The variable _geoCoordinateWatcher is an instance of the location service class that you'll use to access and retrieve location data. Note that you will be using GeoPositionAccuracy.High, which will use the phone device's GPS, and for this to work you must use the real Windows Phone device. If you need to simulate the location service, you can refer to the previous section in this chapter or Chapter 18 to simulate fake GeoCoordinateWatcher service. Note that you'll also be setting MovementThreshold to 100 meters so that the PositionChanged event fires every 100 meters, and you'll be plotting your current location on the Bing Maps map.

GeoCoordinateWatcher has StatusChanged and PositionChanged events that notify the application whenever the new updated position is received from the GPS.

As for bingMap, you will hide the Microsoft Bing Maps logo and copyright in order to make things cleaner and make more space for other controls for the application. Finally, in order to use the map control at all, you must set ClientTokenCredentialsProvider to the value of the application key you obtained when you registered at the Bing Maps site.

```
GeoCoordinateWatcher _geoCoordinateWatcher;


public MainPage()
{
    InitializeComponent();
    // Add your own BingMap Key
    bingMap.CredentialsProvider =
new ApplicationIdCredentialsProvider("ADD-YOUR-OWN-KEY");

    // Remove Bing Maps logo and copyrights in order to gain
    // extra space at the bottom of the map
    bingMap.LogoVisibility = Visibility.Collapsed;
    bingMap.CopyrightVisibility = Visibility.Collapsed;

    // Delcare GeoCoordinateWatcher with high accuracy
    // in order to use the device's GPS
    _geoCoordinateWatcher = new GeoCoordinateWatcher(GeoPositionAccuracy.High);
    _geoCoordinateWatcher.MovementThreshold = 100;

    // Subscribe to the device's status changed event
    _geoCoordinateWatcher.StatusChanged +=
        new EventHandler<GeoPositionStatusChangedEventArgs>(
_geoCoordinateWatcher_StatusChanged);

    // Subscribe to the device's position changed event
    // to receive GPS coordinates (longitude and latitude)
    _geoCoordinateWatcher.PositionChanged +=
        New EventHandler<GeoPositionChangedEventArgs<GeoCoordinate>>(
_geoCoordinateWatcher_PositionChanged);
}
```

Responding to StatusChanged and PositionChanged GeoCoordinateWatcher Events

In GeoCoordinateWatcher, StatusChanged fires when the GPS status changes and PositionChanged fires when the GPS receives new a position. In StatusChanged, if the received status is Disabled, you must notify the user that the device's location service is disabled and must be turned on. You can enable the location service on the device by going to Settings ➤ Location ➤ Turn on the location service.

Note here that the PositionChanged event will not fire until the position of the phone has changed by at least 100 meters as specified by MovementThreshold. When the StatusChanged event fires, txtStatus will be updated, and when the PositionChanged event fires, the locator icon you have added to the Bing Maps layer will be moved accordingly.

```
        private void _geoCoordinateWatcher_PositionChanged(object sender,
GeoPositionChangedEventArgs<GeoCoordinate> e)
        {
            Deployment.Current.Dispatcher.BeginInvoke(() => ChangePosition(e));
        }

        private void ChangePosition(GeoPositionChangedEventArgs<GeoCoordinate> e)
        {
            SetLocation(e.Position.Location.Latitude,
e.Position.Location.Longitude, 10, true);
        }

        private void _geoCoordinateWatcher_StatusChanged(object sender,
GeoPositionStatusChangedEventArgs e)
        {
            Deployment.Current.Dispatcher.BeginInvoke(() => StatusChanged(e));
        }

private void StatusChanged(GeoPositionStatusChangedEventArgs e)
        {
            switch (e.Status)
            {
                case GeoPositionStatus.Disabled:
                    txtStatus.Text = "Location Service is disabled!";
                    break;
                case GeoPositionStatus.Initializing:
                    txtStatus.Text = "Initializing Location Service...";
                    break;
                case GeoPositionStatus.NoData:
                    txtStatus.Text = "Your position could not be located.";
                    break;
                case GeoPositionStatus.Ready:
                    break;
            }
        }
```

Starting the Location Service: GeoCoordinateWatcher

When the user clicks the Start button, the location service will start. TryStart will return false if the phone's location service is disabled. If the location service is disabled, a message box is displayed to the user, instructing the user to enable the location service on the phone.

```
private void btnStart_Click(object sender, RoutedEventArgs e)
{
    if (!_geoCoordinateWatcher.TryStart(true, TimeSpan.FromSeconds(5)))
    {
        MessageBox.Show("Please enable Location Service on the Phone.",
"Warning", MessageBoxButton.OK);

    }
}
```

Plotting the Location on the Bing Maps MapLayer

BingMap has a SetView method that allows you to set the current view on the screen using the location data, latitude and longitude, received from GeoCoordinateWatcher. The zoomLevel property indicates how far into the location the map will be zoomed. BingMap also has MapLayer, which can set the position of the map layer with respect to the received location. To make things interesting, let's animate bingMapLocator with simple color blinks.

```
private void SetLocation(double latitude, double longitude,
double zoomLevel, bool showLocator)
    {
        Location location = new Location(latitude, latitude);
        bingMap.SetView(location, zoomLevel);
        MapLayer.SetPosition(locator, location);
        if (showLocator)
        {
            locator.Visibility = Visibility.Visible;
            BlinkLocator.Begin();
        }
        else
        {
            locator.Visibility = Visibility.Collapsed;
            BlinkLocator.Stop();
        }
    }
}
}
```

Testing the Finished Application

To test the application, press F5. The result should resemble Figure 14–4. Remember that you must have a real phone device to be able to use real GPS. In the following section, you'll utilize Bing Maps geocoding service to convert the address into geocode of longitude and latitude in order to plot the address on the Bing Maps Silverlight control.

Plotting an Address on a Bing Maps Map and Working with the Bing Maps Service

Microsoft provides three main services hosted on the cloud to be used by any clients, including Windows Phone devices.

- *GeoCodeService* allows an address to be converted to longitude and latitude or converts geocode into an address. The web service can be consumed by accessing the URL at http://dev.virtualearth.net/webservices/v1/geocodeservice/geocodeservice.svc.

- *RouteService* includes services such as calculating the distance between two addresses, providing driving and walking directions from address to address, and step-by-step navigation. The web service can be consumed by accessing the URL at http://dev.virtualearth.net/webservices/v1/routeservice/routeservice.svc.

- *SearchService* provides location-based search results. For example, based on the submitted address, it will find restaurants in a five-mile radius. The web service can be consumed by accessing the URL at http://dev.virtualearth.net/webservices/v1/searchservice/searchservice.svc.

In the following section, you will be using GeoCodeService to convert any address into geocode (longitude and latitude) and plot the address on the Bing Maps Silverlight Control. Through the demo, you will learn how to access the Bing Maps service using the credentials you received when you registered.

The following demo interface will contain a text box where you can enter an address to be plotted on the map and a button to invoke a method to convert the address using the Bing Maps geocode service. It then plots the geocode onto the Bing Maps Silverlight control, as shown in Figure 14–9.

Figure 14–9. AddressPlottingDemo application

Creating the AddressPlottingDemo Application

To set up the BingMapDemo project, follow the steps you used for previous examples in this book:

1. Open Microsoft Visual Studio 2010 Express for Windows Phone on your workstation.

2. Create a new Windows Phone Application by selecting File ➤ New Project on the Visual Studio command menu. Select the Windows Phone Application template, and name the application AddressPlottingDemo.

3. In order to use Bing Maps control in Windows Phone, you must reference `Microsoft.Phone.Controls.Maps` and `System.Device`.

Adding a Service Reference to the Bing Maps GeoCodeService

In order to use the Bing Maps GeoCodeService, you need to add a service reference to your project.

1. In Solution Explorer, right-click the References folder and choose Add Service Reference.

2. When the Add Service Reference window pops up, enter `http://dev.virtualearth.net/webservices/v1/geocodeservice/geocodeservic e.svc` into the Address field and press Go.

3. You see a list of services. In the Namespace text box, enter BingMapGeoCodeService. You should see a result similar to Figure 14–10.

Figure 14–10. *Adding a service reference*

4. Click OK and you should see BingMapGeoCodeService in Solution Explorer, as shown in Figure 14–11.

Solution 'AddressPlottingDemo' (1 project)
- **AddressPlottingDemo**
  - Properties
  - References
    - Microsoft.Phone
    - Microsoft.Phone.Controls.Maps
    - Microsoft.Phone.Interop
    - mscorlib
    - system
    - System.Core
    - System.Device
    - System.Net
    - System.Runtime.Serialization
    - System.ServiceModel
    - System.Windows
    - System.Xml
  - Service References
    - BingMapGeoCodeService
  - App.xaml
  - ApplicationIcon.png
  - Background.png
  - MainPage.xaml
    - MainPage.xaml.cs
  - ServiceReferences.ClientConfig
  - SplashScreenImage.jpg

Figure 14–11. Bing Maps GeoCodeService in Service References folder

Coding the User Interface

AddressPlottingDemo has a very simple UI, consisting of the textblock for capturing the address, the button to invoke a method for plotting the address onto the map, and the Bing Maps Silverlight control.

Declaring the UI Resources

The namespaces you see in the following code snippet are typically declared by default when you first create a Windows Phone project. In particular, namespace xmlns:phone="clr-namespace:Microsoft.Phone.Controls;assembly=Microsoft.Phone" allows you to add common Windows Phone controls to the application main page.

```
<phone:PhoneApplicationPage
    x:Class="AddressPlottingDemo.MainPage"
    xmlns="http://schemas.microsoft.com/winfx/2006/xaml/presentation"
    xmlns:x="http://schemas.microsoft.com/winfx/2006/xaml"
    xmlns:phone="clr-namespace:Microsoft.Phone.Controls;assembly=Microsoft.Phone"
    xmlns:shell="clr-namespace:Microsoft.Phone.Shell;assembly=Microsoft.Phone"
    xmlns:d="http://schemas.microsoft.com/expression/blend/2008"
    xmlns:mc="http://schemas.openxmlformats.org/markup-compatibility/2006"
    xmlns:BingMap="clr-
namespace:Microsoft.Phone.Controls.Maps;assembly=Microsoft.Phone.Controls.Maps"
    mc:Ignorable="d" d:DesignWidth="480" d:DesignHeight="768"
    FontFamily="{StaticResource PhoneFontFamilyNormal}"
    FontSize="{StaticResource PhoneFontSizeNormal}"
    Foreground="{StaticResource PhoneForegroundBrush}"
    SupportedOrientations="Portrait" Orientation="Portrait"
    shell:SystemTray.IsVisible="True">
```

Creating the Main Page

The main page consists of the Bing Maps Silverlight control, a button, and an address textblock to capture the user address input. Notice on the bingMap control that CopyrightVisibility and LogoVisibity are set to Collapsed, giving you much more needed real estate on the screen.

```
<Grid x:Name="LayoutRoot" Background="Transparent">
    <Grid.RowDefinitions>
        <RowDefinition Height="Auto"/>
        <RowDefinition Height="*"/>
    </Grid.RowDefinitions>

    <StackPanel x:Name="TitlePanel" Grid.Row="0"
                Margin="12,17,0,28">
        <TextBlock x:Name="ApplicationTitle"
                Text="AddressPlottingDemo"
                Style="{StaticResource PhoneTextNormalStyle}"/>
    </StackPanel>

    <Grid x:Name="ContentPanel" Grid.Row="1" Margin="12,0,12,0">

        <BingMap:Map Name="bingMap"
                Width="425" Height="513"
                Margin="0,0,19,25"
                CopyrightVisibility="Collapsed"
                LogoVisibility="Collapsed"
                VerticalAlignment="Bottom" HorizontalAlignment="Right">
            <BingMap:Pushpin Name="bingMapLocator"
                    Background="Transparent">
                <BingMap:Pushpin.Content>
                    <Ellipse Fill="Red" Width="20" Height="20"
                        Name="locator" />
                </BingMap:Pushpin.Content>
```

```
                </BingMap:Pushpin>
            </BingMap:Map>
            <TextBox Height="72" Margin="110,10,6,0" Name="txtAddress"
                    Text="4237 Salisbury Rd, Suite 114 Jacksonville FL, 32216"
                    VerticalAlignment="Top" />
            <TextBlock Height="30" HorizontalAlignment="Left"
                    Margin="33,32,0,0" Name="textBlock1"
                    Text="Address" VerticalAlignment="Top" />
            <Button Content="Show on map" Height="72"
                    Name="btnPlot" Margin="17,68,192,556"
                    Click="btnPlot_Click" />
        </Grid>
    </Grid>
</phone:PhoneApplicationPage>
```

Coding the Application

One of most important things to notice in this demo application is its use of the Bing Maps geocode service to convert a street address to longitude and latitude measures so that it can be plotted on the map. Also, in order to use the Bing Maps geocode service, you must provide the Bing Maps credential that you created during the registration.

Specifying the Namespaces

Once the service is referenced, you will be able to declare the namespace of the Bing Maps geocode service, AddressPlottingDemo.BingMapGeoCodeService. You are including System.Linq because you will be using Linq to query returned GeoCodeResults with the highest confidence.

```
using System.Windows;
using Microsoft.Phone.Controls;
using AddressPlottingDemo.BingMapGeoCodeService;
using Microsoft.Phone.Controls.Maps;
using System.Collections.ObjectModel;
using System.Linq;
```

Initializing Variables

The GeocodeServiceClient variable _svc is a proxy class that lets you connect to the Bing Maps geocode service to geocode the address in order to plot on the map. Note that you need to subscribe to GeocodeCompleted event in order to receive results that contains longitude and latitude.

```
        GeocodeServiceClient _svc;
        public MainPage()
        {
            InitializeComponent();

            // instantiate Bing Maps GeocodeService
            _svc = new GeocodeServiceClient("BasicHttpBinding_IGeocodeService");
```

```
                    _svc.GeocodeCompleted += (s, e) =>
                        {
                            // sort the returned record by ascending confidence in order for
                            // highest confidence to be on the top.
            // Based on the numeration High value is
                            // at 0, Medium value at 1 and Low voule at 2
                            var geoResult = (from r in e.Result.Results
                                             orderby (int)r.Confidence ascending
                                             select r).FirstOrDefault();
                            if (geoResult != null)
                            {
                                this.SetLocation(geoResult.Locations[0].Latitude,
                                    geoResult.Locations[0].Longitude,
                                    10,
                                    true);
                            }
                        };
                }
```

Handling the Button Event That Plots Address Data onto the Bing Maps Map

When btnPlot is clicked, you will be making a web service request to the Bing Maps geocode service to convert txtAddress.Text to return geocoordinates in longitude and latitude. When the GeoCodeCompleted event is raised, you will receive multiple results that contain only the highest confidence level. Using GeoCodeResult, you will be making a call to SetLocation that will plot the location on the Bing Maps Silverlight control.

```
private void SetLocation(double latitude, double longitude,
double zoomLevel, bool showLocator)
        {
                // Move the pushpin to geo coordinate
                Microsoft.Phone.Controls.Maps.Platform.Location location =
new Microsoft.Phone.Controls.Maps.Platform.Location();
                location.Latitude = latitude;
                location.Longitude = longitude;
                bingMap.SetView(location, zoomLevel);
                bingMapLocator.Location = location;
                if (showLocator)
                {
                    locator.Visibility = Visibility.Visible;
                }
                else
                {
                    locator.Visibility = Visibility.Collapsed;
                }
        }

        private void btnPlot_Click(object sender, RoutedEventArgs e)
        {
                BingMapGeoCodeService.GeocodeRequest request =
```

```
new BingMapGeoCodeService.GeocodeRequest();

            // Only accept results with high confidence.
            request.Options = new GeocodeOptions()
            {
                Filters = new ObservableCollection<FilterBase>
                {
                    new ConfidenceFilter()
                    {
                        MinimumConfidence = Confidence.High
                    }
                }
            };


            request.Credentials = new Credentials()
            {
                ApplicationId = "Put-Your-BingMap-Credential-Id"
            };

            request.Query = txtAddress.Text;

            // Make asynchronous call to fetch the geo coordinate data.
            _svc.GeocodeAsync(request);
        }
```

Testing the Finished Application

To test the application, press F5. The result should resemble the display shown in Figure 14–9. Enter an address into Address text box and press the "Show on map" button. You should see the pushpin move from its current position to the coordinates provided by the Bing Maps geocode service.

Summary

In this chapter, you learned how to start the location service to receive the position in latitude and longitude. Upon receiving the position, you passed the location data into the Bing Maps control and use the Bing Maps map layer to indicate your current GPS position. This simple but powerful concept will help you create your own location-aware application. Also, you learned how to utilize the Bing Maps geocode service, which converts the address to geocoordinates so you can plot the address location on the map.

In Chapter 15, you will learn how to use the media elements of the phone to play video and audio as well as stream movies and sounds from external sites. You will also learn how media elements play a significant role in making sound effects in a game.

CHAPTER 15

Media

In today's smartphone era, content is everything. Think of YouTube, which provides fun videos to the masses through the Internet. Now smartphones, too, have the ability to play high-quality movies, music, and more, anywhere. What was once possible only on a desktop computer can now be done with the smartphone you carry all the time, regardless of whether you are near a cell tower or Wi-Fi connection.

Windows Phones come equipped with powerful media features for developers and designers to use to create compelling applications that can play back music, audio, and video in a host of formats. A good example of such functionality can be found at the NBC Olympics web site, where the Olympic games were streamed live, then archived, and can now be viewed again in high definition (`www.nbcolympics.com/video/index.html`). The NBC Olympic video player includes a BOSS button, which, when clicked, pauses the video player and pops up a full-screen display that resembles Microsoft Excel, creating the impression for you-know-who that you are working really hard. Another example are the pay-per-view fighting matches from the Ultimate Fighting Championship (UFC) that are streamed live at `http://modules.ufc.com/live/`.

MediaElement provides more than just a simple video player. Windows Phone provides the ability to play videos and sounds, listen to FM radio, interact with the music and video hub, and launch Windows Marketplace to allow the user to buy songs.

In this chapter, you will learn how to embed media in your application and customize a media player control to play videos and sounds using MediaElement. You'll also learn to use MediaPlayerLauncher, which activates the stand-alone media player application that ships with Windows Phone. (Please refer to Chapter 5 for more information on how to direct users to Windows Marketplace to buy your application. Also, this chapter won't be covering FMRadio API but you can find information on it at `http://msdn.microsoft.com/en-us/library/ ff769541(VS.92).aspx`.)

Introducing MediaElement

MediaElement is a Windows Phone control that you can add to an application to play video and sound. It first appeared with .NET and was later ported to Silverlight and then to Windows Phone. When the MediaElement control is placed on the Visual Studio or Blend Design view, you will see only a rectangle, which is not what you would expect of a video or audio player. This is because the MediaElement control is left in somewhat of a blank slate to give designers full control over the look of the play, stop, pause, mute, and seek buttons. For developers, MediaElement exposes APIs for full control of a player's play, stop, pause, mute, and seek behavior, as well as stream buffering, the progress of downloads, and volume control.

You'll want to use MediaElement when you are creating an application that requires more than a simple media player and you want it to be a part of your application—not something you have to exit the application to access. Also, MediaElement provides flexibility to customize the look and add more functionality, like being able to share videos via Twitter, Facebook, SMS, or e-mail; you can even allow the user to add ratings and comments. Another option is creating a video player that offers chapters plus thumbnails of each chapter.

MediaPlayerLauncher is more useful if you simply want to play video or audio using the default media player of the Windows Phone. The default media player that comes with Windows Phone supports basic functions such as play, pause, move forward, move backward, and play time elapsed. MediaElement will support a variety of video and audio formats. See Table 15–1 for the most commonly used formats that are supported by Windows Phone; a complete list can be found at `http://msdn.microsoft.com/en-us/library/ff462087(VS.92).aspx`.

Table 15–1. Media Formats Supported on Windows Phone

Media Type	Supported Formats
Audio	WAV, MP3, WMA, MP4
Video	WMV, MP4, AVI
Images	JPEG, PNG, GIF, BMP, TIF

The first demo will show you a technique to stream a video file from the Internet or play a video file that's part of the application content using MediaElement, and then you will learn to play the same video content using MediaPlayerLauncher.

Working with Video

In this demo, you will build a media player (for video and audio) that can play, stop, pause, mute, and seek (which is a video player function that lets you move the video forward or backward to any position); the UI is shown in Figure 15–1. You will learn to stream video content from the Internet as well as play content that is part of the application. (Note that you won't want to package the video as part of the phone application because video or audio files are very large).

In the real world, you must think about the strategy of deploying media content to the Web and allowing the phone application to simply play the URL. In Chapter 13, you learned about caching the image download into the isolated storage. The same technique can be used to download video or music content the first time and then save it into isolated storage.

Another approach is to store video content on a Windows IIS media server and take advantage of the smooth streaming technology for HD-quality content and Microsoft DRM protection the server provides. Netflix, for example, uses DRM technology to secure the content of its streaming videos. Microsoft DRM provides a platform to protect digital materials and deliver content that can be played on any device. Also, IIS media server can effectively distribute the HD video content to low-bandwidth and low-performing computers via smooth streaming technology. If you would like to learn more about DRM using IIS media streaming server, please refer to `http://msdn.microsoft.com/en-us/library/cc838192(VS.95).aspx`, as you will not be learning about this advanced topic in this chapter.

Yet another way to store video content is in the cloud using Microsoft Azure. Please refer to Chapter 3 for Windows Azure data store.

Figure 15–1. *Media Player Demo application*

You will build the demo application in three major steps. First you will create a Windows Phone project. Then you will build the user interface of the media player and you'll finish up by wiring up the commands in the code that respond to the user.

Creating the MediaPlayerDemo Project

To create the Video Demo project, follow the steps from previous examples in this book.

1. Open Microsoft Visual Studio 2010 Express for Windows Phone on your workstation.

2. Create a new Windows Phone Application by selecting File ➤ New Project on the Visual Studio command menu. Select the Windows Phone Application template, name the application MediaPlayerDemo, and click OK.

Building the User Interface

You will build the user interface in Visual Studio with XAML (for building simple controls, it's faster to work with the XAML code). Go to Solution Explorer, open `MainPage.xaml`, and replace the XAML you find there with the following code snippets.

Declaring the UI Resources

The namespaces you see in the following code snippets are typically declared by default when you first create the Windows Phone project. The namespace `xmlns:phone="clr-namespace:Microsoft.Phone.Controls;assembly=Microsoft.Phone"` allows you to add common Windows Phone controls required to build this demo: buttons, textblocks, text boxes, list boxes, sliders, and media elements.

```
<phone:PhoneApplicationPage
    x:Class="MediaPlayerDemo.MainPage"
    xmlns="http://schemas.microsoft.com/winfx/2006/xaml/presentation"
    xmlns:x="http://schemas.microsoft.com/winfx/2006/xaml"
    xmlns:phone="clr-namespace:Microsoft.Phone.Controls;assembly=Microsoft.Phone"
    xmlns:shell="clr-namespace:Microsoft.Phone.Shell;assembly=Microsoft.Phone"
    xmlns:d="http://schemas.microsoft.com/expression/blend/2008"
    xmlns:mc="http://schemas.openxmlformats.org/markup-compatibility/2006"
    FontFamily="{StaticResource PhoneFontFamilyNormal}"
    FontSize="{StaticResource PhoneFontSizeNormal}"
    Foreground="{StaticResource PhoneForegroundBrush}"
    SupportedOrientations="Portrait" Orientation="Portrait"
    mc:Ignorable="d" d:DesignWidth="480" d:DesignHeight="768"
    shell:SystemTray.IsVisible="True">
```

Building the Main Page and Adding Media Player Components

Next, add the code shown in Listing 15–1, which creates the common media controls the application will use, like play, pause, stop, mute, and seek. You will be using the Slider control to implement the function that will allow the user to see how much time is elapsed in playing the media content. Also, by clicking the Slider, the user can skip backward and forward. You will also be adding labels to track video buffering and video downloading status using the textblocks. Lastly, a button called btnMediaPlayerLauncher will launch the default Windows Phone's media player to play the media content.

Listing 15–1. Custom Media Player Main Page and UI (XAML)

```
<phone:PhoneApplicationPage
    x:Class="MediaPlayerDemo.MainPage"
    xmlns="http://schemas.microsoft.com/winfx/2006/xaml/presentation"
```

```xml
xmlns:x="http://schemas.microsoft.com/winfx/2006/xaml"
xmlns:phone="clr-namespace:Microsoft.Phone.Controls;assembly=Microsoft.Phone"
xmlns:shell="clr-namespace:Microsoft.Phone.Shell;assembly=Microsoft.Phone"
xmlns:d="http://schemas.microsoft.com/expression/blend/2008"
xmlns:mc="http://schemas.openxmlformats.org/markup-compatibility/2006"
FontFamily="{StaticResource PhoneFontFamilyNormal}"
FontSize="{StaticResource PhoneFontSizeNormal}"
Foreground="{StaticResource PhoneForegroundBrush}"
SupportedOrientations="Portrait" Orientation="Portrait"
mc:Ignorable="d" d:DesignWidth="480" d:DesignHeight="768"
shell:SystemTray.IsVisible="True">

<Grid x:Name="LayoutRoot" Background="Transparent">
    <Grid.RowDefinitions>
        <RowDefinition Height="Auto"/>
        <RowDefinition Height="*"/>
    </Grid.RowDefinitions>

    <StackPanel x:Name="TitlePanel" Grid.Row="0" Margin="24,24,0,12">
        <TextBlock x:Name="PageTitle" Text="MediaPlayerDemo" Margin="-3,-8,0,0"
                   Style="{StaticResource PhoneTextTitle1Style}" FontSize="48" />
    </StackPanel>

    <Grid x:Name="ContentGrid" Grid.Row="1">
        <MediaElement Height="289" HorizontalAlignment="Left"
                      Margin="26,148,0,0" x:Name="mediaPlayer"
                      VerticalAlignment="Top" Width="417"
                      AutoPlay="False"/>
        <Button Content="&gt;" Height="72"
                HorizontalAlignment="Left" Margin="13,527,0,0"
                x:Name="btnPlay" VerticalAlignment="Top" Width="87"
                Click="btnPlay_Click" />
        <Button Content="O" Height="72"
                HorizontalAlignment="Right" Margin="0,527,243,0"
                x:Name="btnStop" VerticalAlignment="Top" Width="87"
                Click="btnStop_Click" />
        <Button Content="||" Height="72" Margin="0,527,313,0"
                x:Name="btnPause" VerticalAlignment="Top"
                Click="btnPause_Click" HorizontalAlignment="Right" Width="87" />
        <Slider Height="84" HorizontalAlignment="Left"
                Margin="13,423,0,0" Name="mediaTimeline"
                VerticalAlignment="Top" Width="443"
                ValueChanged="mediaTimeline_ValueChanged"
                Maximum="1" LargeChange="0.1" />
        <TextBlock Height="30" HorizontalAlignment="Left"
                   Margin="26,472,0,0" Name="lblStatus"
                   Text="00:00" VerticalAlignment="Top" Width="88" FontSize="16" />
        <TextBlock Height="30"
                   Margin="118,472,222,0" x:Name="lblBuffering"
                   Text="Buffering" VerticalAlignment="Top" FontSize="16" />
        <TextBlock Height="30"
                   Margin="0,472,82,0" x:Name="lblDownload"
```

```
                    Text="Download" VerticalAlignment="Top" FontSize="16"
    HorizontalAlignment="Right" Width="140" />
              <Button Content="Mute" Height="72"
                    HorizontalAlignment="Left" Margin="217,527,0,0"
                    Name="btnMute" VerticalAlignment="Top" Width="89"
                    FontSize="16" Click="btnMute_Click" />
              <TextBlock Height="30" HorizontalAlignment="Left"
                    Margin="315,551,0,0" Name="lblSoundStatus"
                    Text="Sound On" VerticalAlignment="Top" Width="128" />
              <Button Content="Use MediaPlayerLauncher" FontSize="24" Height="72"
                    HorizontalAlignment="Left" Margin="13,591,0,0"
                    Name="btnMediaPlayerLauncher" VerticalAlignment="Top"
                    Width="411" Click="btnMediaPlayerLauncher_Click" />
              <TextBox x:Name="txtUrl" Height="57" Margin="91,33,8,0"
                    TextWrapping="Wrap" VerticalAlignment="Top" FontSize="16"

    Text="http://ecn.channel9.msdn.com/o9/ch9/7/8/2/9/1/5/ARCastMDISilverlightGridComputing_ch9.wm
    v"/>
              <TextBlock x:Name="lblUrl" HorizontalAlignment="Left" Height="25"
                    Margin="8,48,0,0" TextWrapping="Wrap" Text="Video URL:"
                    VerticalAlignment="Top" Width="83" FontSize="16"/>
              <TextBox x:Name="txtBufferingTime" Height="57" Margin="151,78,0,0"
                    TextWrapping="Wrap" VerticalAlignment="Top" FontSize="16"
    HorizontalAlignment="Left" Width="86" Text="20"/>
              <TextBlock x:Name="lblBufferingTime" HorizontalAlignment="Left"
                    Height="25" Margin="8,93,0,0" TextWrapping="Wrap"
                    Text="Buffering Time (s):" VerticalAlignment="Top"
                    Width="139" FontSize="16"/>
        </Grid>
    </Grid>

</phone:PhoneApplicationPage>
```

Once you have loaded the XAML code, you should see the layout shown in Figure 15–2. In the next section, you will add code to respond to UI events and implement MediaElement's behaviors.

Figure 15–2. *MediaPlayerDemo Design view*

Coding the Application

In Solution Explorer, open `MainPage.xaml.cs` and replace the code you find there with the following C#
code blocks to implement the media player's functions.

Specifying the Namespaces

Begin by listing the namespaces the application will use. The inclusion of `Microsoft.Phone.Tasks` will
allow you to launch Windows Phone's default media player. As for the MediaElement, it is declared in
the XAML page, which you will simply reference here by the control's name. Also, you'll need to add
reference to `Microsoft.Xna.Framework` that you will be using to check if background music is currently
being played before playing your own video. This is necessary in order to pass the "Applications that
Play Music section 6.5.1." marketplace certification.

```
using System;
using System.Windows;
using System.Windows.Media;
using Microsoft.Phone.Controls;using Microsoft.Phone.Tasks;
using Microsoft.Xna.Framework;

using Microsoft.Xna.Framework.Media;
```

```
namespace MediaPlayerDemo
{
    public partial class MainPage : PhoneApplicationPage
```

Initializing Variables

The variable _updatingMediaTimeline is an extremely important variable that stops the infinite loop in this demo. By setting _updatingMediaTimeline to true while the media timeline (Slider control) is being updated during the CompositionTarget.Rendering event, the media's backward and forward event will wait to be processed until the timeline update is completed. Another way to look at this complexity is to see the purpose of the Slider control that is responsible for displaying the timeline of the media being played. But the Slider control is also responsible for allowing the user to interact to drag the slider forward or backward in order to move the media position. _updatingMediaTimeline will allow only one specific behavior to happen in the Slider control, thereby avoiding unwanted application behavior.

```
        private bool _updatingMediaTimeline;

        public MainPage()
        {
            InitializeComponent();

            _updatingMediaTimeline = false;

            // rewinds the media player to the beginning
            mediaPlayer.Position = System.TimeSpan.FromSeconds(0);
```

Handling Video Download Progress

As the video file download progresses, you will be receiving the percentage of the file downloaded and you will be displaying the progress updates back to the user by updating the lblDownload.

```
        // Download indicator
        mediaPlayer.DownloadProgressChanged += (s, e) =>
            {
                lblDownload.Text = string.Format("Downloading {0:0.0%}",
mediaPlayer.DownloadProgress);
            };
```

Handling Video Buffering

You will be setting video BufferingTime property, and as the video buffering time progresses, you will receive a callback where you will update lblBuffering.

```
                // Handle media buffering
                mediaPlayer.BufferingTime =
                                    TimeSpan.FromSeconds(Convert.ToDouble(txtBufferingTime.Text));
                mediaPlayer.BufferingProgressChanged += (s, e) =>
                    {
                        lblBuffering.Text = string.Format("Buffering {0:0.0%}",
mediaPlayer.BufferingProgress);
                    };
```

Showing Time Elapsed in the Media Player

CompositionTarget.Rendering is a frame-based event that will fire once per frame, allowing you to update the media timeline (Slider control) that reflects how much of the media is played. By default, the event will fire 60 times in one second. You can check this by checking the value of Application.Current.Host.Settings.MaxFrameRate. By using the CompositionTarget.Rendering event, you will be able to see the smooth media player timeline filling up as the media plays.

```
                // Updates the media time line (slider control) with total time played
                // and updates the status with the time played
                CompositionTarget.Rendering += (s, e) =>
                    {
                        _updatingMediaTimeline = true;
                        TimeSpan duration = mediaPlayer.NaturalDuration.TimeSpan;
                        if (duration.TotalSeconds != 0)
                        {
                            double percentComplete =
mediaPlayer.Position.TotalSeconds / duration.TotalSeconds;
                            mediaTimeline.Value = percentComplete;
                            TimeSpan mediaTime = mediaPlayer.Position;
                            string text = string.Format("{0:00}:{1:00}",
                                (mediaTime.Hours * 60) + mediaTime.Minutes, mediaTime.Seconds);

                            if (lblStatus.Text != text)
                                lblStatus.Text = text;

                            _updatingMediaTimeline = false;
                        }
                    };
            }
```

■ **Tip**   When defining the event handler of `CompositionTarget.Rendering`, you can use the lambda expression to create a delegate that contains the programming logic. For example, you can rewrite `CompositionTarget.Rendering += (s, e) => { … }` by first declaring the event handler `CompositionTarget.Rendering += new EventHandler(CompositionTarget_Rendering)` and then creating a method `void CompositionTarget_Rendering(object sender, EventArgs e) { … }`. Using the lambda expression technique makes the code much more readable, and in this demo project, gives you the ability to group the relevant code together. For more information on the lambda expression, please refer to `http://msdn.microsoft.com/en-us/library/bb397687.aspx`.

Implementing the Pause Button

When the Pause button is clicked, invoke MediaElement.Pause to pause the media player. Note that you are updating the Status label, communicating to the user the media is in pause mode. Occasionally, for unknown reasons, the media player may not be able to pause. You can use mediaPlayer.CanPause to make sure you can pause; otherwise, set the Status label to warn the user it could not pause.

```
private void btnPause_Click(object sender, RoutedEventArgs e)
{
    if (mediaPlayer.CanPause)
    {
        mediaPlayer.Pause();
        lblStatus.Text = "Paused";
    }
    else
    {
        lblStatus.Text = "Can not be Paused. Please try again!";
    }
}
```

Implementing the Stop Button

When the stop button is clicked, invoke MediaElement.Stop to stop the media player and then rewind the media player back to the beginning and update the Status label as Stopped.

```
private void btnStop_Click(object sender, RoutedEventArgs e)
{
    mediaPlayer.Stop();
    mediaPlayer.Position = System.TimeSpan.FromSeconds(0);
    lblStatus.Text = "Stopped";
}
```

Implementing the Play Button

When the play button is clicked, invoke MediaElement.Play to play the media player. But before you can play, you must check to make sure no background music is being played. For example, if the user is using the phone to play music and then he enters your application, your application must confirm with the user that you will be playing your own video or music which will interrupt his already playing music. If you don't confirm with the user the permission to play the music, your application will fail the "Applications that Play Music section 6.5.1" of the market certification. The **CanPlay** method uses XNA media framework's MediaPlayer to check if the GameHasControl to play the sound, which will tell you if the user entered your application playing his or her own music.

```
private void btnPlay_Click(object sender, RoutedEventArgs e)
{
    if (this.CanPlay())
    {
        mediaPlayer.Play();
    }
}

private bool CanPlay()
{
    bool canPlay = false;

    FrameworkDispatcher.Update();
    if (MediaPlayer.GameHasControl)
    {
        canPlay = true;
    }
    else
    {
        if (MessageBox.Show
        ("Is it ok to stop currently playing music and play our animal sounds?"
        , "Can play our sounds?"
        , MessageBoxButton.OKCancel) == MessageBoxResult.OK)
        {
            canPlay = true;
            MediaPlayer.Pause();
            AboutViewModel.Instance.CanPlay = true;
        }
        else
        {
            canPlay = false;
            AboutViewModel.Instance.CanPlay = false;
        }
    }

    return canPlay;
}
```

Implementing the Mute Button

When the Mute button is clicked, set MediaElement.IsMuted to true in order to mute the sound or set it to false to turn on the sound.

```
private void btnMute_Click(object sender, RoutedEventArgs e)
{
    if (lblSoundStatus.Text.Equals("Sound On",
StringComparison.CurrentCultureIgnoreCase))
    {
        lblSoundStatus.Text = "Sound Off";
        mediaPlayer.IsMuted = true;
    }
    else
    {
        lblSoundStatus.Text = "Sound On";
        mediaPlayer.IsMuted = false;
    }

}
```

■ **Note**   To mute the player, you could also have set MediaElement.Volume to zero instead of setting the IsMuted property to true, as shown here.

Implementing Seek

When the Slider control that displays the timeline of the media is clicked or dragged, MediaElement.Position moves either forward or backward, depending on the user's input on the Slider control. Figure 15–3 shows dragging the slider to the right in order to move forward in the video timeline.

```
private void mediaTimeline_ValueChanged(object sender,
                                        RoutedPropertyChangedEventArgs<double> e)
{
    if (!_updatingMediaTimeline && mediaPlayer.CanSeek)
    {
        TimeSpan duration = mediaPlayer.NaturalDuration.TimeSpan;
        int newPosition = (int)(duration.TotalSeconds * mediaTimeline.Value);
        mediaPlayer.Position = new TimeSpan(0, 0, newPosition);
    }
}
```

Figure 15–3. Dragging the slider to skip the video

■ **Note** Using MediaElement.Position, you can jump to any part of the media. This is very useful when you want to create chapters in a movie similar to those you see in DVD players.

Implementing the MediaPlayerLauncher

When the MediaPlayerLauncher button is clicked, invoke the MediaPlayerLauncher task to launch the default Windows Phone media player.

```
private void btnMediaPlayerLauncher_Click(object sender, RoutedEventArgs e)
{
    MediaPlayerLauncher player = new MediaPlayerLauncher();
```

```
            player.Media = new
Uri("http://ecn.channel9.msdn.com/o9/ch9/7/8/2/9/1/5/
ARCastMDISilverlightGridComputing_ch9.wmv");
            //player.Media =
//          new Uri("ARCastMDISilverlightGridComputing_ch9.wmv",
//                          UriKind.Relative);
            //player.Location = MediaLocationType.Data;
            player.Show();
        }
```

■ **Note** In the commented code where MediaPlayerLauncher is going to play the content that is part of the application, you can see that player.Location is set to MediaLocationType.Data, which means that it will look at the isolated storage for the file named `ARCastMDISilverlightGridComputing_ch9.wmv`. Refer to Chapter 13 for the isolated storage demo where the file was downloaded the first time and then saved into the isolated storage for later access. If you set player.Location to MediaLocationType.Install, the media file must be added to the application as the content; also, the media source's `Uri` must have UriKind.Relative, which basically means the file is part of the application. The only problem with this is that the size of the application install will get much bigger.

Testing the Finished Application

To test the application, press F5. The result should resemble Figure 15–1. Try clicking each button: Play, Pause, Stop, and Mute. As the movie plays, take note of the buffering and downloading progress status. You can also drag the slider back and forth to skip around the movie scenes. Feel free to enter your favorite movie link.

In this demo, you created a custom media player and then launched the default Windows Phone media player. Both MediaElement and MediaPlayerLauncher accessed the video content on the Web because video files are typically very big. But if you are adding simple sound effects to an application, it's not always ideal to download the contents from the Web; a better solution is to package the sound along with the application. This is especially true if you are planning to create a game where all the graphical and media assets are packaged as the part of the application. In the next demo, you will learn how to add sound effects to an application.

Adding Sounds to an Application

Sounds can be used in applications and games. In the first demo, you played video, but you can also use MediaElement to play music files or to create sound effects in a game. In this demo, you will learn how to apply a sound effect to an animated object—in this case, a flying robot. Such sound effects are essential to games.

Figure 15–4 shows the UI of the demo application. When you press the Play button, the robot flies diagonally toward the bottom right-hand corner of the screen. When it reaches an edge, the robot will bounce several times while making a swoosh sound to give the animation that dash of realism it needs to satisfy gamers.

Figure 15–4. Robot sound demo

You will build the RobotSoundDemo in three steps. Start by creating a Windows Phone project. Then you'll build the UI, and then you'll add the code to handle control events.

Creating the RobotSoundDemo Project

To create the Video Demo project, follow the steps from previous examples in this book.

1. Open Microsoft Visual Studio 2010 Express for Windows Phone on your workstation.

2. Create a new Windows Phone Application by selecting File ➤ New Project on the Visual Studio command menu. Select the Windows Phone Application template, name the application RobotSoundDemo, and click OK.

Building the User Interface

Before you can build the user interface, you need to add the following three files to the project:

- Robot.xaml

- Robot.xaml.cs

- sound18.wma

Once you have successfully added these files to the project, you see the following list of files in the Solution Explorer window, as shown in Figure 15–5.

```
Solution 'RobotSoundDemo' (1 project)
▲  RobotSoundDemo
    ▷   Properties
    ▷   References
    ▷   App.xaml
        ApplicationIcon.png
        Background.png
    ▷   MainPage.xaml
    ▲   Robot.xaml
            Robot.xaml.cs
        sound18.wma
        sound26.wma
        SplashScreenImage.jpg
```

Figure 15–5. RobotSoundDemo project after adding the assets

All three files are included in the source code that is distributed with this book; located in your unzipped directory of the source codes (c:\[where you unzipped]\Codes\ch15\Assets) are the assets necessary for this demo. Robot.xaml and Robot.xaml.cs are the vector graphic versions of the robot and sound18.wma is the sound effect file for when the robot moves.

Selecting the UI Resources

You will be adding the namespace of the robot asset you just added to the project using xmlns:uc="clr-namespace:RobotSoundDemo". This namespace will allow you to add the robot user control using the XAML code that looks like <uc:Robot x:Name="ucRobot" …>.

```
<phone:PhoneApplicationPage
    x:Class="RobotSoundDemo.MainPage"
    xmlns="http://schemas.microsoft.com/winfx/2006/xaml/presentation"
    xmlns:x="http://schemas.microsoft.com/winfx/2006/xaml"
    xmlns:phone="clr-namespace:Microsoft.Phone.Controls;assembly=Microsoft.Phone"
```

```
xmlns:shell="clr-namespace:Microsoft.Phone.Shell;assembly=Microsoft.Phone"
xmlns:d="http://schemas.microsoft.com/expression/blend/2008"
xmlns:mc="http://schemas.openxmlformats.org/markup-compatibility/2006"
xmlns:uc="clr-namespace:RobotSoundDemo"
FontFamily="{StaticResource PhoneFontFamilyNormal}"
FontSize="{StaticResource PhoneFontSizeNormal}"
Foreground="{StaticResource PhoneForegroundBrush}"
SupportedOrientations="Portrait" Orientation="Portrait"
mc:Ignorable="d" d:DesignWidth="480" d:DesignHeight="768"
shell:SystemTray.IsVisible="True">
```

Adding Robot Animation to the Main Page Resource Section

In the Main Page resource section, add the robot storyboard animation of moving from top left corner to bottom right. The bouncing EasingFunction is added to the robot's movement, which will cause the robot to bounce toward the end of the movement.

```
<phone:PhoneApplicationPage.Resources>
        <Storyboard x:Name="MoveRobot">
                <DoubleAnimationUsingKeyFrames
Storyboard.TargetProperty="(UIElement.RenderTransform).(CompositeTransform.TranslateX)"
Storyboard.TargetName="ucRobot">
                        <EasingDoubleKeyFrame KeyTime="0" Value="0"/>
                        <EasingDoubleKeyFrame KeyTime="0:0:0.6" Value="244">
                                <EasingDoubleKeyFrame.EasingFunction>
                                        <BounceEase EasingMode="EaseOut"/>
                                </EasingDoubleKeyFrame.EasingFunction>
                        </EasingDoubleKeyFrame>
                </DoubleAnimationUsingKeyFrames>
                <DoubleAnimationUsingKeyFrames
Storyboard.TargetProperty="(UIElement.RenderTransform).(CompositeTransform.TranslateY)"
Storyboard.TargetName="ucRobot">
                        <EasingDoubleKeyFrame KeyTime="0" Value="0"/>
                        <EasingDoubleKeyFrame KeyTime="0:0:0.6" Value="421">
                                <EasingDoubleKeyFrame.EasingFunction>
                                        <BounceEase EasingMode="EaseOut"/>
                                </EasingDoubleKeyFrame.EasingFunction>
                        </EasingDoubleKeyFrame>
                </DoubleAnimationUsingKeyFrames>
        </Storyboard>
</phone:PhoneApplicationPage.Resources>
```

Building the Main Page and Adding Components

This demo has a very simple UI that contains a Play button to animate the robot and a MediaElement to play the sound effect. Note that MediaElement.Source is set to sound18.wma, whereas in a previous demo you set the source to the URL. This is because sound18.wma is a type of content. You can verify this by right-clicking the sound18.wma file in Solution Explorer to observe its properties, as shown in Figure 15–6.

Figure 15–6. Sound18.wma file of a type of Content

```
<Grid x:Name="LayoutRoot" Background="Transparent">
    <Grid.RowDefinitions>
        <RowDefinition Height="Auto"/>
        <RowDefinition Height="*"/>
    </Grid.RowDefinitions>

    <StackPanel x:Name="TitlePanel" Grid.Row="0" Margin="24,24,0,12">

        <TextBlock x:Name="PageTitle" Text="RobotSoundDemo" Margin="-3,-8,0,0"
Style="{StaticResource PhoneTextTitle1Style}" FontSize="56" />
    </StackPanel>

    <Grid x:Name="ContentGrid" Grid.Row="1">
        <uc:Robot x:Name="ucRobot" Margin="24,27,264,442" RenderTransformOrigin="0.5,0.5"
>

            <uc:Robot.RenderTransform>
                    <CompositeTransform/>
            </uc:Robot.RenderTransform>
        </uc:Robot>
        <Button Content="Play" Height="72" HorizontalAlignment="Left"
                Margin="6,333,0,0" Name="btnPlay"
                VerticalAlignment="Top" Width="160"
```

```
            Click="btnPlay_Click" />
    <MediaElement x:Name="robotSound" Height="100"
                VerticalAlignment="Bottom" Margin="176,0,204,69"
                Source="sound18.wma" AutoPlay="False"/>
    </Grid>
</Grid>

</phone:PhoneApplicationPage>
```

Once you've loaded the XAML code, you should see the layout shown in Figure 15–7. Now it's time to wire up the events to animate the robot and play the sound effect in the next section.

Figure 15–7. *RobotSoundDemo in Design view*

Coding the Application

In Solution Explorer, open `MainPage.xaml.cs` and replace the code there with the following code C# code blocks.

Specifying the Namespaces

Add reference to `Microsoft.Xna.Framework` because you will be using it to check if background music is currently being played before playing your own video. This is necessary in order to pass the "Applications that Play Music section 6.5.1." marketplace certification.

```
using System.Windows;
using Microsoft.Phone.Controls;
using Microsoft.Xna.Framework;
using Microsoft.Xna.Framework.Media;
```

Adding an Event to Handle Play Button Click

When the Play button is clicked, the MoveRobot animation will be played; at the same time, the sound effect of the robot moving will also be played.

```
private void btnPlay_Click(object sender, RoutedEventArgs e)
{
    if (CanPlay())
    {
        MoveRobot.Begin();

        robotSound.Stop();
        robotSound.Source = new System.Uri("sound26.wma", System.UriKind.Relative);

        System.Threading.Thread.Sleep(50);
        robotSound.Play();
    }
}

private bool CanPlay()
{
    bool canPlay = false;

    FrameworkDispatcher.Update();
    if (MediaPlayer.GameHasControl)
    {
        canPlay = true;
    }
    else
    {
        if (MessageBox.Show("Is it ok to stop currently playing music?", "Can stop
music?", MessageBoxButton.OKCancel) == MessageBoxResult.OK)
        {
            canPlay = true;
            MediaPlayer.Pause();
        }
        else
        {
```

```
            canPlay = false;
        }
    }

    return canPlay;
}
```

Testing the Finished Application

To test the finished application, press F5. The result should resemble the screenshot in Figure 15–4. Test your work by clicking the play button, which should cause the robot to fly to the bottom right-hand corner of the screen, making a swoosh sound as it goes. When the robot reaches the bottom, watch it bounce several times.

Summary

In this chapter, you streamed media content from the Web or from the resource of the application and then played video and audio using MediaElement and MediaPlayerLauncher. You also applied basic sound effects to an animation using MediaElement.

In Chapter 16, you will learn how to interact with the Windows Phone's photo application, which will allow you to create your own version of a photo altering application or interact with the phone's camera to capture and manipulate an image.

Working with the Camera and Photos

Today, consumers assume that any cell phone they purchase will be able to take photos, and that the quality of photos taken will come close to the quality of photos taken with any entry-level digital camera. Furthermore, the latest mobile devices, and especially the Windows Phone 7 device, allow for the integration of their photo capabilities with the various applications that run on them. For instance, taking a picture with the phone, adding a caption to it, and immediately uploading it to a social media web site are common capabilities of all smartphone platforms today.

In this chapter, you will learn how the Windows Phone 7 platform implements yet another level of integrated user experience when it comes to the picture-taking capabilities of the phone and your application. You will learn how to build an application that takes photos, saves them, lets the user open them, and then sends them to Twitpic, a remote cloud service where they can be embedded in Twitter messages.

A lot of the code you will write in this chapter will have to be physically deployed and debugged on a real Windows Phone 7 device—after all, it's not possible to take a real picture with the emulator or test many features of the pictures application (it is, however, possible to take a "dummy" picture of a small square moving around the emulator perimeter, which proves extremely useful for testing). We highly recommend that before you proceed with this chapter, you get your hands on an actual Windows Phone 7 device. You should also install the necessary Zune software that allows debugging on that device and connect the device to your development machine (for more information on using Zune software to debug a photo application using a physical device, see Chapter 4).

Introducing Windows Phone 7 Photo Features

Before you delve into developing a Windows Phone 7 application that snaps photos and manipulates them, it's important to understand the model for working with photos on this device. As explained in greater detail in Chapter 19, each application deployed to the device runs in its own *sandbox*, or execution environment. This execution sandbox prevents third-party applications from *directly* accessing common data stores on the phone, such as photos or contact lists, and prevents them from directly invoking the applications that ship with a Windows Phone device, such as the camera or a messaging application. So how can you build an application that can take pictures, manipulate them, save them to the phone, and then later access those pictures for uploading to the cloud? The answer is through *launchers* and *choosers* as shown in Table 16–1 and 16–2.

Table 16–1. Launchers

Launchers	Description
EmailComposeTask	Opens the default device e-mail composer.
MarketPlaceDetailTask Opens	detailed product information.
MarketPlaceDetailTask	Opens to the Marketplace within specified category.
MarketPlaceReviewTask	Opens the product review for the specified product.
MarketPlaceSearchTask	Opens the MarketPlace search result based on the search term specified.
MediaPlayerLauncher	Opens the default device MediaPlayer.
PhoneCallTask	Opens the Phone application with specified number ready to dial.
SearchTask	Opens the default search application.
SmsComposeTask	Opens the messaging application.
WebBrowserTask	Opens the default device web browser to the specified URL.

Table 16–2. Choosers

Choosers	Description
CameraCaptureTask	Opens the Camera application to capture the image.
EmailAddressChooserTask	Opens the Contact application to choose an e-mail.
PhoneNumberChooserTask	Opens the Phone application to choose a phone number.
PhotoChooserTask	Opens the Photo Picker application to choose the image.
SaveEmailAddressTask	Saves the provided e-mail to the Contact list.
SavePhoneNumberTask	Saves the phone number to the Contact list.

The Windows Phone Launchers and Choosers framework is a collection of APIs you can use to indirectly access core Windows Phone applications, like the phone or contact list, to perform a specific task. Launchers can launch a phone application but return no data. A chooser, such as a photo chooser, on the other hand, returns data to the application that calls it. In other words, the difference between launchers and choosers lies in the fact that the former do not return result to the calling function, but the latter do. Tables 16–1 and 16–2 list all of the launchers and choosers that ship with the Windows Phone platform today and how each is used. The CameraCaptureTask is a chooser that is of particular interest for you in this chapter. This chooser launches the built-in Windows Phone camera application, allowing a user of a third-party application to snap photos and for that application to retrieve them for its own purposes by handling the chooser's Completed event. You will write code to capture photos shortly, but before you do that, it's important to understand one more basic concept when working with launchers and choosers—the application execution model and application tombstoning (for a more thorough and detailed look at the Windows Phone application life cycle, refer to Chapter 10).

As you know by now, the initial version of the Windows Phone 7 platform does not support multitasking due to the excessive demands it puts on the battery and other resources on the device. Microsoft has announced that by the end of 2011, Windows Phone will receive support for multitasking; however, the principles outlined later will still be valid even after the version of Windows Phone with multitasking support ships. Launchers and choosers are, in essence, separate applications that are launched from within your application. Since, at the time of this writing, support for multitasking does not yet exist, your application effectively terminates when launchers or choosers are used. This termination is known as *tombstoning*, and it has direct implications on programming Windows Phone 7 devices that use launchers and choosers, such as the photo management applications you will build in this chapter. The difference between application tombstoning and application termination is that when an application is tombstoned, it is fully expected to be resumed upon completion of the launcher or chooser. Upon resuming, the application should continue in the same state that it was left off in, with data specific to the application session before tombstoning properly preserved. It is up to the application programmer to ensure that this happens and that the data gets properly restored. Therefore, if your application gathered a lot of unique data prior to launcher or chooser call, that data must be properly preserved. For thorough details on how to preserve this data, refer to Chapter 10.

Using a Chooser to Take Photos

The very first application that you will write will take photos and bring them inside your application. The first application will also lay the foundation for the rest of this chapter, since you will enhance and add features to this application as you go along. You will, therefore, create a basic navigation system in this first step for your application using an Application Bar and a standard set of icons that ship with the Windows Phone 7 Development Tools (which you downloaded and installed in Chapter 2). You'll find the icons for a 32-bit system at C:\Program Files\Microsoft SDKs\Windows Phone\v7.0\Icons and for a 64-bit system at C:\Program Files (x86)\Microsoft SDKs\Windows Phone\v7.0\Icons.

As mentioned, you will use choosers to implement photo manipulation features on Windows Phone 7. To take photos, you will use the CameraCaptureTask chooser to take the photo and bring that photo inside your application. Follow this demo to accomplish these tasks.

Creating a New Project and Building the User Interface

In the first part of the demo, you will create a new project and add necessary user interface elements to allow photo manipulation in the future sections of this chapter.

1. Launch Visual Studio 2010 Express for Windows Phone, and create a new Windows Phone Application project. Name it PhotoCapture.

You will create an Application Bar with three icons. The first button of the Application Bar will be for taking photos, which is the subject of the current demo. The second button will be for opening previously taken photos. Finally, the third button will be for saving photos to the phone.

2. Create a separate folder within your application to store Application Bar icons. To do that, right-click the name of the project within Solution Explorer, choose Add ➤ New Folder, and name that folder images.

3. You will use the standard Application Bar icons that came pre-installed with Developer Tools for Windows Phone. By default, the icons are installed in the `C:\Program Files\Microsoft SDKs\Windows phone\v7.0\Icons` folder. Within that folder, go to the subfolder called dark, and, using Windows Explorer, copy the following icons into the images folder within your application: `appbar.feature.camera.rest.png`, `appbar.folder.rest.png`, and `appbar.save.rest.png`.

4. Now you need to make the icons part of your solution. Highlight all three icons, and press F4 to bring up the Properties dialog. For the Build Action property, specify Content. Then, select Copy Always for the Copy to Output Directory property.

5. With icons ready for use in the Application Bar, you are ready to add an Application Bar to `MainPage.xaml` (for an in-depth explanation of how to add and use an Application Bar within your application, please refer to Chapter 7). Open `MainPage.xaml`, and paste the following code at the end of the XAML file just before the `</phone:PhoneApplicationPage>` closing tag. This XAML replaces the auto-generated template for the Application Bar:

```
<phone:PhoneApplicationPage.ApplicationBar>
    <shell:ApplicationBar IsVisible="True">
        <shell:ApplicationBar.Buttons>
            <shell:ApplicationBarIconButton x:Name="btnCamera" Text="Take Photo"
IconUri="images/appbar.feature.camera.rest.png" Click="btnCamera_Click"/>
            <shell:ApplicationBarIconButton Text="Open Photo"
IconUri="images/appbar.folder.rest.png"/>
            <shell:ApplicationBarIconButton Text="Save Photo"
IconUri="images/appbar.save.rest.png"/>
        </shell:ApplicationBar.Buttons>
    </shell:ApplicationBar>
</phone:PhoneApplicationPage.ApplicationBar>
```

■ **Note** The btnCamera_Click event handler will be called when the user clicks the Take Photo button. You will write code for this event handler in the next section.

6. Finally, you need to add an Image control to show the photos taken within your application. From the Toolbox, drag and drop an Image control onto the `MainPage.xaml` design surface, place it in the middle, and size it to be about half of the available screen space. Name it imgPhoto.

Writing Code to Take Photos with CameraCaptureTask

Although you may lose a bit of flexibility when programming with launchers and choosers, it is hard to dispute how easy they have made working with common phone tasks, such as taking pictures. In the following steps, you will launch a PhotoCapture application and wire up a callback event to invoke when that application completes.

1. Open `MainPage.xaml.cs` (right-click `MainPage.xaml` and select View Code). Add the following using statements to the very top of the code page:

   ```
   using Microsoft.Phone.Tasks;
   using Microsoft.Phone;
   ```

2. Add the following class-level variables within the `MainPage` class (right above the MainPage constructor):

   ```
   private CameraCaptureTask cameraCaptureTask;
        byte[] imageBits;
   ```

3. Add the following code for the `btnCamera_Click` method. This will invoke the PhotoCapture application when the user clicks the first button in the Application Bar:

   ```
           private void btnCamera_Click(object sender, EventArgs e)
   {
           cameraCaptureTask.Show();
           }
   ```

4. You are now ready to write event handler code that will be invoked when the CameraCaptureTask chooser completes its work (the user has taken a picture) and control returns to your application. When control returns to your application, the photo taken by the user is passed in as one of the arguments to the callback function; you will take that photo and show it in the imgPhoto image control that you have added previously. Add the following method, which will be executed when the chooser completes, to `MainPage.xaml.cs`:

   ```
           private void PhotoChooserTaskCompleted(object sender, PhotoResult e)
           {
                   if (e.ChosenPhoto != null)
                   {
                           imageBits = new byte[(int)e.ChosenPhoto.Length];
                           e.ChosenPhoto.Read(imageBits, 0, imageBits.Length);
                           e.ChosenPhoto.Seek(0, System.IO.SeekOrigin.Begin);

                           var bitmapImage = PictureDecoder.DecodeJpeg(e.ChosenPhoto);
                           this.imgPhoto.Source = bitmapImage;
                   }
           }
   ```

5. You need to tell your application's instance of CameraCaptureTask that the `PhotoChooserTaskCompleted` method must be invoked upon its completion. You will do this within the MainPage() constructor using the following two lines of code:

```
cameraCaptureTask = new CameraCaptureTask();
cameraCaptureTask.Completed += PhotoChooserTaskCompleted;
```

You are now ready to run the application. Note that for this demo, it is not completely necessary to deploy your application to the physical device, since the emulator provides limited simulated photo-taking capabilities (the aforementioned small rectangle moving around the phone area).

6. Press F5 to run the application on the emulator, and then press the camera button in the Application Bar to be presented with the Windows Phone 7 PhotoCapture application. Press the button in the upper right-hand corner to simulate photo-taking within the emulator (notice how this simulation consists of a black rectangle moving around the screen's perimeter), and then press the Accept button to accept the photo. You should see a phone screen similar to the one shown in Figure 16–1 with your application displaying the captured image. Of course, if you deploy this application to the actual Windows Phone 7 device, the photos that you take will look a bit more exciting.

Throughout the rest of this chapter, you will continue enhancing this application by wiring the rest of the Application Bar icons, getting familiar with the Model-View-ViewModel pattern (covered in Chapter 3), and integrating your application within the Windows Phone 7 experience, including handy image uploads to Twitter.

Figure 16–1. *Results of PhotoCapture on Windows Phone 7 emulator*

Using a Chooser to Open Photos

In the previous section, you learned how to use the CameraCaptureTask chooser to take photos with your phone. In this section, you will learn how to open previously taken photos on your phone using the PhotoChooserTask chooser. As you have already seen, launchers and choosers do make the lives of developers a lot easier by simplifying and abstracting the most common tasks within the Windows Phone 7 Application platform.

In this section, you will enhance the application you have built by adding functionality to the second button of the Application Bar—Opening Photos. Windows Phone 7 has several locations, or "folders" so to speak, where the photos are located. Those "folders" are Camera Roll, Saved Pictures, and Pictures Library. Inside Pictures Library, there are general-purpose photos provided by Microsoft that help you in your programming efforts. Since you have already created a user interface for the application in the previous section, in this section you will add code implementing the photo browsing and retrieving functionality.

1. Launch Visual Studio 2010 Express for Windows Phone, and open the PhotoCapture project that you created in the previous section.

2. Open `MainPage.xaml.cs`, and paste the following class-level variable declaration right above the MainPage() constructor:

    ```
    private PhotoChooserTask photoChooserTask;
    ```

3. You need to specify that the PhotoChooserTaskCompleted will be the callback function invoked upon completion of the PhotoChooserTask chooser. You do this via the following two lines of code inside the MainPage() constructor:

    ```
    photoChooserTask = new PhotoChooserTask();
    photoChooserTask.Completed +=
            new EventHandler<PhotoResult>(PhotoChooserTaskCompleted);
    ```

4. As the final step of this demo, you will need to add logic to launch the chooser when the user clicks the second button in the Application Bar. To accomplish this, open the `MainPage.xaml` file, locate the line of XAML code that starts with `<shell:ApplicationBarIconButton Text="Open Photo",` and indicate that `btnOpenPhoto_Click` must be called when that button is clicked.

    ```
    <shell:ApplicationBarIconButton Text="Open Photo"
    IconUri="images/appbar.folder.rest.png" Click="btnOpenPhoto_Click"/>
    ```

5. Now, switch back to `MainPage.xaml.cs` and paste the `btnOpenPhoto_Click` function definition, which will launch the PhotoChooserTask chooser.

    ```
    private void btnOpenPhoto_Click(object sender, EventArgs e)
    {
            photoChooserTask.Show();
    }
    ```

Press F5 to run application. Now, if you click the Open Photo button in the Application Bar, you should be able to browse through photos on the emulator or (better) on the phone, select a photo, and have it presented to you in the application window.

Being able to navigate to a photo on the phone and display it within an application is certainly important, but hardly a useful feature by itself. However, as you will see shortly, you can use the PhotoChooserTask chooser to select photos to upload to a cloud service, such as TwitPic, as well as for loading images inside the application in order to manipulate them (by cropping, adding shapes to them, altering their color composition and such) and then resaving them back onto the phone or uploading them to a social media site. Although altering photos within an application is slightly beyond the scope of this chapter, you will learn how to save photos onto the phone in the next section. Saving photos could also be used together with CameraCaptureTask from the first demo in this chapter to save photos taken using that chooser.

Saving Photos to the Phone

In the prior sections, you have seen how choosers can be used to make the taking and opening of photos a breeze on a Windows Phone 7 device. Unfortunately, things become a bit more complicated when it comes to saving photos onto the device, since there are no choosers available to aid you with this task. In fact, the Windows Phone 7 platform does not provide any mechanism you can use to get the job done. So how can you do it? Enter the Windows Phone XNA library.

In this book, we have not covered the XNA Framework on Windows Phone 7 for a reason. The XNA Framework is a very powerful mechanism for programming graphics-intensive interfaces and, as such, is used primarily for game development, whereas Silverlight is used for the vast majority of line-of-business applications. This book is about learning to build line-of-business applications. At times, however, you have to resort to using a mix of technologies to get things done, and saving photos onto the Windows Phone 7 device is one example of such a situation. The Microsoft.Xna.Framework.Media library provides the SavePicture method, which saves a given array of bytes to the Saved Pictures location on the phone. The following demo demonstrates how to add save capabilities to the PhotoCapture application you have built so far.

Adding a Status Message

The user interface built as part of the first demo of this chapter has an Application Bar button already defined for saving images. Therefore, you need to make only a small enhancement to the user interface to allow the user to see whether the status of the save was successful or not.

Open MainPage.xaml and add a TextBlock right below the image control. Name it txtStatus and clear its Text property. With user interface enhancements complete, you are ready to add the code that saves photos to the Media Library.

Writing Code to Save Photos with the XNA Framework

Before you can use a method from the XNA Framework, you must first add a reference to the Xna.Framework.Media library. To accomplish this, right-click the name of the project (PhotoCapture) in Solution Explorer, select Add Reference, and then double-click the Microsoft.Xna.Framework assembly. Notice how a warning dialog comes up, telling you that there's a possibility of unexpected behavior—click Yes to complete adding a reference. Follow the rest of the steps to implement photo-saving functionality within your application.

1. Open MainPage.xaml.cs and add the following using statement to the top of that page:

   ```
   using Microsoft.Xna.Framework.Media;
   ```

2. The following method does all the work of saving a photo into the Media Library. Note specifically the SavePicture method, which saves the array of bytes passed into the Media Library.

```
private void btnSave_Click(object sender, EventArgs e)
{
        try
        {
                var library = new MediaLibrary();
                library.SavePicture("PhotoCapture Photo", imageBits);

                txtStatus.Text = "Successfully saved photo.";
        }
        catch (Exception ex)
        {
        txtStatus.Text = "Failed to save photo. Exception: " + ex.Message;
        }
}
```

3. What remains is to tie the btnSave_Click method with the click event of the Save button on the Application Bar. You will do it by editing the XAML of the MainPage.xaml file. Locate the line that starts with <shell:ApplicationBarIconButton Text="Save Photo" and change it to look like the following:

```
<shell:ApplicationBarIconButton Text="Save Photo"
        IconUri="images/appbar.save.rest.png" Click="btnSave_Click"/>
```

You are now ready to run the application on the Windows Phone 7 emulator. Press F5 to start the application, and then press the Camera button on the Application Bar (first button) to take a picture and have it loaded inside your application. Then, press the Save button on the Application Bar; you should get a status message that the image was successfully saved. Now, if you use the middle button of the Application Bar to see photos available, you should see a screen like the one shown in Figure 16–2, with three separate photo "folders," each displayed in a separate tile.

Figure 16–2. The Saved Pictures "folder" is available once at least one photo has been saved there.

Integrating Your Application with Windows Phone 7

So far in this chapter, you have built a stand-alone application that uses choosers and parts of the XNA Framework to manage photos snapped with a Windows Phone camera. What's unique about the Windows Phone 7 Framework, however, is that it encourages you to have your application make use of built-in phone applications to perform certain tasks. The Photo application, for example, provides hooks to make the functionality of an application like PhotoCapture available to users without having to explicitly launch it. Those hooks are the Extras and the Share commands, which are found on the context menus of each photo where the context menu is displayed when you press the photo for a few seconds.

Both Extras and Share features are best explained by actually observing them at work. With the real Windows Phone 7 device in hand, click the Pictures hub, select the "folder" to view the photos from (Camera Roll, for example), and then select a specific photo from the list. Click the ellipsis (…) at the bottom of the screen. When the context menu appears, you'll see an Extras option displayed at the very bottom. This Extras option is available for you to integrate or tie into. You will use it in the next demo to launch the PhotoCapture application so that you can choose a picture, save it to your TwitPic, and share it with your Twitter friends.

■**Note**   You will only see the Extras command if there's an application on the phone that implements the integration with Windows Phone Picture Viewer; as such, if you currently don't have any applications deployed to your Windows Phone device that implement the Extras functionality, you will not be able to see this menu option. You will learn how to build such an integration in the next section.

The context menu that pops up when you press the picture also includes a Share command. The Share option is also available when photos are being viewed as a list rather than one at a time. If you click the Share command, you will notice that it offers several ways to share the photo with the world. In the following section, you will learn to build an application that will use TwitPic as a cloud store for the photos on the phone, and as such will add TwitPic as one of the options on the Share menu.

■**Note**   Up to this point in the chapter, it has been possible (although a bit quirky) to run code against the Windows Phone 7 emulator. The features discussed in the next two sections are not available on the emulator; to see them in action, you must deploy applications onto the real Windows Phone 7 device.

Using Extras to Launch an Application

The Windows Phone 7 platform is all about providing the best possible phone usage experience to consumers. When consumers look at a photo on the phone, they are using an application known as a Single Photo Viewer (SPV) that provides applications to extend the viewer's functionality via the Extras command of the context menu. In this section, you will further enhance the PhotoCapture application to take advantage of the Extras feature within the Photos application. The PhotoCapture application will be using PhotoChooserTask or CameraCaptureTask to allow the user to select or take a picture once it has been invoked via the Extras feature.

To integrate with SPV, an application needs the following:

1.   An `Extras.xml` file in its root directory with markup to the Extras feature.

2.   Code to properly read and load or manipulate the photo selected in the Extras dialog.

You will implement both requirements in the next section.

Adding an Extras.xml File to the Project

Adding an `Extras.xml` file is very straightforward; the only potential difficulty may be in the fact that the content of that file has to be precise. Make sure you either copy and paste this content from the source code available with this book, or type it in very carefully.

3.   Right-click the project name, select Add ➤ New Item, and then select XML file. Make sure (this is important!) you name it `Extras.xml`.

4. Double-click the `Extras.xml` file to open it. Paste the following contents inside that file, which will enable the Windows Phone 7 framework to locate those applications ready to implement the Extras functionality:

```
<Extras>
    <PhotosExtrasApplication>
        <Enabled>true</Enabled>
    </PhotosExtrasApplication>
</Extras>
```

5. In the Properties window, make sure to set the Build Action property to Content and the Copy To Output property to Copy Always for the this file (click the file and press F4 to bring up the Properties dialog).

Make sure you save `Extras.xml`. Now you can move on to the next step.

Adding Code to Navigate to a Photo

To properly retrieve the photo that the user selected through the Extras feature, the application must override the OnNavigatedTo event in `MainPage.xaml.cs`. The steps here show you how to do that:

6. Open `MainPage.xaml.cs` and add the following using statement to the top of the page:

```
using System.Windows.Navigation;
```

7. The reference to the `Microsoft.Xna.Framework` assembly should still be in the project from the prior demos; however, if you start a new project that implements the Extras functionality, make sure to add a reference to that assembly and the following using statement to properly refer to the Media Library. You will also need `System.Windows.Media.Imaging` to work with the image source.

```
using Microsoft.Xna.Framework.Media;
using System.Windows.Media.Imaging;
```

8. Paste the following `OnNavigatedTo` method. Note how the basic operation is that of reading a QueryString passed in, determining if you have a value for the parameter token, and then trying to retrieve the photo from the Media Library by that token ID.

```
protected override void OnNavigatedTo(NavigationEventArgs e)
{
    try
    {
        IDictionary<string, string> queryStrings =
        this.NavigationContext.QueryString;
        if (queryStrings.ContainsKey("token"))
        {
            MediaLibrary library = new MediaLibrary();
            Picture picture =
library.GetPictureFromToken(queryStrings["token"]);
```

```
                             BitmapImage bitmap = new BitmapImage();
                             bitmap.SetSource(picture.GetImage());
                             WriteableBitmap picLibraryImage = new
WriteableBitmap(bitmap);

                             imgPhoto.Source = picLibraryImage;
                    }

              }
              catch (Exception ex)
              {
                      Dispatcher.BeginInvoke(() => txtStatus.Text = ex.Message);
              }
       }
```

9. Deploy the application to the phone. Then, from the phone's Start screen, select the Pictures hub, pick any picture collection, and select an individual picture of your choice. Click the ellipsis at the bottom of the screen, and select Extras. You should see the PhotoCapture application listed on the next screen that comes up. Clicking the PhotoCapture application should start the application and load the selected photo into the Image control—exactly the expected behavior.

In the next section, you will walk through the steps needed to extend the Share dialog for the photos. The concepts you use to extend the Extras and Share features are very similar; the differences, as you will see shortly, are in the details of the file name and the query string key.

Using Share to Upload PhotoCapture Snapshots to TwitPic

In this demo, you will make more changes to the PhotoCapture application to take advantage of the Share extensibility feature within the Photos application. For simplicity, the PhotoCapture application will load the selected image onto its main screen. In the next section, you will complete the circle and write code to send the image to the TwitPic cloud service for easy reference from the Twitter messages.

As with your implementation of Extras, to extend the Share option to include it, an application needs the following:

1. An E0F0E49A-3EB1-4970-B780-45DA41EC7C28.xml file in its root directory enabling the application's integration with the Share feature; this is not a typo—the XML file must be named exactly like that for the application to belong to the Share feature.

2. Code to properly read and/or share the photo selected in the Share dialog.

You will implement both requirements in the next section.

Adding an E0F0E49A-3EB1-4970-B780-45DA41EC7C28.xml File to the Project

Adding this strangely named XML file is very straightforward; the only potential difficulty may be the fact that the name is completely unreadable, so it's a good idea to copy and paste it from the downloadable source code for this book.

3. Right-click the project name, select Add ➤ New Item, and then select XML file. Make sure (this is important!) you name it E0F0E49A-3EB1-4970-B780-45DA41EC7C28.xml.

4. While the contents of the file may not be very important, be sure to go to the Properties window and set the Build Action property to Content and the Copy To Output property to Copy Always for the this file (click the file and press F4 to bring up the Properties dialog).

Make sure you save this XML file before moving onto the next step.

Adding Code to Navigate to the Selected Photo

To properly retrieve the photo that the user selected through the Extras feature, the application must override the OnNavigatedTo event in MainPage.xaml.cs. The steps here show you how to do that:

5. If you are continuing from the Extras demo, you already have all the necessary references and using statements in place. However, if you were to start a new project, make sure that you have a reference added to Microsoft.Xna.Framework and the following using statements are in place:

```
using System.Windows.Navigation;
using Microsoft.Xna.Framework.Media;
```

6. Paste the following OnNavigatedTo method (or add to that method if you are continuing from the Extras demo). Note how the basic operation is that of reading a query string passed in, determining whether there is a value for the Field parameter, and then trying to retrieve the photo from the Media Library by that token ID.

```
try
{
        IDictionary<string, string> queryStrings =
        this.NavigationContext.QueryString;

        if (queryStrings.ContainsKey("FileId"))
        {
                MediaLibrary library = new MediaLibrary();
                Picture picture =
library.GetPictureFromToken(queryStrings["FileId"]);

                BitmapImage bitmap = new BitmapImage();
                bitmap.SetSource(picture.GetImage());
                WriteableBitmap picLibraryImage = new WriteableBitmap(bitmap);
                imgPhoto.Source = picLibraryImage;
        }
}
catch (Exception ex)
{
        Dispatcher.BeginInvoke(() => txtStatus.Text = ex.Message);
}
```

7. Deploy the application to the phone.

Now you're ready to test your implementation so far. Just as you did for your Extras integration, from the phone's Start screen, select the Pictures hub on your phone, pick any picture collection, and select an individual picture of your choice. Click the ellipsis (…) at the bottom of the screen, and select Share. You should see Upload to PhotoCapture as one of the options that come up. Clicking that option should start the application and load the selected photo into the Image control—the behavior you expect.

Now you're ready to upload the photos to TwitPic, which is the primary hosting service for photos destined for Twitter, the hottest social media network today. Silverlight (in general) and Silverlight on Windows Phone 7 (in particular) differ from other applications in the fact that they rigorously enforce a non-blocking user interface principle: everything, including communications over the network, must happen asynchronously. TwitPic cloud service provides a RESTful API that allows programmers to send messages to that service as long as you conform to the expected message format. In the next section, you will write code against that API to upload the photo to TwitPic.

Adding an Upload Button to the UI

On the user interface front, you will need to add an additional button that will trigger the upload of the photo to TwitPic. Figure 16–3 illustrates one possible placement of this button. Name the button btnUpload, and set its caption to TwitPic.

Writing Code to Transfer an Image to TwitPic

Because network access on Windows Phone 7 must be performed asynchronously, it takes quite a bit of code to properly construct the RESTful web service request. Most of the code, however, is repetitive, and all of the major points are summarized in these step-by-step instructions.

8. Right-click the project name in Solution Explorer, select Add Reference, and then select System.Xml.Linq.

9. Add the following using statements to the top of the page:

```
using System.IO;
using System.Text;
using System.Xml.Linq;
```

10. Open MainPage.xaml.cs and paste the UploadPhoto function written here. This will be the only function that will be invoked when the photo upload needs to take place. This function sets the URL and the type of the request, and then it invokes the asynchronous BeginGetRequestStream, which packages the photo and the user credentials.

```
public void UploadPhoto()
{
        HttpWebRequest request =
        (HttpWebRequest)WebRequest.Create("http://twitpic.com/api/upload");
        request.ContentType = "application/x-www-form-urlencoded";
        request.Method = "POST";
        request.BeginGetRequestStream(new
AsyncCallback(GetRequestStreamCallback),
        request);
}
```

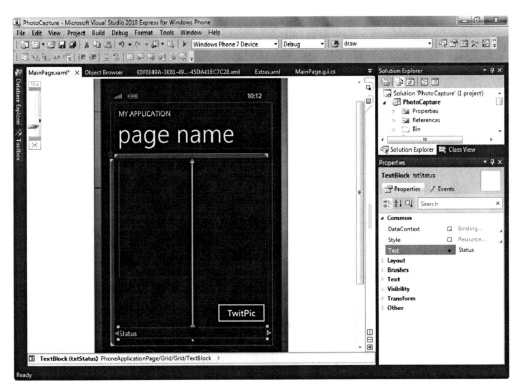

Figure 16–3. User interface for uploading photos to TwitPic

11. Add the following code to define the asynchronous function
GetRequestStreamCallback that does all of the packaging of proper parameters;
note that the exact form of the message was dictated by TwitPic, and this
method simply conforms to it:

▪ **Note**　The TwitPic API is sensitive to even slightly malformed messages, so be sure you copy/paste this method from the source code that comes with this book instead of manually retyping it and risking making a mistake.

```
private void GetRequestStreamCallback(IAsyncResult asynchronousResult)
{
    try
    {

        HttpWebRequest request = (HttpWebRequest)asynchronousResult.AsyncState;
        string encoding = "iso-8859-1";
        // End the operation
        Stream postStream = request.EndGetRequestStream(asynchronousResult);
```

```
        string boundary = Guid.NewGuid().ToString();
        request.ContentType = string.Format("multipart/form-data; boundary={0}",
        boundary);

        string header = string.Format("--{0}", boundary);
        string footer = string.Format("--{0}--", boundary);

        StringBuilder contents = new StringBuilder();
        contents.AppendLine(header);

string fileHeader = String.Format("Content-Disposition: file; name=\"{0}\";
        filename=\"{1}\"; ", "media", "testpic.jpg");
        string fileData = Encoding.GetEncoding(encoding).GetString(imageBits, 0,
        imageBits.Length);

        contents.AppendLine(fileHeader);
        contents.AppendLine(String.Format("Content-Type: {0};", "image/jpeg"));
        contents.AppendLine();
        contents.AppendLine(fileData);
        contents.AppendLine(header);
        contents.AppendLine(String.Format("Content-Disposition: form-data;
        name=\"{0}\"", "username"));
        contents.AppendLine();
        contents.AppendLine("BeginningWP7");

        contents.AppendLine(header);
        contents.AppendLine(String.Format("Content-Disposition: form-data;
        name=\"{0}\"", "password"));
        contents.AppendLine();
        contents.AppendLine("windowsphone7");

        contents.AppendLine(footer);

        // Convert the string into a byte array.
        byte[] byteArray =
        Encoding.GetEncoding(encoding).GetBytes(contents.ToString());

        // Write to the request stream.
        postStream.Write(byteArray, 0, contents.ToString().Length);
        postStream.Close();

        // Start the asynchronous operation to get the response
        request.BeginGetResponse(new AsyncCallback(GetResponseCallback), request);
    }
    catch (Exception ex)
    {
        Dispatcher.BeginInvoke(() => txtStatus.Text = ex.Message);
    }
}
```

12. Add the GetResponseCallback function that will asynchronously receive the results of the upload (Success or Fail) and parse that result out using LINQ to XML:

```
private void GetResponseCallback(IAsyncResult asynchronousResult)
{
    try
    {

        HttpWebRequest request =
(HttpWebRequest)asynchronousResult.AsyncState;
        // End the operation
        HttpWebResponse response =
            (HttpWebResponse)request.EndGetResponse(asynchronousResult);
        Stream streamResponse = response.GetResponseStream();
        StreamReader streamRead = new StreamReader(streamResponse);
        string responseString = streamRead.ReadToEnd();

        XDocument doc = XDocument.Parse(responseString);
        XElement rsp = doc.Element("rsp");
string status = rsp.Attribute(XName.Get("status")) != null ?
rsp.Attribute(XName.Get("status")).Value :
rsp.Attribute(XName.Get("stat")).Value;

        // Close the stream object
        streamResponse.Close();
        streamRead.Close();

        // Release the HttpWebResponse
        response.Close();

    }
    catch (Exception ex)
    {
        Dispatcher.BeginInvoke(() => txtStatus.Text = ex.Message);
    }
}
```

13. Now you need to call the UploadPhoto method when the user clicks the TwitPic button. Open MainPage.xaml in Design view, and double-click the TwitPic button. Inside the btnUpload_Click method, paste the following line of code:

```
UploadPhoto();
```

You are now ready to run the application. Fortunately, you can test the upload to TwitPic functionality in this demo by using Windows Phone emulator; you don't need to deploy to the actual device. Set the Windows Phone 7 emulator as your deployment target, click F5, and when the application comes up, click the camera button (the first button on the Application Bar). Take a picture, accept it, and then click the TwitPic button. If no errors were reported in the status TextBlock, you should see your image on TwitPic's web site, as shown in Figure 16–4.

■ **Note** Once you successfully upload photos from your phone to TwitPic, the response XML from TwitPic contains a mediaurl node with the URL of your image. You can parse out that URL in a way that is similar to parsing out the status in the previous code. Your application can then make use of that URL by, for example, constructing an HTML page with that URL and showing it within the Web Browser control or doing anything else with it that your imagination can dream up.

Figure 16–4. Image uploaded to TwitPic

Summary

In this chapter, you worked extensively with photos on a Windows Phone 7 device. You used choosers to take pictures and loaded previously saved pictures. You also learned a bit about the XNA Framework and how it helps you work with the Media Library. You then explored the integration options available between the Windows Phone 7 built-in application for photos and your application. Finally, you uploaded photos that you took with your Windows Phone 7 device to TwitPic, a photo-sharing site used extensively by Twitter.

In the next chapter, you will look into push notifications, a powerful mechanism for mimicking multi-tasking and providing timely notifications about important events.

CHAPTER 17

Push Notifications

One day in the somewhat distant future, smartphones and other mobile appliances will ship with batteries that last for weeks without the need to recharge them. But until that day arrives, Windows Phone 7 software developers must write applications that use energy sparingly, since a resource-intensive program—such as one that uses the built-in cellular or Wi-Fi radio continuously—can quickly drain a Windows Phone battery. To prevent this from happening, Microsoft has built a number of safeguards into the Windows Phone application platform to ensure that the phone battery lasts as long as possible. One such safeguard prohibits any third-party application from running in the background while another is executing in the foreground, a feature that is also known as multitasking.

Given this limitation, how do you build an application that needs to be—or at least needs to appear to be—always running, providing your users with important alerts and messages, such as when to buy or sell stocks or take cover from bad weather? In the Windows Phone 7 world, the answer is push notifications, also referred to as Windows Phone Notifications (WPN). In a nutshell, push notifications allow a user of an application to receive notification messages even when it is not running (currently on Windows Phone 7, any time an application is not in the foreground, it is not running).

In this chapter, you'll learn how notifications work on the Windows Phone, the WPN types that Microsoft provides, and the steps you need to follow to use them in an application. You will build a simple phone application that can receive and process push notifications, and you'll create a simple service that can create and send them. The service will notify the user when the price of Microsoft stock changes (stock symbol MSFT). Without further ado, let's start experimenting with this powerful technology available for Windows Phone 7.

Understanding Push Notifications

The Windows Phone 7 platform provides developers with three types of push notifications: *toast* notifications, *tile* notifications, and *raw* notifications. All three types follow the same basic principles of operation and processing, yet differ in the way they display notifications. Toast and tile notification types are used only when the application is not running; raw notifications are used to continuously receive messages while the application is running in the foreground. Let's discuss each notification type in detail.

Toast Notifications

Toast notifications are displayed as overlays at the top of a phone's screen. Only a message title and a line of text can be controlled by the service or an application sending ("pushing") a toast notification; the icon that appears on the left side of a toast notification is the default icon for the application deployed on the Windows Phone 7 device. You can display toast notifications only when an application is not running; if an application is running when a toast notification is sent, it is not displayed on the phone screen.

Toast notifications are used to display information that is timely and urgent. An example of toast notification is shown in Figure 17–1, where it appears as "Time to buy!" text at the top of the phone screen. Here, a notification has been received about Microsoft stock becoming an attractive buy. If the user chooses to tap (or click) the toast notification, an application opens up, allowing users to take additional actions within the application.

Figure 17–1. Sample toast notification

Tile Notifications

Tile notifications can alter the contents of any application tile that is pinned to the Quick Launch area of the phone initial screen (also referred to as Start Experience/Start Screen in Microsoft documentation). Tile notifications are used to communicate information visually, by displaying, say, dark clouds with rain to represent a rapidly approaching storm. Generally, an application tile is a visual representation of an application and its contents or functionality. An application tile typically contains an icon and two strings, and tile notifications can change any of these elements, as well as the background of each tile. To change a tile's background image, a tile notification must include a URI that points to the new image, a

URI that can be either local or cloud-based. The string at the bottom of an application tile is referred to as the *tile title*. The string in the middle and slightly to the right is referred to as the *tile counter*.

Figure 17–2 shows the same Windows Phone 7 Start screen as Figure 17–1, but with an update to the PNClient application tile, which has changed the tile's text to "MSFT +2" and set the count property to 2. By continuously updating the tile with new text and images, an application can keep a user informed without the need to launch the application.

Raw Notifications

The third and final type of push notification is the raw notification, which can be used to continuously send messages or updates to a Windows Phone 7 application that is running in the foreground. Contrast this with toast and tile notifications, which are used to send updates to an application when it is not running front and center on the Windows Phone 7 device. Unlike toast and tile notifications, all raw notifications are dropped once an application is no longer running in the foreground on the Windows Phone 7 device. Raw notifications are an energy-friendly alternative to constantly polling web services for data; this type of push notification also eliminates the need to keep connections to web services open for prolonged periods of time.

Each notification type has its niche—specific application development scenarios in which it shines (shown in Table 17-1). For instance, if an application receives updates only when it's actively used, such as a chat application, a raw notification is the most appropriate mechanism for transmitting these updates. If an application is ideally suited to communicate updates via the use of visual elements on an ongoing basis, such as weather updates, sports events scores, or stock prices, tile notifications are a more appropriate choice. Finally, if text-based messages are the most appropriate form of communication on an around-the-clock basis (such as e-mail receipts, Facebook friend requests, or news alerts), toast notifications would be most suitable.

Having taken a look at three available push notification types, let's look at the architecture of notification services, since knowing the architecture will help you better understand how to program and troubleshoot push notification services.

Table 17–1. Characteristics of Windows Phone Push Notification Types

PN Type	Must Application Be Running in Foreground?	Must Application Tile be Pinned to Start Screen?	Use
Toast	No	No	Urgent and time-sensitive data (e.g., storm warning)
Tile	No	Yes	Updates (e.g., count of new messages)
Raw	Yes	No	Continuous data (e.g., Twitter client, stock ticker)

Introducing the Push Notifications Architecture

Windows Phone push notifications involve three players, (1) a phone application, (2) a Microsoft service, and (3) a remote web-based service, as illustrated in Figure 17–3. At the heart of push notifications is a service provided by Microsoft called, very appropriately, Microsoft Push Notification Service (MPNS). MPNS "provides a dedicated, resilient, and persistent channel for pushing a notification to a mobile device," according to MSDN documentation. This service is hosted on Microsoft's Azure cloud operating system and is responsible for seamlessly establishing a channel of communication between a Windows Phone 7 device and an application that provides notification data to it. Typically, notifications to Windows Phone 7 devices are provided by a web service (or a "cloud service," as often seen in Microsoft documentation). These cloud services are generally accessible via standard web protocols, such as REST and SOAP, aside from MPNS for data retrieval and updates.

Naturally, you may be wondering what happens when MPNS becomes unavailable for some technical reason. At the moment, the answer is that should that happen, push notifications will not reach their destination; in other words, they will be simply dropped (see the Note below). Hence, push notifications should never be counted on as a reliable form of message delivery.

■ **Note** When programming Push Notifications, there's an additional caveat that you should be aware of: the battery level of the Windows Phone 7 device has direct influence over the receipt of Push Notifications. Currently, there are three different values defined for battery power within the Microsoft.Phone.Notifications namespace: Normal, Low, and CriticalLow. If the power on the device receiving Push Notifications drops from Normal to Low, tile and toast notifications are discontinued, and only Raw will still be sent to the device. When the battery power drops to CriticalLow, all push notifications are discontinued.

Figure 17–2. A tile notification

The Life Cycle of a Notification

Suppose that you're building a mobile stock trading application that consists of a central web service, which gathers and analyzes trading data, and an application running on Windows Phone 7 devices, which displays data to users. Suppose you want the application to notify users whenever there is a significant jump in the value of Microsoft stock, such as might occur right after the official launch of the next version of Windows Phone 7. Architecturally speaking, how would it go about doing that?

First, the application will need to take advantage of Push Notification Services, since this will allow it to keep the user updated on the market conditions even if the user is not constantly running the stock trading app on her Windows Phone 7.

Second, to enable push notifications on Windows Phone 7, a communication channel for notifications must be created between the application and the web service that is collecting stock trading data. In the world of push notifications, a communication channel is represented by a URI that contains all of the information necessary for notifications to reach their destination. A Windows Phone 7 client must request this channel be created, and obtain the URI associated with that communication channel.

Third, the URI of this communication channel must be communicated to the web service that will deliver, or "push" notifications about the market conditions to Windows Phone 7 clients. Once this third step is complete, all three types of push notifications are available to the stock trading application.

Figure 17–3 provides detailed visual representation of how a Windows Phone 7 client application will be able to receive stock trading alerts from the server using MPNS. The steps are sequentially numbered and each numbered step is described in detail below:

1. Windows Phone 7 application contacts MPNS and requests for communication channel inside MPNS to be created.

2. MPNS responds with the URI of communication channel, which is unique for a given Windows Phone 7 device and an application on that device.

3. Windows Phone 7 application communicates the URI of the channel created in Step 2 to the service providing stock quotes.

4. The stock quotes service publishes updates to the URI communicated to it in Step 3.

5. MPNS routes the updates to the proper Windows Phone 7 device and application on that device.

CHAPTER 17 ■ PUSH NOTIFICATIONS

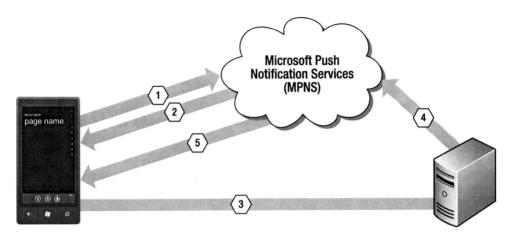

Figure 17–3. Basic push notifications architecture

When the service needs to send notifications to its clients, it contacts MPNS by making a POST request to the unique URIs created for each client (Step 4). These POST requests have to conform to a predefined XML schema set by Microsoft. The type of notification sent (toast, tile, or raw) is determined by one of the header values inside the POST request—namely, the X-NotificationClass header; you will see how to use this header momentarily.

The sections that follow will show you how to write code for the steps that have just been described. Using the Windows Phone 7 emulator, you'll implement an application with both toast and tile notifications.

When programming Windows Phone 7 push notifications, perhaps the most common error that occurs is the PayloadFormat error. Generally, it means that the XML or message format received from the MPNS does not conform to the expected format. If this happens, check whether an XML format expected for tile notifications is used for toast notifications or vice versa.

The Push Notification Framework

The namespace that hosts the APIs to do the push notification heavy lifting is Microsoft.Phone.Notification, and the HttpChannelNotification is its workhorse. Before a notification of any type can be sent, a notification channel must be created. The HttpChannelNotification class allows developers to create a new channel or find an existing (previously created) one using its Open and Find methods correspondingly. When programming push notifications, it is a good practice to check whether the channel has been previously created using the Find operation. You will see how this is done shortly in several upcoming demos. An important note about the Open method: once the channel is open, it is not immediately active. The push notification channel becomes active once it acquires the push notification URI from the MPNS. This URI is acquired in an asynchronous manner, as you will also see in the demos in this chapter.

Other important methods of the HttpChannelNotification class include BindToShellToast and BindToShellTile. These methods are responsible for associating, or binding, a particular HttpChannelNotification channel instance to toast and tile notifications. These methods have corresponding UnbindToShellToast and UnbindToShellTile methods that disassociate toast and tiles subscriptions correspondingly from a given channel. Finally, the Close method of the

`HttpChannelNotification` class closes the channel and removes all the subscriptions associated with that channel.

Push notifications are most appropriate in situations where Windows Phone 7 applications almost fully depend on the data supplied by the server on the web or somewhere else in the cloud. As such, to demonstrate push notifications in action, you must create two separate projects: one project will be a Windows Phone 7 application, and the other project could be either a web-based application, a web service, or, for the purposes of keeping the current example simple, a Windows Forms application. To create the Windows Forms application that will be used as part of the next demo, you will be using a version of Visual Studio that allows the creation of Windows Forms applications—Visual C# 2010 Express. Alternately, you could use other (paid) editions of Visual Studio 2010 to create Windows Forms applications.

■ **Note** Currently, there's a limit of one notification channel per application and the maximum of 15 push notification channels per device. This means if you deploy an application to the device that already has 15 notification channels consumed by other applications, you will get an InvalidOperationException (Channel quota exceeded).

Implementing Toast Notifications

For the toast notifications demo, you will implement a Windows Phone 7 client application that will create a notification channel, and a Windows Forms application that can send the notifications to the Windows Phone 7 application via that channel. The Windows Phone 7 client application will be a single screen application with one button and one text box, as shown in Figure 17–4.

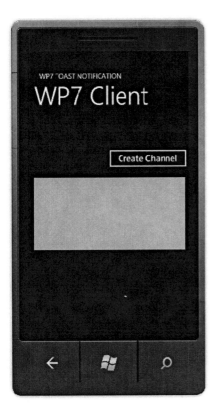

Figure 17–4. Windows Phone 7 application that will create a push notification URI and receive push notifications

The Windows Forms application will consist of the single form shown in Figure 17–5. You will follow this order of program implementation:

1. You will create the Windows Phone 7 Notification client application. This application will establish a notification channel and print the URI of that communication channel into the Output window.

2. You will create and execute the Windows Forms application that will send notifications. You will take the URI of the notification channel that you established in Step 1, paste it into the Push Notifications URL field of this application, and submit the notification.

3. You will verify that you are able to receive toast notifications in the Windows Phone 7 application.

Figure 17–5. Design surface for Windows Phone 7 Notification client application

---

■ **Note** If your application implements toast notifications, per Microsoft Application Certification Requirements, you must ask the user for permission to receive those notifications and you must allow the user to disable such notifications.

Creating a Client Application

The Windows Phone 7 Notification client application will consist of a command button that will create a push notification channel and print its URI into the Debug window. You will also add a text box to the application to display the URI for visual confirmation. Follow these steps to create the application:

1. Launch Visual Studio 2010 Express for Windows Phone and create a new Windows Phone Application project. Name it PNClient.

2. From the Toolbox, drag and drop a text box on the design surface. Rename the text box to txtURI, adjust its width to be the full width of the screen, and adjust its height to be about a quarter of the screen's height. Set the text box's TextWrapping property to Wrap and clear out its Text property.

3. From the Toolbox, drag and drop a button on the design surface. Rename the button to btnCreateChannel and set the Content property to Create Channel. Your Windows Phone 7 design surface should now look like Figure 17–6.

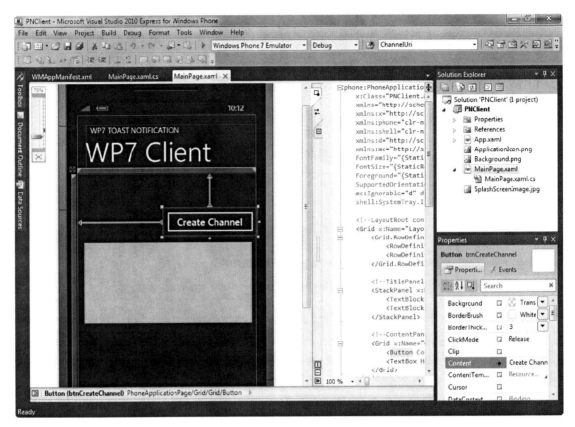

***Figure 17–6.** Windows Forms application that will send push notifications to WP7 app*

4. Add the following using directives to the top of the MainPage.xaml.cs file.

```
using Microsoft.Phone.Notification;
using System.Diagnostics;
```

5. You need to add code that will capture the URI of the notification channel in the Output window. At the top of the code page, right underneath the

```
public partial class MainPage : PhoneApplicationPage
{
```

add the following code

```
Uri channelUri;
public Uri ChannelUri
{
get { return channelUri; }
set
    {
```

```
            channelUri = value;
            OnChannelUriChanged(value);
    }
}

private void OnChannelUriChanged(Uri value)
{
        Dispatcher.BeginInvoke(() =>
        {
                txtURI.Text = "changing uri to " + value.ToString();
        });

        Debug.WriteLine("changing uri to " + value.ToString());
}
```

The last bit of code will print the URI of the push notification channel opened by the application into the Visual Studio Output window, which will allow you to copy and paste that URI into the Windows Forms application that you will be building in the next section. Certainly, in a real-world application, this copy and paste method is not appropriate; a more robust method of exchanging that URI, such as passing it to a web service, would be more appropriate. You will build a more realistic method of exchanging this URI later on in this chapter.

6. Open `MainPage.xaml` in Design view (right-click `MainPage.xaml` in Solution Explorer and select View Designer), double-click the Create Channel button, and make the `btnCreateChannel_Click` event handler look like the following:

```
private void btnCreateChannel_Click(object sender, RoutedEventArgs e)
{
SetupChannel();
}
```

7. Paste the following `SetupChannel` function into the btnCreate_Click event handler (note that you can always download the code available for this book). Here, you use the `HttpNotificationChannel` class to try to find an existing push notification channel or open a new channel with a given channel name.

```
private void SetupChannel()
{
    HttpNotificationChannel httpChannel = null;
    string channelName = "DemoChannel";

    try
    {
        //if channel exists, retrieve existing channel
        httpChannel = HttpNotificationChannel.Find(channelName);
        if (httpChannel != null)
        {
            //If we cannot get Channel URI, then close the channel and reopen it
            if (httpChannel.ChannelUri == null)
            {
                httpChannel.UnbindToShellToast();
                httpChannel.Close();
                SetupChannel();
```

```
            return;
        }
        else
        {
            ChannelUri = httpChannel.ChannelUri;
        }
    BindToShell(httpChannel);
    }
        else
        {
            httpChannel = new HttpNotificationChannel(channelName);
        httpChannel.ChannelUriUpdated += new
EventHandler<NotificationChannelUriEventArgs>(httpChannel_ChannelUriUpdated);
        httpChannel.ShellToastNotificationReceived+=new
EventHandler<NotificationEventArgs>(httpChannel_ShellToastNotificationReceived);

        httpChannel.ErrorOccurred += new
EventHandler<NotificationChannelErrorEventArgs>(httpChannel_ExceptionOccurred);

            httpChannel.Open();
            BindToShell(httpChannel);
    }
    }
    catch (Exception ex)
    {
        Debug.WriteLine("An exception setting up channel " + ex.ToString());

    }
}
```

The code in the SetupChannel() function warrants an explanation, since there is quite a bit going on and it is the nucleus of creating a channel for a Windows Phone 7 Notification client application. In the first few lines, you define a new object of type HttpNotificationChannel, give it a name, and wire up an event to fire when an error occurs. You also wire up an event to fire when the URI of the notification channel changes. Next, you try to find the channel with a given name for the application and then bind it to receive toast notifications (via the BindToShell function shown here). If the channel is found, you'll use an existing channel to obtain the push notification URI and you will not need to wire various httpChannel event handlers. If the channel is not found, you'll create a new one and wire up appropriate httpChannel events. Notice the ShellToastNotificationReceived event—it occurs if your application is running in the foreground when it receives a toast notification. Normally, push notifications are designed to alert that there is something happening when the application is not running and when an application needs to receive a notification. However, occasionally, your application may be running when a toast notification is received—to handle cases like this, ShellToastNotificationReceived event handler is introduced. You will code this event handler in the next step.

8. To handle toast notifications when the application is running in the foreground, add the code below for the ShellToastNotificationReceived event handler. This code will read the notification messages received and print them in the textbox on the screen.

```
void httpChannel_ShellToastNotificationReceived(object sender,
    NotificationEventArgs e)
    {
```

```
                Dispatcher.BeginInvoke(() =>
                {
                        txtURI.Text = "Toast Notification Message Received: ";
                        if (e.Collection != null)
                        {
                        Dictionary<string, string> collection =
                                (Dictionary<string, string>)e.Collection;
                        System.Text.StringBuilder messageBuilder = new
                        System.Text.StringBuilder();
                                foreach (string elementName in collection.Keys)
                                {
                                        txtURI.Text+= string.Format("Key: {0},
Value:
                        {1}\r\n", elementName, collection[elementName]);
                                }
                        }
                });
        }
```

9. To bind a toast notification subscription to a given HttpNotificationChannel instance, you must call the BindToShellToast method of the HttpNotificationChannel class. Underneath the SetupChannel function, paste the following code to accomplish this:

```
        private static void BindToShell(HttpNotificationChannel httpChannel)
        {
                //This is a toast notification
                try
                {
                        httpChannel.BindToShellToast();
                }
                catch (Exception)
                {
                        Debug.WriteLine("An exception occurred binding to shell " +
ex.ToString());
                }
        }
```

10. In the SetupChannel function, you designated the httpChannel_ExceptionOccurred should fire in case of an error. Add this function to your code as defined here:

```
  void httpChannel_ExceptionOccurred(object sender, NotificationChannelErrorEventArgs
        e)
        {
                //Display Message on error
                Debug.WriteLine ( e.Message);
        }
```

11. You also need to add code that will fire if the ChannelUri gets updated:

```
void httpChannel_ChannelUriUpdated(object sender, NotificationChannelUriEventArgs e)
{
                //You get the new Uri (or maybe it's updated)
                ChannelUri = e.ChannelUri;
}
```

At this point, you have finished building the Windows Phone 7 client application and are ready to implement the Windows Forms application for sending notification messages to the mobile device.

Creating an Application to Send Notifications

In the previous section, you wrote a Windows Phone 7 client application that creates a notification channel to the MPN Service to indicate that it wishes to receive push notification messages. By creating a channel, the application has also created an MPNS endpoint to which the web-based application can send POST requests. The endpoint exists on an MPNS server operated by Microsoft and will forward any requests it receives to the appropriate mobile device and application to which the endpoint points.

You can create POST requests from virtually any application environment, including web sites, web services, and desktop applications, making this type of notification architecture very flexible and easy to use. In this example, you will create a Windows Forms application that packages POST requests to the URI generated in the previous section. This application will create POST requests and send them off to the MPNS in the cloud, which will in turn properly route the requests to the mobile devices and applications.

To ensure proper message routing and successful delivery, there are two key pieces of information that any application sending push notifications to a Windows Phone 7 device must supply. Those key pieces of information are the following:

1. *The URI of the notification channel that the service must use to communicate with a Windows Phone 7 device.* It is up to the Windows Phone 7 client application to request the URI and pass it to the service that will use it.

2. *A proper XML message to POST to the URI.* While the format of the XML message is simple, it has to be followed precisely for the notifications to succeed.

The latest MPNS XML template for toast notifications looks like the following, where <Notification Title> and <Notification Text> are the text of the notification title and the text of the toast notification message to be sent to a Windows Phone 7 device:

```
<?xml version="1.0" encoding="utf-8"?>
<wp:Notification xmlns:wp="WPNotification">
 <wp:Toast>
  <wp:Text1><Notification Title></wp:Text1>
  <wp:Text2><Notification Text></wp:Text2>
 </wp:Toast>
</wp:Notification>
```

Now that you know the XML template format of the expected POST request and, using cut and paste, can quickly obtain the URI of the notification channel, you're ready to create an application to dispatch notifications to the Windows Phone 7 client app. Follow these steps:

1. Launch Visual C# 2010 Express (or another edition of Visual Studio that will allow you to create Windows Forms projects) and create a new Windows Forms project. Name it PNServer.

2. Form1.cs is added by default. Double-click it to bring up the design view. From the toolbox, drag three labels and three text boxes and make Form1.cs look like Figure 17–5. Name the text boxes txtURL, txtTitle, and txtText accordingly.

3. Add a Button control onto Form1. Change its text property to Send Notification and change its name to btnSendNotification.

4. Finally, add the label control to the bottom of the form and change its name to lblStatus.

5. Right-click Form1.cs in Solution Explorer and choose View Code (alternately, you can also press F7). Add the following using statements to the top:

```
using System.Net;
using System.IO;
```

6. After the constructor, add the following definition of the XML to be POSTed to MPNS:

```
string ToastPushXML = "<?xml version=\"1.0\" encoding=\"utf-8\"?>" +
    "<wp:Notification xmlns:wp=\"WPNotification\">" +
    "<wp:Toast>" +
    "<wp:Text1>{0}</wp:Text1>" +
    "<wp:Text2>{1}</wp:Text2>" +
    "</wp:Toast>" +
    "</wp:Notification>";
```

7. Switch back to the design view on Form1.cs (by right-clicking Form1.cs in Solution Explorer and choosing View Designer). Double-click the Send Notification button to bring up the btnSendNotification_Click event handler.

You'll use the btnSendNotification_Click event handler, with the help of the .NET HttpWebRequest class to create a POST request to the push notification URI that the Windows Phone 7 client has obtained. The beauty of communication with MPNS is that once this POST request is composed and sent off, MPNS will take care of the delivery of the notification from there. The critical piece of information is the URI to send the POST request to, since that URI is what uniquely identifies both a Windows Phone 7 device and an application to send push notifications to.

Make the btnSendNotification_Click event handler look like the code here:

```
private void btnSendNotification_Click(object sender, EventArgs e)
{
    if (txtURL.Text == string.Empty)
    {
        MessageBox.Show("Please enter a url");
        return;
    }

    if (txtTitle.Text == string.Empty || txtText.Text == string.Empty)
    {
```

```
            MessageBox.Show("Please enter text and title to send");
            return;
    }

    string url = txtURL.Text;

    HttpWebRequest sendNotificationRequest = (HttpWebRequest)WebRequest.Create(url);

    sendNotificationRequest.Method = "POST";
    sendNotificationRequest.Headers = new WebHeaderCollection();
    sendNotificationRequest.ContentType = "text/xml";

    sendNotificationRequest.Headers.Add("X-WindowsPhone-Target", "toast");
    sendNotificationRequest.Headers.Add("X-NotificationClass", "2");

    string str = string.Format(ToastPushXML, txtTitle.Text, txtText.Text);
    byte[] strBytes = new UTF8Encoding().GetBytes(str);
    sendNotificationRequest.ContentLength = strBytes.Length;
    using (Stream requestStream = sendNotificationRequest.GetRequestStream())
    {
        requestStream.Write(strBytes, 0, strBytes.Length);
    }

    HttpWebResponse response = (HttpWebResponse)sendNotificationRequest.GetResponse();
    string notificationStatus = response.Headers["X-NotificationStatus"];
    string deviceConnectionStatus = response.Headers["X-DeviceConnectionStatus"];
    lblStatus.Text = "Status: " + notificationStatus + " : " + deviceConnectionStatus;
}
```

The POST request includes two headers:

- The X-WindowsPhone-Target header defines the notification type. The possible values for this header are toast, token, or not defined. Toast defines the notification of toast type, while token defines a tile notification. If this header is not defined, then it is a raw notification.

- The X-NotificationClass header defines how soon the MPNS should deliver the notification. The value of 2 specifies that the toast notification is to be delivered immediately. Had you specified the value of 12, for example, the MPNS would have been instructed to wait 450 seconds, or seven and a half minutes before notification delivery.

Now it's time to test the application and its service.

Verifying Delivery of Push Notifications

With the Windows Phone 7 Notification client application ready to receive notification messages and the Windows Forms application ready to send them, you are ready to verify the proper delivery of those notifications. Follow these steps to test push notification delivery:

1. First, you will need to obtain the URI of the notification channel. Open the PNClient project created in the "Creating a Client Application" section. Make

sure that you have a connection to the Internet, and press F5 to run the project.

2. Click the Create Channel button and, after a short while, you should see messages (the URI of the notification channel, actually) printed in the text box on the screen—that's a confirmation that the notification URI is available to copy from the Output window.

3. In Visual Studio 2010 Express for Windows Phone, click the Debug ➤ Windows ➤ Output menu option to bring up the Output window. The URI should be printed together with the "changing uri to …" message, as shown in Figure 17–7. Highlight the URI and press Ctrl+C to copy it into the buffer. Make sure to leave the application running in the Windows Phone emulator, since you will be receiving push notifications on this emulator screen.

Figure 17–7. Notification channel URI printed in the Output window

4. Switch to the PNServer Windows Forms project and press F5 to run it. In the Push Notifications URL text box, paste the URI obtained in Step 3 above by pressing Ctrl+V. In the Push Notifications Title and Push Notifications Text

text boxes, you can enter any text—for example, "Time to buy!" and "MSFT up
$2 after WP7 release". Press the Send Notification button.

Remember that push notifications appear on the phone only when the Windows Phone 7
application associated with these notifications is not running in the foreground on the phone. Therefore,
if the PNClient application was running—which is likely—in the foreground when you pressed the Send
Notification button, no notifications will have appeared on the phone screen. To enable them, do the
following; otherwise, skip to the next paragraph.

5. Press the Windows button on the emulator (the middle button on the emulator
    with the Windows logo on it) to switch to the Start screen of the phone, which
    shuts down PNClient application. In the PNServer app, press the Send
    Notification button again.

You should see a toast notification like the one shown in Figure 17–1.

As you can see, creating and receiving push notifications is a somewhat involved process, with a
separate Windows Phone 7 application establishing a notification channel and receiving notifications,
and a separate application sending these notifications to that Windows Phone 7 app. Once you
understand how to work with other types of notifications—namely, tile and raw—you can build a service
that will programmatically acquire and keep track of the connected clients. From an application
development point of view, the good news is that the process of creating other notification types—tile
notifications and raw notifications—is very similar to the process of creating toast notifications
described previously.

In the next section, you will take a look at how to create tile notifications, but instead of creating
everything from scratch, you will concentrate only on the changes needed to the toast notifications
already implemented.

Implementing Tile Notifications

Tile notifications can update the images and texts of application tiles, as you saw in Figure 17–2. Tile
notifications are ideal for applications that convey small amounts of information, especially when that
information changes frequently. For example, weather reports and compass headings are both good
candidates for this category.

■ **Note** There is currently a limitation of 500 push notifications per subscription channel per day on
unauthenticated web services. Later in this chapter, you will learn about overcoming this limitation by setting up
authenticated web services for push notifications.

You will implement the tile notifications application in the same three steps you followed to
implement toast notifications, namely the following:

1. Create a Windows Phone 7 Notification client application. This application will
    establish a notification channel.

2. Create and execute the Windows Forms client. You will take the URI of the
    notification channel that you established in Step 1, paste it into the Push
    Notifications URL text box, and submit push notification to the application.

3. Verify that you are able to receive tile notifications in the Windows Phone 7 application.

Creating a Client Application

You will take the PNClient application that you have created and enhance it to accept tile notifications in addition to toast notifications. You will not recreate the application; rather, you will concentrate on the changes needed to enable tile notifications.

1. Launch Visual Studio 2010 Express for Windows Phone and open the PNClient project.

2. Locate the BindToShell function inside the MainPage.xaml.cs file. Change that function to look like the one here (essentially, you are adding a line to bind this application to tile notifications):

```
private static void BindToShell(HttpNotificationChannel httpChannel)
    {
    try
        {
        //toast notification binding
    httpChannel.BindToShellToast();
        //tile notification binding
        httpChannel.BindToShellTile();
        }
        catch (Exception)
        {
    //ignore exceptions at the moment
        }
    }
```

These are all the changes you need to make to the PNClient application to enable tile notifications.

Creating an Application to Send Notifications

There are a few changes that you need to make to code that sends push notifications to enable tile notifications processing. First, you'll need to use a different XML schema for tile notifications, as shown here:

```
<?xml version=\"1.0\" encoding="utf-8"?>
<wp:Notification xmlns:wp="WPNotification">
 <wp:Tile>
  <wp:BackgroundImage><URI to Image></wp:BackgroundImage>
  <wp:Count><Count Message></wp:Count>
  <wp:Title><Title Message></wp:Title>
 </wp:Tile>
</wp:Notification>
```

The <URI to Image> element specifies the location, which is either local or remote, of the background image used to update the application tile. <Count Message> is the counter text (the one almost at the center of the tile) to set on the tile and the `<Title Message>` is the message text to set at the bottom of the application tile.

■ **Note**   In the current implementation of Push Notifications for Windows Phone 7, to set the background image to an image located on the Internet, you must specify the location of that image when creating a Windows Phone 7 Notification client application. While this is certainly not very flexible (you would have to know beforehand all of the images that you will be using to update tiles), Microsoft generally does not encourage the use of remote images for tile updates, limiting the maximum allowed size of those images to 80KB and emphasizing in documentation that the use of remote resources leads to excessive battery drain.

Follow these steps to make changes for tile notifications:

1. Open the PNServer project and open code for the `Form1.cs` file (right-click `Form1.cs` in Solution Explorer and select View Code).

2. Now, you will define the XML schema information inside the code. Paste the following string declaration to the top of the file, right underneath the `string ToastPushXML` declaration:

```
string TilePushXML = "<?xml version=\"1.0\" encoding=\"utf-8\"?>" +
        "<wp:Notification xmlns:wp=\"WPNotification\">" +
        "<wp:Tile>" +
        "<wp:Count>{0}</wp:Count>" +
        "<wp:Title>{1}</wp:Title>" +
        "</wp:Tile>" +
        "</wp:Notification>";
```

3. Inside the btnSendNotification_Click event handler, change the following two lines of code

```
sendNotificationRequest.Headers.Add("X-WindowsPhone-Target", "toast");
sendNotificationRequest.Headers.Add("X-NotificationClass", "2");
```

to

```
sendNotificationRequest.Headers.Add("X-WindowsPhone-Target", "token");
sendNotificationRequest.Headers.Add("X-NotificationClass", "1"); //- tiles
```

4. Finally, you need to change the string that gets sent to the Windows Phone 7 application. To accomplish that, change the following line of code inside the btnSendNotification_Click event handler from

```
string str = string.Format(ToastPushXML, txtTitle.Text, txtText.Text);
```

to

```
string str = string.Format(TilePushXML, txtTitle.Text, txtText.Text);
```

These are all of the changes that you need to make to enable tile notifications on the Windows Phone 7 device. You are now ready to test tile notifications on the Windows Phone 7 emulator.

Verifying Delivery of Push Notifications

Having made changes to both the client and the server portions of the code to enable tile notifications, it's time to take them for a spin.

Just as with toast notifications, you need to obtain the URI of the notification channel.

1. Open PNClient project, make sure that you have a connection to the Internet, and press F5 to run the project.

2. Click the Create Channel button and, after seeing the URI printed on the screen, copy it to the clipboard from the Output window.

Remember that tile notifications appear on the phone only when a Windows Phone 7 application associated with these notifications is not running in the foreground on the phone and (this is important!) only when the application tile is available on the Windows Phone 7 Start screen.

3. To pin the application tile onto the Start screen, with the PNClient application running, click the phone's Windows button, and then click the arrow (➤) to open the Windows Phone 7 Options screen, shown in Figure 17–8.

4. Click and hold the left mouse button down (also referred to as "long click") to bring up the pop-up menu shown in Figure 17–8.

5. Click the Pin to Start option.

Now, you should see the PNClient application tile on the Start screen, together with the Internet Explorer tile.

6. Switch to the PNServer Windows Forms project, and press F5 to run it.

7. In the Push Notifications URL text box, paste the URI obtained in Step 1. In the Push Notifications Title and Push Notifications Text text boxes, enter text for the counter and tile message accordingly. For example, to get tile notification to appear as in Figure 17–2, enter "2" for Push Notification Title and "MSFT +2" in Push Notification Text field.

Figure 17–8. To receive tile notifications, the application tile must be pinned to the Start screen.

Now you're ready to send and receive tile notifications.

8. Click the Push Notification button in the PNServer application.

You should now see the application tile updated from default to the one containing both the counter text (2) and the message text (MSFT +2).

As you can see, processing tile notifications is only slightly different from processing toast applications. Processing raw notifications is also very similar to the previous demos; however, since raw notifications are received when an application is running in the foreground only, you would need to wire up an event inside the Windows Phone 7 application to process messages received, as you will see in the next demo implementing raw notifications.

Implementing Raw Notifications

Raw notifications represent the third and final type of push notification available on the Windows Phone 7 platform. Unlike tile and toast notifications, however, raw notifications are available to a Windows Phone 7 application only if that application is running in the foreground. If the application is not running in the foreground, even if the application's icon is pinned to the phone's Start screen, raw notifications are simply dropped.

You will implement raw notifications following the same three general steps as implementing toast and tile notifications, namely the following:

1. Create a Windows Phone 7 Notification client application. This application will establish a notification channel.

2. Create and execute a Windows Forms client. You will take the URI of the notification channel that you established in Step 1, paste it into the Push Notifications URL text box, and submit a push notification to the application.

3. Verify that you are able to receive raw notifications in your Windows Phone 7 application.

Creating a Client Application

You will create the RawNotificationPNClient application to accept raw notifications. This application is similar to the PNClient application you have created in the prior sections of this chapter, yet it has subtle differences from that codebase to warrant a separate project.

1. Launch Visual Studio 2010 Express for Windows Phone and create a new Windows Phone Application project. Name it RawNotificationPNClient.

2. From the Toolbox, drag and drop a text box on the design surface. Rename the text box to txtURI, adjust its width to be the full width of the screen, and adjust its height to be about a quarter of screen's height. Set the text box's TextWrapping property to Wrap and clear out its Text property.

3. From the Toolbox, drag and drop a button on the design surface. Rename the button to btnCreateChannel and set the Content property to Create Channel. Once again, your Windows Phone 7 design surface should now look like Figure 17–6.

4. The `Microsoft.Phone.Notification` namespace contains the functionality necessary to establish a push notification channel and receive push notifications; therefore you need to add the following using directive at the top of the `MainPage.xaml.cs` file:

```
using Microsoft.Phone.Notification;
using System.Diagnostics;
```

5. You will now program the button click event handler to create the push notification URL. In the Windows Phone 7 design surface, double-click the Create Channel button and make that button's click event handler look like the following:

```
private void btnCreateChannel_Click(object sender, RoutedEventArgs e)
        {
                SetupChannel();
        }
```

The `SetupChannel` function, which follows, is responsible for creating a channel within MPNS to receive updates from the server and to fire when the error occurs during communication and when the raw notification is received. Remember that raw notifications are available to the application only when it's running; therefore an event handler must be defined in code that processes raw notifications as they come in. The code that binds the raw notification received event to the httpChannel_HttpNotificationReceived event handler function lives inside the `SetupChannel` function:

```
httpChannel.HttpNotificationReceived += new
  EventHandler<HttpNotificationEventArgs>(httpChannel_HttpNotificationReceived);
```

6. Here's the complete implementation of the SetupChannel function. Add the code to your project:

```
private void SetupChannel()
{
        HttpNotificationChannel httpChannel = null;
        string channelName = "DemoChannel";

        try
        {
         //if channel exists, retrieve existing channel
         httpChannel = HttpNotificationChannel.Find(channelName);
         if (httpChannel != null)
         {
         //If you can't get it, then close and reopen it.
         if (httpChannel.ChannelUri == null)
         {
                httpChannel.UnbindToShellToast();
                httpChannel.Close();
                SetupChannel();
                return;
         }
         else
         {
                ChannelUri = httpChannel.ChannelUri;

         //wiring up the raw notifications event handler
                httpChannel.HttpNotificationReceived += new
        EventHandler<HttpNotificationEventArgs>(httpChannel_HttpNotificationReceived);
         }
        }
        else
        {
                httpChannel = new HttpNotificationChannel(channelName);
                httpChannel.ChannelUriUpdated += new

    EventHandler<NotificationChannelUriEventArgs>(httpChannel_ChannelUriUpdated);
        httpChannel.ErrorOccurred += new

        EventHandler<NotificationChannelErrorEventArgs>(httpChannel_ExceptionOccurred)
        ;

                //wiring up the raw notifications event handler
                httpChannel.HttpNotificationReceived += new

    EventHandler<HttpNotificationEventArgs>(httpChannel_HttpNotificationReceived);

                httpChannel.Open();
}
```

```
            }
            catch (Exception ex)
            {

            }
        }
```

What you do with received raw notifications is totally up to you: raw notifications can be simple status messages to be shown in the Windows Phone 7 client application, or they can be directives to the application to perform a given task. In this application, you will simply print a message into the text box with the text of raw notifications received.

7. To print the raw notification, add the following code:

```
            void httpChannel_HttpNotificationReceived(object sender,
HttpNotificationEventArgs e)
                {
                  if (e.Notification.Body != null && e.Notification.Headers != null)
                  {
                System.IO.StreamReader reader = new
                System.IO.StreamReader(e.Notification.Body);
                            Dispatcher.BeginInvoke(() =>
                    {
                      txtURI.Text = "Raw Notification Message Received: " +
reader.ReadToEnd();
                    });
                  }
            }
```

You are very close to completing the client application; what remains is to write an error handling function that will fire off when any errors during communication occur. You will also write a simple event handler that will fire off when the push notification channel URI gets updated.

8. Add the following code to your application:

```
    void httpChannel_ExceptionOccurred(object sender, NotificationChannelErrorEventArgs e)
    {
      //Display Message on error
            Debug.WriteLine ( e.Message);
    }

    void httpChannel_ChannelUriUpdated(object sender, NotificationChannelUriEventArgs e)
    {
      //You get the new Uri (or maybe it's updated)
      ChannelUri = e.ChannelUri;
    }
```

9. Finally, add the following helper code to the top of the MainPage class. This code will print the push notification channel URI into the Debug window; you will need that URI to test the application shortly.

```
    Uri channelUri;

        public Uri ChannelUri
```

```
        {
                get { return channelUri; }
                set
                {
                        channelUri = value;
                        OnChannelUriChanged(value);
                }
        }

        private void OnChannelUriChanged(Uri value)
        {
                Dispatcher.BeginInvoke(() =>
                {
                        txtURI.Text = "changing uri to " + value.ToString();
                });

                Debug.WriteLine("changing uri to " + value.ToString());
        }
```

With the client application complete, press F5 to make sure that the application compiles and runs. In the next section, you will be building a server piece to send raw notifications to this client application.

Creating an Application to Send Notifications

Sending raw notifications from the server is simpler than sending Tiles or Toasts: there are no XML templates for message formatting for raw notifications. You will reuse the PNServer project created in the prior sections and edit the button click event handler for raw notifications processing. Follow these steps to accomplish that:

1. Open the PNServer project and open code for the Form1.cs file (right-click Form1.cs in Solution Explorer and select View Code).

2. Replace the btnSendNotification_Click event handler with the following code. Note how the X-NotificationClass header value is set to 3 and how the X-WindowsPhone-Target header value is left blank to indicate that this is a raw notification.

```
        private void btnSendNotification_Click(object sender, EventArgs e)
        {
                if (txtURL.Text == string.Empty)
                {
                        MessageBox.Show("Please enter a url");
                        return;
                }

                if (txtTitle.Text == string.Empty || txtText.Text == string.Empty)
                {
                        MessageBox.Show("Please enter text and title to send");
                        return;
                }
```

```
    HttpWebRequest sendNotificationRequest =

        (HttpWebRequest)WebRequest.Create(txtURL.Text);

            sendNotificationRequest.Method = "POST";
            sendNotificationRequest.Headers = new WebHeaderCollection();
            sendNotificationRequest.ContentType = "text/xml";

            sendNotificationRequest.Headers.Add("X-WindowsPhone-Target", "");
            sendNotificationRequest.Headers.Add("X-NotificationClass", "3"); //-
raw
            string str = string.Format(txtTitle.Text + "\r\n" + txtText.Text);
            byte[] strBytes = new UTF8Encoding().GetBytes(str);
            sendNotificationRequest.ContentLength = strBytes.Length;
            using (Stream requestStream =
sendNotificationRequest.GetRequestStream())
                {
                    requestStream.Write(strBytes, 0, strBytes.Length);
                }

        HttpWebResponse response =
            (HttpWebResponse)sendNotificationRequest.GetResponse();
            string notificationStatus = response.Headers["X-NotificationStatus"];
            string deviceConnectionStatus = response.Headers["X-
DeviceConnectionStatus"];
                lblStatus.Text = "Status: " + notificationStatus + " : " +
deviceConnectionStatus;
                }
```

That's all the code necessary to send raw notifications to Windows Phone 7 clients. You are now ready to test raw notifications on the Windows Phone 7 emulator.

Testing Delivery of Raw Notifications

Testing raw notifications is very straightforward: there are no applications to pin to the Start screen—simply start both the client and the server pieces of the application, make sure that the push notification URL is available to both, and fire away! This demo gives more details on testing raw notifications.

1. Just as with toast and tile notifications, you need to obtain the URI of the notification channel. Open the RawNotificationPNClient project, make sure that you have a connection to the Internet, and press F5 to run the project. Click the Create Channel button and, after seeing the URI printed on the screen, copy it to the clipboard from the Output window.

2. Switch to the PNServer Windows Forms project and press F5 to run it. In the Push Notifications URL text box, paste the URI obtained in Step 1. In the Push Notifications Title and Push Notifications Text text boxes, enter "Hello" and "World" correspondingly. Click the Send Notification button.

3. You should now see the message stating that the raw notification has been received and the "Hello World" message on the Windows Phone 7 emulator screen.

As you can see, implementing raw notifications is very similar to implementing tile and toast notifications, albeit a bit simpler. Each one of the notification types has its purposes; use the most appropriate notification type for your circumstances.

You may be shaking your head by now, thinking that the copy and paste method of communicating the push notification channel URL between the client and the server is completely unrealistic for any commercial application. We agree, and we will show you how to automate that communication piece in the next section.

Implementing Cloud Service to Track Push Notifications

In the previous demos, you have used a somewhat unrealistic approach to communicating push notification URLs from the Windows Phone 7 client application to the push notification server. You copied that URL from the Debug window of the client application and pasted it into the server application, where it was used to send tiles, toasts, and raw notifications to the Windows Phone 7 applications. To make the stock alerts application a bit more real-world, however, you must automate the URL communication piece. In this section, you will learn how to do that using a cloud service built with the Microsoft Windows Communication Foundation (WCF) stack of technologies.

Creating a WCF Service to Track Notification Recipients

This section will show you how to enhance the PNServer application built previously by adding a WCF service to it. WCF is a very powerful technology with an array of configuration options for creating and hosting cloud services. You will be building what is known as a *self-hosted service*, which means that it will be hosted within the Windows Forms application and you will write code to initialize and start that service. Another important point about this service is that it will be a *RESTful service*, which, for your purposes right now, means that you can access operations of the service over the properly formatted URLs, as you will see shortly.

Before you create a RESTful WCF service, however, you may need to make a small change in the Visual Studio environment to reference assemblies you need to create that service. The reason for this is that, by default, Visual Studio creates a lightweight profile for client applications, such as Windows Forms or Windows Presentation Foundation (WPF) applications. This lightweight profile omits many web-related assemblies by default because the chances of a true client application needing them are slim.

The setting that controls which assemblies are included or left out is the Target Framework setting, and it is located on your project's Properties page. You need to change this setting from .Net Framework 4 Client Profile to .Net Framework 4. To accomplish this, open the PNServer project if it's not already open, right-click the project name, and then select Properties. Locate the Target Framework setting and set it to .Net Framework 4, as illustrated in Figure 17–9.

Figure 17–9. *To add RESTful WCF service to the Windows Forms application, set the application's target framework to .NET Framework 4.*

Now follow these steps to complete creation of the WCF service. First, before creating the service, you need to include the System.ServiceModel.Web assembly to the PNServer project.

1. Right-click the project name and select Add Reference. Locate the System.ServiceModel.Web assembly in the list, highlight it, and click OK.

Now, you will add WCF service files to the project. Adding the WCF service files will consist of two parts: creating what is known as a *Service Contract*, which will appear in the form of an Interface file, and defining a class that will physically implement the methods defined within the Service Contract.

2. To create the Service Contract, right-click the project name, choose Add ➤ New Item, and then scroll almost all the way to the bottom and pick WCF Service. Name the service Registration Service, and then click OK.

3. Add the following statement to the top of the IRegistrationService.cs file created:

```
using System.ServiceModel.Web;
```

4. Add the following code to the IRegistrationService.cs file:

```
[ServiceContract]
public interface IRegistrationService
{
            [OperationContract, WebGet]
            void Register(string uri);

            [OperationContract, WebGet]
            void Unregister(string uri);
}
```

Note how you defined two operations for the service to perform: Register new Windows Phone 7 clients for push notifications and Unregister them.

Now it's time to add the implementation of the Register and Unregister methods.

5. Double-click the RegistrationService.cs file that Visual Studio added to your project. Make the RegistrationService.cs file look like the code here:

```
public class RegistrationService : IRegistrationService
{
            private static List<Uri> subscribers = new List<Uri>();
            private static object obj = new object();

            public void Register(string uri)
            {
                    Uri channelUri = new Uri(uri, UriKind.Absolute);
                    Subscribe(channelUri);
            }

            public void Unregister(string uri)
            {
                    Uri channelUri = new Uri(uri, UriKind.Absolute);
                    Unsubscribe(channelUri);
            }

            private void Subscribe(Uri channelUri)
            {
                    lock (obj)
                    {
                        if (!subscribers.Exists((u) => u == channelUri))
                        {
                            subscribers.Add(channelUri);
                        }
                    }
            }

            public static void Unsubscribe(Uri channelUri)
            {
                    lock (obj)
                    {
                        subscribers.Remove(channelUri);
                    }
```

```
        }

        public static List<Uri> GetSubscribers()
        {
                return subscribers;
        }
}
```

Take a look closer look at the code that you just added to the `RegistrationService.cs` file. Notice that the `RegistrationService` class implements the `IRegistrationService` interface on the very first line—this is important! Aside from that, the code is pretty straightforward: a collection of push notification URIs is maintained in the static `subscribers` variable, and every client that calls the `Register` method of the service gets added to that list of subscribers. The `lock` function is used to prevent multiple clients changing the same data at the same exact moment in time, possibly resulting in incomplete and unpredictable data.

In the beginning of this section, we said that a WCF service hosted by a Windows Forms application needs initialization code to start up. One of the places this initialization code can go is in the load event of Form1.

6. Here's the code you need to start up the service. Copy it to the load event of Form1 here:

```
        ServiceHost host;
        host = new ServiceHost(typeof(RegistrationService));
        host.Open();
```

You're almost done—you only need to provide some configuration parameters for the WCF service to run.

7. Open the `app.config` file and add the following configuration parameters to the `<system.ServiceModel>` element (you should already have configuration settings defined within `<system.ServiceModel>`, but now you need to make sure those settings match precisely what is pasted here):

```
<system.serviceModel>
        <behaviors>
        <endpointBehaviors>
        <behavior name="EndpointPNServerServiceBehavior">
            <webHttp />
        </behavior>
        </endpointBehaviors>
        <serviceBehaviors>
        <behavior name="">
            <serviceDebug includeExceptionDetailInFaults="true" />
        </behavior>
        </serviceBehaviors>
        </behaviors>
        <services>
        <service name="PNServer.RegistrationService">
        <endpoint address="http://localhost/RegistrationService"
            behaviorConfiguration="EndpointPNServerServiceBehavior"
            binding="webHttpBinding"
            contract="WP7_Push_Notifications.IRegistrationService">
```

```
        </endpoint>
      </service>
    </services>
  </system.serviceModel>
```

In a nutshell, with these settings you have configured your service to listen at the following address: `http://localhost/RegistrationService`. You have also specified that the requests to this service will be coming over the http protocol.

Finally, you will modify the main application form (Form1) and add a Broadcast button that will send a push notification to all subscribed clients. Once clicked, the button click handler will get a list of all clients subscribed and send each one of them a push notification (toast notification in the following code). Here's how to do this:

8. Open `Form1.cs` in Design view and add a button to that form underneath the Send Notification button.

   a. Change the button's text to Broadcast, as shown in Figure 17–10.

   b. Change the button's name to btnBroadcast, double-click it, and make sure that the button's Click event contains the following code:

```
private void btnBroadcast_Click(object sender, EventArgs e)
{
        if (txtTitle.Text == string.Empty || txtText.Text ==
string.Empty)
        {
         MessageBox.Show("Please enter text and title to send");
           return;
        }

        List<Uri> allSubscribersUri =
RegistrationService.GetSubscribers();

        foreach (Uri subscriberUri in allSubscribersUri)
        {
          sendPushNotificationToClient(subscriberUri.ToString());
        }
}
```

Figure 17–10. Main application form with Broadcast button

9. Add the following code to the sendPushNotificationToClient function:

```
private void sendPushNotificationToClient(string url)
{
    HttpWebRequest sendNotificationRequest =
(HttpWebRequest)WebRequest.Create(url);

    sendNotificationRequest.Method = "POST";
    sendNotificationRequest.Headers = new WebHeaderCollection();
    sendNotificationRequest.ContentType = "text/xml";

    sendNotificationRequest.Headers.Add("X-WindowsPhone-Target", "toast");
    sendNotificationRequest.Headers.Add("X-NotificationClass", "2");

    string str = string.Format(TilePushXML, txtTitle.Text, txtText.Text);
    byte[] strBytes = new UTF8Encoding().GetBytes(str);
    sendNotificationRequest.ContentLength = strBytes.Length;
    using (Stream requestStream = sendNotificationRequest.GetRequestStream())
{
 requestStream.Write(strBytes, 0, strBytes.Length);
}

    try
    {
        HttpWebResponse response =
(HttpWebResponse)sendNotificationRequest.GetResponse();
        string notificationStatus = response.Headers["X-NotificationStatus"];
     string deviceConnectionStatus = response.Headers["X-DeviceConnectionStatus"];
```

```
        lblStatus.Text = "Status: " + notificationStatus + " : " +
    deviceConnectionStatus;
    }
    catch (Exception ex)
    {
        //handle 404 (URI not found) and other exceptions that may occur
        lblStatus.Text = "Failed to connect, exception detail: " + ex.Message;
    }
```

Note that the TilePushXML variable was previously defined when we talked about Tile Notifications—specifically, in the "Creating an Application to Send Notifications" section. With the WCF service tracking subscribed clients and sending push notifications complete, it's now time to enhance the client application to call the web service with its push notification URL.

Modifying the Client to Call the WCF Service

The Windows Phone 7 Push Notification client application needs to be modified to call the newly implemented web service with the push notification URL. Previously, we briefly mentioned that the convenience of creating a RESTful WCF service lies in the fact that the operations of that web service can be accessed as URLs. For instance, the URL http://localhost/RegistrationService/Register?uri={0} accesses the Register function of the web service created in the previous section; the uri parameter is supplied on the QueryString. With that in mind, you can go ahead and complete the Windows Phone 7 Push Notification client implementation by creating the functions that will register/unregister a Windows Phone 7 client with the server.

1. Launch Visual Studio 2010 Express for Windows Phone and open the PNClient project.

2. Locate the ChannelUri property getter and setter and change them to the following (notice the use of two new functions, RegisterUriWithServer and UnregisterUriFromServer):

```
public Uri ChannelUri
{
    get { return channelUri; }
    set
    {
        //unregister the old URI from the server
        if (channelUri!=null)
        UnregisterUriFromServer(channelUri);

        //register the new URI with the server
        RegisterUriWithServer(value);

        channelUri = value;
        OnChannelUriChanged(value);
    }
}
```

3. Now add the following two functions to invoke the WCF service that you have created (note that when it comes time to release your service to production, you will be most likely deploying this service somewhere in the cloud):

```
private void RegisterUriWithServer(Uri newChannelUri)
{
    //Hardcode for solution - need to be updated in case the REST WCF service
address change
    string baseUri = "http://localhost/RegistrationService/Register?uri={0}";
    string theUri = String.Format(baseUri, newChannelUri.ToString());
    WebClient client = new WebClient();
    client.DownloadStringCompleted += (s, e) =>
    {
        if (e.Error == null)
            Dispatcher.BeginInvoke(() => {
                txtURI.Text = "changing uri to " +
newChannelUri.ToString();
            });
        else
            Dispatcher.BeginInvoke(() =>
            {
                txtURI.Text = "registration failed " +
e.Error.Message;
            });
    };
    client.DownloadStringAsync(new Uri(theUri));

}

private void UnregisterUriFromServer(Uri oldChannelUri)
{
    //Hardcode for solution - need to be updated in case the REST WCF service
address change
    string baseUri = "http://localhost/RegistrationService/Unregister?uri={0}";
    string theUri = String.Format(baseUri, oldChannelUri.ToString());
    WebClient client = new WebClient();
    client.DownloadStringCompleted += (s, e) =>
    {
        if (e.Error == null)
            Dispatcher.BeginInvoke(() =>
            {
                txtURI.Text = "unregistered uri " + oldChannelUri.ToString();
            });
        else
            Dispatcher.BeginInvoke(() =>
            {
                txtURI.Text = "registration delete failed " + e.Error.Message;
            });
    };
    client.DownloadStringAsync(new Uri(theUri));
}
```

In the preceding code, notice that the URL of the cloud service is hardcoded—this URL must match the URL you have specified in the configuration file (app.config) for the WCF service. Notice also how the event handlers (client.DownloadStringCompleted) are wired up—those event handlers provide the status updates on whether the registration/unregistration succeeded or failed.

At this point, you have completed writing both the server and the client pieces for automated push notification. It is now time to verify that the server is able to keep track and notify its clients appropriately, without the need to manually copy and paste the push notification URL.

Verifying Automated Push Notification Subscriber Tracking

To test automated push notification tracking, the very first thing you have to do is make sure that the WCF service starts up appropriately and that it is able to process requests coming in. Here's how:

1. WCF Services are designed with security in mind, so there are numerous security configuration options for those services. To bypass security configuration options so that they don't take distract from the main points of this chapter and allow you to test the service that you have built, you will need to run the WCF Service project as Administrator. The quickest way to accomplish this is to exit Visual Studio, then right-click on the shortcut to Visual Studio, and choose "Run as Administrator" option. Once Visual Studio comes up, open the PNServer solution. You are now set to run PNServer as Administrator.

2. To verify that the WCF service is indeed ready to accept client connections, set a breakpoint at the first line of the Register function of the RegistrationService class, and then press F5 to start the PNServer application.

3. If the application is running and the Windows form in Figure 17–10 is displayed, then fire up Internet Explorer (or any other browser) and go to the following URL:

   http://localhost/RegistrationService/Register?uri=http://www.microsoft.com

If the breakpoint gets hit after you access this URL, this means that the service is running and it is ready for clients to connect.

If the breakpoint does not get hit and you see a message that the page cannot be displayed, verify that the content in the <system.ServiceModel> section of your app.config file in the PNServer project matches the content of that file described in the section on creating a WCF service. Most likely, some sort of configuration issue is preventing you from properly launching the service.

Once you've confirmed that the service is running, you can observe the automated push notification subscriber tracking in action by following these steps:

4. Launch PNClient application and click the Create Channel button. If you still have the breakpoint set in the Register function of the WCF service, that breakpoint should be hit.

5. To be able to see toast notifications on the phone, you need to pin the application icon to the Start screen. To accomplish this, click the phone's Windows button, and then click the arrow (➤) to open the Windows Phone 7 Options screen, as shown in Figure 17–8. Click and hold the left mouse button (also referred to as a "long click") to bring up the pop-up menu shown in Figure 17–8, and then click the Pin to Start option.

6. With the application icon pinned onto the Start screen, you are ready to receive notifications on the phone. In the PNServer application window, enter the title and the text of the notification message to send and press the Broadcast button. A second or two later, you should see the push notification coming through to the phone.

With clients and cloud service dynamically exchanging push notification URLs and clients accepting push notifications, this is a good point to conclude push notifications demos. The next sections will give you a perspective on using push notifications in the real world and summarize what you have learned in this chapter. The solution that you have built in this chapter provides the full lifecycle implementation of Push Notifications; however, it has a set of limitations that should be considered before deploying it to production. Windows Phone 7 client applications that go down don't unregister themselves from the server; therefore, the server will try to send notifications to non-existent channels. The server lacks persistency—all of the connected client addresses are kept in-memory, which means that they all will be lost should the service be shut down accidentally or on purpose. Finally, there's no centralized scheduling or event-based mechanism for distributing notifications: you have to push the button on the Windows Forms application to distribute the notifications. In the real world, the notifications will most likely be distributed in response to some external events (such as Microsoft stock rising rapidly), and the service has to be smart about handling those.

Using Push Notifications in the Real World

Push notifications provide a scalable framework for Windows Phone 7 applications that lets them receive important messages without the need to continuously run in the background. This approach preserves device resources (processor, Internet connection) and extends battery life. There are many potential uses for Push notifications: from Twitter updates to severe weather alerts to stock market notifications. This chapter demonstrated how you can send push notifications to Windows Phone 7 devices using a Windows Forms application; just as easily, it could be a web-based or cloud-based application that sends those updates. In this chapter, you built a cloud service to programmatically keep track and send notifications to the connected clients. This same cloud service could be further enhanced to send out push notifications on a schedule.

Currently, there is a limit on how many free push notifications can be sent to a single notification channel URI. That limit is 500 notifications per 24 hours per URI. That means that you can send 500 messages per app per device for free for every 24 hours. This limitation is in place to prevent abuse or malicious attacks and possibly spam through a notification channel. To get past the limit of 500 messages per channel in the 24-hour window, follow the guidelines in the next section, "Setting Up Secure Web Services for Push Notifications." The communication channel between the Windows Phone 7 and the Microsoft Push Notification Service is secure, and customers also have an option (for a fee) to secure the channel between their web service and MPNS, as described next.

Setting up Secure Web Services for Push Notifications

In a nutshell, to set up secure web services for Push Notifications, you must acquire an SSL certificate from one of the trusted root Certificate Authorities (a full list can be found at http://msdn.microsoft.com/en-us/library/gg521150(v=VS.92).aspx, and it includes companies like Verisign and RSA Security among others). Once you acquire that certificate, submit it to the Windows Phone Marketplace at the time of application certification. This will allow you to process unlimited push notification messages per secure channel.

Of course, as a prudent developer, you will want to test the secure communication channel between your Windows Phone 7 application, MPNS, and your web service before you reach the application certification step. Microsoft allows you to do so by letting you upload a certificate purchased from trusted CA to the Windows Phone Marketplace ahead of the certification process. Once the certificate is uploaded, you have four months to test secure communication out between your Windows Phone 7 application and your cloud service via Push Notifications. After your application passes certification, the four-month time limit is removed, and you gain access to unlimited push notifications via secure communication channel—truly the best practice for utilizing Microsoft Push Notifications.

Summary

This chapter gave the background and provided an introduction to push notification services. You gained an understanding of various push notification types, as well as the general architecture of push notifications. You implemented all three forms of push notifications: toast, tile, and raw. Finally, you completed the push notifications life cycle by creating a simple yet realistic WCF service to keep track of all Windows Phone 7 clients connecting to it and to broadcast messages to all subscribed clients.

In the next chapter, you will take a look at simplifying and abstracting asynchronous and event-based programming with Reactive Extensions for .Net, also referred to as Rx.Net. With Rx.Net, the implementation of concurrent asynchronous and events-based applications becomes easy and manageable. You could perhaps start thinking about implementing the server portion of Push Notifications using Rx.NET, with notifications broadcasting messages using Rx.NET techniques in response to a given event (such as severe weather alert or a stock price alert).

CHAPTER 18

Reactive Extensions for .NET

For developers, the computing world of today is becoming much more concurrent than just a few short years ago. Computer users expect an ever-increasing computational power from their electronic gadgets, including their mobile devices. Unfortunately, it seems that the only way manufacturers will be able to increase computational speed in the near future is through adding additional processors (instead of making a single processor faster, as has been the case over the last few decades). In the case of processors on personal computers, the industry has already hit a proverbial brick wall, having pretty much reached the maximum computational capacity available on a single processing unit. An average personal computer today comes with two or more processing units, and the number is certain to increase.

Mobile devices still have some processing speed to grow into before they max out the processing power of a single CPU. However, the average phone will soon have several processing units as well. In addition, uninterrupted Internet access on the phone is assumed—resources needed for proper functioning of an application may be spread around the world (in the cloud), but the user is rarely aware of that. A phone application should have the ability to access those resources seamlessly as needed—i.e., it should not stop accepting all input from the user while these resources are accessed. Rather, an application should retrieve the resources without interrupting other functionality of an application—in other words, it should obtain these resources asynchronously. The future for both personal computers and mobile devices is both concurrent and asynchronous.

How do you approach concurrent and asynchronous programming on Windows Phone 7? The answer is, certainly, with great caution, since it's not easy. To help tame that complexity, a powerful framework emerged on the .NET scene at the end of 2009. That framework, called the Reactive Extensions for .NET (also known as Rx.NET), is now available for Windows Phone 7 and provides sophisticated mechanisms to make event processing and asynchronous programming more intuitive. In this chapter, you will learn the concepts behind Reactive Extensions for .NET and build two simple applications using the Rx.NET framework. The first will search and retrieve images on Flickr asynchronously. The second will display the current weather after accepting a ZIP code as input from the user. As with several other chapters of this volume, a whole book could be written on the subject of Reactive Extensions alone, especially since there is a version of Reactive Extensions for JavaScript available as well.

In this chapter, you will learn the basics of Rx.NET and, we hope, leave with a basic understanding and appreciation of this technology. However, to leverage the power of Rx.NET, you need a good understanding of LINQ. Although the examples in this chapter should be relatively easy to understand for the novice C# programmer even without an in-depth knowledge of LINQ, for expert coverage of the topic we recommend the excellent book *Pro LINQ: Language Integrated Query in C#2008* by Joseph C. Ratz (Apress, 2008). Another good resource is "101 LINQ Samples," available for free online at http://msdn.microsoft.com/en-us/vcsharp/aa336746.aspx. Rx.NET also relies heavily on general object-oriented principles; if the concept of interfaces is not familiar to you, it may be a good idea to understand those before reading this chapter. Finally, Rx.NET constructs make extensive use of the newer concepts of the .NET Framework, such as lambda expressions and extension methods. While it will be possible to follow examples in this book without in-depth understanding of either of those concepts, to leverage the power of Rx.NET on your own, you will have to know these features of the .NET Framework.

The power of Reactive Framework can be applied to deal with a wide range of computational issues. This chapter will focus on the way that the framework deals with a problem that is probably as old as the personal computer: how do you provide a responsive user interface while utilizing the full computational resources available? And how can you do so in a manner that makes code readable and easy to manage/maintain?

■ **Note**   The initial release of Rx.NET libraries comes pre-installed on the operating system of every Windows Phone 7 device. However, just like any other technology, the Reactive Extensions library is constantly being enhanced to deliver even more power to the developers. As a Windows Phone 7 developer, you are not "stuck" having to use the version of Rx.NET that comes preinstalled on the devices—you can always go to the Microsoft Data Developer Center (http://msdn.microsoft.com/en-us/data/gg577609) and download the latest libraries available for the phone. Once you reference and use them, they will be distributed together with your application, slightly increasing its footprint.

Introducing Reactive Programming

Rx.NET aims to revolutionize *reactive* programming in the .NET Framework. In reactive programming, you register an interest in something and have items of interest handed over, or pushed to the attention of the application, asynchronously, as they become available. A classic example of an application that relies heavily on the reactive programming model is the spreadsheet, where an update to a single cell triggers cascading updates to every cell that references it. This concept of having things pushed down as they become available is particularly well suited to applications that use constantly changing data sources, such as the weather application that you will be building in this chapter.

Reactive programming is often contrasted with interactive programming, where the user asks for something and then waits for it until it is delivered. To help further differentiate these concepts, let's take a look at a car shopping analogy. Usually, when shopping for a car, you go to a car dealership (or look online) and look at different car makes and models. You pick the ones you like and test-drive them. This arrangement is an example of interactive programming, where you asked for a car and got it in return. In a reactive approach to car shopping experience, you would send a note to a dealership expressing interest in a certain make and model and then continue going on with your daily routine. The dealer locates items of interest and notifies you when they become available.

Let's see if we can carry over this analogy to event processing on Windows Phone 7. For the sample application that you will be building later in this chapter, you will want to read the contents of a text box once it can be determined that no keystroke has occurred a half a second since the previous one. In the sample, this will be taken to mean that the user has finished typing and is ready for the application to do something. If you were to use an interactive approach, you would implement this by wiring up the KeyDown event for the text box, and then checking some sort of timer to see whether enough time had elapsed between keystrokes. In a reactive approach, as you will see shortly, things are much simpler: you express interest in being notified of KeyDown events only after a half-second has elapsed between a user's keystrokes. Once notified of such an event, you take action—searching for photos online, in this case. Before you learn how to search for photos in a reactive manner, however, you will walk through several short examples to get a feeling for how Reactive Extensions implement the core Observer pattern, which forms the basis of the Reactive Framework and is described in detail in the following sidebar.

Rx.NET Subscription Pipeline

To use Rx.NET, there are four basic steps that you have to follow to designate observables and create observers.

1. First, you build or define an Observable (or Subject, as it is called in the Observer pattern described in the sidebar).

2. Then, you subscribe to that Observable (or create an Observer if you follow along with the Observer pattern in the sidebar).

3. Next, you receive data and act on it for as long as the Subject continues to notify the Observer.

4. Finally, when there are no more notifications from the Subject to process, the Observer unsubscribes from the Subject by calling the `Dispose` method.

Rx.NET defines two new interfaces to accommodate this subscription pipeline: IObservable and IObserver. You will learn how to use these interfaces in the next few sections.

THE OBSERVER PATTERN

The Observer pattern is a commonly used technique (pattern) in the world of object-oriented software development. At its basis, it has a Subject object that keeps track of all the objects (referred to as Observers) that want to be notified about changes to the Subject's state. All Observers are automatically notified of any changes to the Subject. The power of this pattern comes from not having to query the Subject for specific changes to its state—the Subject will promptly let Observers know when it gets modified. For detailed description of the Observer pattern, you can refer to *Design Patterns: Elements of Reusable Object-Oriented Software* by Gamma et al (Addison-Wesley, 1994) or you can read about it on Wikipedia at `http://en.wikipedia.org/wiki/Observer_pattern`.

According to Microsoft DevLabs, where the Reactive Extensions library was developed, the objective of Rx.NET is to enable the composition of asynchronous and event-driven programs. Rx.NET uses *observable collections* to enable such composition. In Rx.NET, Observable collections perform the role of the Subject in the Observer pattern. Observable collections gather data associated with a given event or an asynchronous method call and notify everyone who has subscribed to these collections of the changes as they occur. This might sound a bit confusing, so let's jump into code that will allow you to start using key features of Rx.NET right away to build awesome Windows Phone 7 applications.

Implementing the Observer Pattern with Rx.NET

Before you create an application that asynchronously searches photos on Flickr, you will take a short detour to understand the basics of Rx.NET. In the project that follows, you will generate a simple Observable collection using Reactive Extensions for .NET and read values from this collection as they are pushed down to you. Follow these step-by-step instructions.

Creating a Windows Phone Project

First, you will create a new Windows Phone 7 project and add framework elements necessary to make it work on the mobile platform.

1.   Launch Visual Studio 2010 Express for Windows Phone and create a new Windows Phone Application project. Name it RxSample.

In this project, you will observe the messages generated by the Reactive Extensions framework in the text box on the phone screen.

2.   From the Toolbox, select the textblock and drop it on the design surface. Since you are just getting your feet wet with Rx.NET, leave the name of the textblock (textBlock1) unchanged for now and adjust its height and width to occupy the full area of the screen. Highlight the textblock, press F4 to bring up its Properties window, and set the TextWrapping property to Wrap.

On Windows Phone 7, the Rx.Net implementation is contained within two separate assemblies–`Microsoft.Phone.Reactive` and `System.Observable`.

3. Add a reference to `Microsoft.Phone.Reactive` and `System.Observable`
   assemblies by right-clicking and selecting Add Reference.

Adding Code to Create and Read Observable Collections

You will now add code to create an Observable collection, subscribe to it, and read values from it.

1. Import the Rx.NET libraries to current code. To do that, open
   `MainPage.xaml.cs` (right-click `MainPage.xaml` and select View Code) and add
   the following statement to the top of the page:

   ```
   using Microsoft.Phone.Reactive;
   ```

Remember how an Observable collection performs the role of the Subject in the Observer pattern.
In Rx.NET, the `IObservable<T>` interface acts as that Subject. You will now create an Observable
collection that will consist of a range of integer values.

2. In the `MainPage()` constructor, add the following code right after the
   `InitializeComponent()` statement:

   ```
   IObservable<int> source = Observable.Range(5, 3);
   ```

Notice the use of the `Observable.Range` method to create an Observable collection that will consist
of a range of integers from 5 to 7 inclusive (the Range method created three sequential values, from 5 to 7
inclusive).

You will now create an Observer for the source Subject created in Step 2. This Observer object will
be notified of any changes to the source—in this case, every time a new integer is generated, or "pushed
down" to the application. Notice that the Observer object implements IDisposable interface as well.

3. Add the following code to create the Observer:

   ```
   IDisposable subscription = source.Subscribe(x =>
           textBlock1.Text += String.Format(" OnNext: {0}", x),
           ex => textBlock1.Text += String.Format(" OnError: {0}", ex.Message),
           () => textBlock1.Text += " OnCompleted");
   ```

The `Subscribe` method of `IObservable<T>` has several overloads; the one that you just used accepts
three *lambda expressions* (see the "Lambda Expressions" sidebar) as its parameters: the first lambda
expression contains the logic to invoke when another element becomes available to the Observer
(OnNext), the second has logic to invoke if there is an exception in the Observer (OnError), and the last
one contains logic that gets executed when the Subject completes its useful life (OnComplete). The
"completion of useful life" condition varies from Subject to Subject, but generally means that there are
no more elements to receive from the Subject. If you're not familiar with lambda expressions, the
sidebar contains a brief introduction to this newer feature of the .NET Framework.

4. Finally, tell the Observer to discontinue its interest in the Subject's state by
   issuing a `Dispose()` method:

   ```
   subscription.Dispose();
   ```

5. Press F5 to run the application. The Windows Phone 7 emulator screen will
   appear, showing messages OnNext: 5, OnNext: 6, OnNext: 7, and OnComplete,
   as shown in Figure 18–1. The Observable object generated three integer values,
   pushed them down to Observers, and called it quits.

LAMBDA EXPRESSIONS

With the release of C# 3.0, Microsoft borrowed a number of features from the so-called family of functional programming languages. Among these features is the ability to define functions inline known to C# programmers by the intimidating term "lambda expression." At a basic level, lambda expressions are simply functions that differ from "normal" C# functions in their syntax. In your example, x =>textBlock1.Text += String.Format(" OnNext: {0}", x) is a lambda expression that defines a function that accepts x as a parameter and infers its type from context. The textBlock1.Text += String.Format(" OnNext: {0}", x) statement is the body of the function. Note that if you see the "()=>" syntax in the lambda expression, as in the last parameter to the Subscribe function (Step 3), it means that no parameters are being passed in to the lambda expression.

Figure 18–1. Reactive Extensions for .NET first steps

In the previous code, notice how subscription does not implement the IObserver<T> interface. That is because the Microsoft.Phone.Reactive assembly contains a set of extension methods that overload the Subscribe() method of IObservable. These overloaded methods accept OnNext, OnError, and OnCompleted handlers defined by the IObserver<T> interface as lambda expressions, just as described in the previous paragraphs. Hence, in your experiments and samples with Rx.NET in this chapter, you will not have to physically implement the IObserver<T> interface.

The output of your first Rx.NET application (shown in Figure 18–1) is certainly nothing spectacular. But you are just barely skimming the Rx.NET surface here. Imagine subscribing to events, such as keystrokes or data emitted by the location service. Then, imagine having the ability to react to those events only if certain conditions are met. For instance, filter out location values so that only when the location specifies a certain predefined area, the event is raised. In the next section, you will build a small application that uses this filtering approach to make an asynchronous web service call to Flickr once the user has stopped typing text for half a second.

Using Rx.NET Event Handling to Search for Flickr Photographs

In this section, you will build an application that searches Flickr photos asynchronously using Rx.NET. In particular, you will learn how to create Observable data sources from events, as well as how to subscribe to them. The version of Flickr search you'll create is shown in Figure 18–2. The search technique is basic and uses a WebBrowser control to display images; however, this example will allow you to concentrate on learning the Rx.NET techniques for processing events on the Windows Phone 7. In the next example, you will build a Weather Service application that will demonstrate asynchronous programming with Rx.NET. Let's get started.

Creating a Windows Phone Project

First, create a new Windows Phone 7 project for the Flickr image search.

1. Launch Visual Studio 2010 Express for Windows Phone and create a new Windows Phone Application project. Name it FlickrRx.

2. Change the name of the application to Flickr Search, and change the page title to "Rx at Work" (to accomplish this, highlight the application name, press F4, edit the Text property, and then do the same for the page title).

3. Add a reference (by right-clicking and selecting Add Reference) to Microsoft.Phone.Reactive and System.Observable assemblies.

Figure 18–2. Flickr Search with Rx.NET

Adding a User Interface

Now, add some user interface elements to the project. The user interface will consist of a text box, a label, and a WebBrowser control, as shown in Figure 18–3.

4. From the Toolbox, select a text box and drop it on the design surface. Rename the text box to txtSearchTerms. Make the width of the text box equal the width of the screen and clear the Text property. Next, select a textblock, drop it underneath the text box, rename it lblSearchingFor, and resize it to be the width of the screen.

5. From the Toolbox, select the WebBrowser control and drop it on the design surface underneath the textblock. Rename the WebBrowser control webResults and make it the width of the screen.

You should now have something similar to Figure 18–3.

412

Figure 18–3. Flickr Search using Rx.NET screen layout

Adding Logic to Search Flickr for Images

The next step is to add logic to populate the WebBrowser controls with the results of a Flickr image search.

1. Open `MainPage.xaml.cs` (right-click `MainPage.xaml` and select View Code) and paste the following `using` statement at the top of the page:

```
using Microsoft.Phone.Reactive;
```

Now, write code to capture the KeyUp events of the text box. To accomplish this, you will use the FromEvent method of the Rx.NET library, which accepts the name of the object to capture events for, as well as name of the event on that object.

2. Paste the following code immediately following the `InitializeComponent()` statement in the `MainPage()` constructor:

```
var keys = Observable.FromEvent<KeyEventArgs>(txtSearchTerms, "KeyUp");

keys.Subscribe(evt =>
{
  lblSearchingFor.Text = "Searching for ..." + txtSearchTerms.Text;
```

413

```
        webResults.Navigate(new Uri("http://www.flickr.com/search/?q="
        + txtSearchTerms.Text));
    });
```

The first statement creates an Observable data source, keys that will consist of all KeyUp events of the txtSearchTerms text box. The second statement is a lambda expression that creates an Observer on this collection and attempts to update the lblSearchingFor textblock with the text entered into the text box and show the web page representing the results of searching Flickr with the text supplied in the text box. Note the { symbol within the lambda expression—that symbol is used to define a lambda expression whose body has more than one statement within it, as you do in the previous example.

3. Press F5 to run the application. As you type the first character, you should see the WebBrowser control attempting to navigate to the Flickr search page specifying the only character entered as its search criteria. Notice how there is very little visual indication that there's some search or navigation performed behind the scenes. You will improve on that in the sections that follow, where you will create an animation to play while the WebBrowser control is loading with the results of an image search.

Enhancing a Flickr Search with Throttling

At this point, you must certainly be wondering what Rx.NET has added to your toolbox besides the complexities of the Observer pattern. Couldn't you do pretty much everything you have done so far using the standard event handling procedures available to Microsoft developers since the earliest days of Visual Basic (before there ever was VB.NET, that is)? The answer is: Rx.NET has added nothing up until now, and yes, you could have done everything with VB. The power of Reactive Extensions for .NET starts to come through in the next few steps of the example.

First, modify the application as follows:

1. Change the code line declaring an Observable collection above from

```
var keys = Observable.FromEvent<KeyEventArgs>(txtSearchTerms, "KeyUp");
```

to

```
        var keys = Observable.FromEvent<KeyEventArgs>(txtSearchTerms,
                    "KeyUp").Throttle(TimeSpan.FromSeconds(.5));
```

2. Change the code block declaring an Observer from

```
keys.Subscribe(evt =>
{
        lblSearchingFor.Text = "Searching for ..." + txtSearchTerms.Text;
        webResults.Navigate(new Uri("http://www.flickr.com/search/?q="
        + txtSearchTerms.Text));
});
```

to

```
keys.ObserveOn(Deployment.Current.Dispatcher).Subscribe(evt =>
        {
                if (txtSearchTerms.Text.Length>0)
```

```
                    {
                            lblSearchingFor.Text = "Searching for ..." +
txtSearchTerms.Text;

                            webResults.Navigate(new Uri("http://www.flickr.com/search/?q="
+
                            txtSearchTerms.Text));
                    }
        });
```

3. Press F5 to run the application. Click the text box and enter the search terms for photo lookup in Flickr (for example, Barcelona) and watch the WebBrowser control retrieve the images of that beautiful European city from Flickr.

Let's examine the code that you added in the last section. You created an observable collection that consists of all of the KeyUp events generated on txtSearchTerms text box. When you added the Throttle(.5) statement, you effectively told Rx.NET that you wanted to observe only KeyUp events that occur more than half a second apart (0.5 seconds). Assume that an average user will be pressing the keys on the keyboard less than half a second apart; so a half-a-second pause between key presses will tell the application that the user is ready for the Flickr search to launch and the user is ready to "observe" the results of its execution.

In Step 2, you enhanced the application in two ways. First, you added logic not to invoke image search if nothing is entered in the text box (this could happen if the user erased the content with the Backspace key). Second, notice the ObserveOn(Deployment.Current.Dispatcher) construct that was used to help create an Observer. To understand its reason for being and to allow you to peek under the hood of Rx.NET, remove it. As a result, your code for Step 2 will look like the following snippet:

```
keys.Subscribe(evt =>
        {
            if (txtSearchTerms.Text.Length > 0)
            {
                lblSearchingFor.Text = "Searching for ..." + txtSearchTerms.Text;
                webResults.Navigate(new Uri("http://www.flickr.com/search/?q=" +
txtSearchTerms.Text));
            }
        });
```

4. Press F5 to run the application now, and you will see the screen shown in Figure 18–4, where Visual Studio displays an "Invalid cross-thread access" message.

What is happening, as readers familiar with programming User Interface (UI) on the .NET platform know, is that updating UI from a thread other than a UI thread is a tricky undertaking. Under the hood, Reactive Extensions for .NET has created a separate background thread and will be pushing notifications of changes from the Observable data source to the Observers from that thread. This background thread can't modify the UI thread directly.

Figure 18–4. An invalid cross-access thread exception is generated when trying to update UI directly from the background thread.

Fortunately, the creators of Rx.NET have provided a solution to this problem by giving us the `ObserveOn()` extension method in the `Microsoft.Phone.Reactive` assembly. This extension method has several overloads, and one of them accepts a `Dispatcher` object. In the .NET Framework, a `Dispatcher` object maintains a prioritized queue of work items on a specific thread, and here it provides a way for you to observe an Observable data source on the UI thread. In the preceding example, you pass the Deployment.Current.Dispatcher property to the `ObserveOn()` method to get thread-safe access to the current Dispatcher and use it to update visual elements on the phone. The use of a single `ObserveOn()` method is significantly easier than dealing with the Dispatcher's Invoke method, which is a common way to update UI in multi-threaded Silverlight and WPF applications.

Adding an Animation that Plays as Flickr Images Load

You can further enhance the Flickr image search application by adding a simple animation that will play while the web pages with the results of your image search are loading. To do that, you will create an animation in Expression Blend for Windows Phone, subscribe to the Navigated event of the WebBrowser control, and play the animation in code.

Follow these steps to add this feature to your project:

1. Still in Visual Studio for Windows Phone, add a textblock to the phone's design surface and place it between the "Searching for" textblock and the WebBrowser control. Name that textblock lblLoading, set the caption to "Loading Images," and set its Visibility property to Collapsed.

Microsoft Expression Blend for Windows Phone is a powerful application for creating and editing graphics and animations for Windows Phone 7 devices. You have used it in the first part of this book to style controls and for other graphical tasks.

2. To launch Expression Blend and load it with the Flickr project, right-click MainPage.xaml in Visual Studio and select Open in Expression Blend. Microsoft Expression Blend launches with your solution open and ready to edit.

Your animation will be a progress bar in the form of a rectangle that will grow in width as the time passes. This animation will loop indefinitely, so that when it reaches maximum allowable size, the rectangle will go back to its beginning and the animation will be repeated.

3. In Expression Blend, select a Rectangle from the Toolbox, draw a very narrow, almost invisible rectangle right next to the Loading Images textblock, and set its Fill color to red.

Now, create what is called a timeline animation in Expression Blend. Timeline animations are created with the use of the storyboards, so you will create a new storyboard in this step.

4. In the Objects and Timeline window, click the New button (shown in Figure 18–5), name the storyboard loadingImages, and click OK.

The Objects and Timeline panel will now change to display a timeline, and Blend is ready to record your animation.

5. Select the rectangle that you placed on the Windows Phone design surface and click the Record Keyframe button, as shown in Figure 18–6.

6. Next, move the Animation Playhead (the yellow vertical line in the Timeline) to about 1.5 seconds, as shown in Figure 18–7. Click the Record Keyframe button again, and then resize the rectangle to be close to the full phone screen width.

Now you will now set the animation to loop as long as it is active.

7. In Objects and Timeline, click and select the loadingImages storyboard name. Common Properties for the Storyboard dialog appears. Select "Forever" in the Repeat Behavior property of this storyboard.

With the animation now complete, you are ready to show it when the user performs a search for Flickr images.

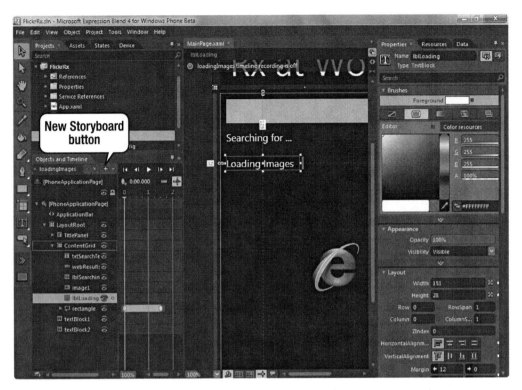

Figure 18–5. Creating a new storyboard animation in Expression Blend

8. Save everything in Expression Blend (File ➤ Save All) and switch back to Visual Studio.

Now you will add code to first show the animation when the search for images is initiated and then stop the animation once that search is complete.

To start the animation once the user initiates search for Flickr images, you will call the Begin method of the loadingImages animation.

In MainPage.xaml.cs, change the code that creates an Observer for the KeyUp event to the following:

```
keys.ObserveOn(Deployment.Current.Dispatcher).Subscribe(evt =>
{
    if (txtSearchTerms.Text.Length > 0)
    {
            lblSearchingFor.Text = "Searching for ..." + txtSearchTerms.Text;
            lblLoading.Visibility=System.Windows.Visibility.Visible;
            loadingImages.Begin();

        webResults.Navigate(new Uri("http://www.flickr.com/search/?q=" +
            txtSearchTerms.Text));
            }
});
```

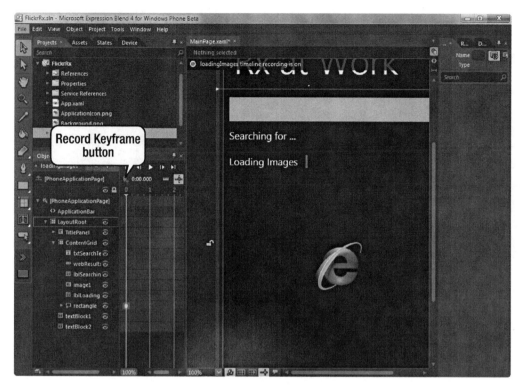

Figure 18–6. Beginning of the Loading Images timeline animation

Once the images load in the WebBrowser control, you will stop the animation by calling the Stop method of the loadingImages animation. To accomplish this, you will use Rx.NET to subscribe to the web browser's Navigated event. Once this subscription receives data, you will stop the animation. The following code accomplishes these tasks.

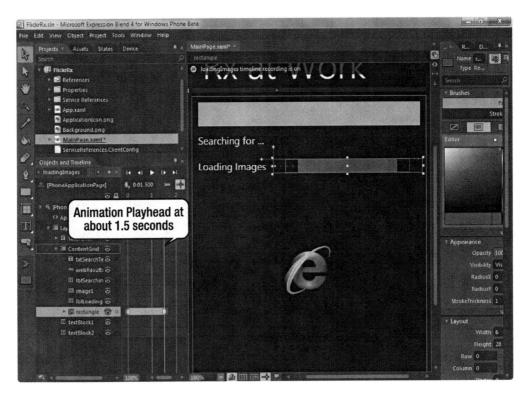

Figure 18–7. End of the Loading Images timeline animation

9. Paste the following code at the end of the MainPage constructor:

```
var browser =
    Observable.FromEvent<System.Windows.Navigation.NavigationEventArgs>(webResults,
"Navigated");

    browser.ObserveOn(Deployment.Current.Dispatcher).Subscribe(evt =>
    {
        loadingImages.Stop();
    lblLoading.Visibility = System.Windows.Visibility.Collapsed;
    });
```

You are now ready to run the application.

10. Press F5, type a keyword into the text box, and observe the animation while the images are being loaded into the browser.

You're still only scratching the surface of Rx.NET and its applications, but you can already see the power of this framework. Using Rx.NET, you can think of virtually any event as an observable data source, whether it's a location service that generates coordinate values (which you can think of as an observable set of position values), accelerometer data, key press events, or web browser events, such as those already demonstrated. Now that you have seen how to create Observable data sources from events using the FromEvent<T> method and how to subscribe to those events, we will expand upon this knowledge in the next section. Specifically, using Rx.NET, you will build a small real-time weather application that will use a publicly available web service to asynchronously retrieve current weather and show a small picture representing current weather for the zip code provided. But before you build this application, you will learn about general design guidelines for using Rx.NET from the Rx.NET Development team.

Rx.NET Design Guidelines

As a sign of maturing platform, Rx.NET has received its own set of design guidelines (available at http://go.microsoft.com/fwlink/?LinkID=205219) to help developers make best decisions when using the library. Some of the recommendations within that document have already been covered in this chapter; for instance, the general guideline to use Rx.NET for asynchronous and event-based computations. In the next few sections, you will get familiar with few more useful strategies for creating robust Rx.NET-based applications.

Consider Drawing a Marble Diagram

If you research Rx.NET on Microsoft web site (and specifically, Channel 9), chances are extremely high you will encounter references to what is known as Marble Diagrams. An example of a Marble Diagram is shown in Figure 18-8, where it depicts the use of the TakeUntil() operator in Rx.NET. In Marble Diagrams, we have input sequences of event-based and asynchronous data that we know about. Marble Diagram helps us understand what would happen to those input sequences as a result of application of Rx.NET operator.

Figure 18-8 is representative of the real-world example of receiving geolocation position on the phone. It assumes that there is data about phone user's location being gathered until the user types in a new location of interest to search for (such as searching for a Starbucks in the immediate neighborhood, for example). Initially, the top data sequence (geoLocationReading) receives data points (each data point is indicated by a small circle, or a marble, on the line corresponding to the geoLocationReading, in Figure 18-8). Then, newLocation sequence starts receiving data and the marbles are drawn on the line corresponding to the newLocation sequence. Notice how as a result of application of the TakeUntil() operator, the resulting sequence (result) gets only the data points (marbles on the line corresponding to the result sequence) of geoLocationReading until the marbles on the newLocation sequence started coming in. Regardless of how many data points (marbles) appeared on either geoLocationReading or newLocation sequences after that fact (indicated by an X in Figure 18-8), the result sequence did not get any additional data points after that fact.

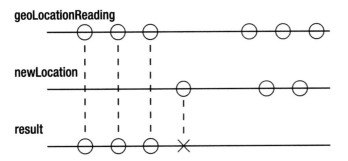

Figure 18–8. *Marble Diagram for the TakeUntil Rx.NET operator*

As with the TakeUntil operator, you can analyze all of the Rx.NET operators by visualizing them on a Marble Diagram and understanding the resulting sequences they produce. Rx.NET design guidelines hint at another area where Marble Diagrams may be helpful: draw a marble diagram of the sequence you would like to create, and then you can deduct which Rx.NET operators you need to use to get to that marble diagram.

Consider Passing a Specific Scheduler to Concurrency Introducing Operators

We stated in the beginning of this chapter that Rx.NET has the power to make parallel programming easier. It does this by abstracting away many issues of threading and concurrency and handling concurrency in a declarative way (there is no need to explicitly create threads, for example). However, even with this concurrency abstraction, we have some control over how the execution of Rx.NET should proceed and the context of how the Rx.NET notifications should be processed. This brings us to a discussion about *schedulers.*

In Rx.NET, it is possible to schedule two things: (1) how (or what thread context) the subscription will execute and (2) how (what thread context) the notification will be published. This context is controlled by the SubscribeOn() and ObserveOn() extension methods of the IObservable<T> interface. Both of those extension methods can accept a property of the static Scheduler class, and the properties available for you to pass in are described next.

- Scheduler.Dispatcher will force the execution on the Dispatcher, which is a class that owns the application thread and internally maintains a queue of work items.

- Scheduler.NewThread will schedule all actions onto a new thread.

- Scheduler.ThreadPool will schedule all actions onto the Thread Pool.

- Scheduler.Immediate will ensure the action is executed immediately.

- Scheduler.CurrentThread will ensure that the actions are performed on the thread that made the original call. This is not the same as Scheduler.Immediate, since actions scheduled on the current thread may be queued for later execution.

The following code is an example of how you would use the schedulers with subscriptions in Rx.NET—notice how you subscribe on a new thread and observe the results of the subscription on the dispatcher:

```
Observable.FromAsyncPattern<WebResponse>(
            webRequest.BeginGetResponse,
            webRequest.EndGetResponse)()
            .SubscribeOn(Scheduler.NewThread)
            .ObserveOn(Scheduler.Dispatcher)
            .Subscribe(
```

The Rx design guidelines deem it as best practice to pass in the scheduler wherever appropriate, so that the concurrency is created in the right place to begin with. Now you know how to accomplish that.

We have touched on a couple of guidelines from *The Rx Design Guidelines* document in this section. There are many other suggestions for building robust, high-performing Rx.NET constructs in this document, so you are encouraged to study it in greater detail. In the next section of this chapter, you will continue practicing using Rx.NET by building a simple weather application, which will also allow us to discuss concepts such as error recover in Rx.NET.

Using Rx.NET with Web Services to Asynchronously Retrieve Weather Data

In this section, you will use a publicly available weather web service located at http://www.webservicex.net/WS/WSDetails.aspx?CATID=12&WSID=68 to retrieve and display current weather for a given ZIP code within the United States. In addition to weather services, there are many other useful web services available at this location, including ZIP code validation and currency conversion. As an exercise in the usage of Rx.NET, you are encouraged to build useful, functional applications that take advantage of these services.

From the development point of view, the weather application will consist of (1) asynchronously capturing user input (a ZIP code), and (2) asynchronously calling the web service and then displaying the current weather for a given ZIP code. Let's go ahead and create the application.

Creating a Windows Phone Project

First, you will create a new project, import all of the libraries, and create service references necessary to make the weather application work.

1. Launch Visual Studio 2010 Express for Windows Phone and create a new Windows Phone Application project. Name it WeatherRx.

2. In MainPage.xaml, change the name of the application to WeatherRx and change the page title to "Weather App" (you are also certainly welcome to name the application and the page according to your preference).

3. Since you will be using Rx.NET to build this application, add a reference (by right-clicking and selecting Add Reference) to Microsoft.Phone.Reactive and System.Observable assemblies.

You need to add a Service Reference to the weather service already mentioned. The weather service is an .asmx web service hosted at www.webservicex.net.

4. To add a reference to this service, right-click the Project Name and select Add Service Reference. In the dialog that comes up, enter the following value in the Address Textbox: http://www.webservicex.net/WeatherForecast.asmx. Press the Go button.

5. The WeatherForecast service should appear on the left. Click the arrow next to it, make sure to select WeatherForecastSoap service, and then rename the namespace to "svcWeather."

6. Your final Add Service screen should look like Figure 18–9.

7. Press the OK button.

Figure 18–9. Adding a Service Reference to the weather web service

Creating a User Interface

For the application, your goal is to create a screen that looks like the one shown in Figure 18–10. To assist in that objective, the XAML for visual elements that appear after the page title is pasted here. You can also copy and paste this XAML from the sample code available in the download section for this chapter.

1. Open MainPage.xaml and add the following code:

```
<!--ContentPanel - place additional content here-->
        <Grid x:Name="ContentGrid" Grid.Row="1">
            <TextBox Height="72" HorizontalAlignment="Left" Margin="0,51,0,0"
Name="txtZipCode" Text="" VerticalAlignment="Top" Width="480" />
            <TextBlock Height="53" HorizontalAlignment="Left" Margin="6,13,0,0"
Name="lblLegend" Text="Enter Zip Code Below for Current Weather" VerticalAlignment="Top"
Width="462" />
            <TextBlock Height="30" HorizontalAlignment="Left" Margin="6,129,0,0"
Name="lblWeatherFahrenheit" Text="Current Weather, Fahrenheit " VerticalAlignment="Top"
Width="435" />
            <Image Height="150" HorizontalAlignment="Left" Margin="241,213,0,0"
Name="imgWeather" Stretch="Fill" VerticalAlignment="Top" Width="200" />
    <TextBlock Height="30" HorizontalAlignment="Left" Margin="6,162,0,0"
Name="lblCelsius" Text="Current Weather, Celsius" VerticalAlignment="Top" Width="435" />
    <TextBlock Height="30" Margin="6,379,39,0" Name="lblStatus" Text=""
VerticalAlignment="Top" />
        </Grid>
    </Grid>
```

Notice how in addition to the textblocks that will hold the current weather information, the XAML also creates an image control that will show a visual representation of the current weather (e.g., sunny, raining, snowing, etc.). Notice also that the last </Grid> statement closes the LayoutGrid element, not shown in the preceding fragment.

Figure 18–10. WeatherRx design layout

Adding Logic to Get Weather Information

With design elements and proper references in place, you are ready to add code to the application. In this example, you will split the code into multiple functions for enhanced readability.

1. Open `MainPage.xaml.cs` (by clicking `MainPage.xaml` and selecting View Code) and add the following using statements to the top of the page:

    ```
    using Microsoft.Phone.Reactive;
    using System.Windows.Media.Imaging;
    ```

2. Add the following code after the `InitializeComponent()` statement of the `MainPage()` constructor:

    ```
    WireUpWeatherEvents();
    WireUpKeyEvents();
    ```

Here, you are wiring up web service events and keystroke events in separate functions, a technique that will become very useful in the subsequent sections of this chapter when you deal with error recovery.

3. Create the WireUpWeatherEvents function and its supporting GetWeatherSubject function by pasting the following code. Note how you have created a separate function (GetWeatherSubject) to return an Observable collection from the weather web service event.

```
private void WireUpWeatherEvents()
{
        var weather = GetWeatherSubject();
weather.ObserveOn(Deployment.Current.Dispatcher).Subscribe(evt =>
        {
                if (evt.EventArgs.Result.Details != null)
                {
                lblWeatherFahrenheit.Text = "Current Weather, Fahrenheit: " +
                evt.EventArgs.Result.Details[0].MinTemperatureF.ToString() + "
                - " +
                evt.EventArgs.Result.Details[0].MaxTemperatureF.ToString();

                lblCelsius.Text = "Current Weather, Celsius: " +
                evt.EventArgs.Result.Details[0].MinTemperatureC.ToString() + "
                - " +
                evt.EventArgs.Result.Details[0].MaxTemperatureC.ToString();

                imgWeather.Source = new BitmapImage(new
                Uri(evt.EventArgs.Result.Details[0].WeatherImage,
                UriKind.Absolute));
                }
        },
    ex => { lblStatus.Text = "Sorry, we encountered a problem: " + ex.Message; }
   );
}

private IObservable<IEvent<svcWeather.GetWeatherByZipCodeCompletedEventArgs>>
GetWeatherSubject()
   {
      var weather =
Observable.FromEvent<svcWeather.GetWeatherByZipCodeCompletedEventArgs>(weatherClient,
"GetWeatherByZipCodeCompleted");
      return weather;
   }
```

4. Create the WireUpKeyEvents function that will define an Observable collection from the KeyUp events and create subscription to that collection by adding the following code:

```
private void WireUpKeyEvents()
      {
      var keys = Observable.FromEvent<KeyEventArgs>(txtZipCode,
            "KeyUp").Throttle(TimeSpan.FromSeconds(1)).DistinctUntilChanged();
      keys.ObserveOn(Deployment.Current.Dispatcher).Subscribe(evt =>
            {
                if (txtZipCode.Text.Length >= 5)
                {
```

```
            weatherClient.GetWeatherByZipCodeAsync(txtZipCode.Text);
                    }
            });
        }
```

5. Press F5 to run the application. You should see a screen prompting you to enter the US ZIP code to retrieve the current weather for. If you enter your ZIP code, you should get a reasonable estimate of your current weather, both on the Fahrenheit and Celsius scales. You should also see a small picture with a visual representation of the current weather conditions. Figure 18–11 shows sample output for the Jacksonville, FL area (ZIP code of 32202).

Let's spend some more time dissecting the tools you used to build this application. First, you used Rx.NET to create an Observable collection from the asynchronous responses to the weather web service calls. You used the following statement to create that collection:

```
var weather =
        Observable.FromEvent<svcWeather.GetWeatherByZipCodeCompletedEventArgs>(weatherClient,
        "GetWeatherByZipCodeCompleted");
```

You then defined an Observer for this data source, so that when the data is pushed from the web service to Observers, you take action by displaying that data in the User Interface.

Next, you created an Observable collection of the KeyUp events in the txtZipCode text box and created an Observer for that collection. As a result, whenever users pause their typing for one second, the Observer on the keys data source will validate whether five or more digits have been entered in the Zip Code field. Then, it goes ahead and calls the function GetWeatherByZipCodeAsync, which in turn invokes an asynchronous request to the weather web service.

It's important to note the asynchronous nature of all these calls—if you had other functionality built into the application, you could continue using it while the asynchronous request completes. As stated several times, the asynchronous processing is an area that Rx.NET was specifically designed to address.

If you have done some form of asynchronous programming prior to Rx.NET, you can certainly appreciate that single code line. Prior to Rx.NET, in an asynchronous method design pattern in .NET, two methods were provided. The first method started the computation, and the second method acquired the results of the computation. If there was more than one asynchronous operation, even just the simple ones illustrated in the weather example, the management of those multiple methods quickly became a headache. The fact that Rx.NET also attempts to parallelize asynchronous requests across all available cores is a hefty bonus to an already generous benefits package of clarity and powerful querying of Observers.

Figure 18–11. Sample output of WeatherRx application for ZIP code 32202

Handling Errors in Rx.NET

In the world of asynchronous programming, and especially in the world of distributed asynchronous programming, errors are a fact of life and should be expected. Rx.NET Observers provide a separate OnError event handler to deal with unforeseen errors that may arise. For instance, to make the WeatherRx application more robust, let's add an OnError handler to the weather.Subscribe call. The resulting code would look like this:

```
weather.ObserveOn(Deployment.Current.Dispatcher).Subscribe(evt =>
    {
                if (evt.EventArgs.Result.Details != null)
                {
                    lblWeatherFahrenheit.Text = "Current Weather, Fahrenheit: " +
                    evt.EventArgs.Result.Details[0].MinTemperatureF.ToString() + "
                    - " +
                    evt.EventArgs.Result.Details[0].MaxTemperatureF.ToString();

                lblCelsius.Text = "Current Weather, Celsius: " +
```

```
                              evt.EventArgs.Result.Details[0].MinTemperatureC.ToString() + "
                                - " +
                              evt.EventArgs.Result.Details[0].MaxTemperatureC.ToString();

                     imgWeather.Source = new BitmapImage(new
                              Uri(evt.EventArgs.Result.Details[0].WeatherImage,
                     UriKind.Absolute));
                     }
        },
  ex =>    {
           Deployment.Current.Dispatcher.BeginInvoke(() => lblStatus.Text = ex.Message);
                     }
  );
```

Note the somewhat cryptic (it's a lambda expression and it uses a lambda expression within its own body) use of the Deployment.Current.Dispatcher.BeginInvoke statement to get around cross-thread access issues discussed previously. In the preceding code, the OnError handler simply displays the exception text, but there is nothing stopping you from dissecting an error thoroughly and providing a possible corrective action. For instance, if the web service is not available at the address specified, you may retry your call to a different location of the web service. Rx.NET also has exception handling operators Catch, Finally, OnErrorResumeNext, and Retry, which aid in recovering from errors. You will explore some of them in the next section as we discuss some potential ways of handling intermittently available data connections on the phones.

Handling Data Connection Issues with Rx.NET

On a phone, slow or lost data connections are a fact of everyday life. Ideally, phone applications should detect such connections and provide a recovery mechanism to deal with them. Two potential ways to deal with slow or lost connectivity on the phone are: (1) let the user decide whether the application should retry what it was doing before the connection timed out or lost, and (2) provide an automated retry mechanism.

Rx.NET can aid in both scenarios. Furthermore, Rx.NET includes a special Timeout operation that will generate a timeout error if it does not receive data, such as a web service callback, from its Observable within a user-specified interval. Let's take a look at the Timeout operation in action. Let's change the WireUpWeatherEvents function to time out if it does not get any data for two seconds:

1. Replace the WireUpEvents() function of the WeatherRx application with the following code:

```
private void WireUpWeatherEvents()
{
        var weather = GetWeatherSubject();
        weather.ObserveOn(Deployment.Current.Dispatcher)
                .Timeout(TimeSpan.FromSeconds(2))
        .Subscribe(evt =>
        {
                if (evt.EventArgs.Result.Details != null)
                {
                lblWeatherFahrenheit.Text = "Current Weather, Fahrenheit: " +
                evt.EventArgs.Result.Details[0].MinTemperatureF.ToString() + "
                 - " +
                evt.EventArgs.Result.Details[0].MaxTemperatureF.ToString();
```

```
                    lblCelsius.Text = "Current Weather, Celsius: " +
                    evt.EventArgs.Result.Details[0].MinTemperatureC.ToString() + "
                    - " +
                    evt.EventArgs.Result.Details[0].MaxTemperatureC.ToString();

                    imgWeather.Source = new BitmapImage(new
                    Uri(evt.EventArgs.Result.Details[0].WeatherImage,
                    UriKind.Absolute));
                    }
            },
            ex =>    {
                    Deployment.Current.Dispatcher.BeginInvoke(() => lblStatus.Text
                    = ex.Message);
                    }
            );
    }
```

Now run the application and notice how after two seconds, it immediately times out and displays the timeout exception text on the emulator. What happened? You did not even get a chance to specify the ZIP code!

Your code needs a little refactoring, or changing around. In the code so far, you subscribed to the web service's events immediately on application launch, and since you did not get any data two seconds after the launch of the application, that subscription timed out. The change that you need to make is to subscribe to the web service's events right before you invoke that web service, yet you have to be careful to create this subscription just once.

2. Remove the call to WireUpWeatherEvents from the MainPage constructor and place it within the WireUpKeyEvents function, like so:

```
        private void WireUpKeyEvents()
        {
        var keys = Observable.FromEvent<KeyEventArgs>(txtZipCode,
        "KeyUp").Throttle(TimeSpan.FromSeconds(1)).DistinctUntilChanged();
                keys.ObserveOn(Deployment.Current.Dispatcher).Subscribe(evt =>
                {
                        if (txtZipCode.Text.Length >= 5)
                        {
                                WireUpWeatherEvents();

    weatherClient.GetWeatherByZipCodeAsync(txtZipCode.Text);
                        }
                });
        }
```

Now the timeout feature should work properly. Notice, however, that it will most likely take slightly more than two seconds to return a valid response from the Weather service.

Rx.NET also provides a Retry method that optionally takes a parameter for the number of times to retry to re-subscribe to the Observable collection. If you don't specify that parameter, Rx.NET will try to re-subscribe to the Observable collection indefinitely. One way to deal with an absent or slow connection is to retry the subscription two or three times, and then, if unsuccessful, give the user the option to either retry once more or cancel. You will see how to give the user this option in the next section.

Revising WeatherRx to Manage Slow Data Connections

To modify the WeatherRx application, you will first add buttons to the UI to allow the user to either retry the failed connection or to exit gracefully. Then, you will add code to the application to react to the events on these new User Interface elements.

To add the new elements to the WeatherRx UI, do the following:

1. Open MainPage.xaml and add two buttons right below the lblStatus textblock, as shown in Figure 18–12. Name the first button btnRetry and set its Content property to Retry. Name the second button btnQuit and set its Content property to Quit. Set the Visibility of both buttons to Collapsed.

Figure 18–12. *Weather application with error recovery elements*

On retry, you will recreate the Observable connection to the weather web service, if it's needed, and then invoke the web service again.

2. Double-click the Retry button and add the following handler code to the btnRetry_Click function:

```
private void btnRetry_Click(object sender, RoutedEventArgs e)
{
        btnQuit.Visibility = System.Windows.Visibility.Collapsed;
        btnRetry.Visibility = System.Windows.Visibility.Collapsed;
        lblStatus.Text = "";

        WireUpWeatherEvents();
        weatherClient.GetWeatherByZipCodeAsync(txtZipCode.Text);
}
```

If the user selects Quit, let's simply hide the buttons and the exception text.

3. Double-click the Quit button and add the following code to the btnQuit_Click
    function:

```
private void btnQuit_Click(object sender, RoutedEventArgs e)
{
        btnQuit.Visibility = System.Windows.Visibility.Collapsed;
        btnRetry.Visibility = System.Windows.Visibility.Collapsed;
        lblStatus.Text = "";
}
```

Finally, you will need to ensure there is only one subscription to the weather web service at any
given time.

4. To ensure that there's only one subscription, first declare a module level
    variable by adding the following statement:

```
IObservable<IEvent<GetWeatherByZipCodeCompletedEventArgs>> _weather;
```

5. Next, change the GetWeatherSubject function to the following:

```
private void GetWeatherSubject()
{
        if (_weather == null)
        {
        _weather =
        Observable.FromEvent<svcWeather.GetWeatherByZipCodeCompletedEventArgs>
        (weatherClient, "GetWeatherByZipCodeCompleted");
        }
}
```

6. Finally, change the WireUpWeatherEvents method to look like the following
    (notice how the timeout value is now set to a more reasonable five seconds as
    well):

```
private void WireUpWeatherEvents()
{
        GetWeatherSubject();
        _weather.ObserveOn(Deployment.Current.Dispatcher)
        .Timeout(TimeSpan.FromSeconds(5))
        .Subscribe(evt =>
        {
                if (evt.EventArgs.Result.Details != null)
```

```
                                          {
                                          lblWeatherFahrenheit.Text = "Current Weather, Fahrenheit: " +
                                          evt.EventArgs.Result.Details[0].MinTemperatureF.ToString() + " - " +
                                          evt.EventArgs.Result.Details[0].MaxTemperatureF.ToString();

                                          lblCelsius.Text = "Current Weather, Celsius: " +
                                          evt.EventArgs.Result.Details[0].MinTemperatureC.ToString() + " - " +
                                          evt.EventArgs.Result.Details[0].MaxTemperatureC.ToString();

                                          imgWeather.Source = new BitmapImage(new
                                          Uri(evt.EventArgs.Result.Details[0].WeatherImage, UriKind.Absolute));
                                      }
                                  },
                                  ex =>
                                  {
                                          Deployment.Current.Dispatcher.BeginInvoke(() => lblStatus.Text =
                ex.Message);
                                  Deployment.Current.Dispatcher.BeginInvoke(() =>
                                  btnQuit.Visibility=System.Windows.Visibility.Visible);

                                  Deployment.Current.Dispatcher.BeginInvoke(() => btnRetry.Visibility =
                                  System.Windows.Visibility.Visible);
                                  }
                         );
              }
```

This example illustrates one approach to handling connection issues on Windows Phone 7 devices: you specify a timeout period, and if you don't get a response within that period, you prompt the user to retry or to quit.

Handling Multiple Concurrent Requests with Rx.NET

So far, the weather application that you have created is sending as many requests for weather data as the user types in ZIP codes. When the data comes back from the weather web service, the order that this data comes back in is not guaranteed. For example, if the user first types in 32207 (Jacksonville) and then types in 10001 (New York City), the weather results for Jacksonville may come in behind New York City, yet the user would not realize that she's seeing Jacksonville's weather when New York's ZIP code still remains on the screen. It would be great if there were a solution that gave an application the power to cancel out all weather requests that occurred prior to the latest one, i.e., in this example, a request for Jacksonville weather is canceled as soon as request for New York City weather is made.

Rx.NET provides such a solution. There are two operators in Rx.NET—TakeUntil() and Switch—that allow for cancellation of operations that occur prior to the latest operation and are still "in-flight," or are still pending the return values. Through the use of an elegant LINQ query, these operators tie together Observable collections, as you will see shortly. But first, there is some bad news: in the current implementation of .NET Framework on Windows Phone 7, it is impossible to link the beginning of the asynchronous SOAP web service invocation to the end of that invocation. The root of the problem is the exclusion of the CreateChannel method implementation in the Windows Communication Foundation libraries on Windows Phone 7. Microsoft had to slim down and optimize .NET Framework on the phone, and the loss of this method for the time being seems to be due to those optimization efforts.

Nevertheless, the technique for canceling in-flight requests still applies to the clients with full .NET Framework installed (Windows Forms and WPF applications) and to the Silverlight platform. For the weather application, you will "fake" the technique of canceling those requests by creating a new Observable collection for the weather service each time a user types in a new ZIP code. Note, however, that the Observable subscriptions that you will be creating listen for any completed weather service requests, and not the specific ones. In other words, your implementation of canceling in-flight requests on Windows Phone 7 is currently incomplete and not reliable. Here, each one of these subscriptions would process both Jacksonville and New York City weather from the example, and the order that this weather data comes in would be irrelevant. This is due to the aforementioned limitation in the current implementation of Windows Phone 7 framework—at present, you can't link the beginning of the SOAP web service call to the end of that service call on this platform.

To make the cancellation of operations on the Observable collections possible while those operations are in-flight, you will change the code around to expose Observable collections to LINQ queries.

Follow these steps to make operation cancellation possible:

7. At the top of the MainPage class (right above the constructor), paste the following code to declare a module-level Observable collection for the KeyUp events of the ZIP code text box:

```
IObservable<IEvent<KeyEventArgs>> _keys;
```

8. Expose the Observables for both the KeyUp event of the ZIP code text box and for the web service callback by adding the following two methods to your code:

```
private IObservable<IEvent<GetWeatherByZipCodeCompletedEventArgs>> GetWeatherSubject()
        {
        return
        Observable.FromEvent<svcWeather.GetWeatherByZipCodeCompletedEventArgs>(weather
        Client, "GetWeatherByZipCodeCompleted");
        }

        private void GetKeys()
        {
                if (_keys == null)
                {
        _keys = Observable.FromEvent<KeyEventArgs>(txtZipCode,
        "KeyUp").Throttle(TimeSpan.FromSeconds(1)).DistinctUntilChanged();
                }
        }
```

The magic that makes the cancellations work appears in the next code snippet. Pay particularly close attention to the LINQ query; it establishes the relationship between the Observable collection for the KeyUp events and the Observable collection for the web service callbacks. Note that had Windows Phone 7 framework supported what is referred to as the Asynchronous pattern for web service calls (with the use of BeginXXX/EndXXX methods), you could have established a direct relationship between key sequences and web service invocations. However, with the following code, you have only a loose or indirect relationship between those two, since each subscription listens for any and all responses from the weather web service, and not just for specific ones. Right after the LINQ statement, there is a Switch() operator that instructs the application to dispose of the old subscription to the weather web service once there is a new key sequence awaiting in the _keys Observable collection.

9. Add the following code to the application:

```
private void WireUpWeatherEvents()
```

```
        {
                GetKeys();
                var latestWeather = (from term in _keys
                        select GetWeatherSubject()
                        .Finally(() =>
                        {
                Deployment.Current.Dispatcher.BeginInvoke(() =>
                Debug.WriteLine("Disposed of prior subscription"));
                        })
                ).Switch();

                latestWeather.ObserveOnDispatcher()
                        .Subscribe(evt =>
                        {
                                if (evt.EventArgs.Result != null)
                                {
                lblWeatherFahrenheit.Text = "Current Weather, Fahrenheit: " +
                evt.EventArgs.Result.Details[0].MinTemperatureF.ToString() + "
                - " +
                evt.EventArgs.Result.Details[0].MaxTemperatureF.ToString();

                lblCelsius.Text = "Current Weather, Celsius: " +
                evt.EventArgs.Result.Details[0].MinTemperatureC.ToString() + "
                - " +
                evt.EventArgs.Result.Details[0].MaxTemperatureC.ToString();

                imgWeather.Source = new BitmapImage(new
                Uri(evt.EventArgs.Result.Details[0].WeatherImage,
                UriKind.Absolute));
                                }
                        },
                ex => {
                                        Deployment.Current.Dispatcher.BeginInvoke(()
=>lblStatus.Text = ex.Message);
                        }
                );
        }
```

Notice the .Finally statement in the code. Its purpose is to print a "Disposed of prior subscription" message into the Output windows when one Observable collection is being removed and replaced with the newer one. This occurs when there is a new event in the _keys module-level Observable collection.

Finally, you need to make some minor changes to the WireUpKeyEvents function, namely, the Observable sequence generation for the KeyUp event on the ZIP code has been moved into a separate GetKeys method.

10. Replace the WiredUpKeyEvents() function with the following code:

```
private void WireUpKeyEvents()
{
        GetKeys();
        _keys.ObserveOn(Deployment.Current.Dispatcher).Subscribe(evt =>
        {
                if (txtZipCode.Text.Length >= 5)
```

```
                        {
        weatherClient.GetWeatherByZipCodeAsync(txtZipCode.Text);
                        }
                });
        }
```

You are now ready to run the application.

11. Press F5 and observe that the application behavior is virtually unchanged from the previous examples: you still type in the ZIP code and receive weather information for that ZIP code. However, behind the scenes, you will notice the messages printed in the Output window indicating that there are Observable sequences being disposed of in accordance to the new data (ZIP codes typed in) available in the key sequence observable collection.

Perhaps in the very near future, you will see a CreateChannel method available on the Windows Phone 7 platform. Once that happens, you could very easily enhance the previous example with the code linking the beginning and end of an asynchronous web service call through the Observable.FromAsyncPattern method. For right now, however, you can still take advantage of this extremely powerful feature of Rx.NET in Silverlight or on clients running the full version of .NET Framework.

Summary

This chapter provided a general overview of Reactive Extensions for .NET and their implementation of the Observer pattern. You built two applications that demonstrated the features of Rx.NET, including event representation as Observable data sources and seamless concurrent asynchronous processing and error handling. You learned about Marble Diagrams and some of the main design guidelines for building Rx.NET applications. You observed techniques for managing unreliable data links and the principles of cancellation of in-flight operations using the Rx.NET framework. As concurrent programming becomes more and more the norm, Rx.NET provides a powerful framework for asynchronous and parallel programming, including programming for the cloud. We have touched on the subject of Rx.NET lightly, but we hope that you have gained an appreciation for this technology and will take the initiative to learn (and, most importantly, practice!) Rx.NET development techniques on your own.

In the next and final chapter of this book, you will learn how to make your Windows Phone 7 applications more secure. You will learn about the common threats to mobile devices and the steps you must take to protect yourself and your customers from unwanted and potentially harmful attention.

CHAPTER 19

Security

Because everything about the design and operation of Windows Phone 7 targets consumers, it is only natural that Microsoft has carefully thought through the ways to protect consumers from both intended and unintentional harm. Windows Phone 7 ships with a compelling set of built-in security features that go towards accomplishing that goal. The capabilities of the Windows Phone 7 platform allow the data to be protected both in transit and on the device. Because of the centralized application certification process, consumers gain confidence that no malicious applications are downloaded and installed on their devices (unlike some competing platforms, which are increasingly becoming infested with malware). And should the phone be lost or stolen, each device comes with a free web-based tool that allows you to remotely control the phone, including locking and wiping all data on that phone.

In this chapter, you will learn how the Windows Phone Marketplace certification process acts as a gatekeeper and allows only legitimate applications to be present on the device. Then you'll look at the ways you can ensure that your Windows Phone 7 application can receive, transmit, and store sensitive data in a secure manner. Finally, you'll take a look at the free support for remote lock and data wipe that Microsoft provides to protect lost or stolen Windows Phones.

We will lead you through an analysis of Windows Phone 7 security features along the following four domains: application security, network security, data security, and device security. You will also learn how to use the tools Windows Phone 7 platform has to address specific security concerns associated with each domain.

Understanding Application Security

Ideally, all Windows Phone 7 applications would come from legitimate sources and behave like good citizens. However, experience shows that many applications break rules and that safeguards must be put in place to prevent malicious behavior. On the application security front, Windows Phone 7 platform includes the safeguards to verify the identity of the author of the application and sandboxes the execution of each mobile application. In the next few sections, you will explore these safeguards in detail.

Windows Phone Marketplace

For a moment, let's travel a couple of decades back in time. The early years of Windows XP were not happy ones at Microsoft. The whole world was upset with the company for allowing its operating system to be exploited by multiple malicious programs. Even though Windows XP shipped with safeguards that could prevent those exploits, the activation of those safeguards was left up to the user, and that activation rarely happened. What Microsoft quickly learned from that experience was that it must take a lot of responsibility to protect its user base from both known and potential harm.

Because mobile devices contain huge amounts of personal information and by their nature are frequently lost or misplaced, application monitoring is all the more necessary. For Microsoft to assume this responsibility for Windows Phone 7 applications, it must have as much control as possible over the applications built and deployed onto its platform, while still encouraging developer creativity as much as possible. To facilitate this dual goal of being autocratic and democratic at the same time, Microsoft has created a Windows Phone Marketplace. Windows Phone Marketplace is the single online distribution point for all Windows Phone 7 applications. The objectives of Windows Phone 7 Marketplace and the way it achieves those objectives are described in the following sections.

Non-Repudiation: Proof of the Integrity and Origin of Data

The first objective of Windows Phone Marketplace is to confirm the identity of an application's author. In the Internet era, attempts to claim false identity are extremely common—every day, millions of e-mails claim to come from an online bank or an African prince. In a similar fashion, without a centralized approval mechanism, any malicious Windows Phone 7 application could claim to be genuine and capture the user's personal information. In software security, the concept of *non-repudiation* refers to the guarantee that the application indeed came from the source it claims to have come from. On the Windows Phone 7 platform, the origin and safety of applications are confirmed during the application certification, a required step for all Windows Phone 7 applications. (Note that the application certification process is covered in Chapter 5, and a lot of the material on the following pages is repeating that same information as it relates to Windows Phone 7 security). During application certification, the developer submits her application to the Windows Phone Marketplace and pays a fee, at which point Microsoft runs a series of automated and manual tests to confirm application safety and, to some extent, reliability.

Currently, no application can be loaded onto the phone without going through Windows Phone Marketplace. While there is a possibility that this policy will be revisited in the future to allow enterprise customers to bypass Windows Phone Marketplace, at the time of this writing it is only a possibility. All Windows Phone 7 developers must sign up for the marketplace and must provide legitimate proof of their identity to the marketplace before any of the applications they create are available for installation on users' phones. Once their identity is verified, application developers receive a code-signing certificate. This digital certificate verifies that the application was created by the specified company or individual, fulfilling the concept of non-repudiation mentioned previously.

Intellectual Property Protection

Software piracy is a huge problem affecting both giants of software development like Microsoft as well as small one-person shops trying to building mobile applications. To help safeguard from piracy, Microsoft requires that a valid application license issued by the Windows Phone Marketplace be present on the Windows Phone 7 device before it allows the execution of an application. This means that even if somebody figures out how to load an application onto the device without going through Windows Phone Marketplace, the application will not run since the license key for that application will not be available.

Safe Application Behavior

The Windows Phone Marketplace application approval process includes a suite of certification tests to prohibit risky applications from being loaded onto users' phones. Risky applications may contain malware or viruses themselves, or they may contain code constructs that could allow malicious code execution.

All applications submitted to Windows Phone Marketplace will be subject to malicious software screening, which will attempt to confirm that applications are free from viruses and malware. After successful completion of those tests, additional tests are performed to confirm that an application is written using only type-safe Microsoft Intermediate Language (MSIL) code. Writing applications in MSIL avoids public enemy #1, as software buffer overruns were called in *Writing Secure Code* by Michael Howard and David LeBlanc (Microsoft press, 2001). In addition, an application must not implement any security-critical code, since Windows Phone Application Platform does not allow an application to run security-critical code. You will revisit MSIL and briefly learn about security-critical code on mobile devices at the end of this chapter.

To get a better idea of how the Windows Phone Marketplace submission process helps improve the security of a user's device, let's walk through the steps involved in submitting an application to the marketplace.

Submitting an Application to Windows Phone Marketplace

In this example, you will prepare a package for your application to submit to Windows Phone Marketplace and learn the steps involved in successfully publishing an application to the marketplace, beginning with the creation of a XAP file. Let's get started.

Generating a XAP Submission File

The submission file that Windows Phone Marketplace requires is a XAP file that gets generated when the Windows Phone 7 application is built. An XAP file is a zip file containing all elements an application needs to run. To generate a XAP file, you must first build your application, as described in the following steps:

1. Open your Windows Phone 7 application project inside Visual Studio Express for Windows Phone.

2. Set the Solution Configuration option to Release if it presently isn't, as shown in Figure 19–1.

3. In Solution Explorer, right-click the name of the solution and select Build. At this point, if the build succeeds, Visual Studio creates the `ProjectName`.xap file, where `ProjectName` is the name of your solution.

4. Locate the `ProjectName`.xap file you created in Step 3. Open Windows Explorer and navigate to the project's directory and the `bin/Release/` folder. You should find there a file named `ProjectName`.xap. This is the file that you will upload to the marketplace.

The next step is to log in to Windows Phone Marketplace and submit the XAP file you just created.

Uploading the XAP File to Marketplace

Before uploading files to Windows Phone Marketplace, you must create Windows Phone Marketplace login credentials at http://create.msdn.com/. To do this, once you open the Marketplace web site, click the Register for the Marketplace link and follow the step-by-step wizard to create your username and password for the Marketplace. With login credentials created, follow the following step-by-step guide to submit your application to the marketplace.

1. Login to Windows Phone Marketplace (http://create.msdn.com/) and create a new application submission.

2. When prompted, locate the XAP file that you created in the previous section (remember, it's in the bin/Release/ folder of the project's directory) and follow instructions to upload it to the Marketplace.

3. Enter a description for your application, select its category, and upload an icon for it.

4. Next, choose the countries that you would like your application to be available in and set the pricing.

5. While you are busy entering application details (description, category, pricing), Marketplace is at work validating the XAP file. This is the step that confirms that the XAP file is valid and can be passed on for further testing of its reliability and security.

6. If basic XAP file validation fails, you will get a failure notification and will have to start the process over.

7. If validation succeeds, you will be presented with a screen that lets you make your application available to customers right away once it passes certification or wait until you decide to publish.

8. The automated process within Windows Phone Marketplace opens up the submitted XAP file and updates the application manifest file (WMAppManifest.xml) with a unique product identifier and which hub on the Windows Phone 7 device (for example, Media + Video hub) this application belongs to. In addition, the header file called WMAppPRHeader.xml is created; it will be used to protect digital rights to your application. Finally, an additional update to the application manifest file listing all of the security capabilities of an application is performed and the application is repackaged into a new XAP file. This new XAP file is then deployed to the actual Windows Phone 7 device at the Marketplace for certification testing.

Figure 19–1. Before deploying your application, make sure to set Solution Configuration to Release.

Certification testing consists of both manual and automated verification that the application complies with the rules set by Microsoft regarding content, security, performance, and reliability of Windows Phone 7 applications. If an application violates any of these provisions, it is not published and you get a failure report with details of the problem-causing behavior.

If the application successfully passes certification tests, the XAP file is signed and becomes available for installation from the Windows Phone Marketplace according to the option you selected in Step 5.

▨**Note** When you update your application, you will have to go through the same certification steps as the original application. Chapter 5 outlines the update process in detail.

Sandboxed Execution and the Execution Manager

Sandboxed execution refers to the concept that each application runs in its own environment, or sandbox, so that it has no access to applications running in different sandboxes on the same device. Windows Phone 7 platform implements this concept of sandboxed execution. Applications running on the same Windows Phone 7 device are isolated from each other and must communicate with services provided by the Windows Phone 7 platform by using a well-defined standard mechanism. System files and resources are shielded from user applications. To store and retrieve application and configuration data, applications must use isolated storage, which is designed to be protected from access by any application other than the currently running one. For in-depth information on working with isolated storage, please refer to Chapter 13.

To further ensure security and responsiveness of the Windows Phone 7 platform, Microsoft has built in separate provisions to make it even more secure. These provisions include the use of the Execution Manager, as well as granting only the rights an application absolutely requires to function.

The Execution Manager monitors application resource usage in accordance with certain defined conventions. For instance, the Execution Manager may terminate an application in the background if it deems that an application in the foreground is not very responsive. Similarly, the Execution Manager may dismiss an application if it makes an excessive number of requests for phone resources.

The Windows Phone Application Platform also tries to minimize the number of privileges granted to an application. For instance, if an application does not require the use of the location services library, Windows Phone will create a custom execution environment for the application that does not include the rights to that library. This way, the number of potential exploits (or "attack surface," as it is referred to in the computer security industry) against the application is minimized.

Implementing Network Security

If your application accesses sensitive data over the network, it is critical that this data is encrypted during transit from the remote location to the Windows Phone 7 device. Similarly, if your application requires authentication, it is important to implement a secure authentication mechanism within your application. Windows Phone 7 platform allows you to accomplish both of these objectives. Any time you have to transmit sensitive data from a remote location, you should use Secure Sockets Layer (SSL) protocol, an industry standard for encrypting data. And if your environment requires secure authentication, it is possible to use digital certificates on a Windows Phone 7 device for that authentication, eliminating the need for user names and passwords.

In the next sections, you will walk through establishing SSL connections and configuring a certificate for secure authentication on a Windows Phone 7 device.

Securing Connections with SSL

Secure Sockets Layer protocol is a sophisticated way of securing connections between the client (Windows Phone 7 device) and cloud service, and it utilizes the concepts of asymmetric cryptography and certification authority (CA) hierarchies. When a Windows Phone 7 device initiates a secure connection to the remote service, it requests that service's certificate. That certificate is checked and the certification authority that issued that certificate is determined. Once the CA of the certificate is known, Windows Phone 7 client then checks its own installed list of certification authorities. If it finds a certification authority in its list, that implies that a trust relationship between the Windows Phone 7 device and the CA has been previously established, and that a secure connection between the phone and the remote server can be created.

Windows Phone 7 devices come with several certification authorities pre-installed. This means that, most of the time, establishing an SSL connection will be a seamless experience. As long as the remote service obtained its certificate from a very well-known certification authority (such as VeriSign, for example), SSL connections can be created both from Internet Explorer on the phone and from application code. The following example demonstrates how to test if you can establish a secure connection to the remote server (PayPal) that has a certificate issued by a well-known CA (VeriSign).

Testing and Opening an SSL Connection

In this brief example, you will test if you can establish a secure connection to a remote server (PayPal), and then you will write a small Windows Phone 7 application that programmatically loads secure content from the PayPal web site.

1. The quickest way to test whether a connection to a secure web site can be established is to open up Internet Explorer on Windows Phone 7 Emulator or a Windows Phone 7 device and type the URL of a secure remote server. Launch Windows Phone 7 Emulator by clicking Start ➤ All Programs ➤ Windows Phone Developer Tools ➤ Windows Phone 7 Emulator. Once the emulator loads, click the Internet Explorer icon and type in https://www.paypal.com to go to the secure PayPal site. You should see the main screen of the PayPal web site.

▓ **Tip** It may get quite tiresome having to click all of the keyboard buttons on the emulator. To enable the use of computer keyboard in the emulator window, you can press the PgUp key once the emulator loads up. To discontinue using the keyboard in the emulator, press the PgDn key.

---

2. Now, you will create a small Windows Phone 7 application that will access the PayPal site via a secure connection. You could access any secure remote service in a similar manner, but only if that service has a certificate issued by a CA that Windows Phone 7 device trusts. In the next section of this chapter, you will go through creating, exporting, and installing the self-signed certificates, which is a bit more complicated.

3. As usual, launch Visual Studio 2010 Express for Windows Phone and create a new Windows Phone 7 Application project. Name that project SSLConnection and click OK. MainPage.xaml is presented in the Designer.

4. From the toolbox, drag and drop the WebBrowser control onto the design surface. Make the width and height of that control to be the full width and height of available design surface on MainPage.xaml.

5. Switch to code view (right-click MainPage.xaml and select View Code) and add the following code to the MainPage() constructor. This code will create a WebClient object, register the callback function for that object (which you will write in the next section), and create a request to retrieve the contents of www.paypal.com securely.

```
WebClient client = new WebClient();
        client.OpenReadCompleted += new
                OpenReadCompletedEventHandler(HandleResponse);
        client.OpenReadAsync(new Uri("https://www.paypal.com"));
```

6. Write the HandleResponse callback function for the request. This function will display the contents of whatever was returned as a result of the previous request to https://www.paypal.com.

```
void HandleResponse(object sender, OpenReadCompletedEventArgs e)
{
        StreamReader reader = new StreamReader(e.Result);
        string res = reader.ReadToEnd();
        webBrowser1.NavigateToString(res);
}
```

7. Press F5 to run the application. You should see the PayPal page displayed in the web browser window.

As you can see from the previous example, establishing a secure connection to the remote service is fairly straightforward if a remote service has a certificate issued by a major CA with whom Windows Phone 7 has an existing trust relationship. Just remember to use https protocol instead of http when accessing a remote web service securely. But certificates issued by a major certification authority can be expensive, and may not be necessary if all users of remote service trust that the service is legitimate. In addition, you may want to experiment or test your secure service without spending a lot of money on the certificates. Self-signed SSL certificates offer the same degree of data protection in transit (data is encrypted using SSL), without the expense of using the certification authority. There is a slight administrative overhead in issuing and installing those certificates, but you will easily tackle it in a few steps in the next example.

Creating a Self-Signed Certificate

There are three steps to enabling the use of self-signed certificates on Windows Phone 7 device: first, you have to create a self-signed certificate; second, you have to export that certificate for installation on the mobile device; and third, you have to install that certificate on the Windows Phone 7 device. Creating and exporting the self-signed certificate steps occur on the server where the secure service resides. Installing the certificate, of course, happens on each device that will need to establish a secure connection to the service using a self-signed certificate.

Internet Information Services (IIS) is the web server software written by Microsoft. IIS has evolved significantly over the years, and the most current version in production as of this writing is IIS version 7.5. With IIS 7.5, creating self-signed certificates and enabling SSL using those certificates is much easier than with previous versions of IIS. IIS 7.5 comes with Windows 7 by default, and the following example assumes that you are using IIS7.5 installed on a Windows 7 machine. The example also assumes that both the server and the Windows Phone 7 client (the emulator) reside on the same machine.

1. Open IIS Manager by clicking Start ➤ Control Panel ➤ Administrative Tools ➤ Internet Information Services (IIS) Manager.

2. Create a new web site by right-clicking the Sites node on the left and choosing Add Web Site. Name the site WP7Server and fill in the rest of the web site properties as shown in Figure 19–2.

■ **Note** The physical path setting for the new site on your computer may certainly be something else than what is shown in Figure 19-2, but be sure to make the Port setting something other than the default 80, otherwise IIS might complain that port 80 is already taken (note how it is set to 8888 in Figure 19-2).

Figure 19–2. IIS 7.5 new web site properties dialog

Next, you will issue a self-signed certificate.

    3.   Click the root machine node on the left, and then click the Server Certificates node, as shown in Figure 19–3. This should bring up a dialog listing all of the certificates currently registered on the machine.

Figure 19–3. IIS 7.5 Server Certificates node

4. Click the Create Self-Signed Certificate link on the right-hand side of the dialog. Then, specify a name for that certificate when prompted—for example, wp7cert.

Next, you will enable SSL on the new web site that you created. To do this, you will need to create a binding of that web site to the https protocol.

5. In the list of sites, click WP7Server and then click Bindings on the right-hand side, as illustrated in 19–4.

Figure 19–4. Web site bindings link

6. To create an https binding for the site, so that traffic to and from the site can be encrypted using SSL, click Add Binding. When the dialog shown in Figure 19–5 comes up, select https type binding and select the wp7cert certificate from the certificates list. This certificate will be used to encrypt traffic between the web site and your Windows Phone 7 client application.

Figure 19–5. Adding https site binding

Finally, you need to create some content to browse to on the secure web site. In the real world, this would most likely be the service returning some sort of sensitive data, such as financial or security information. However, for this example, you will simply create an HTML file and save it onto the server.

7. Open Notepad and paste the following HTML into it:

```
<html>
<h1>Hello, Windows Phone 7</h1>
</html>
```

8. Save the HTML file you created to the physical path for the web site that you specified in Step 2 (referenced in Figure 19–2) and name the file index.html. For example, if you kept your Physical Path setting as C:\WP7Server\ in Step 2, then you will save the HTML file as C:\WP7Server\index.html.

■ **Note** You may be getting a "Permission Denied" error when you try to save the HTML file (we did). If so, make sure that the currently logged-in user has permissions to write to that folder and try again.

You are now ready to test out your self-signed certificate.

9. On your computer, open Internet Explorer and navigate to https:/*machinename*/, where machinename is the name of your computer (for example, wp7server). You should see the "Hello, Windows Phone 7" message in the browser.

Now let's test whether you can access secure data from your Windows Phone 7 application.

10. From your Windows Phone 7 emulator, open Internet Explorer and navigate to https:/machinename/. The very first time you start up the emulator, you will see a screen like the one shown in Figure 19–6, the absence of trust relationship error message. If you click Continue, however, you will be able to establish SSL connections to the web server from both the browser on the Windows Phone 7 device and the applications.

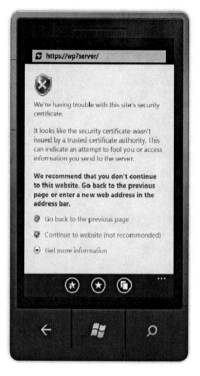

Figure 19–6. Certificate authority error on the Windows Phone 7 Emulator

Exporting a Self-Signed Certificate

It is possible to establish secure connections between mobile applications executing on the Windows Phone 7 and remote services, such as Microsoft Exchange, using self-signed certificates.

The first step in establishing a secure connection with the use of a self-signed certificate between the client and the server is to export the certificate from the server. The next example shows you how to do this; it assumes that you are using Internet Explorer 8 to export certificates and that you have created a self-signed certificate using the steps in the previous section.

1. On the server, open Internet Explorer, and click Tools ➤ Internet Options. If the menu bar with Tools menu option is not visible, press the Alt key.

2. In the window that comes up, click the Content tab, and then click the Certificates button. In the Certificates dialog that comes up, select the Trusted Root Certification Authorities tab. The self-signed certificate that you created

should be listed in this tab—you can scan the Friendly Name column and look for wp7cert, as shown in Figure 19–7.

Figure 19–7. List of trusted root CAs, with self-signed certificate highlighted

3. Click on the Export button, and then click the Next button. On the next screen, select "No, do not export the private key" (the default option) and click Next.

4. On the next screen, choose the DER Encoded binary X.509 format (default option) and click Next. Finally, select the folder to export certificate into, name the file wp7cert (make sure to put it somewhere you can find it later!), click Next, and then click Finish. You should get a message notifying you that the export was successful.

With the certificate exported, you are now ready to finalize the trust relationship between the Windows Phone 7 device and the server secured by a self-signed certificate. You will do that in the next section.

Installing Self-Signed Certificate on Windows Phone 7

The easiest way to install a self-signed certificate on Windows Phone 7 device or emulator in the first release of Windows Phone 7 Framework is to simply e-mail it. Then, let the built-in Windows Phone 7 features recognize the certificate file and properly install it on the device. The next few steps will guide you through this process.

1. Open or navigate to your e-mail program; for instance, if you use Hotmail as your default e-mail, log in and create an e-mail message to yourself. In that e-mail, add an attachment—the exported self-signed certificate in the `wp7cert.cer` file you created in the previous example. Send e-mail to yourself.

2. From the Windows Phone 7 device or emulator, access the e-mail message you just sent. Once you click the `wp7cert.cer` attachment, the Windows Phone 7 should prompt you to open the certificate file. Go ahead and click (or tap) the screen to get the Install Certificate prompt shown in Figure 19–8. Then, click the Install Certificate button. After the installation, click the OK button.

You are now familiar with how to secure data in transit from a remote service to the Windows Phone 7 device. You have seen how to use SSL with both trusted third-party certificates from established certification authorities and self-signed certificates. In the next section, you will take a look at securely storing data on your Windows Phone 7 device by encrypting it.

Implementing Data Security

In this section, you will learn how to secure data that gets stored on a Windows Phone 7 device. While the data in isolated storage is sandboxed for each application—i.e., an application cannot access the contents of isolated storage of another application—it is still important to encrypt sensitive data stored on the device. Encrypting data makes it impossible for anybody other than the data owner to read that data, something that is especially critical for enterprise users. Windows Phone 7 provides a powerful subset of .NET encryption classes, which make data encryption not only possible, but extremely easy on this device. The following data encryption algorithms are supported on Windows Phone 7:

- AES
- HMACSHA1
- HMACSHA256
- Rfc2898DeriveBytes
- SHA1
- SHA256

As you will see in the next example, many of these algorithms complement each other to provide a robust data encryption strategy for Windows Phone 7 devices. But first, let's briefly review the purpose of each of the supported encryption algorithms.

AES (stands for Advanced Encryption Standard) is a symmetric encryption algorithm, which means that it uses the same key (password) to encrypt and decrypt data. Since the key used to encrypt/decrypt data could be easy to guess by iterating through words in a dictionary in an automated manner, an additional secret key is added during the encryption process.

Figure 19–8. Installing certificates via e-mail

This additional key is called *salt* and is usually a random set of bits, such as an employee identification number, that is used to make the AES-encrypted message harder for intruders to decrypt.

HMACSHA1 and HMACSHA256 algorithms both generate a unique message authentication code (MAC) from the data and password supplied. Both algorithms use the same approach to generating MAC: they take data and hash it with the secret key using standard hash function SHA1 and SHA256 correspondingly. The difference between HMACSHA1 and HMACSHA256 lies in the strength of the message generated: HMACSHA1 output is 160 bits long while HMACSHA256 generates results that are 256 bits in length.

Finally, Rfc2898DeriveBytes is an algorithm that relies on the HMACSHA1 function to generate a strong key, using the password and salt values supplied, to be used to encrypt and decrypt data.

■**Note** Do not store password or salt values in application code. It is extremely easy to peek at compiled .NET code using tools such as Ildasm.exe, Red Gate Reflector or even a simple text editor and retrieve the value of the password/salt. At the end of this chapter, you will learn how to protect your application code from possible decompilation by obfuscating it; however, even with obfuscation, the password and salt values should never be stored inside application code.

In the first data security example, you will experiment with HMACSHA1 and HMACSHA256 algorithms to observe the keys that those algorithms generate from the input and password/salt values supplied. In the second example, you will encrypt and decrypt data on the device using the AES algorithm.

Using HMACSHA1 and HMACHSHA256

Both HMACSHA1 and HMACSHA256 functions are one-way: once the message authentication code is generated using either of those functions, it is impossible to recreate the original message from the generated MAC. This makes those functions ideal for storing values of security codes: the only way to produce a match of the MAC on those values is to supply a valid password and security code. The following example demonstrates how to generate HMACSHA1 and HMACSHA256 messages.

Creating a User Interface

Your application interface will consist of textboxes to accept a message and a password to create a MAC from, and it will show the MAC generated using both HMACSHA1 and HMACSHA256 algorithms.

1. Open Visual Studio Express for Windows Phone and create a new project called HMACTest.

2. Make MainPage.xaml look like Figure 19–9. For reference, the XAML of this page is pasted here (and don't forget that you can also download all code samples for this book):

```
<!--LayoutRoot contains the root grid where all other page content is placed-->
<Grid x:Name="LayoutRoot" Background="Transparent">
        <Grid.RowDefinitions>
        <RowDefinition Height="Auto"/>
        <RowDefinition Height="*"/>
        </Grid.RowDefinitions>

    <!--TitlePanel contains the name of the application and page title-->
    <StackPanel x:Name="TitlePanel" Grid.Row="0" Margin="24,24,0,12">
        <TextBlock x:Name="ApplicationTitle" Text="MY APPLICATION"
Style="{StaticResource PhoneTextNormalStyle}"/>
        <TextBlock x:Name="PageTitle" Text="HMAC Test" Margin="-3,-8,0,0"
Style="{StaticResource PhoneTextTitle1Style}"/>
    </StackPanel>
```

```
        <!--ContentPanel - place additional content here-->
        <Grid x:Name="ContentGrid" Grid.Row="1">
            <Button Content="Generate" Height="72" HorizontalAlignment="Left"
Margin="149,437,0,0" Name="button1" VerticalAlignment="Top" Width="160" Click="button1_Click"
/>
            <TextBox Height="72" HorizontalAlignment="Left" Margin="149,23,0,0"
Name="txtMessage" Text="" VerticalAlignment="Top" Width="317" />
            <TextBlock Height="99" HorizontalAlignment="Left" Margin="21,216,0,0"
Name="textBlock1" Text="TextBlock" VerticalAlignment="Top" Width="445" TextWrapping="Wrap" />
            <TextBlock Height="114" HorizontalAlignment="Left" Margin="24,321,0,0"
Name="textBlock2" Text="TextBlock" VerticalAlignment="Top" Width="442" TextWrapping="Wrap" />
            <TextBlock Height="30" HorizontalAlignment="Left" Margin="21,44,0,0"
Name="textBlock3" Text="Message:" VerticalAlignment="Top" Width="122" />
            <TextBlock Height="30" HorizontalAlignment="Left" Margin="21,129,0,0"
Name="textBlock4" Text="Key:" VerticalAlignment="Top" />
            <TextBox Height="72" HorizontalAlignment="Left" Margin="149,101,0,0" Name="txtKey"
Text="" VerticalAlignment="Top" Width="246" />
        </Grid>
    </Grid>
```

Coding the Application Logic

The next step is to add logic that takes advantage of the cryptography classes on Windows Phone 7 to show Message Authentication Codes.

1. Add the following using directive to the top of the page:

    ```
    using System.Security.Cryptography;
    ```

2. Because you want all of the encryption logic to happen on the button click, add an event handler to the Click event of the Generate button. To do that, double-click the Generate button and paste the following code inside the handler. Note how after declaring the HMACSHA1 and HMACSHA256 classes, all of the magic happens in the ComputeHash function, which returns an array of bytes that you convert to the hexadecimal string.

    ```
            string message = txtMessage.Text;
            string key = txtKey.Text;

            System.Text.UTF8Encoding encoding = new System.Text.UTF8Encoding();

            byte[] keyByte = encoding.GetBytes(key);

            HMACSHA1 hmacsha1 = new HMACSHA1(keyByte);
    HMACSHA256 hmacsha256 = new HMACSHA256(keyByte);

    byte[] messageBytes = encoding.GetBytes(message);
    byte[] hashmessage = hmacsha1.ComputeHash(messageBytes);
            textBlock1.Text = ConvertToString(hashmessage);

            hashmessage = hmacsha256.ComputeHash(messageBytes);
            textBlock2.Text = ConvertToString(hashmessage);
    ```

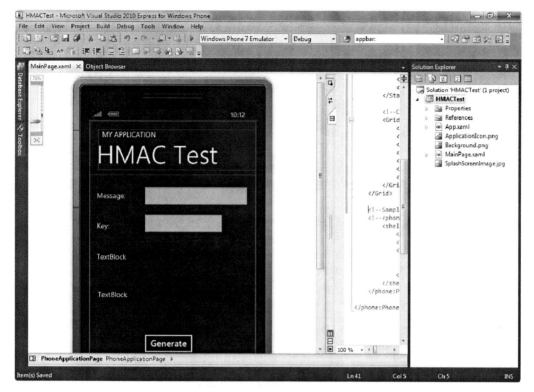

Figure 19–9. User interface for the HMACTest application

3. Finally, paste the contents of the ConvertToString helper function that converts a byte array passed in to the hexadecimal string.

```
public static string ConvertToString(byte[] buff)
{
        string sbinary = "";

        for (int i = 0; i < buff.Length; i++)
        {
                //hex-formatted
                sbinary += buff[i].ToString("X2");
        }
        return (sbinary);
}
```

Press F5 to run the application. Enter some message text (for example, "Hello, World") and key (for example, "test") and observe the MAC values generated using the HMACSHA1 algorithm (top TextBlock) and HMACSHA256 algorithm (bottom TextBlock). Notice that not only does the length of the MACs differ, but the MACs themselves are completely different from each other.

In the next example, you will encrypt and decrypt data using AES.

Using Rfc2898DeriveBytes and AES to Encrypt Data

To encrypt data from prying eyes on a Windows Phone 7 device, you need a strong encryption mechanism that, in turn, relies on the strong key to make encryption withstand all of the known attempts to break it. The Rfc2898DeriveBytes algorithm, available on Windows Phone 7, creates a very strong key for use in AES encryption from the password and salt values passed in. This example demonstrates how to use both of these algorithms in combination on a Windows Phone 7 device.

Creating a User Interface

The interface will prompt the user for data to encrypt and for a password and salt to use for that encryption. The interface will also have two buttons—one for encryption and the other one for decryption of data.

1. Open Visual Studio Express for Windows Phone and create a new project called AESEncryption.

2. Make the MainPage.xaml page look like the one shown in Figure 19–10. For convenience, the XAML of this page is pasted here:

```
<!--LayoutRoot contains the root grid where all other page content is placed-->
<Grid x:Name="LayoutRoot" Background="Transparent">
    <Grid.RowDefinitions>
        <RowDefinition Height="Auto"/>
        <RowDefinition Height="*"/>
    </Grid.RowDefinitions>

    <!--TitlePanel contains the name of the application and page title-->
    <StackPanel x:Name="TitlePanel" Grid.Row="0" Margin="24,24,0,12">
        <TextBlock x:Name="ApplicationTitle" Text="CLASSIFIED" Style="{StaticResource
PhoneTextNormalStyle}"/>
        <TextBlock x:Name="PageTitle" Text="AES Encryption" Margin="-3,-8,0,0"
Style="{StaticResource PhoneTextTitle1Style}"/>
    </StackPanel>

    <!--ContentPanel - place additional content here-->
    <Grid x:Name="ContentGrid" Grid.Row="1">
        <TextBox Height="65" HorizontalAlignment="Left" Margin="6,41,0,0"
Name="txtDataToEncrypt" Text="" VerticalAlignment="Top" Width="462" />
        <TextBlock Height="30" HorizontalAlignment="Left" Margin="20,21,0,0"
Name="textBlock1" Text="Data to encrypt" VerticalAlignment="Top" Width="419" />
        <TextBox Height="72" HorizontalAlignment="Left" Margin="6,334,0,0"
Name="txtPassword" Text="" VerticalAlignment="Top" Width="462" />
        <TextBlock Height="30" HorizontalAlignment="Left" Margin="20,310,0,0"
Name="textBlock2" Text="Password" VerticalAlignment="Top" Width="346" />
        <TextBox Height="72" HorizontalAlignment="Left" Margin="6,426,0,0" Name="txtSalt"
Text="" VerticalAlignment="Top" Width="462" />
        <TextBlock Height="36" HorizontalAlignment="Left" Margin="21,403,0,0"
Name="textBlock3" Text="Salt" VerticalAlignment="Top" Width="304" />
```

```
        <Button Content="Encrypt" Height="72" HorizontalAlignment="Left"
Margin="20,504,0,0" Name="button1" VerticalAlignment="Top" Width="160" Click="button1_Click"
/>
        <Button Content="Decrypt" Height="72" HorizontalAlignment="Left"
Margin="296,504,0,0" Name="button2" VerticalAlignment="Top" Width="160" Click="button2_Click"
/>
        <TextBlock Height="30" HorizontalAlignment="Left" Margin="24,101,0,0"
Name="textBlock4" Text="Encrypted Data" VerticalAlignment="Top" Width="432" />
        <TextBox Height="72" HorizontalAlignment="Left" Margin="8,123,0,0"
Name="txtEncryptedData" Text="" VerticalAlignment="Top" Width="460" />
        <TextBlock Height="27" HorizontalAlignment="Left" Margin="21,197,0,0"
Name="textBlock5" Text="Decrypted Data" VerticalAlignment="Top" Width="435" />
        <TextBox Height="72" HorizontalAlignment="Left" Margin="13,221,0,0"
Name="txtDecryptedData" Text="" VerticalAlignment="Top" Width="460" />
      </Grid>
    </Grid>
```

Figure 19–10. User interface for the AESEncryption application

Coding the Application Logic

AES encryption in the .NET Framework is implemented via a class called AesManaged. The following code uses this class, together with the Rfc2898DeriveBytes class to encrypt the data.

1. Add the following using directive to the top of the page:

```
using System.Security.Cryptography;
using System.IO;
using System.Text;
```

2. Code the Encrypt method. The Encrypt method takes data to encrypt, password and salt as parameters, and returns a string. Notice how the Encrypt method creates the Rfc2898DerivedBytes class and uses that class to generate a strong key from the password and salt combination; that key is later used by the AesManaged class to encrypt data.

```
public string Encrypt(string dataToEncrypt, string password, string salt)
{
    AesManaged aes = null;
    MemoryStream memStream = null;
    CryptoStream crStream = null;

    try
    {
//Generate a Key based on a Password and Salt
        Rfc2898DeriveBytes rfc2898 = new Rfc2898DeriveBytes(password,
        Encoding.UTF8.GetBytes(salt));

        //Create AES algorithm with 256 bit key and 128-bit block size
        aes = new AesManaged();
        aes.Key = rfc2898.GetBytes(aes.KeySize / 8);
        aes.IV = rfc2898.GetBytes(aes.BlockSize / 8);

        memStream = new MemoryStream();
        crStream = new CryptoStream(memStream, aes.CreateEncryptor(),
        CryptoStreamMode.Write);

        byte[] data = Encoding.UTF8.GetBytes(dataToEncrypt);
        crStream.Write(data, 0, data.Length);
        crStream.FlushFinalBlock();

        //Return Base 64 String
        return Convert.ToBase64String(memStream.ToArray());
    }
    finally
    {
        //cleanup
        if (crStream != null)
            crStream.Close();
```

```
                if (memStream != null)
                    memStream.Close();

                if (aes != null)
                        aes.Clear();
                }
                }
```

3. Code the Decrypt method. The Decrypt method is the inverse of Encrypt: it
    takes data to decrypt, password and salt as parameters, and returns an input
    string. Since AES is a symmetric algorithm, the same password and salt values
    must be used to decrypt data as were used to encrypt it. The Decrypt method
    initializes the Rfc2898Bytes key and uses it to create Decryptor for data.

```csharp
public string Decrypt(string dataToDecrypt, string password, string salt)
        {
                AesManaged aes = null;
                MemoryStream memStream = null;
                CryptoStream crStream = null;

        try
        {
                Rfc2898DeriveBytes rfc2898 = new Rfc2898DeriveBytes(password,
                Encoding.UTF8.GetBytes(salt));
                aes = new AesManaged();
                aes.Key = rfc2898.GetBytes(aes.KeySize / 8);
                aes.IV = rfc2898.GetBytes(aes.BlockSize / 8);

                memStream = new MemoryStream();
                crStream = new CryptoStream(memStream, aes.CreateDecryptor(),
                CryptoStreamMode.Write);
                byte[] data = Convert.FromBase64String(dataToDecrypt);
                crStream.Write(data, 0, data.Length);
                crStream.FlushFinalBlock();

                byte[] decryptBytes = memStream.ToArray();
                return Encoding.UTF8.GetString(decryptBytes, 0, decryptBytes.Length);
        }
        finally
        {
                if (crStream != null)
                        crStream.Close();

                if (memStream != null)
                        memStream.Close();

                if (aes != null)
                        aes.Clear();
                }
        }
```

4. Add code to call the Encrypt method when the user clicks the Encrypt button. Double-click the Encrypt button in MainPage.xaml and add the following code to the click event handler:

```
txtEncryptedData.Text = Encrypt(txtDataToEncrypt.Text, txtPassword.Text,
    txtSalt.Text);
```

5. Finally, add code to call the Decrypt method when the user clicks the Decrypt button. Double-click the Decrypt button in MainPage.xaml and add the following code to the Click event handler:

```
txtDecryptedData.Text = Decrypt(txtEncryptedData.Text, txtPassword.Text,
txtSalt.Text);
```

Press F5 to run the application. Enter some data (for example, "Classified Information"), a password (for example, "test"), and salt (note that it must be at least 8 characters long, otherwise AES classes will throw an exception), and observe the values being encrypted in the Encrypted Data textbox. Press Decrypt and you should see the original text in the Decrypted Data field. Note that if you enter the password or salt values that are different between encryption and decryption, the application will raise an error.

Now that you understand the cryptography framework on the Windows Phone 7, it's time to take a look at the physical security of the device.

Understanding Device Physical Security

With Windows Phone 7, customers rarely have to worry about sensitive data ending up in malicious hands if the device is lost or stolen. This is because several standard features that come complimentary with the phone make it possible to feel confident about the security of the device at no extra charge. In this section, you will walk through the Windows Phone 7 physical security safeguards that Microsoft provides. All of these features are accessible at http://windowsphone.live.com. You will need to create a Microsoft Live ID if you don't have one already and properly associate it with your Windows Phone 7 device.

- **Map It**: Using this feature, Windows Phone 7 users are able to see the location of their phones using Bing maps.

- **Ring It**: Using this option, you can instruct the phone to ring for 60 seconds using a special ringtone, even if the ring tone has been turned off.

- **Lock It and Display a Message**: You can also lock the phone from the web site and display a custom message to instruct people who may have found your phone on how to get in touch with you.

- **Erase It**: Finally, if all is lost and there is no hope of recovering the phone, you can remotely wipe all of the data from that phone and reset it to factory settings.

As you can see, the Windows Phone 7 security story is very compelling, especially for the first generation of this device. You can expect this story to become better and more feature-rich in the very near future. Certainly, more and more features from the full .NET Framework will find their way onto the phone, which should further contribute to the security of the device.

Meeting Certification Requirements

Microsoft documentation on security in Windows Phone 7 lists explicit requirements regarding application code. In this chapter, you will gain an understanding of what types of application behavior are not tolerated by Microsoft.

Application Must Implement MSIL Code

Microsoft imposes a requirement on Windows Phone 7 application developers to use managed code to construct their applications. Strong typing, bounds checking, and memory management features of managed code help minimize the most common types of attacks (also referred to in the security community as *attack vectors*) on both the application and the Windows Phone 7 application platform.

Generally, if you use C# language with its default settings, you will be in compliance with this restriction imposed by Windows Phone Marketplace. The problems will arise, however, if you venture into unsafe C# code territory, which can be enabled by using the unsafe keyword in a method signature. In addition to the unsafe keyword, applications with unsafe code must be compiled with a special switch, as shown in Figure 19–11. As an example of unsafe code, consider the following code, which uses a simple SquarePtrParam function to accept a pointer variable (non-MSIL code) and perform pointer arithmetic on it:

```
public partial class MainPage : PhoneApplicationPage
{
    unsafe public MainPage()
    {
        int i=5;
        InitializeComponent();
        SquarePtrParam(&i);
        PageTitle.Text = i.ToString();
    }

    // Unsafe method, using a pointer to square the number
    unsafe static void SquarePtrParam(int* p)
    {
        *p *= *p;
    }
}
```

The good news for Windows Phone 7 developers is that while the previous code is a perfectly valid .NET code, the Windows Phone 7 templates in Visual Studio disable the option to compile unsafe code. This option is generally found under Project ➤ Properties ➤ Build tab, and the check box "Allow Unsafe Code" is grayed out on Windows Phone 7 templates, making the option of writing unsafe application for Windows Phone 7 a challenging exercise. And even though it is possible to work around this limitation by modifying the project file (.csproj) using a text editor and specifying the <AllowUnsafeCode> attribute, it is certainly not worth the trouble because Windows Phone Marketplace will reject the application anyway.

Figure 19–11. *Applications that implement unsafe code must be compiled with a special switch.*

Application Must Not Implement Any Security-Critical Code

With .NET version 4.0, Microsoft has moved away from the complexities of its Code Access Security (CAS) model and towards a simpler model it calls the Transparent Security model. The first transparency rule set was initially introduced in .NET 2.0 and then expanded to Transparency Level 2 in .NET 4.0. With Transparency Level 2, code is segregated into three types: transparent code, security-safe-critical code, and security-critical code. These types are discussed in the following sections.

Transparent Code

In the transparent category, there are applications that run in a sandbox, which are pretty much all of the Windows Phone 7 applications that you will ever write, and these applications have a limited permission set granted by the sandbox. That means that as a developer you don't have to be concerned about checking security policies when you write your applications, as long as you don't try to perform any operation deemed not accessible by the transparent code. For reference purposes, here is the list of tasks that transparent applications are not permitted to perform:

- Directly call critical code

- Perform an Assert operation or elevation of privilege

- Contain unsafe or unverifiable code

- Call native code or code that has the SuppressUnmanagedCodeSecurityAttribute attribute

- Call a member that is protected by a LinkDemand

- Inherit from critical types

Security-Safe-Critical Code

In the security-safe-critical category, there is code that is fully trusted but is still callable by transparent code. It exposes a limited surface area of full-trust code. Correctness and security verifications happen in security-safe-critical code.

Security-Critical code

Finally, there is a category of code that can't be called by transparent code. This is usually security-critical code that typically implements system-level functionality and has unlimited access to Windows Phone resources, making it a perfect place to embed malicious behavior. Therefore, Microsoft disallows this type of code; to successfully pass Windows Phone Marketplace certification criteria, applications must not implement any security-critical code. In addition, applications must not invoke native code via PInvoke or COM Interoperability.

You will most likely never have to worry about the ins and outs of the Transparent Security model when you program for Windows Phone 7. But in case you decide to try to implement unsafe or security-critical code in your application, remember that Marketplace certification tests will quickly uncover this type of behavior and deny entry to your application.

Capability List

To protect users' privacy and enforce developer accountability, Windows Phone Marketplace fully discloses to the user whether an application is relying on any of the following services for proper operation:

- Gamer Services
- Location Services
- Media Library
- Microphone
- Networking
- Place Phone Calls
- Push Notifications
- Sensors
- Web Browser

These capabilities are requested on a Windows Phone 7 device when an application developer submits her application for certification. Only the requested capabilities are granted, protecting device users from unexpected behavior of potentially privacy-intruding applications.

Obfuscating Your Application Code

The clarity and speed of writing your application in managed .NET languages (C# or VB.NET) and avoiding unsafe code constructs are very appealing features of the Windows Phone 7 platform. Unfortunately, from a security and intellectual property perspective, managed languages have one significant drawback: they can easily be de-compiled or reverse-engineered using tools such as ildasm.exe or Red Gate Reflector, potentially exposing your application source code to anybody who has access to your application's .xap file. That means that the programming logic that you may have spent days or weeks tweaking could be easily copied by your competition or could be easily eavesdropped on for a possible attack on your application.

To illustrate how easy it is to peek inside your compiled application, let's use the Red Gate Reflector tool and open up one of the compiled assemblies that you have created earlier in this chapter.

▓ **Note** Reflector was a free tool for the longest time; however, it appears that Red Gate started charging for its use recently. You can still download a 14-day evaluation trial of this tool from http://reflector.red-gate.com/download.aspx.

Launch Reflector (by double-clicking on Reflector.exe from the location you downloaded it to) and click on File ➤ Open Assembly. Navigate to AESEncryption.dll, which should be located inside the Bin/Debug/ folder of the AESEncryption project created in the previous section (AESEncyrption.dll is created automatically for you in the Debug folder when you run the application inside the emulator). Once you open that assembly, expand AESEncryption ➤ AESEncyrption.dll ➤ AESEncryption ➤ MainPage node and click on the Encrypt method. You should see something similar to Figure 19-12, with virtually all of your code for the Encrypt method exposed in the right pane.

Figure 19–12. Encrypt method of the AESEncryption project in Reflector

Obfuscation serves to protect intellectual property in your code from the prying eyes of Reflector and other such tools. There are several .NET obfuscation products on the market, including Dotfuscator, DeepSea, and Crypto. The one you will be taking a look in this chapter is Dotfuscator because full version of Dotfuscator for Windows Phone 7 will be freely available to you to try out first before making a decision to buy, but the basic principles of hiding code should be applicable to all of the products mentioned above.

■ **Note**   You can download a copy of Dotfuscator for Windows Phone 7 from PreEmptive Solutions website at www.preemptive.com/know-more/windows-phone-7.

Follow the steps in this example to obfuscate the code from the AESEncryption project.

1. Start by launching Dotfuscator from Start ➤ All Programs ➤ Dotfuscator.

2. When the Select Project Type dialog comes up, select Create New Project. On the Input Files menu bar, select the Add New Input (the folder icon) and navigate to the AESEncryption.xap file. Note how Dotfuscator understands that Windows Phone 7 applications consist of .xap files, while we had to navigate to the .dll file when we used Reflector, since Reflector is not currently customized to work with Windows Phone 7 applications. Make a mental note

of it for now—you will come back to this minor difference in the way these two programs function shortly.

3. By default, Dotfuscator is not set to obfuscate anything in the assembly. You must tell the application that you want the assembly obfuscated and variables hidden. To do so, go to the Settings tab. Set Disable Control Flow to No, and set Disable String Encryption to No, as shown in Figure 19-13.

Figure 19–13. `Enabling Dotfuscator settings for code obfuscation`

4. Still on the Settings tab, click on the Build Settings node and make sure to set Destination Directory to a folder that you can easily locate on your computer such as `C:\Projects\Dotfuscated\`.

5. You are now ready to create an obfuscated version of your .xap file. To do that, click on the Build button in Dotfuscator, as shown in Figure 19-13. Once the Build completes, you should have a new .xap file generated in the Output Directory that you configured in Step 4.

6. You are now ready to peek inside the obfuscated file to determine whether the code has indeed been made unreadable to Reflector. However, Reflector can only understand .dll assemblies and not .xap files generated for Windows Phone 7 applications. Recall how a .xap file is simply a renamed .zip file containing several files, including application resource files and a .dll

assembly within it. Rename the obfuscated .xap file to have a .zip extension and peek inside that file.

7. Extract the AESEncryption.dll assembly from the obfuscated .xap file generated in Step 5. From within Reflector, navigate to that assembly and open it.

8. Expand AESEncryption ➤ AESEncyrption.dll ➤ AESEncryption ➤ MainPage node and click on the Encrypt method. Instead of code in the right pane, you should now see something similar to Figure 19-14, making the logic of that method unreachable to tools like Reflector and ildasm.

This example should give you the basic idea on obfuscating managed .NET code. You can tweak settings inside Dotfuscator to ensure that you application's intellectual property is properly secured. Note, however, that you should always deploy your obfuscated device to your (unlocked) Windows Phone 7 device for testing. Sometimes, the obfuscator tools get a bit ambitious and scramble the information that is expected by the Windows Phone 7 platform in a certain format, resulting in application failing to properly load and launch. Always test your .xap before submitting it to the Marketplace for certification!

Figure 19–14. Obfuscated Encrypt method

Summary

In this last chapter of the book, you learned about the facilities that the Windows Phone 7 platform provides to secure data in transit and on devices, as well as how it imposes a set of rigorous tests to confirm the identity of the application developer and ensure that the applications in Windows Phone Marketplace don't contain malicious code. You have also looked at making your code unreadable, or obfuscated, to tools like ildasm and Reflector. The Windows Phone 7 device also provides security for the device itself, giving users the ability to remotely find, ring, or erase all data from the phone. Windows Phone 7 has already implemented a strong set of security features, and those features will only get more and more comprehensive.

Index

■ C

CPSIA information can be obtained at www.ICGtesting.com
Printed in the USA
243311LV00009B/4/P